A·N·N·U·A·L EDITIONS

African American History

First Edition

00/01

EDITOR

Rodney D. Coates
Miami University

Rodney D. Coates, professor of sociology and director of Black World Studies at Miami University, received a B.A. from Southern Illinois University in 1975, and an M.A. and a Ph.D. from the University of Chicago. He has written, reviewed, and taught extensively in the areas of social theory, social stratification, race and ethnic relations, and social historical analysis.

Dushkin/McGraw-Hill
Sluice Dock, Guilford, Connecticut 06437

Visit us on the Internet
http://www.dushkin.com/annualeditions/

Credits

1. Africa: Ancient and Colonial
Unit photo—photo by Captain Hurley/American Museum of Natural History.
2. The Beginning of the Atlantic Slave Trade
Unit photo—courtesy of the Library of Congress.
3. Colonial America
Unit photo—Lithograph of the lower deck of a slave ship © by Corbis/Bettmann.
4. The Civil War
Unit photo—painting by Thomas Nast of "Regiment into Charleston, South Carolina, February 21, 1865," courtesy of the Museum of Fine Arts, Boston.
5. Reconstruction and Emancipation
Unit photo—courtesy of the Library of Congress.
6. African-Americans and the Beginning of the 20th Century
Unit photo—students studying at Tuskegee Institute courtesy of the Library of Congress.
7. African-Americans from the Great Depression to World War II
Unit photo—Tuskegee Airmen, pilots of the 99th U.S. Fighter Squadron of the USAAF, © by Corbis/Bettmann.
8. Modern Civil Rights
Unit photo—Rosa Parks, December 21, 1956, © by United Press International.
9. Contemporary Debates and Issues
Unit photo—Million Man March, October 16, 1995, © by Porter Gifford/Gamma Liaison.

Copyright

Cataloging in Publication Data
Main entry under title: Annual Editions: African American history. 2000/2001.
    1. Afro-Americans—History. 2. Slavery in the United States. I. Coates, Rodney D., *comp.*
II. Title: African American history.
ISBN 0–07–233372–3   973'.0496073

First Edition

Cover painting, *Inspiration*, by Aaron Douglas. From the collection of John Hope Frankin.

Printed in the United States of America   1234567890BAHBAH543210   Printed on Recycled Paper

Members of the Advisory Board are instrumental in the final selection of articles for each edition of ANNUAL EDITIONS. Their review of articles for content, level, currentness, and appropriateness provides critical direction to the editor and staff. We think that you will find their careful consideration well reflected in this volume.

EDITOR

Rodney D. Coates
Miami University

ADVISORY BOARD

Beverly G. Bond
University of Memphis

Lena Boyd-Brown
Prairie View A&M University

Olen Cole Jr.
North Carolina Agricultural and Technical State University

Andrew J. DeRoche
Front Range Community College

Ernest D. Green
Otterbein College

Lenworth Gunther
Essex Community College

Deborah Newman Ham
Morgan State University

Charles Herod
SUNY–Plattsburgh

Albert E. Jabs
Shaw University

Stanley W. Johnson
Fayetteville State University

William M. King
University of Colorado Boulder

Wilma King
University of Missouri Columbia

Jerome McDuffie
University of North Carolina Pembroke

John J. Navin
Coastal Carolina University

Arthur Pitz
Black Hawk College

Linda Reed
University of Houston

Charles K. Ross
University of Mississippi

Arwin Smallwood
Bradley University

EDITORIAL STAFF

Ian A. Nielsen, Publisher
Roberta Monaco, Senior Developmental Editor
Dorothy Fink, Associate Developmental Editor
Addie Raucci, Senior Administrative Editor
Cheryl Greenleaf, Permissions Editor
Joseph Offredi, Permissions/Editorial Assistant
Diane Barker, Proofreader
Lisa Holmes-Doebrick, Program Coordinator

PRODUCTION STAFF

Brenda S. Filley, Production Manager
Charles Vitelli, Designer
Lara M. Johnson, Design/Advertising Coordinator
Laura Levine, Graphics
Mike Campbell, Graphics
Tom Goddard, Graphics
Eldis Lima, Graphics
Juliana Arbo, Typesetting Supervisor
Jane Jaegersen, Typesetter
Marie Lazauskas, Typesetter
Kathleen D'Amico, Typesetter
Larry Killian, Copier Coordinator

Editors/Advisory Board

Staff

To the Reader

In publishing ANNUAL EDITIONS we recognize the enormous role played by the magazines, newspapers, and journals of the public press in providing current, first-rate educational information in a broad spectrum of interest areas. Many of these articles are appropriate for students, researchers, and professionals seeking accurate, current material to help bridge the gap between principles and theories and the real world. These articles, however, become more useful for study when those of lasting value are carefully collected, organized, indexed, and reproduced in a low-cost format, which provides easy and permanent access when the material is needed. That is the role played by ANNUAL EDITIONS.

New to ANNUAL EDITIONS is the inclusion of related World Wide Web sites. These sites have been selected by our editorial staff to represent some of the best resources found on the World Wide Web today. Through our carefully developed topic guide, we have linked these Web resources to the articles covered in this ANNUAL EDITIONS reader. We think that you will find this volume useful, and we hope that you will take a moment to visit us on the Web at **http://www.dushkin.com** to tell us what you think.

The study of Africans in the Americas provides a uniquely rich vantage point by which we can view ourselves and our past. The African American is at once part of and set apart from the American experience that defines the United States. Our knowledge regarding this rich history is increasing at such a rapid rate that both scholars and students have difficulty keeping pace. While many would content themselves with the more recent history, let us say the last three decades, history is only meaningful when placed within the larger and wider historical context of the last five centuries. It is through this process that we are able to see the transformative powers that Africans have had on the Americas and how subsequently the Africans have been transformed.

African American history cannot be limited to a few events, a few dates, or a few persons. It is rather the sum total of millions of regular people who have dreamed, lived, loved, worked, and died to create a people, a community, and a nation. Often ignored, the struggles of blacks have served as the *leitmotif* defining the American character. Consequently, wrapped up in this process has been the story of America, its race and gender relations, its place in global politics and affairs, its past, its present, and its destiny. American indentity and its soul, to a great degree, is defined by its African roots.

Annual Editions: African American History 00/01, contains a number of features designed to facilitate learning. These include a *table of contents*, where you can find summaries for each of the articles with key concepts in boldface; a *topic guide* to help you locate specific articles by subject matter or individuals; a comprehensive *index;*

and *World Wide Web* sites that can be used to further explore topics addressed in the articles. These sites are cross-referenced by number in the topic guide.

The first edition of *Annual Editions: African American History 00/01* constitutes an effort to present a balanced and objective appraisal of the black experience in the Americas. Toward that end a variety of source material has been selected, ranging from primary and scholarly articles to secondary and more journalistic (historical) essays. The hardest part of this process was not that of finding suitable material but of selecting material from the tremendous array of available sources. The reader, in all likelihood, will agree with some of these selections and disagree with others. Some readers probably would have liked more attention spent in some areas and less in others. It is for this reason that we encourage both teachers and students to evaluate the strengths and weaknesses of this edition and to share your thoughts with us.

This is an entirely new adventure for *Annual Editions* and this author. With your help it can only get better. If you have any suggestions for new articles please complete and mail in the postage-paid *article rating form* included in the back of the book. You will help in making this even better the next time around.

Rodney D. Coates
Editor

Contents

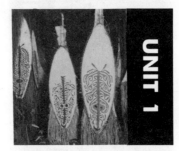

The concepts in bold italics are developed in the article. For further expansion please refer to the Topic Guide and the Index.

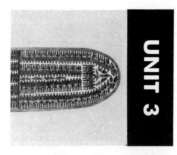

UNIT 3

Early America

Four selections in this section consider the experience of slavery in America. Topics considered include conditional antislavery, the impact on women, and slave insurrections.

UNIT 4

The Civil War

Seven selections in this section review African American experiences before and during the American Civil War.

The concepts in bold italics are developed in the article. For further expansion please refer to the Topic Guide and the Index.

The concepts in bold italics are developed in the article. For further expansion please refer to the Topic Guide and the Index.

UNIT 5

Reconstruction and Freedom

Four articles in this section examine what Reconstruction meant to the recently freed slaves and how their newly won freedom impacted on African American society.

UNIT 6

African Americans and the Beginning of the Twentieth Century

Four selections in this section examine the challenges faced by African-Americans in the tumultuous times leading up to the Depression.

The concepts in bold italics are developed in the article. For further expansion please refer to the Topic Guide and the Index.

UNIT 7

African Americans from the Great Depression to World War II

Four selections in this section consider the interaction of African Americans and the white majority during the 1930s and 1940s.

The concepts in bold italics are developed in the article. For further expansion please refer to the Topic Guide and the Index.

Modern Civil Rights

Three articles in this section look at some key events that affected modern civil rights in America.

Contemporary Debates and Issues

Four selections in this section consider some of the challenges faced by today's African American.

The concepts in bold italics are developed in the article. For further expansion please refer to the Topic Guide and the Index.

The concepts in bold italics are developed in the article. For further expansion please refer to the Topic Guide and the Index.

Topic Guide

This topic guide suggests how the selections and World Wide Web sites found in the next section of this book relate to topics of traditional concern to African American history students and professionals. It is useful for locating interrelated articles and Web sites for reading and research. The guide is arranged alphabetically according to topic.

The relevant Web sites, which are numbered and annotated on pages 4 and 5, are easily identified by the Web icon (◎) under the topic articles. By linking the articles and the Web sites by topic, this ANNUAL EDITIONS reader becomes a powerful learning and research tool.

TOPIC AREA	TREATED IN	TOPIC AREA	TREATED IN
Abolition	7. Founding Fathers, Conditional Antislavery 12. Long Road to Abolition 13. Struggle for Black Freedom before Emancipation ◎ **1, 2, 3, 4, 5, 6, 7, 8, 9, 20**		33. Black Deprivation–White Privilege 34. Rights Group Suing Florida for Failure to Educate Pupils ◎ **1, 2, 3, 4, 5, 6, 7, 8, 9, 29, 30, 31, 33, 34**
Activism	10. American Slave Insurrections before 1861 11. "All We Want Is Make Us Free!" 13. Struggle for Black Freedom before Emancipation 14. Jacksonville Mutiny 24. Claude McKay and the New Negro of the 1920's 30. Negro Is Your Brother 31. South's History Rises 32. Black Women Activists ◎ **1, 2, 3, 4, 5, 6, 7, 8, 9**	**Civil War**	14. Jacksonville Mutiny 15. Pride and Prejudice in the American Civil War 16. Forgotten Rebels: Blacks Who Served the Confederacy 17. Gallantry under Fire ◎ **1, 2, 3, 4, 5, 6, 7, 8, 9, 18, 19, 20**
		Colonial America	3. Under the Whiplash 4. Who Was Responsible? 6. Multitude of Black People . . . Chained Together 7. Founding Fathers, Conditional Antislavery 8. "Us Colored Women Had to Go through a Plenty" 9. Negro Craftsmanship in Early America 10. American Slave Insurrections before 1861 ◎ **14, 15, 16, 17**
Affirmative Action	33. Black Deprivation–White Privilege ◎ **1, 2, 3, 4, 5, 6, 7, 8, 9**		
Africa and Africans	1. Nile Kingdoms 2. Our Third Root 3. Under the Whiplash 4. Who Was Responsible? 6. Multitude of Black People . . . Chained Together ◎ **5, 10, 11, 12, 13**	**Culture**	1. Nile Kingdoms 2. Our Third Root 24. Claude McKay and the New Negro of the 1920's ◎ **10, 11, 22, 25**
Black Workers	9. Negro Craftsmanship in Early America 27. Work and Hope: African American Women in Southern California during World War II ◎ **14, 15, 16, 27**	**Emancipation**	13. Struggle for Black Freedom before Emancipation 18. Reconstruction 21. "Sweet Dreams of Freedom" ◎ **20, 21**
Civil Rights	18. Reconstruction 28. Desegregation of the Armed Forces 29. Sacrifice Play: The Negro Baseball Leagues Remembered 30. Negro Is Your Brother 31. South's History Rises 32. Black Women Activists	**Lynching**	22. When White Hoods Were in Flower ◎ **1, 2, 3, 4, 5, 6, 7, 8, 9, 26**
		Military	13. Struggle for Black Freedom before Emancipation 14. Jacksonville Mutiny

2

◉ AE: African American History

The following World Wide Web sites have been carefully researched and selected to support the articles found in this reader. If you are interested in learning more about specific topics found in this book, these Web sites are a good place to start. The sites are cross-referenced by number and appear in the topic guide on the previous two pages. Also, you can link to these Web sites through our DUSHKIN ONLINE support site at *http://www.dushkin.com/online/*.

The following sites were available at the time of publication. Visit our Web site—we update DUSHKIN ONLINE regularly to reflect any changes.

General sources

1. African American History: Historical Text Archive
http://www.msstate.edu/Archives/History/USA/ Afro-Amer/afro.html
Mine this in-depth site for genealogy, the African American experience in states and regions, people, history, slavery, art and literature, and much more.

2. African American History
http://www.ukans.edu/~usa/index.html
This index at the University of Kansas's African American History site includes information on the *Amistad,* American slave narratives, and African slave trade research.

3. The African-American Mosaic
http://lcweb.loc.gov/exhibits/african/afam001.html
This Library of Congress Resource Guide for the study of black history and culture is divided into four sections: colonization, abolition, migration, and the WPA.

4. African Americans
http://home.san.rr.com/jg/USHistory3AfricanAmer.html
From this highly recommended Web site travel to many interesting sites, including the Schomburg Center for Research in Black Culture, and the Black History Museum.

5. Africana.com
http://www.africana.com
Called the Black Lane on the Information Highway, this site includes Encarta Africana, archives, virtual scholars, and a new media center. It contains up-to-date cultural information and reviews of books, films, videos and events.

6. The Black Market.com
http://theblackmarket.com/blksites.html
Billled as "Other Black Sites," this site leads to a wide range of fascinating and different sites: women, professional organizations, newspapers, religious sites, music-related sites, colleges and universities, and more.

7. A Deeper Shade of History: Events and Folks in Black History
http://www.ai.mit.edu/~isbell/HFh/black
New to the Web is this Black History database, where you can look up facts by a particular week, month, or year as well as by topic. Includes good biographical information.

8. Education First: Black History Hotlist
http://www.kn.pacbell.com/wired/BHM/bh_hotlist.html
This collection of sites will lead you to Slavery and African American History, African American and "Buffalo" Soldiers, the Civil Rights Movement and Protests, Twentieth Century Oral History, African American Leaders, and Issues in the News.

9. Encyclopaedia Brittanica Guide to Black History
http://blackhistory.eb.com
This Guide to Black History offers 600 informative articles, illustrated with film clips and audio recordings, in an easy-to-access format: Eras in Black History, Timeline to Achievements, Articles A to Z.

Africa: Ancient and Colonial

10. Africa's Ancient Empires and States
http://artsedge.kennedy-center.org/aoi/resources/ hg/ancient.html
This section of the Kennedy Center's African Odyssey Interactive covers the Nile Valley: Nubia and Egypt; the Western Sudanic Empires of Ghana, Mali, and Songhai; and the Legacy of Slavery and Colonialism.

11. Links to Learn More about Ancient Africa
http://www.mrdowling.com/609-links.html
Mr. Dowling's Virtual Classroom on Ancient Africa covers the Nok, the Phoenicians and Carthage, trade in ancient Africa and many other ancient Africa links.

The Beginnings of the Atlantic Slave Trade

12. Economics of the African Slave Trade
http://dolphin.upenn.edu/~vision/vis/MAR-95/5284.html
Anika Francis at the University of Pennsylvania offers this short essay on the Web.

13. Trans-Atlantic Slave Trade
http://library.advanced.org/13406/contents.html
This four-page description of the trans-Atlantic slave trade covers the period 1450 through 1750.

Early America

14. Chronicling Black Lives in Colonial New England
http://www.csmonitor.com/durable/1997/ 10/29/feat/feat.1.html
This article by Lee Lawrence is a fascinating account of colonial New England attitudes and actions toward African Americans, both slave and free.

15. Museum of Afro-American History Boston
http://www.afroammuseum.org/trail.htm
This museum features a tour of the Black Heritage Trail Online. It explores the history of Boston's nineteenth century community from the vantage point of the Afro-Americans who have lived there as early as 1638.

16. Seacoast New Hampshire Black History
http://www.seacoastnh.com/blackhistory
Here is an account of New Hampshire's African American history, which begins in Portsmouth in 1645.

17. Weevils in the Wheat: Free Blacks and the Constitution, 1787–1860
http://www.apsanet.org/CENnet/thisconstitution/ horton.html
This interesting article was written by James Oliver Horton, associate professor of American civilization at George Washington University, and discusses the relationship of African Americans to the Constitution before the Civil War.

The Civil War

18. Civil War
http://members.aol.com/teachpdlaw/civilwar.htm
This very complete site of Civil War links contains sections on the confessions of Nat Turner, an excellent unit on slavery, the underground railroad, specific portraits of African Americans, and the history of African American troops.

19. The Civil War: The Black Defenders Fight for Freedom
http://www.wanonline.com/blackhistory/1999/blackhistory19996065.html
Offered by the World African Network and CNN Interactive, this article by Deborah G. Simmons celebrates Black History Month 1999. It contains many related links.

20. The Roots of Individualist Feminism
http://www.zetetics.com/mac/fem1.htm
This article, by Wendy McElroy, has been excerpted from *Freedom, Feminism, and the State.* The relation between slavery, abolitionism, and feminism date to the early 1830s. Feminist attitudes pre– and post–Civil War are described here.

Reconstruction and Freedom

21. Ancestry.com—African American Family Research
http://www.ancestry.com/magazine/articles/afamres2.htm
What happened to African Americans after December 18, 1865, when the thirteenth Amendment officially ended slavery in the United States? Read on.

22. Reconstruction
http://members.aol.com/teachpdlaw/civilwar.htm#Reconstruction
Several links to information about Reconstruction are available at this site. They include Jim Crow laws, timelines, and a Reconstruction timetable and other information.

African Americans and the Beginnings of the Twentieth Century

23. Black Creativity and Intellect Invent the Harlem Renaissance
http://www.wanonline.com/blackhistory/1999/blackhistory19996127.html
This article about the Harlem Renaissance is a celebration by Donald Jackson Jr. of Black History Month 1999.

24. Ida B. Wells, Crusader for Justice
http://clem.mscd.edu/~hatter/wells.html
Ida B. Wells's interesting story is told in this article. She is an excellent example of a late-nineteenth-century/early-twentieth-century African American female activist.

25. A Literary Exploration of the Harlem Renaissance
http://www.wanonline.com/blackhistory/1999/blackhistory19996136.html
This short essay by Dolores Bundy is an excellent introduction to the Harlem Renaissance.

26. The Most Atrocious Crime
http://www.pioneerplanet.com/archive/cent/dox/cent15.htm
This account of a lynching in Duluth, Minnesota, in 1920 is shocking but revealing.

African Americans from the Great Depression to World War II

27. Marcus Garvey, Father Divine and the Gender Politics of Race Difference and Race Neutrality
http://muse.jhu.edu/demo/american_quarterly/48.1satter.html
Beryl Satter's essay provides many insights about issues of race in the period of the 1920s to the 1950s.

28. Lest We Forget . . . World War II
http://www.coax.net/people/lwf/ww2.htm
Compiled by Bennie J. McRae Jr., this site contains links to every possible African American connection to World War II from Lena Horne and the Red Tail Project, to the 761st Tank Battalion, to Black Americans Awarded the Medal of Honor.

Modern Civil Rights

29. Civil Rights Oral History Bibliography
http://www-dept.usm.edu/~mcrohb
This bibliography is divided into three parts: a listing of every interview that was found, a list of the archives with contact information, and a subject index. Related sites, history of the research, and transcripts are also available.

30. The National Civil Rights Museum Web Site
http://www.midsouth.rr.com/civilrights
Take an Interactive Tour of the museum at this site for a comprehensive overview of the civil rights movement in exhibit form.

31. Seattle Times: Photo Tour of the Civil Rights Movement
http://www.seattletimes.com/mlk/movement/PT/phototour.html
Photo pages reflect the national civil rights movement.

Contemporary Debates and Issues

32. AFRO-America: The Afro-American Newspapers Home Page
http://www.afroam.org
History, culture and current information about the African American community are available here. Some of the exhibits in the history museum section include Tuskegee Airmen and the Million Man March.

33. NAACP Home Page
http://www.naacp.org
The National Association for the Advancement of Colored People maintains this Web presence, which includes NAACP news and programs and links, as well as sections headed Image Awards, Report Card, Supreme Court, Census 2000, and Education Summit.

34. Southern Poverty Law Center
http://www.splcenter.org
This nonprofit organization combats hate, intolerance, and discrimination through education and litigation. Teaching Tolerance is its education project. Militia Task Force and Klanwatch are part of its intelligence project. Also visit Law Center Information and Legal Action.

We highly recommend that you review our Web site for expanded information and our other product lines. We are continually updating and adding links to our Web site in order to offer you the most usable and useful information that will support and expand the value of your Annual Editions. You can reach us at:
http://www.dushkin.com/annualeditions/.

Unit Selections

1. **The Nile Kingdoms,** Scott MacLeod

2. **Our Third Root: On African Presence in American Populations,** Luz María Martínez Montiel

Key Points to Consider

❖ What is the significance of learning about the Nubian presence in Egyptian history?

❖ After reading "The Nile Kingdoms," what were the greatest discoveries uncovered at the archaeological sites? What place does ancient Sudan have in African history?

❖ Why might there be resistance to discussing the African roots of American culture?

❖ Do you agree or disagree with the idea that today African cultures are returning to their origins? Defend your answer.

❖ Describe your thoughts about the slave trade and its economic and cultural consequences throughout the world today.

 **Links** **www.dushkin.com/online/**

These sites are annotated on pages 4 and 5.

Africa, and its ancient civilizations, have been either ignored or misunderstood throughout history—for most of this century, and before histories of Africa started with nineteenth century European colonialism. Explorers and historians have long been aware that the upper Nile region is occupied by a people of Nubian descent. Unfortunately, Western archaeologists, often thought of Nubian culture as the spillover of Egyptian civilization. As African nations have achieved their independence this historical picture has changed. A new generation of historians are providing a new vision of the African past. New interpretations now provide an expansive and remarkable accounting of precolonial Africa. Now we see revealed a rich and autonomous development of Nubian cultures for hundreds of miles along the Nile Valley.

Equally misunderstood in history is America's involvement in the colonization of Africa. America's connection to Africa is most dramatically examined in the context of Liberia. Liberia stands out as one African nation that, because of its ties to America, resisted European colonization efforts. As Britain, France, and other European powers forced colonialism upon much of Africa, the small black nation faced both hostility and intrigue. England, France, and Germany all aggressively sought to grab Liberian land.

Americans are reluctant to acknowledge the African influences and contributions, which would entail recognizing that Africans have been contributing to American culture since the sixteenth century. "Just as in the Ancient African kingdoms, certain areas represent agglomerations where Africanness is preserved and taught: Harlem, Bahia, Palenque San Basilio, Santiago in Cuba, Matanzas, Barlovento." African cultural development in the Americas represents not only resistance to assimilation but also fosters what Luz Montiel refers to as "the syncretic movements and the movements that result in the cultural conquest of the nonblack world."

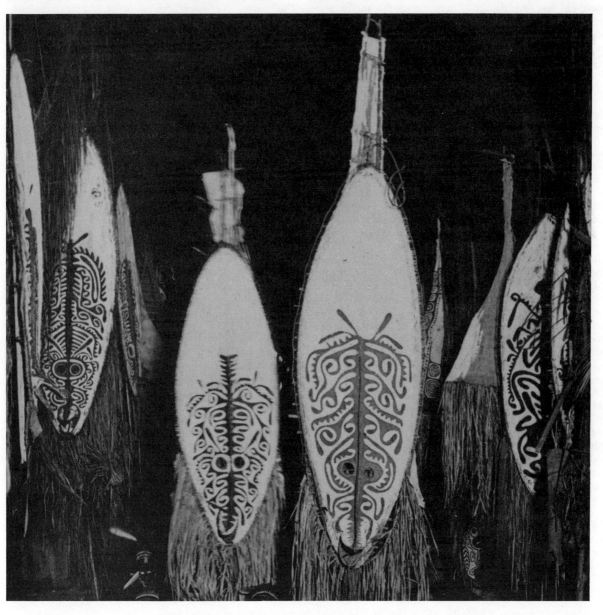

<u>ARCHAEOLOGY</u>

THE NILE KINGDOMS

AFTER DECADES OF DIGGING AND DEBATE, A GREAT NUBIAN CIVILIZATION
IS REVEALED AS A LEADING POWER IN THE ANCIENT WORLD

BY SCOTT MACLEOD/PARIS

The bare-backed warriors march in royal procession, heads held high, hands grasping bows and arrows. This stirring scene is captured in a magnificent limestone relief from the ancient Egyptian Temple of Hatshepsut dating back to 1500 B.C. Yet there's something wrong with this tableau. The soldiers don't have the lean, aquiline features of ancient Egyptians; they have dark brown skin, full lips, large nostrils and layered locks of curly black hair. They are not, in fact, Egyptian infantrymen at all, but Nubians—or to use the term in vogue among archaeologists, Sudanese.

Explorers have long been aware that ancient peoples inhabited the lands of the upper Nile River in what is today modern Sudan. But because of an obsession by Western archaeologists with Egypt's brilliant kingdoms, these Nubian cultures were regarded as little more than spillovers of Egyptian civilization. When Nubians were noticed at all, they were depicted as one of Egypt's defeated enemies or—as in Hatshepsut's shrine—mercenaries in the service of Egypt.

All that is changing, thanks to the remarkable work of excavators from Sudan and various Western countries at several dozen archaeological sites strung hundreds of miles along the Nile from the capital, Khartoum, to the Egyptian border. Digging quietly but steadily since the 1960s, they have uncovered what experts now believe was not only an autonomous culture on the Nile, but one of the greatest civilizations in all of African history. The evidence for such conclusions is finally available in Sudan: Ancient Kingdoms on the Nile, currently at the Institut du Monde Arabe in Paris and moving to the Netherlands and Germany over the course of the next 18 months.

This collection of some 468 statues, ceramics, jewelry and other objects—celebrated as the most spectacular presentation of Nubian antiquities ever organized—was marshaled from nine museums around the world. Taken together, the exhibits reveal a civilization as profound as it was powerful, a richly inventive society influenced by Egyptian, Mediterranean, African—and even Arabian—cultural currents, but distinctive from earliest times. "After a tremendous number of major finds in the

past 20 years, we know a lot more about these kingdoms and their power," says Timothy Kendall, associate curator at the Museum of Fine Arts in Boston. "Sudan was not an Egyptian kingdom but one rooted in central Africa." Adds Dietrich Wildung, curator of the Egyptian Museum in Berlin: "This is nothing less than the discovery of a new dimension of the ancient world. Until now, Nubia has been a no-man's land."

Although not the most dazzling visually, many experts regard the displays of recently discovered Neolithic pottery and burial talismans as the most significant items in the exhibition. The finds predate similar discoveries in Egypt, thus indicating a pre-existing, indigenous Nubian civilization. According to Hassan Hussein Idris, director of Sudan's National Board for Antiquities and Museums, the finds even suggest that Nubia "provided part of Egypt's formative roots" rather than the other way around.

This is just one example of how researchers have been getting Nubia wrong since the beginning of Western excavations in Sudan. For example, when the American Egyptologist George Reisner went digging in the Upper Nile region in 1913, he thought he had discovered an Egyptian colonial outpost. But as the exhibition makes clear, what he actually uncovered was Kerma, the seat of the first great Nubian kingdom, which existed from 2500 to 1500 B.C. The Egyptian statuary and ceramics Reisner found in Kerma were probably objects the Nubians received as gifts or pillaged in battle. Certainly, Nubia's reputation for military prowess dates from this period.

During most of the 1,000-year reign of the Kingdom of Kerma, it was the Egyptians who evidently had the most to fear. The pharaohs built huge fortresses along the Nile to beat back Nubian advances and xenophobic motifs depicting aggression against the Nubians proliferated in Egyptian art of the period.

Field discoveries made over the past decade have strengthened understanding of the most glorious period of them all, the Kingdom of Kush which stretched from 900 B.C. to A.D. 350. At its zenith, King Taharqo ruled over Egypt in what is known today as

Egypt's 25th Dynasty, lasting from 750 to 656 B.C. During this time, the Nubians considered themselves the rightful heirs to an ancient Nile kingdom that embraced both Egypt and Nubia. Famed for their wisdom and piety, they were humane and generous towards defeated enemies. Yet such was the influence of Egyptian culture that the Nubians appropriated Amun, the Egyptian god, for their own ram-headed deity. They even believed Amun's sources of divinity were located in Thebes as well as in their own city of Napata.

The Sudan exhibition instructs as it delights by solving mysteries that have vexed curators for years. The Sudanese government's generous policy of allowing excavators to keep half of their findings once encouraged archaeological missions to Sudan's remote sites. But it also resulted in the separation of many pairs of discovered treasures. In the show, several important sets of objects—such as gold earrings and the bronze legs of a funerary bed adorned by geese, unearthed by a Boston expedition in 1919—are reunited for the first time. Perhaps the most thrilling reunion is that of a granite statue of King Sobekhotep V with its base, which is inscribed with Egyptian hieroglyphics. The Berlin Museum acquired the statue in 1889 in Luxor, while the intrepid Reisner found the base in Kerma and took it to Boston in 1913. A Danish Egyptologist discovered the connection—and hence the statue's identity—only in 1990.

But the exhibit's showstopper is the Ferlini Treasure of exquisite gold amulets, signet rings, necklaces and other items of fine jewelry. An Italian physician, Ferlini accompanied Ottoman viceroy of Egypt Mohammed Ali on his invasion of Sudan in 1821, and discovered the hoard by blasting pyramids open. The booty belonged to Queen Amanishakheto, one of Nubia's most powerful rulers. The items were scattered and many wound up divided between museums. The inclusion of the reunited treasure in the show is, to many archaeologists, a crowning achievement. In some respects, the entire exhibition is a reunion of sorts, giving back ancient Sudan its rightful place in African history.

Our Third Root

On African Presence in American Populations

Luz María Martínez Montiel

The recognition of Africa's contribution to American culture involves accepting an inheritance that is both part of the national heritage and part of the identity and cultural profile of each of our societies. By encouraging its complete assimilation into our history, this recognition also involves the study and dissemination of the culture, which in turn will enable the millions of Afro-Americans spread across the continent to participate in the process of building the future. Once properly recognized, this cultural heritage will produce a rich form of *métissage* and generate pluralism.

Roger Bastide applied the term *Amériques noires* (black Americas) to the cultures created by Africans and preserved by their descendants. When we use the term *Amérique africaine* (African America) in the same sense, we mean it to encompass all that the black man has created, from economic structure to community representation, including techniques of production, types of work, systems of understanding and thought, and the arts and traditions. American cultural movements challenge us to accept our roots. As we begin to better understand our identities, we become more specific and more universal. African cultures, forcefully transformed into American cultures, are returning to their origins.

Africans have been present in America since the first decades of the sixteenth century. According to Du Bois, the number of men and women seized from the African continent approximates 15 million, while De la Roncière puts it at 20 million; if, however, to these numbers are

From *Diogenes*, Autumn 1997, pp. 165-185. © 1997 by Luz María Martínez Montiel. Reprinted by permission.

added those who died in the slave ships during the voyage (35 percent), in the slave pens on the African coast (25 percent), or on the journey from the interior of the continent to the ports (50 percent), as well as the victims of the manhunt (50 percent), a more precise idea of the number sacrificed can be had.

Afro-Americans have developed what is known as *folk-life* in specialized language: a synthesis of African and European traits that took root in America and thus became "native." This is a language whose form has developed its own motifs, styles, and structures. Music and rhythm continue to be an essential mechanism of integration in Africa, and by inheritance, in America, accompanying a great number of social and religious activities in all cultures on both continents. In the United States in particular, they have the functional role of accompanying community activities: tradition is a solid, surviving link between Africa and America. Some forms and techniques have been adapted and incorporated into local societies in Latin America and in the Caribbean. The resulting combinations demonstrate the *métissage* that is at work in the cultural development of countries and peoples who share the same origin.

The oral tradition and the value accorded to the spoken word are other traits that reveal the similarities between descendants of slaves. In South America the oral tradition is present in the *creole culture* in which everyone participates. In a new cultural history this tradition should be brought to the forefront for the study of popular literature and oral tradition are fundamental to the rewriting of the history of Afro-American societies.

America is one in its entirety, but diverse in its plurality. No future is possible without the total participation, as is their right, of the full range of ethnicities that constitute it. Any rejection of our roots, whether Indian, European, or African, will prevent us from eradicating the racist conceptions that, in one way or another, interpolate our identities, *for any people that rejects itself is committing suicide.*

The study of African slavery in America begins with the system of slavery and black trade on the other side of the Atlantic. Despite the particularities due to the complexity of the subject, we find a common denominator of American origin at the heart of the problem: the Negro, that is, the African converted into a slave, into merchandise. To study the Negro as a cultural product requires seeing him within two contexts: on one hand, the slave trade that kidnapped him from his own environment to sell him in America, and on the other, the system of slavery that subjected him to forced labor during the American colonial regime. Reconstructing the scope and nature of the Negro's culture means going even further back into his origins.

From a more current theoretical perspective, documentary resources are available in American and European countries waiting to be catalogued and put to use through diverse and clearly defined research methods. Some of these works should make a priority of examining the positions and evolution of the Christian church's doctrine concerning the trade, for the church had its own interest in providing support for the African slave trade throughout the seventeenth and eighteenth centuries.

What is most needed, however, is a comprehensive study of the role of Africans and Afro-Americans in the economic, social, and cultural development of America. This would require the collaboration of numerous specialists from all of the different countries who have had and still have populations of African descent. A complete study of the trade, of slavery, and of their economic and cultural consequences throughout the world, requires a catalog and inventory of all available American sources of documentation.

In many cases, the printed matter and existing bibliographies on the subject have never traveled beyond their native country, despite an increasing interest in the spread and growth of Afro- American values. In taking up the black man as a theme and as a protagonist in literature, poetry, music, dance, sculpture, and painting, countless cultural expressions work to this end. The black man is not only found in the domain of the fine arts: his natural and ancestral milieu is that of popular culture, which is where we must search for him, for it is here that he has made his greatest contributions.

In the last fifty years, specialists with diverse political backgrounds have studied the economic relationship between blacks and other marginalized minorities in the United States, the Caribbean, and South America. In reviews and other periodicals, blacks continue to be a theme, but one consistently treated with respect to *subculture* and the various migratory movements toward the industrial centers of northern countries. This phenomenon provokes the disintegration of the family, inter-ethnic clashes, and the formation of ghettos in poor areas. Today the subject of minorities and their assimilation into dominant cultures is returning to the forefront.

At the time of the independence of our American countries, the status of the black man rose from slave to citizen. Questions were of course raised about his ability to assimilate Anglo-Saxon or Latin models of culture. It was thought that his strange culture, with its different customs and forms of thought and perception, would prevent, or at least pose serious obstacles to, the integration of Africans into American societies and Western culture. Regarding this issue, it is of interest to take a look at the Afro-American religions, which had in fact captured the attention of some of the first researchers,

such as Nina Rodriguez in Brazil and Fernando Ortiz in Cuba. In Haiti, it was at first thought that voodoo, the religion of the black rural masses, was the major hindrance to the economic and social development of the island. It was in this country, however, that the negritude movement got its start, a movement demanding among other things the reevaluation of formerly misunderstood and despised local religions, taught to be "superstitions." The North American occupation of Haiti revived the elite's nationalism and produced a realization that led to the cultural unity of all Haitians and, finally, to their embrace of their African heritage.

Some authors believe that science has severed its last links to ideology in these last decades. This rupture has indeed encouraged the systematic application of scientific analyses and theories to the study of surviving African culture. However, it cannot really be asserted that the links between science and ideology have been thoroughly severed: absolute neutrality and objectivity seem impossible to obtain in this era, still plagued with problems of racial and ethnic integration across the world and in particular throughout America, where integration has known periods of violence.

In the Caribbean, ancient forms of the *santeria* cults, which are of Nigerian origin, are reappearing in the form of large religious movements. These religions are practiced by fully active ethnic groups who are in the process of reinterpreting their own traditions. Such reports bear witness to a new return to the African roots of these so called syncretic religions. There are other examples; in daily practice the religion of Yoruba origin (*santeria*), usually considered a *cosa de negros* (a black affair), includes an increasing number of nonblack participants in the countries in which it is practiced. These collective rituals of religious communion have resulted in the "Africanization" of whites. Such manifestations of identification with Africa prove that, contrary to what has been thought, slavery has not totally destroyed black culture. Assimilation must be considered with respect to the extent of disorder instigated by the white man on the reorganization of black nuclear structures according to the options and models offered by the dominant society. In the course of a long process of *métissage*, blacks, whites, and Indians have all contributed to new forms of living and dancing, new beliefs, and even new culinary recipes.

In light of the above, we can now call upon the proposition made by Bastide in his work, "the ideology of negritude, born in the West Indies, claims to reground the black American in his ancestral culture; the wise man who studies the problems of Afro-Americans finds himself implicated, whether he wants it or not, in an agonizing debate, for the America of tomorrow depends on the conclusions that he makes."

Several authors have agreed on the "gesture" of independence, by which the insurgent armies of America predominantly lined up their ranks with black people and representatives of castes *who had already opposed a resistance to colonial forces*. In fact, one recognizes the important role that they played in the liberation of our continent, for it is reasonable to assume that it was the dark-skinned who undermined the core of colonial power by blazing the road to freedom in America. The validity of this theory is proven by Haiti's example.

The opposition between blacks and Indians was reinforced, even legally so, by outlawing, for example, mixed marriages. In this way, it was ensured that black descendants of Indians, who inherited the mother's status at birth, would not go free. A great number of lawsuits attest to the racial rivalry between blacks and Indians. This is not to say that the rivalry was formerly nonexistent; it is to say that as a result of white power, the laws in question served to reinforce it.

One of the greatest achievements of the anthropological sciences in the last century is the recognition that no society exists without culture and that all human groups have a cultural heritage that cannot be dissolved or abolished by a change in economic structure, as long as it persists in the official discourse and in educational institutions, both public and private.

In America, the factors that characterize cultural revolution are also found in the strength of precolonial cultures—the results of the *métissage* that occurred throughout the centuries of colonial domination, and the transformations that took place after independence. On this subject, Leopold Zea quotes Vascortelos who wrote: "in Spanish America, Nature will no longer repeat her partial trials. There will no longer be a race of a single color with particular traits, the kind that would emerge from an Atlantis fallen into oblivion. The future race will not be a fifth or sixth one, destined to surpass those that preceded it; what will be born is the definitive race, the race of synthesis, or the integrated race, steeped in the wisdom and blood of all people, and as a result, more capable of proving the possibility of true brotherhood and a truly universal vision." Zea ends thus, "All equal amongst each other as a result of their differences, but none sufficiently different that some could be considered more or less 'men' than others."

From the conquest of America to the present day, South American countries have been oriented toward the assimilation of Western values, but the search for identity by the populations produced by *métissage* remains a subject of vital importance today. The history of the last centuries is in part an account of the failures and successes in the search for a national culture. In the new history, all the cultural processes and movements, such as negritude, that have contributed to

forging the identity of a plural and multiethnic people must be gathered together.

In order to activate all facets of identity, to write a history that includes our Amerindians and blacks in addition to the Europeans, we must write a new history. To achieve this we must use the museums of our many American countries to create spaces that serve to disseminate the existence of our third African root and all of its contents.

Aureola Molina, the thinker of Vera Cruz notes, "history doesn't unfold by itself but follows the people closely: those who do not value their past are incapable of imagining a future in keeping with the mark that they have made in history."

As for the rest it is up to the American peoples to have the last word on their identity and on the preservation of their traditions.

Sources of Documentation on the Trade and African Enslavement

Our primary sources of data are made up of the numerous works written on the slave trade, the forced immigration of Africans, and the study of African communities in America. The first represent the resources used in the pioneering works of this century; the second is comprised of the work of historians, anthropologists, sociologists, etc., dedicated to synthesizing the initial collection of documents. These initial works describing the black man in America are generally of an ethnographic nature, based on first hand accounts of the customs, rituals, and beliefs of the descendants of African slaves. Even if they involve judgments that fail to totally understand their subject, their testimony is very valuable in reconstructing America's social and cultural history.

Documentary resources, the necessary base from which a complete vision of the trade can be arrived, should not only provide for the causes and consequences of slavery, but also help determine the volume of traffic, broken down by era, period, and century, as well as its form and the consequences of the massive migration of Africans to America, Europe, and Africa. Some authors have even used existing documents as a base from which to study other aspects of the slave trade, such as the personality traits of the procurers, their commercial relationships, and their social status, that is, the world of slave traders from the factory bosses, to the ship owners, the slave brokers, the shippers, etc.[1]

The first stories of the trade are best documented in Spanish archives, even though the first brokers were Portuguese. Historians have established that the supervision of the trade was divided between the Indian council (*Consejo de Indias*), the Chamber of Commerce (*Casa de Contratación*), and the Finance Council (*Consejo de Hacienda*). The boats were registered in Seville and the ac-

counts were kept at the General Audit Court (*Contaduría Mayor de Hacienda*). The General Indian Archives represent thus the first documented source concerning the trading, the General Archives of Simanca follow as do the Historic Provincial Archives of Valladolid and the National Historical Archives of Madrid, as well as the Naval Museum and the Library of the Royal Academy of History.[2]

Although much documentation on the trade exists in the European countries involved, they have not been sufficiently studied, despite their obvious importance. Portugal, Great Britain, France, and, in other respects, the Netherlands, all possess very rich documentary inheritances which are well enough organized to be useful. The oral tradition, which takes up where archival evidence is ignored, makes reference to the demographic drain suffered by the African continent. Slavery has become a part of the body of myths and legends maintained by the oral tradition of the African peoples, but even so it remains an insufficiently explored and potentially valuable line of research.

The information on the documentation concerning Africans and their American descendants has yet to be logically organized in the countries of the New World. The organized resources that we currently possess are those thanks to the efforts of international organizations such as UNESCO who have taken the preservation of this information to heart. The many meetings that have focused on the cultural relations between Africa and Latin America have yielded a series of recommendations for both short- and long-term action. At last, the need for a center of documentation and information specializing in the study of African culture in Latin America has been recognized. The final document of the 1964 meeting further suggests the exchange of facsimiles, documents, bibliographies, and documentary files between Africa and Latin America. In support of this suggestion, they underlined the need for a catalogue of cultural, institutional, and other available collections, specific to the issues concerning Afro-Latino-Americans in Africa, America or any other country that has an historical interest in the matter.

Over one hundred volumes worth of documents and works on this theme and related details can be cited. Only the essential ones will be mentioned here, those sources that will most benefit from a wide distribution. This is only the beginning of a new investigation that has posed numerous difficulties to the experts, for the creation of a catalogue of documents relating to the theme of blacks in America demands that all of the archives be organized in accordance with international systems. The libraries and archives of different American countries have all adopted varying systems of classification. In each case the criteria used were those that were directly related to the research underway at the time. In Latin America, documents were organized in a system based on colonial affairs. It is only in the last twenty-five years that blacks have emerged as a theme of research (still in the developmental stages for some institutions) with rubrics covering slavery, the trade, slave revolts, and other subjects of interest such as emancipation and liberation.

Once accepted as an object of study, blacks became the subject of highly-specialized books by authors recognized in the field of human and social sciences. In generaL the primary centers of documentation are to be found in the capitals of Latin-American countries, as are the majority of specialists and institutions. In certain cases, however, several cities house important archives within a single country, such as Seville, Simancas, and Valladolid in Spain or Cordoba, Jalapa, and Mexico City in Mexico. These centers of documentation must be hierarchized.

A certain reticence can be felt with respect to this theme and added to the list of factors disfavoring the adequate classification of material related to blacks in the Latin American archives. In many countries the history taught does not give an account of the influx and presence of Africans in each American region. Even universities do not offer consistent courses on black cultures. The prejudices born of slavery have contributed to the negation of Africa and to the ban on teaching its cultures at all levels of the system, from kindergarten to higher education. Only in these last decades have historical studies taken Africa and its cultures, art, and folklore into account. Literature, anthropology, and sociology have served as a vector of dissemination for African cultures. There nonetheless remains a lot to do, for university chairs devoted to Afro-American cultures are the exception rather than the rule. Even amongst the programs of study with a focus on Latin America, there are only a few institutions of higher education and research who take the past and present of Asia and Africa into account. The old prejudices have not been completely dispelled. Few historians have really objectively evaluated the ethnic and social development of the American continent despite the recent emphasis by black-culture specialists on the participation of Africans in the social struggles of the colonial era and in the wars of independence.

Still, the progress of history itself has obliged the historians and other scientists to widen the field of their research. They are now publishing works that pose theoretical questions: about the significance of the regime of slavery in America; about the economic correlation between American countries on a global level during the period of slavery; and about the process of the development and decline of the regime of slavery in America, to name only a few of the most interesting themes.

While the works addressing the life of blacks in America already number the hundreds, their production is very uneven, and there are extreme differences between the publications of various countries. In all of Latin America there exist only a few reviews that focus on the theme or themes relative to black Americans, and of these, some are limited to just a few issues (this was the case with *Afroamerica* which published only three issues).

In countries with a strong Amerindian population such as Peru, Mexico, Ecuador, and Bolivia, the presence of black culture is not of quite the same proportion as it is in Brazil, Venezuela or Colombia where the black population is historically strong and has left a large lineage. This explains the importance of the documentation of blacks in these countries, as it does the importance of the direct study of Afro-American communities.

Ecuador offers only a few isolated monographs based on archival documents; in Bolivia and Chile the bibliography on blacks is quite reduced and, in fact, specialized works are rare. Specialized bibliographies such as the Afro-Paraguayan one by Paulo de Carvalho Neto or the Uruguayan one by Alfonso Pereda Valdéz are rather exceptional.

In two countries, Cuba and Brazil, African influence has preserved the folklore and the traditions. Most of the studies of documentation and actual populations of African descent have been carried out there. In these countries, the study of black cultures does take place in the universities where they teach the different languages still used in religious rites, and a special importance is accorded to the study of recent migrations from Brazil toward Africa.

On the Term "Afro-American"

In their respective domains, history, sociology, ethnology, and other disciplines all grapple with the African presence in America, which now forms a collective that we call *African America*. The results of slavery have become a global reality in which the traces of our ancestors are manifest and alive, where Africanness is a substance not only biological but also a product of history and cultural roots. Its territory is not defined, though it is easy to observe the weight of its representation in certain regions, in people's faces, in their devotion to the inescapable use of drums, in the continuity of *afro-synthetic* ritual. There are nuances in demographic distribution across the map, but the African constituency covers the entire country, from Canada to Argentina and from the Pacific to the Atlantic. It is the link that has built, through slavery, the complex chain of the world of *métissage*. Perhaps the concept of Afro-American arises from a methodological need for a term that designates the African element spread throughout the peoples of the continent; this would be a term similar to Latin America or Spanish America, drawing attention to the makeup of the occidental world via a name (Spanish or Latin) of a part of their land. These terms have, however, held the black person at a distance, separating him from America and negating his position as a cultural agent in Latin America; in addition, the African sector is kept separate in English and Dutch speaking countries. In other words, Latin America is exclusive as a result of its European mold, while African America includes all Americans who have African roots whether their language be French, English or Spanish.

The term *Amerindian,* which underlines the persistence of pre-colonial cultures in predominantly Indian regions, must also be considered. A broad and politically engaged term, it designates in particular the America weakened by the devastating actions of conquest. "Amerindian," like "Afro-American," is an inclusive term that unites the original cultures of the entire continent, or in any case, what is left of them. This term designates the country's most distant history, that of its Old World founders. It stands as an epilogue, defends them from complete destruction, and represents five centuries of unfailing survival.

African America has no more of a frontier and is no more homogenous than *Amerindian*. Just as in the ancient African kingdoms, certain areas represent agglomerations where Africanness is preserved and taught: Harlem, Bahia, Palenque San Basilio, Santiago in Cuba, Matanzas, Barlovento. . . . Contemporary diasporas originate in these places, fostering resistance to assimilation, but also fostering the syncretic movements and the movements that result in the cultural conquest of the *nonblack* world.

In Mexico, the term "Afro-American" took on its conceptual dimension at the time of the first Inter-American Demographic Congress which took place in the capital. The International Institute of Afro-American studies was founded on 20 October 1943 with the review *Afroamerica* as the periodical mouthpiece of the Institute. The two would last for only a brief duration: the review only published three issues; 1 and 2 in the first volume and 3 in the second, despite the fact that the most prestigious Afro-Americanists were involved in the review's promotion: M. Herskovits, A. Lokce, R. Price, J. Price Mars, A. Ramos, F. Ortiz, G. Aguirre Beltrán, J. Le Reverand, and Jorge A. Vivó, among others.

On 5 July 1946 Aguirre Beltrán's work *La población negra de México* came out. The sequel would be published in 1958 under the name *Cuijla, esbozo etnográfico de un pueblo negro*. Since then, and until 1976, the Center of Higher Research of the National Institute of Anthropology and History

(INAH) has initiated the Afro-American Conference which still functions in various capacities.

Documentation

The following summary of UNESCO catalogues will give an idea of the resources currently available.

ARGENTINA—*Nation's General Archives*: the most significant source of information on blacks. *National Library Archives*: here are found works on blacks, slaves and slavery within the country. *Archives of the Library of Congress*: documents relating to blacks. *Archives of the Minister of External Relations and of the Cult*: documents on the terms of the slave trade and the traffic in blacks. *Archives of the National Institute of Anthropology*: details of the folklore of black populations. *Archives of the Buenos Aires Customs*: details on the traffic of blacks and the trade. In certain private libraries and archives one can also find old and new materials treating blacks.

BOLIVIA—*Historical Archives of Potosí*: the material concerning blacks is spread throughout the documentation: documents about black slaves refer to those employed to work in a metal foundry. *Ecclesiastical Archives*: baptism records of black slaves. *National Archives of Bolivia*: documents corresponding to the colonial and nationalist periods. *National Library of Bolivia*: printed materials from the colonial era on blacks in the history of Bolivia.

BRAZIL—paradoxically, this country does not possess a great number of documents concerning blacks, although there are royal maps, decrees, rulings, and a somewhat reduced set of documentation. As is well known, most of the official documents concerning slaves were destroyed in 1890, when the slaves were liberated and slavery was abolished. This resulted from the idea that slavery was a stain which should disappear forever. By granting the legitimacy of this generally held opinion, the abolitionist confederation, which harbored the most fervent defenders of black liberty among its ranks, demanded and obtained from the Financial Minister of the provisional government of the Republic, the abolitionist Ruy Barbosa, the destruction by fire of all papers, books and documents relating to slaves, the registration of slaves, the "ingenuos" (the sons of slaves born after the emancipation), the free sons of slaves' wives, and the emancipated sexagenarians, for as was stated in the minister's order, it was the duty of the Republic to destroy all vestiges of slavery for the honor of the fatherland.[3]

In spite of this enormous loss, one can still find documentation in the *National Archives*, at the *Brazilian Historic and Geographical Institute*, in the *Archives of the*

State of Bahia and in many libraries such as the National Library. In retrospect, the Brazilian bibliography on this subject remains extensive and deep. It is a collection of the most significant aspects of the lives of blacks in Brazil. Among Brazilian authors, there are in particular: Raymundo Nina Rodríguez, Arthur Ramos (already mentioned), Manuel Querino, René Ribeiro, Octavio Iani, Henrique Cardoso, L.A. Costa Pinto, and Tales de Acevedo, from among so many others that to list them all would take too long.

COLOMBIA—the *Historic National Archives of Colombia*: documentary resources on mines, lands, introduction of populations, ornaments, taxes, and a large section on the subject of the black population or slaves called "Negros y Esclavos" in the *Historical Archives of Antioqía*. The documentation corresponds to colonial and independent periods. There is a more specific department containing a section on slaves including various documents referring to the black population.

CUBA—*General Archives*: whose catalog was developed by specialists from the *Institute of the History of the Academics of the Sciences in Cuba* who published a catalog summarizing documentary resources. A good number of Cuban archival materials were transferred to Spain. Those that refer the most closely to colonial life must be consulted in the *General Archives in India*. In any case the materials referring to the blacks abound in the section entitled *Historic Archives*. There one can find facts by which to study the trade and piracy in close relation to the trafficking of slaves. One mustn't forget that in Cuba, as in other countries, provincial or regional archives should be the object of thorough, fundamental research.

CHILE—the *National Archives of Chile* have assembled all historical documentation of a public character which can be found in the country: the acts, notary records, and those of the court are particularly pertinent to the study of blacks.

DOMINICAN REPUBLIC—the *General Archives of the Nation*: here one finds different sections corresponding to different historical periods—the Spanish colonial era, the French colonial era, Haitian domination, etc. *Cathedral Archives*: black baptism, marriage and death records.

ECUADOR—*Municipal Archives of Quito*: one of the principal centers of documentary research; the most significant section is the book of Chapters (Cabildos). *Archives of the Legislative Power*: references to slaves and to emancipated slaves. *Archives of Archevêché*: details in various documents on the blacks' enslavement. *Guayaquil Archives*: references to blacks in several cities.

EL SALVADOR—*General National Archives*: the documentation is dispersed throughout and there is no section devoted to the black population.

GUATEMALA—*General Government Archives*: the "Colony" section devotes itself mainly to titles from the registry, royal patronage, government decrees; the references to blacks are important in the section dedicated to royal warrants.

HONDURAS—*Honduran General Archives*: scattered references to blacks.

MEXICO—*General National Archives*: archives of great importance concerning history; here we find close to 25,000 volumes. Sections that refer to the subject of blacks: the Inquisition, royal warrants, interrogations of parties, ordinances, favors, Jesus Hospital, history, and patrons. The significant characteristic of these archives is that other institution's resources have been added to them. Now we will attempt to classify exhaustively the places where, unless otherwise indicated, the sections containing materials on blacks are found. *Financial Historical Archives*: many materials on blacks. *Mexico City Hall Archives*: materials relating to slavery. *Notary Archives of the District Federal Department*: multiple details concerning blacks. The State's notary and parish records are very important and remain mostly unexplored.

NICARAGUA—*Nicaraguan National Archives*: completely destroyed by the earthquake in 1931. *Parish Archives*: a source of information concerning baptisms, deaths, marriages and births among blacks.

PANAMA—*National Archives*: the judicial section is of special interest for it contains testimony referring to the sale of slaves. In the index one will find maps of concessions, documents referring to the introduction of black slaves, to the dark-skinned revolt, to the distribution of blacks, to the war against the dark-skinned, to punishments and misdemeanors, to alliances between dark-skinned and corsairs, to the liberation and rights of blacks, in addition to important documents on this topic.

PARAGUAY—*Paraguayan National Archives*: documents on blacks. *Parish Archives*: also, documents on blacks.

PUERTO RICO—*General Puerto Rican Archives*: numerous contracts of purchase/sale as well as details of marriages, escapes, emancipation, and testimony of blacks. *Parish Archives*: here we find documents relating to blacks and mulattos. *Municipal Archives of San Juan*: details concerning slaves and freed blacks, mulattos etc. *Carnegie Public Library*: details on slaves and slavery. *Library of Athénée of Porto Rico*: here one finds a collection of minutes from sessions of Spanish courts, with acts by deputies and debates concerning the slavery question.

PERU—*Peru National Archives*: rich information on blacks. Here we find materials from the king's coffers, customs, and from the Court of Accounts and Finance. *Archives of the Minister of Foreign Relations*: documents relating to slaves. *Cuzco Archives*: references to black slaves. *National Library*: one documentation concerning blacks.

URUGUAY—*General National Archives* and *Parish Archives*: in these we find birth records related to slaves and to affairs concerning emancipation, testimonies, sales, etc. The documents that are found in the *General National Archives* contain details of the capture of slaves, the permits for their sale, the licenses for the purchases of boats destined for the trade, hunts for blacks, census, emancipation, etc. One also finds an equally interesting list of slaves as a part of the goods owned by inhabitants of Montevideo. *Archives of the Montevideo Customs*: lists slave ships with the names of the vessels, their nationality, equipment, and the number of slaves. *National Library*: an important resource concerning general information on blacks in Uruguay.

VENEZUELA—The principal source of documentation pertaining to blacks is found in the *General National Archives*. One should next mention the *Archevêché Archives* and certain primary registries such as those in Caracas and the parish archives which are of great interest.

Bibliography

I. Regional bibliography English-speaking America

The works in Mexican libraries concerning black, English-speaking cultures are few in number and often treat the sociological phenomenon of blacks in actual societies. There are, however, few works that approach the subject from a historical perspective.

In *1713* the political events that enabled England to gain supremacy over other European powers guaranteed it monopoly of the trade in Spanish-American territories for a period of thirty years. The monopoly included the transport of slaves to Peru. During these years and until the beginning of the eighteenth century, the Anglo-Saxons established their presence on the isthmus by means of the slave trade, maintaining equal control over re-exportation, in effect, the economy of Panama. In 1739, three years before its term, the agreement with the English came to an end. Later, however, other licenses would be granted to the Friers of London. They were directly involved in Panamanian trading from 1752 to 1753 and from 1758 to 1761. During this time, Jamaica was definitively transformed into the principal reserve of slaves offering merchandise to the Caribbean slave traders.

The French succeeded the English, taking advantage of freed licenses granted to individuals such as Barboteau between 1743 and 1745, and Malhorty between 1746 and 1748. From 1764 to 1779 they revived the conditions of the eighteenth century by granting a monopoly agreement to the Cádiz traders of the Aristegui and Aguirre society. In truth, the pivotal bulk of the trade remained Flemish and English, the slaves being exported, as we have seen, from Jamaica, the great slaving port of the Caribbean.

Loren Katz, William. *Teacher's Guide to American Negro History*. Quadrangle Books, Chicago, 1968.

Carreras, Julio Angel. *Breve historia de Jamaica*. La Havane, Ed. Ciencias Sociales, 1984.

Various Authors. *El moviemiento negro en Estados Unidos—Now*. La Havane, Ensayos Unstituto del Libro, 1967.

Nichols, J.L. *The New Progress of a Race*. Naperville, DLI, J.L.Nichols, 1929.

Hoover, Dwight W. *Understanding Negro History*. Chicago, Quadrangle Books, 1968.

Herskovits, Melville I. *The Myth of Negro Past*. Boston, Beacon Press, 1941.

Just Butcher, Margaret. *El Negro en la cultura norteamericana*. Mexico, Letras, 1958.

Minas, Siendo W. *Slavery, Colonialism and Racism*. New York, W.W.Norton, 1974.

Cueto, Mario G. del. *Historia, economía y sociedad en los pueblos de habla ingles del Caribe*. La Havane, Ed. Ciencias Sociales, 1982.

Millette, James. *El sistema colonial inglès en Trinidad (1783–1810)*. La Havane, Casa de las Américas, 1985.

Lobat, R.P. *Viajes a las islas de la América*. La Havane, Casa de las Américas, 1979.

Cavalcanti, Cristina. "El movimiento rastafari y la lucha por la identidad," in *El Caribe Contemporáneo*, no. 10, Mexico, UNAM, 1987.

The dark skinned communities of Guyane did not manage to form a geographically determined entity and were, in fact, considered a group of tribes out of which four groups were distinguishable: *saramaca, auca*, also known as *djuka, boni* and *matawaai*.

Misunderstood for a long time, the *"bushmen"* of the Guinea forests abruptly caught the interest of the ethnologists who thought they were discovering, by studying them, a culture that conserved its African purity, the origin of which could be located in the *agni-ashanti* zone.

Gaslinga, Cornelio Ch. *Los holandeses en el Caribe*. La Havane, Casa de las Américas (Serie Estudios), 1983.

Lamur, H.E. *The Demographic Evolution of Surinam, 1920–1970*. La Haye, Martinus Nyhoff, 1973.

Groot, Silvia W. *Djuka society and Social Change*. Pays-Bas, Te assien par Van Gorcum, 1969.

Kom, A. *Nostros esclavos de Surinam*. La Havane, Casa de las Américas, 1981.

The French-speaking Caribbean

The special attention devoted to the French speaking areas of the Caribbean is essentially thanks to Haiti, where the first great slave revolt occurred. That revolt is considered the precedent for all such actions that occurred in Latin America. The rest of the islands, that is to say the Little West Indies, including Guadeloupe and Martinique, which continued under a permanent colonial system until our time, have acquired a particular connotation. The isolation, more than the language barrier, was the result of the psycho-social status of the two islands, who did not go beyond their borders, and released little information to the outside world.

Apart from its legendary aspect, the Haitian revolution is considered the first victory of revolted slaves in history because the French were soundly routed. After the revolution, the territory left the colonial sphere, and the social group that had formerly been oppressed by the colonial powers became the new power and government. This antecedent broke the ground for a whole body of serious thought on the liberation of blacks, and their cultural situation and identity while assimilated to the values of white culture.

Dathorne, O.R. *Caribbean Aspirations and Achievements*. Florida, Association of Caribbean Studies, 1985.

Franco, José Luciano. *Ensayos sobre el Caribe*. La Havane, Ed. Ciencias Sociales, 1980.

Cesaire, Aimé. *Cuaderno de un Retorno al país natal*. Mexico, ERA, 1969.

Gisler, Antoine, C.S.S.P. *L'esclavage aux Antilles françaises*. Fribourg, Ed. Univ., 1965.

Price-Mars, Jean. *Así habló el tío*. La Havane, Casa de las Américas, 1968.

Von Graferstein, Johanna. *América Latina. Una breve Historia: Haïti*. Mexico, Alianza, 1988.

Textos de la historia de Centroamérica y el Caribe: Haïti 1, Mexico, Nueva Imagen, 1988.

Textos de la historia de Centroamérica y el Caribe: Haïti 2, Mexico, Nueva Imagen, 1989.

Bellati, Felice. *Alaou Haiti*, Ban. Ed. Leonardo da Vinci, 1964.

Casimir, Jean. *La cultura oprimida*. Mexico, Nueva Imagen, 1980.

Metraux, Alfred. *Ler Vaudou haïtien*. Paris, Gallimard, 1968.

Larose, Serge. *L'exploitation agricole en Haïti*. Montréal, Centre des Recherches Caraïbes, 1976.

Vera, Pedro Jorge. *Haití*. La Havane, Casa de las Américas, 1967.

Labelle, Micheline. *Idéologie de couleur et classes sociales en Haïti*. Montréal, 1978.

Hurbon, Laënec. *Culture et Dictature en Haïti*. Port-au-Prince, Henri Deschamps, 1987.

Fouchard, Jean. *Les Marions de la Liberté*. Paris, Ed. de l'Ecole, 1972.

II. General bibliography of the historical development of slavery

Van Sertina, Y. *Ils y étaient avant Christophe Colomb*. Paris, Flammarion, 1981.

Saco, J.A. *Historia de la esclavitud de la raza africana en el Nuevo Mundo y, en especial, los países Américo-hispanos*. La Havane, Cultura, 1938.

Curtis, P.D. *The Atlantic Slave Trade*. A census. Madison/Londres, Univ. of Wisconsin Press, 1969.

Franco, J.L. *Comercio clandestino de esclavos*. La Havane, Ed. Ciencias Sociales, 1985.

Klein, H.S. *La esclavitud africana en América Latina y el Caribe*. Madrid, Alianza Ed., 1986.

Mannix, D.P. et Cowley, M. *Historia de la trata de los negros.* Madrid, Alianza Ed., 1970.

Scelle, G. *La traite négrière aux Indes de Castille. Contrats at traites d'asiento.* Paris, 1906.

Chaunu, H.P. *Séville et l'Atlantique (1504–1650).* Paris, 1956–1959.

Mellafe, R. *Breve historia de la esclavitud en América Latina.* Mexico, SEP/SETENTAS, 1973.

Vila Vilar, E. *Hispano-América y el comercio de esclavos. Los asientos portugeses.* Séville, EEHA/CSIC, 1977.

Herskovits, M. *The Myth of the Negro Past.* Boston, 1941.

Morner, M. *La mezcla de razas en la historia de América Latina. Vigencia de los cultos afroamericanos.* Buenos Aires, Fernando Garcia Cambeiro, 1986.

Bastide, R. *Las Américas negras.* Mexique, Alianza Ed., 1967.

Gallardo, J.E. *Presencia africana en la cultura de América Latina. Vigencia de los cultos afroamericanos.* Buenos Aires, Fernando Garcia Cambeiro, 1986.

Carvalho-Neto, P. *El folclore de las luchas sociales.* Mexique, Siglo XXI, 1973.

Price, R. *Sociedades cimarronas. Comunidades esclavas rebeldes en las Américas.* Mexique, Siglo XXI, 1981.

Moura, C. *O Negro. De bom escravo a mau a'dado.*

Jahn, J. *Manuel de Littérature Neo-Africaine, du XXIe siècle à nos jours, de l'Afrique à l'Amérique.*

Verger, P. *Flux et reflux de la traite des nègres entre le golfe de Beniu et Bahia de Todos os Santos.* Paris, Mouton, 1968.

Arrazola, R. *Palenque, primer pueblo libre de América (Historias de las sublevacones de esclavos en Cartagens).* Cartagena, Ed.Hernández s.d.

Brito Figueroa, F. *Las insurrecciones de Los negros en la sociedad colonial venezolana.* Caracas, Ed. Cantaclaro, 1961.

Carniero, E. *O Quilombo dos Palmares.* Ed. Civil. Brasileira, 1966.

Kapsoli, W. *Sublevaciones de esclavos en el Perú.* Lima, Univ. Ricardo Palma, DUI, 1975.

Carneiro Da Cunha, M. *Negros, estrangeiros. Os escravos liberto e sua volta a africa.* São Paulo, Brasiliense, 1985.

Olinto, A. *Brasileiros na Africa.* La Havane, Ed. Ciencias Sociales, 1968.

Sanacino, Rodolfo. *Los que volvieron a Africa.* La Havane, Ed. Ciencias Sociales, 1968.

Bastide, R. *Blancos e negros em São Paulo.* São Paulo, Comp. Ed. Nacional, 1959.

Dzidzienyo, A. *The Position of Blacks in Brazilian Society.* London, rapp. no. 7, Miority Rights Group, 1971.

Toplin, R.B. *Slavery and Race Relations in Latin America.* Westport/London, Greenwood Press, 1974.

Alvarez Nazario, M. *El elemento afronegroide en el español de Puerto Rico. Contribución al estudio del negro en América.* San Juan, Inst. Cult. Puertorriqueña, 2nd ed., 1974.

De Granada, G. *Estudios sobre un àrea dialectal hispanoamericana de población negra. Las tierras bajas occidentales de Columbia.* Bogota, inst. Caro y Cuervo, 1977.

Magenny, W.W. "Africa en Venezuela: su herencia lingüística y su cultura literaria," in *Montalban,* no. 15, Caracas, 1985.

Ballagas, E. *Antología de la poesía hispanoamericana.* Madrid, Aguilar, 1935; "Situación de la poesiá afroamericana" in *Revista Cubana de Educación,* vol. 21, Havana, January 1946.

Pereda Valdes, Y. "El negro en la literatura iberoamericana" in *Cuadernos,* no. 19, Paris, 1956.

Ramos Guedes, J.M. *El negro en la novela venezolana.* Caracas, 1980.

Anson, L.M. *La negritud.* Ed. Revista de Occidente, 1971.

Guillen, N. *Antologia mayor.* La Havane, Instituto del Libro, 1969.

Feijoo, S. *El negro en la literatura folclórica cubana.* La Havane, Ed. Letras Cubanas, 1980.

Leon, A. *Música folclórica cubana.* La Havane, Biblioteca Nacional José Martí, 1964.

Ramon y Rivera, L.F. *La música afrovenezolana.* Caracas, Universidad Central de Venezuela, 1971.

Roberts, S. "Danza negra en América" in *Todo la Danza,* nos. 1 and 7, Buenos Aires, 1975.

Ortiz Oderigo, N. *Aspectos de la cultura africana en el Río de la Plata.* Buenos Aires, Ed. Plus Ultra, 1974.

Vasquez Rodriguez, R.F. *La práctica musical de la población negra en Perú.* La Havane, Ed. de Ciencias Sociales, 1985.

Valente, V. *Sincretisimo religioso afrobrasiliero.* São Paulo, Ed. Nacional, 1950.

Verger, P. F. *Les dieux yoruba an Afrique et au Nouveau Monde.* Paris, PUF, 1982.

Aguirre, Beltrán, Cuijla, G. *Esbozo etnográfico de un pueblo negro.* Mexiquem Fondo de Cultura Económica, 1943.

Introducción a la cultura africana en América Latina, Paris, UNESCO 1979, 2nd ed.

Las culturas del Caribe. Documentos de la Reunión de Expertos sobre el Caribe, en Santo Domingo, 18–22 Sept. 1978, Paris, UNESCO, 1981.

Franco, F.J. *Los negros, los mulatos y la nación dominicana.* Santo Domingo, Ed. Nacional, 1969.

Ortiz, F. *Ensayos etnográficos* (sélection. de Miguel Barnet et Angel L. Fernàndez). La Havane, Ed. de Ciencias Sociales, 1984.

Ramos, A. *Aculturação Negra no Brasil.* São Paulo, Comp. Ed. Nacional, 1942.

III. *Unpublished sources*

ARA Algemeen Ryksarcheif (Archives générales du Gouvernement), La Haye, West Indische Oude Compagnie.

Réunions du XIXe siècle, no. 1–13: acts, secret minutes, reports, transcripts, warrants.

Chambre d'Amsterdam, no. 14–18: acts, commisions, instructions, resolutions.

Verspreide West Indische Stukken, no. 501.

Nieum Nederland, no. 2–6.

Suriname no.463,764,766,767,768,769,770, 973, 1117.

Collectie Rademaeker zaken Oude Wic. 1621–1674, no. 77–84.

Collectie Fagel.

West Indische Compagnie. Nieuwe compagnie.

Chambre d'Amsterdam, no. 52,452,467.

Maps and Papers of Curaçao, no. 1160.

Resolucheboeken van de Staten General, 1580–1680.

Bueno De Mesquita, J.A. et al. Geshuedkundige tydtafel van Suriname Paramaribo, 1924.

Gedenkboek Nederland Curazao, 1634–1934, Amsterdam, 1934.

Cordoba Bello, Eleazar. *Compañías holandesas de navegación,* Seville, 1964.

Berkis, Alexander V. *The Reign of Duke James in Courland,* 1638–1682, Lincoln, Nebraska, 1960.

Eurvens, P.A. "De eerste jood up Curzao" in West Indische Gids, XII, 1930.

Notes

1. E. Vila Vilar, *Hispanoamericana y el comercio de los esclavos* (Seville, 1977), p.9.
2. *Ibid.*
3. Various authors, "Introducción al estudio de los repositorios documentales sobre los africanos y sus descendientes en América" in *Introdución a la cultura africana en América Latina,* pp. 47–122.

Unit 2

Key Points to Consider

❖ Describe the history of slavery as presented in the essay "Under the Whiplash."

❖ Who was responsible for the African slave trade?

❖ Who or what would you consider to be the main impediment to the phasing-out of the slave trade in the nineteenth century?

❖ What insights are gained by seeing slavery from the vantage point of a slave?

 **Links**   **www.dushkin.com/online/**

These sites are annotated on pages 4 and 5.

While slavery has existed throughout antiquity, the institution of slavery was devised by the Greek city-state. Oruno Lara points out that under this system "the slave became a commodity" or what Aristotle referred to as "a piece of property which is animate." Modern slavery, beginning with the start of the Atlantic slave trade, has many similarities to previous slave systems. No one knows exactly how many African and Malagasy captives were sold in the slave markets of the Caribbean and the Americas. In both periods "a variety of methods . . . were used to dehumanize and degrade (the slave), (to) deprive them of their personality and make them different from other human beings, who were not chattels." The Atlantic slave trade added race and racism to the equation. Runaway slaves often banded together in armed struggle or revolt against the system. From its inception, there were but two ways for a slave to gain freedom—to escape or to be emancipated.

The question of responsibility is often asked with respect to the Atlantic slave trade. Elikia M'Bokolo argues that slave raiding, while popular among Europeans, was extremely costly and unpredictable. Precolonial lineage or state societies along the African coast were therefore forced, compelled, or enticed to provide a more efficient means for acquiring slaves. Over time trading networks were established that secured slaves from deep within the African continent.

Many of the colonial governments in America attempted to deter slavery through the passage of import taxes. Unfortunately, as pointed out by William Riddell, every act of any American colony to reduce the slave trade was met with opposition by the British Empire. Continuous circumventions and exclusions actually served to encourage the slave trade in the colonies.

The conditions of slavery have been well documented. But it should be remembered that slavery, with all its horrors and insults, had a very human face. The narrative of Olaudah Equiano vividly recounts the shock and isolation that he felt during the Middle Passage to Barbados. He notes that the ship was a continuous source of his fear, pain, and struggle for survival. From his reports we learn of those slaves who were not docile but a few "somehow made through the nettings and jumped into the sea." Death was preferred "to such a life of misery."

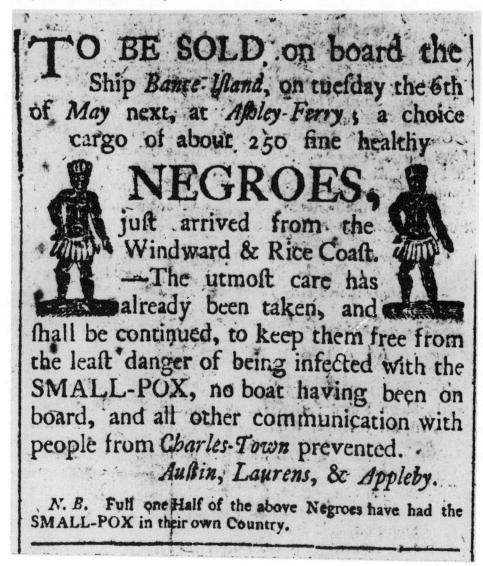

Under the whiplash

by Oruno D. Lara

Slavery existed in early times, but it was in the Greek city-state that the slave became what Aristotle called "a piece of property which is animate"

■ Forced labour existed in a variety of forms throughout Antiquity—in the Egypt of the Pharaohs, the Middle East (Babylon and Assyria), and Greece and Italy. However, slavery as an institution, in which the slave became a commodity or what Aristotle called "a piece of property which is animate", was first devised by the Greek city-states.

Slavery is essentially a relationship in which one person dominates another. It is based on the power of a master, who imposes his will by force and threats. The slave system was created and maintained by violence. Whipping slaves was not only a means of inflicting punishment on them but of dominating them, making an impression on them and reminding them of their state of servitude. Slaves were kept apart from one another. The alternatives before them were "abject submission", escape or rebellion.

This domination was justified by the "original alienation" of the slaves and their status as "people without honour". Stripped of any rights or title, they no longer had any family history, ancestry or issue. Completely isolated, they could not receive or hand down any heritage. In their state of rootless alienation, they were tools whose owners could treat them as they saw fit. Masters had a whole array of physical or symbolic instruments which they could use to control the bodies of their slaves.

When did the slave system start to go into decline, or rather to be replaced?[1] In Italy, the first imperial measures against the breaking-up of slave families were promulgated in the year 325 of our era. According to some historians, however, the ancient form of slavery is considered as having ended under the reign of Charlemagne. Even so, the Church at that time was still a considerable owner of slaves. The Anglo-Saxon theologian Alcuin, one of Charlemagne's closest advisers, owned 20,000 slaves in the four abbeys under his control. Almost 20 per cent of Europe's population in Charlemagne's time consisted of slaves. Some forms of medieval slavery continued to exist from the ninth to the fifteenth centuries and gradually faded out only when they were superseded by the African and Asian slave trades.

Exploitation and torture

How many men, women and children left Africa in the holds of the slave ships? How many African and Malagasy captives were sold on the slave markets of the Caribbean and mainland America? The answer is that they were probably tens of millions, but we shall never know the exact figure because there are no reliable

---

ORUNO D. LARA, of Guadeloupe, is a historian who heads the Caribbean-America Research Centre at the University of Paris X-Nanterre. His published works include *Les Caraïbes* (1986), *Caraïbes en construction: espace, colonisation, résistance* (2 vols. 1992) and, in collaboration with Nelly Schmidt, *Les abolitions de l'esclavage, Une longue marche* (Centre national de documentation pédagogique, Paris, 1993).

Reprinted with permission from the *Unesco Courier,* October 1994, pp. 8-10.

The Same Seed

Please reflect that the man you call your slave was born of the same seed, has the same good sky above him, breathes as you do, lives as you do, dies as you do! You may see him free, he may see you a slave—the odds are level.

SENECA

Letters to Lucilius,

65–65 A.D.

statistics. In this respect, the stumbling-block historians have to contend with lies in the conditions and practices of the trade, both legal and illegal, which went on from the mid-fifteenth century to the closing decades of the nineteenth century.

The slaves of Antiquity, like those of modern times, had to submit to the sexual demands of their masters. Prostitution was only one feature of the relationship. Trimalchio, one of the characters in the *Satyricon* of Petronius, the Roman author of the 1st century A.D., says: "For fourteen years, I was the light of my master's eyes. There is no shame in doing what your master orders you to do. In the meantime, I also kept my mistress happy".

A variety of methods, such as changing slaves' names, inflicting corporal punishment on them or torturing them, were used to dehumanize and degrade them, deprive them of their personality and make them different from other human beings, who were not chattels. This was the sole purpose of the practice whereby all male slaves, regardless of their age, were called "boy"—*pais* in Greek, *puer* in Latin.

Attempts have been made to minimize, and indeed conceal, the many acts of physical cruelty meted out on slaves, and to deny the existence of torture in Greece and Italy. Torture was practised in Athens, however, and the instruments used are well-known to specialists. As Demosthenes noted, freedmen differed from slaves because the latter had to answer for all their crimes with their bodies. What we do not know, however, is whether the slave-owners of Antiquity displayed the same refinement as the planters of the Americas in inflicting cruelty on their slaves. The atrocities perpetrated by the latter have provided material for a large num-

ber of books on the subject and are borne out by irrefutable eyewitness accounts.

A totalitarian system based on racism

There were two ways of escaping from slavery: emancipation or flight. Emancipation meant that the slaves were no longer chattels. In Greece, they became "metics", resident aliens who were free but were debarred from discharging political obligations, whereas in Rome they automatically acquired Roman citizenship. Their legal status changed from being that of an object to that of a person recognised by law. The emancipated slaves of Antiquity were able to become absorbed into the mass of the population within the space of one or two generations. The poet Horace, whose father was an emancipated slave, complains in his *Satires* of having sometimes been insulted about his origins.

This was by no means the case of the emancipated slaves of the Caribbean and the Americas, for whom the colour of their skin was the indelible mark of their slave origins. Writing in 1776, the colonist Hilliard d'Auberteuil noted that "In San Domingo, for the sake of our own interests and security, we show such contempt for the black race that anybody descending from it . . . is marked with an indelible stain".[2] In Brazil, emancipation was regarded as a powerful form of pressure whereby slave-owners were able to keep control over their slaves and sow discord among them. In the Spanish colonies of the Caribbean, a system of gradual emancipation, known as *coartación*, under which slaves could buy back their freedom in instalments, was introduced in the sixteenth century. The emancipated slaves remained dependent on their masters and were therefore obliged to respect and honour them or work for them.

Slavery in the Caribbean was more than an institution with its own laws and customs and methods of keeping order. It was literally a "totalitarian" system of economic, political, social and sexual exploitation based on force, violence and the ideology of racism. The ceremonial in which the slaves were integrated into the system was meant to blot out their past and their culture, and kill them as free men and members of society. It was only by making a bid for freedom that the black *cimarrón*, the runaway slave, could regain his identity as a man (by again using his African name) and his will to work.

In Greece and Italy, and also in Roman-occupied Egypt, slave-owners had specially designed instruments, in the shape of metal chains and collars, to prevent the slaves from escaping. If slaves did escape, the owners offered rewards through public announcements or called on the authorities or engaged professional slave-hunters known as *fugitivarii.*

What fate lay in store for the runaway slaves? They could flee into the bush and form small bands living off robbery. One account from the third century B.C. tells of a celebrated example on the island of Chios, at some unknown date. A band of runaway slaves had sought refuge in a rugged, forest-covered mountain region, under the leadership of a chief called Drimacos. They successfully resisted several punitive expeditions until Drimacos eventually concluded a formal agreement with the authorities. He gave an undertaking to protect the property of Chios and only to accept as members of his band those slaves who had "suffered intolerably" and returned the others to their masters. On his death, he was raised to the dignity of "benevolent hero".

In the course of history, only four slave revolts took on the proportions of actual warfare, with thousands of armed men on either side, pitched battles, sieges and the occupation of towns. The first three took place in Sicily and Italy over the period from 140 to 70 B.C. The fourth was the major insurrection on the island of San Domingo, which culminated in the independence of Haiti in January 1804.

---

[1]"Slavery is not a moral category: it is an institution which provides a large fraction of the labour force. As long as that force is necessary, slavery cannot merely go into decline, it has to be replaced". Moses I. Finley, *Ancient Slavery and Modern Ideology,* New York, Penguin, 1983.

[2]Hilliard d'Auberteuil, *Considérations sur l'état présent de la colonie française de Saint Domingue (1776–1777).*

Who Was Responsible?

Africans were above all victims of the slave trade, but some of them were partners in it.

Elikia M'Bokolo

Elikia M'Bokolo, Zairean historian, is director of studies at the Ecole des Hautes Etudes en Sciences Sociales in Paris. He is the author of many works on African history, cultures and development problems, including L'Afrique au 20e siècle, le continent convoité (1985) *and* Afrique noire, Histoire et civilisations, 19–20e siècles (1992).

To judge from the number of countries taking part in it, the slave trade must have been for Europeans both a profitable business and, considering the number of years it lasted, a familiar fact of life. Even so, in some of the ports involved in the trade, like Nantes, the slave-traders themselves were reluctant to call it by its name and instead spoke of it in more veiled terms as the "matter".

What about the Africans? Were they merely its victims or were they conscious and consenting partners in a business arrangement with whose terms they were perfectly familiar?

A controversial question

There has always been heated debate over the part played by Africans in the slave trade. For a long time, the slave-traders took refuge behind what they saw as the irrefutable argument that the Africans made a regular practice of selling their fellow Africans, and that if the Europeans refused to buy slaves from them, other people—meaning the Arabs, who also used black slaves, among others—would hasten to do so. Nowadays, African intellectuals and statesmen contend that these exchanges were always unequal (in that human beings were bought with baubles) and that the Europeans always resorted to violence to get the Africans to co-operate against their will.

For historians the story is not quite as simple as that, in the first place because our criteria are not the same as those of 500 or even 150 years ago. We believe that if only one slave had been shipped across the Atlantic, it would have been one too many. But did Africans think like this in the past? Secondly, the slave trade, which went on for almost four centuries, was a very complex process involving a very wide variety of power relationships and participants whose interests and responses were bound to have changed with the course of time. This has prompted the British historian Basil Davidson to say that the "notion that Europe altogether imposed the slave trade on Africa is without any foundation in history. . . . [it] is as baseless as the European notion that institutions of bondage were in some way peculiar to Africa."[*]

From slave-raiding to slave-trading

The first method by which the Europeans acquired African slaves was through straightforward abduction. Striking examples of this can be found in the celebrated *Crónica dos Feitos da Guiné (Chronicle of the Discovery and Conquest of Guinea)*, written by the Portuguese Gomes Eanes de Zurara in the mid-fifteenth century. When the Europeans landed on the coasts of Africa, they stopped at random at places they thought might be suitable for their purpose and set out on man-hunts. This was not without its risks, however, as evidenced by the massacre in 1446 of almost all the members of the expedition led by Nuno Tristao near the Cap Vert peninsula in present-day Senegal. This was not the only such massacre, but it certainly shows that the Africans were determined to fight against enslavement.

The drawbacks of slave-raiding were that its outcome was uncertain and it was incapable of catering for the constantly growing demand, when the plantations and mines of the Americas had to be supplied with slave la-

---

[*]Basil Davidson, *Black Mother, The Years of the African Slave Trade*, Boston/Toronto, Little, Brown and Company, 1961.

Reprinted with permission from the *Unesco Courier*, October 1994, pp. 11-14.

bour. The Portuguese were the first to switch from merely seizing captives to actually trading in slaves, following a suggestion made by Prince Henry the Navigator in 1444 and subsequently followed by Portuguese sovereigns until the end of the fifteenth century. However, even after this trade had become a routine matter, raiding continued to provide slave-traders with an additional source of supply. The so-called "roving" trade—in which slaving ships sailed along the coast and captured slaves at various places until they had a full consignment—often took the form of armed incursions against villages situated near to the coast. When countries engaged in the slave trade, they often began by organizing raiding expeditions, as did the first vessels hailing from the "twelve colonies" (the future United States of America) in the first half of the seventeenth century.

By that time, however, the leading European nations had imposed a code of ethics of a kind on the slave trade. The English, Portuguese and French agreed to make a joint declaration to the effect that the slave trade was justified only when it involved slaves duly sold by Africans. Forts were built along the coastline in order to organize the trade and at the same time to instill a healthy sense of fear among the Africans. The message they conveyed was perfectly clear: "Sell us slaves—and we shall leave it to you to choose them as you see fit—or else we shall take the slaves we need at random."

The slave trade was therefore a one-sided relationship, founded and maintained on the threat of force. We once again have to agree with Basil Davidson when he says, "Africa and Europe were jointly involved. . . . Europe dominated the connection, shaped and promoted the slave trade, and continually turned it to European advantage and to African loss."

Thinking of the millions of my brothers

Each morning, when I wake up, I have the taste of death in my mouth. . . . But, after doing a few physical exercises, I open the windows of my bedroom. They overlook the sea and, away in the distance, I can just make out the island of Gorée. And when I think of the millions of my black brothers who were shipped from there to destinations where misfortune and death awaited them, I am compelled not to despair. Their story goads me on. . . .

LÉOPOLD SÉDAR SENGHOR

Affairs of state and lineage societies

At its height, the slave trade was regarded by Africans as a kind of diabolical plot in which they had to be accomplices or perish. Hence almost all the lineage or state societies of the African seaboard were compelled to become involved in it. They did this in ways and under conditions which differed significantly from one region to another and from one period to another.

The social history of pre-colonial Africa shows that slavery was a widespread institution in states where, in some instances, a domestic trade in slaves already existed for military or economic reasons. However, a distinction has to be made between those states which maintained relations with the outside world and those which did not. The former were quicker and more ready to join in the slave-trade cycle. This was true of the states bordering the Sahel, which were already in the practice of selling slaves, among other goods, to their Arab and Berber partners, who actually went on to sell some of them to the Europeans. The chronicler Alvise de Ca' da Mósto, who took part in a Portuguese expedition to Senegambia in 1455–1456, reported that the local sovereigns were skilled at taking advantage of the new competition that was growing up between the trans-Saharan trade and the Atlantic trade by selling slaves to the Arabs and Berbers in exchange for horses, and other slaves to the Portuguese in exchange for European goods.

The situation was by no means the same in those states which had no trading links with the outside world. The part these played in the slave trade is a pointer to the ambiguous and contradictory attitudes they displayed and the difficulties they faced when they came to take decisions, often under duress. The kingdom of Kongo, one of the most powerful in Africa at the time of its encounter with the Portuguese at the end of the fifteenth century, is a typical example. In the view of contemporary historians, its economic, political and social standing was on a par with that of Portugal. From the time of the very first contacts, the Kongo nobility became converts to Christianity and the king saw fit to address the Portuguese sovereign as "my brother". Yet the fact was that the slave trade had already started, in violation of the agreements, both tacit and formal, concluded between the two states. A number of letters, in which the king of Kongo protested against the seizure of slaves, including members of noble families, have survived to the present day. There is still some controversy as to what was really the motive behind these protestations. Some historians regard them as being an outburst of nationalist sentiment, but others look upon them more as a sign of the concern of the country's aristocracy not to allow so lucrative a business to slip through their hands. In any event, the kingdom did not survive the impact of the slave trade for very long. The same drama was to be played out to varying degrees elsewhere in Africa.

The kingdom of Dahomey was also exposed to the bitter experience of the slave trade. In the mid-eighteenth century, it took over the port of Ouidah, one of the main centres of the trade in the Gulf of Guinea. The king of Dahomey regarded the port—where there was a growing buildup of firearms—as posing a threat to the security of his possessions, since the slave trade gave it a tactical advantage over its neighbours. Once they took control of Ouidah, the rulers of Dahomey were caught in a vicious circle: in order to maintain a strong state, they needed rifles and gunpowder, but to obtain these they had to sell slaves to the Europeans. The answer was really very straightforward: since the sale of the kingdom's own subjects was strictly forbidden, powerful armies were raised to raid neighbouring peoples and make war on them for the purpose of taking slaves.

Unlike states, lineage societies did not have any means of obtaining slaves by force. In such cases, servitude was based on complex practices in which various categories of social outcasts, such as criminals, misfits, sorcerers and victims of natural or economic disasters, were relegated to being slaves. Even so, this would not have been sufficient to turn the slave trade into the vast and lasting business it became. Other means were therefore found of meeting the Europeans' demands. For example, in the city of Arochukwu ("the voice of Chukwu", the supreme deity), in the Niger delta, a celebrated oracle whose authority was respected by all the population was called on to designate those who, for whatever reason, were condemned to be sold into slavery. This practice continued until the beginning of the nineteenth century.

In other regions, especially in central Africa, trading networks were gradually established, extending from the coast deep into the interior. All the goods exported or imported via these networks—predominantly slaves—transited through the heads of the lineages. In Gabon and Loango in particular, the coastal so-cieties forming the key links in these trading networks had a highly developed ranking social order based on the extent to which their members were involved in the slave trade. Kinship relations, which are fundamental in lineage societies, gradually gave way to relations based on fortunes made in the trade, which came to dictate people's standing in society.

Africans and the abolition of the slave trade

On the African side, however, the basis of the slave trade was very precariously balanced. The part played by Africans in the trade cannot be discussed without reference to the part they played in its abolition. In a one-sided view of history, the role of Europeans—philosophers, thinkers, men of religion and businessmen—is too often stressed, while that played by the Africans is left in the shade. Some people have even gone so far as to tax the Africans with being the main impediment to the phasing-out of the trade in the nineteenth century. Nothing could be further from the truth.

Outside Africa, the resistance of the victims of the slave trade—which took a variety of forms, including the "Back to Africa" movement, the founding of "Maroon" communities and even armed insurrection, like that in San Domingo in 1791—was primarily instrumental in calling the whole institution of slavery into question. Those who had managed to escape its clutches took a very active but often unacknowledged part in the campaign for abolition. They included people like Ottobah Cuguano, who had been born in Fantiland, in present-day Ghana, had been a slave in the West Indies, and published his *Thoughts and Sentiments on the Evil and Wicked Traffic of Slavery* in London in 1787. In 1789, another African, Olaudah Equiano, alias Gustavus Vassa, a native of Iboland, in Nigeria, published, again in London, *The Interesting Narrative of the Life of Olaudah Equiano, or Gustavus Vassa the African, written by himself*. These books played a significant role in the movement of opinion which led to the abolition of the slave trade.

In Africa itself, all through the "years of trial" of the slave trade, along with slaves, blacks continued to sell the produce of their soil and subsoil, such as timber, ivory, spices, gold, vegetable oils, and others besides. Changing European demand was sufficient for the Africans to turn to a more "legal" form of commerce.

ENCOURAGEMENT OF THE SLAVE-TRADE

Much has been said and written of the callous greed of the American Colonies in their insistence upon Negro slavery and the African slave-trade. Most, perhaps all, of the blame may be deserved; but, to their credit be it said, some of the provinces did all in their power to check the latter, but were balked by the higher authority at Westminster in the interest of English trade. The Old British Empire, as it existed before it was rent in twain by the American Revolution to make way for the grander and better New British Empire, was frankly built on the model of the Roman Empire in which colonies and provinces were supposed to exist not for the benefit of colonists and provincials but of the mother country. Every act of any American colony was closely scrutinized with a view of its effect on English trade and commerce.

All the examples of interference by the Privy Council with colonial legislation which I shall adduce are during the decade before the Declaration of Independence and are taken from official sources.[1]

Let us begin with the Old Dominion. Virginia, in April, 1767, having already an import duty of ten per cent on slaves brought into the colony, imposed a further duty of ten per cent payable by the purchaser. This was disallowed.[2]

The story is not very creditable to the home authorities. An act of 1728 for laying a duty on slaves imported into Virginia had been disallowed as harmful to English trade since it would work a practical prohibition of the importation of slaves into Virginia.[3] In 1731, however, the governors of the American colonies were instructed to give the royal assent to laws laying moderate duties upon Negroes imported, provided such duties were paid by the purchaser, the colonial, and not by the importer.[4] Virginia thereupon laid an import duty of ten per cent and this was suffered to pass; but an additional ten per cent laid in 1767 was too much; and this, as we have seen, was disallowed by the Privy Council at Westminster.

The Old Dominion did not relax her efforts to check the villainous traffic. In December, 1769, another act was passed imposing an import duty of fifteen per cent on slaves in addition to the existing duty of ten per cent and also payable by the purchaser. Now, the Privy Council recognized that the effect, as it was the obvious intention, would be the entire prohibition of the importation of slaves into Virginia. They also were now convinced both from principle and experience that the distinction between duties paid by the buyer and those paid by the importer was fallacious and the operation of either mode was the same. The former mode wherein the purchaser and not the slave trader paid the duty had "without Complaint from the Merchants of this Kingdom [England] universally prevailed in all Colonies which import Slaves"; and the Privy Council would not have interfered "had these Duties in the present Case been confined within the Limits of Moderation: But when the privilege of laying moderate Duties payable by the purchaser is extended so far as to have the effect of a prohibition, the objections made ... in the year 1729 do stand forth in their full force and extent. For which Reason and forasmuch as the Merchants of Bristol, Liverpool and Lancaster have both by their Representatives and by Memorials stated ... the prejudice which these Laws will be to the Trade and Commerce of those Ports ...", they were disallowed, December 4, 1770. The governor was given specific instructions not to give the royal assent to any law increasing the import duty on slaves beyond the ten per cent already imposed.[5]

The following year, an address by the House of Burgesses of Virginia was sent by Lord Dunmore, the Governor of Virginia, to Lord Hillsborough, Secretary of State, and by him to the Privy Council, who, December 19, 1771, referred it to the Board of Trade. This address humbly prayed His Majesty to remove all restraints from his governors which prevented them from "assenting to such Laws as might check the Importation of Slaves into

---

[1] *Acts of the Privy Council of England—Colonial Series, Vol. V, A.D. 1766–1783:* London, *The King's Printer*, 1912, an instructive publication, admirably edited and printed.
[2] *Do. do.,* Vol. V, pp. 164, 165—August 12, 1768.
[3] *Do. do.,* Vol. III, pp. 64, 65.
[4] *Do. do.,* Vol. V, p. 287.

[5] *Do. do.,* Vol. V, pp. 286–8, where the whole interesting story is told. It is somewhat amusing to note the absurd fallacy of the effect of the incidence of the duty upon the purchaser rather than the importer (or manufacturer) having force with the hard-headed group of men in Westminster; but it is not dead yet in all quarters.

From the *Journal of Negro History*, January 1927, pp. 22-32. © 1927 by the Association for the Study of African-American Life and History, Inc. Reprinted by permission.

the Colonies from the Coast of Africa, The Importation of such Slaves having long been considered as a Trade of great Inhumanity and under its present Encouragement, they have too much reason to fear will endanger the very Existence of His Majesty's American Dominions."[6] This address does not seem to have been so much as considered until July 31, 1772; but in the meantime in April, 1772, an act was passed in Virginia laying an additional five per cent import duty on slaves. This, of course, under his Instructions, the governor could not assent to—and it was disallowed, April 7, 1773.[7] The attempt was not renewed.

Georgia was not more successful. In September, 1773, an act was passed obliging masters of vessels and other transient persons, importing Negroes, &c., to pay tax for the same. It was in vain that the Assembly solemnly declared that it was not intended by the act to levy a duty but only to compel transient traders to contribute to the support of the Government of Georgia. The Board of Trade and their lawyer, Mr. Jackson, K.C., saw through the subterfuge, especially as a very great part of the expense of the Government of Georgia was "defrayed out of the Revenue of Great Britain." The act was disallowed, December 19, 1773.[8]

Pennsylvania was no more fortunate. In February, 1773, she passed an act levying an additional import duty of £10 on every slave. The Board of Trade said that it was "probably intended as a prohibition on this article of trade—to the prejudice of a very important branch of British Commerce"; and it was promptly disallowed, July 6, 1774.[9]

Even Jamaica had the same experience. Her act of February, 1774, imposing an additional duty of 40 s. a head on slaves imported, payable by the importer, was disallowed, February 27, 1775, the merchants alleging "that this additional Duty is such a Burthen having already amounted to upwards of £15,000 upon twenty-six Cargoes that without Your Majesty's Interposition for their relief they can no longer with any hope of gain carry on the Slave Trade to that Island."[10]

Some of the horrors of the slave-trade are incidentally made to appear. For example in an appeal by Jasper Hall, merchant of Kingston, Jamaica, in 1768, it appears that he had his agent in England fit out a ship for the coast of Africa for a cargo of slaves to put in at Jamaica for orders whence to convey them, but not to sell them on that island. The ship took on a cargo of slaves and arrived at Jamaica in October, 1762. She was leaky, and some of the slaves were sickly and wanted landing for the recovery of their health. They were landed at Kingston "to the number of 630, many of whom being taken with the Small Pox and 400 Inoculated, they necessarily continued in the Island till the January following, when all that remained alive, being but 521 were . . . reshipped . . . for the Havannah. . . ."[11] It is appalling to think of one hundred and nine unfortunates meeting death by disease in this way, and yet they may have been more fortunate in escaping the fate of the survivors sent in slavery to Cuba.

—WILLIAM RENWICK RIDDELL

OSGOODE HALL, TORONTO,
    October 2, 1926

GENERAL NOTE

It is not to be supposed that the interference with the colonies began only a very short time before the Declaration of Independence. Some account of transactions in earlier times concerning the Colonies, and more or less germane, is added here.

VIRGINIA

Virginia as early as 1710 and again in 1718 passed acts which laid a duty of £5 per head on Negroes imported. These were found to reduce the number usually imported and considered necessary for the colony and "a hindrance to the Negro trade as well as a burden upon the poorer planters." They were, however, not so serious as to call for action by the home government. But in 1723, another duty, though less in amount, being 40/—per head, was provided for by an act which came up for consideration by the Privy Council, this being referred to the Board of Trade Committee of the Privy Council. The Board of Trade reported that it would "Discourage the Planting and Cultivating Navall Stores especially in the two new Counties where great Numbers of Negroes will be wanting"; and, April 17, 1724, recommended the disallowance of the act: it was disallowed accordingly, April 30. *Do. do.*, Vol. III, p. 64.

January 29, 1726, Samuel Jacob and other British merchants complained of being forced to pay duty about April 30, 1724, on certain Negroes imported notwithstanding the disallowance of the act: *do. do.*, p. 123.

---

[6]*Do. do.*, Vol. V, p. 288.

[7]*Do. do.*, Vol. V, pp. 362, 3.

[8]*Do. do.*, Vol. V, pp. 403, 4. It may be of interest to note other legislation of Georgia as to slaves. By the Imperial Act of 1732, 5 George II, c. 7, s. 4, Negroes in the American plantations were made real estate—See my article *The Slave in Canada*, JOURNAL OF NEGRO HISTORY, V (July, 1920), p. 13, n. 12. And it was the policy of the American Colonies to make slaves real estate descendible to the heir with the land. In 1766, however, Georgia made slaves chattels personal. This act seemed objectionable to the Board of Trade and their counsel, Sir Mathew Lamb, as thereby the slaves "might be separated and taken from the lands, so that the plantations might sink and become useless in the hands of the heir for want of the slaves that would be taken therefrom." The act was accordingly disallowed, June 26, 1767: *do. do.*, Vol. 5, pp. 40, 41. A similar act of Virginia in 1752 had been disallowed: *do. do.*, p. 177. In 1771, the Governor of Georgia asked for Instructions, and he was instructed to assent to a bill making slaves chattels personal as in the neighboring colony of South Carolina: *do. do.*, pp. 176, 7.

[9]*Do. do.*, Vol. V, pp. 398, 9.

[10]*Do. do.*, Vol. V, pp. 406, 7. It will be observed that 7,500 slaves were imported into Jamaica within the year, an average of 288 to a ship.

---

[11]Although Hall refused to sell any of the slaves in Jamaica, when he came to reship them, Malcolm Laing, the Receiver General of the Island, demanded 10 s. a head duty on the 630 landed—£315—and 20 s. a head on the 521 exported—£521, £836 in all. Hall paid under protest and sued for the money. The trial court, July, 1763, gave him judgment; but his was reversed, August 16, 1766, by the Court of Appeals: Hall appealed to the King in Council and his appeal was allowed, July 15, 1768. *Do. do.*, pp. 52–55. He sold the slaves in Hispaniola, the market in Havana being a monopoly.

An act of 1723 concerning servants and slaves was disallowed, August 29, because it would amount "almost to a prohibition of the transportation of felons from Great Britain"—*do. do.*, p. 55.

[In 1748–9, Virginia was allowed to make Slaves personal estate, repealing an act of 1705 and two later acts making them real estate. *Do. do.*, Vol. IV, pp. 131, 2, 8, 9.]

Another act placing a duty of 40 s. per head on imported Negroes passed in 1728 met the same adverse report, July 31, 1729, as it "would discourage the trade of this Kingdom (*i.e.*, England) with Virginia, raise the price of tobacco and discourage settlement in the two new counties for want of sufficient slave labour": it was disallowed, August 18. *Do. do.*, pp. 64, 65. The new counties were Spotsilvania and Brunswick, *do. do.*, p. 244; the former called after Colonel Spottswood: *do. do.*, p. 246.

GEORGIA

An act had been passed by Georgia for rendering the colony more defensible by prohibiting the importation and use of black slaves or Negroes except under special restrictions and regulations. In 1750, legislation was passed for the repeal of this act. The matter was referred to the Board of Trade, November 18, 1750. *Do. do.*, Vol. IV, pp. 107, 108.

SOUTH CAROLINA

An act passed August 20, 1731, to impose an import duty on Negroes of £10 per head was disallowed as excessive. *Do. do.*, pp. 393–5.

NEW YORK

A New York act in 1734 imposed an import duty of "five Ounces of Seville, Pillar or Mexico Plate or Forty Shillings in Bills of Credit of that Colony . . . on every Slave (Male or Female) of four years of age and upwards imported directly from Africa"—from any other place, £4, payable by the importer. This, though questioned, was allowed to come into force. *Do. do.*, Vol. III, pp. 422, 423.

Not as bearing upon our subject but as of interest from another point of view, I note an act of *Antigua*.

ANTIGUA

This Island passed an act, September, 1744, to prevent Papists settling, as it required certain oaths within three months of any person's arrival which they could not take: and it also punished anyone who encouraged any Papist to reside upon the Island " . . . by hiring or purchasing them as Servants or leasing them or giving them any Lands to dwell on." The act was disallowed, November 28, 1746. *Do. do.*, Vol. IV, pp. 73, 74.

JAMAICA

Two acts of Jamaica, complained of in 1724, seem to have been purely revenue acts as not only was a duty imposed on import but also on export of Negroes. *Do. do.*, pp. 72. In two years the export duty of the South Sea Company amounted to £4737. But they were complained of by the South Sea Company and Merchants trading to Jamaica who said 15 s. per head on import and 30 s. per head on export was "a Burthen to British Trade and Navigation." The Assembly then reduced the duty to 10 s. and 20 s. respectively for import and export. This also was disallowed, October 13, 1732. *Do. do.*, pp. 159–162. August

1, 1733, the Assembly levied a duty of 10 s. per head on all Negroes imported and unsold and also on all to be imported—the South Sea Company and Merchants of London, Bristol and Liverpool appealed against the Bill and it was disallowed, May 10, 1735; but a reasonable import duty was authorized to be imposed. *Do. do.*, pp. 164–167. (An act of July 13, 1730, to render "free Negroes and Mulattoes more useful," by making them work, was disallowed, November 25, 1731, as "destructive of former laws in favour of Negroes freed for faithful services and particular merit . . . and their descendants." *Do. do.*, pp. 344, 345.)

In 1754, a Mr. Fornichon, who from ignorance of the laws of Jamaica had employed another's slave and been sentenced to a fine of £50 and imprisonment for a year, was let off his fine. *Do. do.*, Vol. IV, pp. 270, 271.

In 1766, by the Act 6 George III, c. 49, ss. 5, 12, Jamaica and Dominica were permitted to export Negroes brought in by British ships, Jamaica charging an export duty of £1 10 for each Negro exported in a foreign vessel; but Dominica could charge only an import duty to the same amount.

The Act of 1773, 13 George III, c. 73, s. 4, repealed these provisions and substituted an import duty of 2 s. 6 d. on each Negro brought into Dominica and a similar export duty for Jamaica.

ST. VINCENT

An act of 1767–8 levying a tax on lands and slaves was considered May 24, 1771, and adversely criticized: *do. do.*, Vol. V, pp. 302–306.

GRENADA

In 1769, a complaint was laid before the Privy Council against Robert Melvill, the Governor of the Island, alleging *inter alia* that he "did permit John Graham, Peter Gordon, and other Justices of the peace of the Island of Grenada, to use the severest and most Cruel Tortures upon the Bodies of five Negroes Suspected of Committing Murder, and this with a view to induce them to confess the said Crime and to accuse their Master Monsieur La Chancellerie; which Accusation after repeated Tortures was actually extorted from them, and the said La Chancellerie was thereupon apprehended and imprisoned and they, the said Negroes Condemned to death upon their own Confession thus Extorted; which Sentence would probably have been executed upon the said Negroes if the most respectable Inhabitants of the Colony had not remonstrated against such illegal and unnatural proceedings, which occasioned a delay of their execution, until the Matter was represented to the King's Ministers, who ordered the prisoners to be Liberated nevertheless three had died from injuries they had received by the Torture together with their long Confinement before the said Order arrived; Notwithstanding which the said Justices were still continued by the said Robert Melvill in the Commission of the peace." *Do. do.*, Vol. V, at p. 226. It does not appear what was the result.

That the inhabitants of some at least of the colonies were not unanimous in the desire to prevent the further important of Negroes can be seen from the following:

PENNSYLVANIA

The Assembly early in 1761 passed a Bill intituled "An Act for laying a Duty on Negroes and Mulatto Slaves imported into this Province": this was laid before the Lieutenant-Governor James Hamilton for his Assent, February 28, 1762. At the same time a petition was presented in the following terms:

"A Petition from the Merchants against the Bill for Duty on the Negroes.
"To the Honourable JAMES HAMILTON, Esquire, Lieutenant Governor of the Province of Pennsylvanie, &c., &c.,
'The Petition of Divers Merchants of the City of Philadelphia, Trading to His Majesty's Coloneys in the West Indies,
'Humbly Sheweth:
'That we are informed there is now a Bill Before your Honour for your assent, laying a Duty on the importation of Negros, and that it is to take place immediately on the publication.
'We, the subscribers, ever desirous to extend the Trade of this Province, have seen, for some time past, the many inconveniencys the Inhabitants have suffer'd for want of Labourers and artificers, by numbers being inlisted for His Majesty's Service, and near a total Stop to the importation of German and other white Servants, have for some time encouraged the importation of Negros, and acquainted our friends and correspondents in several parts of His Majesty's dominions (who are no Way apprehensive of a Bill of this Nature), that an Advantage may be gained by the Introduction of Slaves, which will Likewise be a means of reducing the exorbitant price of Labour, and, in all probability, bring our Staple Commoditys to their usual prices; And as many of us have embarked in this Trade through the motives before mentioned, We humbly beg your honour will take into consideration the hardships we shall Labour under by such a Law taking immediate effect, when we have it not in our power to countermand our Orders or advise our friends; therefore humbly pray that such time may be allowed (before the Law takes place) as your honour shall think most Conducive to extricate your petitioners from the impending danger.
'Philadelphia, 1st March, 1761.

'John Bell,	Banjamin Levy,
Humphry Robinson,	Henry Harrison
Reed & Pettit,	John & Jos. Swift.
William Coxe,	John Nixon,
Charles Baths,	Daniel Rundle.
Philip Kearney, jr.,	Francis & Relfe,
James Chalmers,	Stoker & Fuller,
Joseph Wood,	Scott & McMichael,
Willing, Morris & Co.,	John Inglis,
Thos. Riche,	David McMurtrie,
David Franks,	Saml. & Archa. McCall.
Hu. Donnaldson,	Joseph Marks.' "

The Bill named Richard Pearne as the collector of these duties and the Lieutenant-Governor returned it for amendment by striking out this unconstitutional provision, March 10: the amendment was made and the bill again, March 14, laid before the Lieutenant-Governor and assented to, April 11, 1761. *Minutes of the Provincial Council of Pennsylvania*, Harrisburg, 1852, Vol. VIII, pp. 575, 576, 578, 583, 601.

While this act with others of the same year was referred by the Privy Council to the Committee for the Plantations, it was allowed to come into effect; *Acts. &c.,* Vol. IV, p. 808.

That being a Negro Slave was not in old Pennsylvania wholly without its advantages may be seen from the following extract from the Minutes of the "Council held at Philadia, the 25th of ffebry., 1707" (February 25, 1708) "A Petition from Wm. Rightton & Robt. Grace, directed to the Govr. alone, being presented to him, the Govr. thought fitt to lay it before the Council,

and desire their advice therein. The matter of which Petition was, That Toney, a Negroe Slave of the said Righton, and Quashy, a like Slave of the said Grace's, were lately at a Special Court held for that purpose in this Town, condemned to Death for Burglary proved agst. them; But for asmuch as it will be of very great Damage to the Petitrs. should their sd. slaves lives be taken, since there is no provision in this Govmt. as is Usual in other places, for a Competent restitution to the Owners who lose their Slaves by the hand of Public Justices.

"Therefore, the humbly pray, that in Mercy to the said Owners the lives of their slaves may be spared, & that they may be suffered to transport them, & instead of Death, that they may have the Liberty to inflict on ym. such Corporal Punishmt. as may be requisite, for a Terror, to others of their Colour, wch the said Owners will take care to have duly executed upon ym." "All wch being taken into Consideration, the Board thought fitt to give it as their Opinion, that the Death of these Slaves would be a greater Loss to the Owners than they could well bear, and therefore seeing there is no Provision made for restitution for the Loss by the Publick, it may be as convenient to make the Slaves Examples of Terror to others of their Complexion, by a most Severe Corporal Punishmt., and that the Petitioners may have Liberty to transport them as requested.

"And it is hereupon Resolved, that the Owners may have Liberty to punish their Slaves, notwithstanding the Sentence of Death pass'd upon them, wch in case they will perform in the following Manner; the said Sentence shall be taken off, and their Owners shall transport them to their own benefit and advantage.

"That the Punishment shall be as follows: They shall be led from the Market place, up Second Street, & down thro' the front street to y Bridge, with their arms extended & tied to a pole across their Necks, a Cart going before them, and that they shall be severely Whipt all the way as they pass, upon the bare back and shoulders; this punishmt. shall be repeated for 3 market days successively; in the meantime they shall lie in irons, in the prison, at the Owners Charge, untill they have such an Opportunity as shall best please them for transporation; All of which being duly perform'd, the Sentence of Death shall be entirely remitted." *Minutes of the Provincial Council of Pennsylvania*. Philadelphia, 1852, Vol. II, pp. 405, 406.

There was trouble in earlier times over Sunday meetings of Negroes in Philadelphia. We read the following minute of an item of business at a meeting of "A Council Head at Philadelphia on a Tuesday, the yth (11th) of July, 1693":

"Upon the Request of some of the members of Councill, that an ordr made by the Court of Quarter Sessions for the Countie of philadelphia the 4th July instant, (proceeding upon a presentment of the grand Jurie, for the bodie of the sd Countie,) agt the tumultous gatherins of the negroes of the towne of philadelphia, on the first dayes of the weeke, ordering the Constables of philadelphia, or anie other person whatsoever, to have power to take up negroes, male or female, whom they should find gadding abroad on the said first dayes of the week, without a tickett from their Mr., or Mrs, or not in their Compa, or to carry them to goale, there to remain that night, & that without meat or drink, & to cause them to be publickly whipt next morning, with 39 Lashes, well Laid on, on their bare backs, for which their sd Mr., or Mris. should pay 15d to the whipper att his deliverie of ym to yr Mr., or Mris. & that the sd order should be Confirmed by the Lievt. Governor and Councill.

"The Lievt. Governor & Councill Looking upon the sd presentment to proceed upon good grounds, & the ordr of Court to be reasonable & for the benefit of the Inhabitants of the towne of philadelphia, & that it will be a means to prevent further mischeifs that might ensue upon such disorders of negroes, doe ratifie & confirme the same, & all persons are required to put the sd ordr in execu'n." *Do. do.,* Vol. I, pp. 380, 381.

"A MULTITUDE OF BLACK PEOPLE . . . CHAINED TOGETHER"

Olaudah Equiano

Olaudah Equiano vividly recounts the shock and isolation that he felt during the Middle Passage to Barbados and his fear that the European slavers would eat him.

Their complexions, differing so much from ours, their long hair and the language they spoke, which was different from any I had ever heard, united to confirm me in this belief. Indeed, such were the horrors of my views and fears at the moment, that if ten thousand worlds had been my own, I would have freely parted with them all to have exchanged my condition with that of the meanest slave of my own country. When I looked around the ship and saw a large furnace of copper boiling, and a multitude of black people of every description chained together, every one of their countenances expressing dejection and sorrow, I no longer doubted my fate. Quite overpowered with horror and anguish, I fell motionless on the deck and fainted. When I recovered a little, I found some black people about me, and I believe some were those who had brought me on board and had been receiving their pay. They talked to me in order to cheer me up, but all in vain. I asked them if we were not to be eaten by those white men with horrible looks, red faces and long hair. They told me I was not.

I took a little down my palate, which, instead of reviving me as they thought it would, threw me into the greatest consternation at the strange feeling it produced, having never tasted such liquor before. Soon after this, the blacks who had brought me on board went off and left me abandoned to despair.

I now saw myself deprived of all chance of returning to my native country or even the least glimpse of hope of gaining the shore, which I now considered as friendly. I even wished for my former slavery in preference to my present situation, which was filled with horrors of every kind.

There I received such a salutation in my nostrils as I had never experienced in my life. With the loathesomeness of the stench and the crying together, I became so sick and low that I was not able to eat, nor had I the least desire to taste anything. I now wished for the last friend, Death, to relieve me.

Soon, to my grief, two of the white men offered me eatables and on my refusing to eat, one of them held me fast by the hands and laid me across the windlass and tied my feet while the other flogged me severely. I had never experienced anything of this kind before. If I could have gotten over the nettings, I would have jumped over the side, but I could not. The crew used to watch very closely those of us who were not chained down to the decks, lest we should leap into the water. I have seen some of these poor African prisoners most severely cut for attempting to do so, and hourly whipped for not eating. This indeed was often the case with myself.

I inquired of these what was to be done with us. They gave me to understand we were to be carried to these white people's country to work for them. I then was a little revived, and thought if it were no worse than working, my situation was not so desperate. But still I feared that I should be put to death, the white people looked and acted in so savage a manner. I have never seen among my people such instances of brutal cruelty, and this not only shown towards us blacks, but also to some of the whites themselves.

One white man in particular I saw, when we were permitted to be on deck, flogged so unmercifully with a large rope near the foremast that he died in consequence of it, and they tossed him over the side as they would have done a brute. This made me fear these people the more, and I expected nothing less than to be treated in the same manner.

I asked them if these people had no country, but lived in this hollow place? They told me they did not but came from a distant land. "Then," said I, "how comes it that in all our country we never heard of them?"

They told me because they lived so far off. I then asked where were their women? Had they any like themselves? I was told they had.

"And why do we not see them" I asked. They answered, "Because they were left behind."

I asked how the vessel would go? They told me they could not tell, but there was cloth put upon the masts by the help of the ropes I saw, and then vessels went on, and the white men had some spell or magic they put in the water when they liked in order to stop the vessel when they liked.

I was exceedingly amazed at this account, and really thought they were spirits. I therefore wished much to be from amongst them, for I expected they would sacrifice me. But my wishes were in vain—for we were so quartered that it was impossible for us to make our escape.

At last, when the ship we were in had got in all her cargo, they made ready with many fearful noises, and we were all put under deck, so that we could not see how they managed the vessel.

The stench of the hold while we were on the coast was so intolerably loathsome, that it was dangerous to remain there for any time . . . some of us had been permitted to stay on the deck for the fresh air. But now that the whole ship's cargo were confined together, it became absolutely pestilential. The closeness of the place and the heat of the climate, added to the number of the ship, which was so crowded that each had scarcely room to turn himself, almost suffocated us.

This produced copious perspirations so that the air became unfit for respiration from a variety of loathsome smells, and brought on a sickness among the slaves, of which many died—thus falling victims of the improvident avarice, as I may call it, of their purchasers. This wretched situation was again aggravated by the galling of the chains, which now became insupportable, and the filth of the necessary tubs [toilets] into which the children often fell and were almost suffocated. The shrieks of the women and the groans of the dying rendered the whole a scene of horror almost inconceivable.

Happily perhaps for myself, I was soon reduced so low that it was necessary to keep me almost always on deck and from my extreme youth I was not put into fetters. In this situation I expected every hour to share the fate of my companions, some of whom were almost daily brought upon the deck at the point of death, which I began to hope would soon put an end to my miseries. Often did I think many of the inhabitants of the deep much more happy than myself. I envied them the freedom they enjoyed, and as often wished I could change my condition for theirs. Every circumstance I met with, served only to render my state more painful and heightened my apprehensions and my opinion of the cruelty of the whites.

One day, when we had a smooth sea and moderate wind, two of my wearied countrymen who were chained together (I was near them at the time), preferring death to such a life of misery, somehow made through the nettings and jumped into the sea. Immediately another quite dejected fellow, who on account of his illness was suffered to be out of irons, followed their example. I believe many more would very soon have done the same if they had not been prevented by the ship's crew, who were instantly alarmed. Those of us that were the most active were in a moment put down under the deck, and there was such a noise and confusion among the people of the ship as I never heard before to stop her and get the boat out to go after the slaves. However, two of the wretches were drowned, but they got the other and afterwards flogged him unmercifully for thus attempting to prefer death to slavery.

I can now relate hardships which are inseparable from this accursed trade. Many a time we were near suffocation from the want of fresh air, which we were often without for whole days together. This, and the stench of the necessary tubs, carried off many.

Source: *The Interesting Narrative of the Life of Olaudah Equiano or Gustavus Vassa the African* (London, 1789).

Unit Selections

7. **The Founding Fathers, Conditional Antislavery, and the Nonradicalism of the American Revolution,** William W. Freehling

8. **"Us Colored Women Had To Go through a Plenty": Sexual Exploitation of African-American Slave Women,** Thelma Jennings

9. **Negro Craftsmanship in Early America,** Leonard Price Stavisky

10. **American Slave Insurrections before 1861,** Harvey Wish

Key Points to Consider

❖ Do you agree or disagree with the statement that the Founding Fathers were ambivalent to slavery while striving to reach the goal of individual freedom? Defend your answer.

❖ What evidence is there that the plight of female slaves was different from that of their male counterparts?

❖ What types of skills did African slaves bring to the Americas?

❖ While many African slaves had experience in manual African arts and crafts, what happened to these traditional skills among later generations of transplanted blacks? Is that still true today? Explain.

❖ Describe slave insurrections that occurred prior to 1861 in both the North and the South.

 **Links**   **www.dushkin.com/online/**

These sites are annotated on pages 4 and 5.

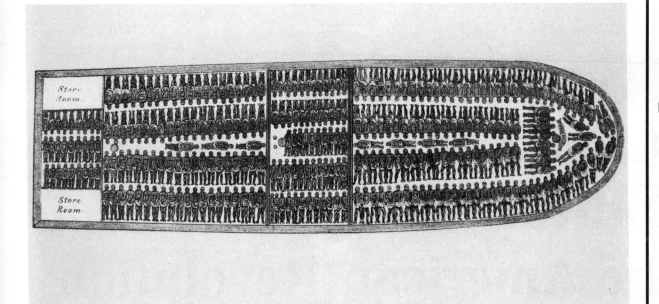

While sparking the American Revolution, with its goal of individual freedom, the Founders at best were ambivalent when it came to slavery. The issue is even more confusing when one considers that the same people who were espousing the rights of man were also slaveholders. This duplicity, William Freehling argues, accounts for the fact that the Founders were reluctant abolitionists and only marginally supported the antislavery process. Their conditional antislavery position produced several roadblocks to total emancipation, freedom, and justice for blacks in America. Their conditional aspiration to free black slaves was counterbalanced by their greater desire to build white republics.

Black women in eighteenth century Pennsylvania, serving as slaves, indentured servants, or free persons, were nevertheless constrained in their activities. African American female slaves were more affected and afflicted by "rule of the patriarch" than the "white women in the Big House." Thelma Jennings points out that female servitude was "more severe than male bondage because these women had to bear children and cope with sexual abuse in addition to doing the work assigned to them."

The slave, contrary to myth, often was quite skilled, his crafts highly sought after. African craftsmen developed a variety of skills such as spinners, butchers, carpenters, cooks, coopers, distillers, and goldsmiths, to name just a few. African skilled laborers were found in every province of colonial America. Skills acquired by slaves during their captivity served to increase their value and often allowed them to earn their freedom.

The notion of a docile slave is only preserved in old movies and fiction. In actuality, several notable slave insurrections and rebellions paved the way for abolition and the eventual freedom of blacks. Throughout the colonial period, African slaves revolted in both the North and South. American slave insurrections before 1861 are profiled in an article by Harvey Wish.

The Founding Fathers, Conditional Antislavery, and the Nonradicalism of the American Revolution

William W. Freehling

By 1972, two years after publishing "The Editorial Revolution," I more clearly understood that the story of the events of 1860 must begin with the Founding Fathers. But I still hoped that my narrative of disunion could begin in 1850. I thus decided to publish my thoughts on the earlier history separately. The resulting first version of this essay, entitled "The Founding Fathers and Slavery," appeared in the American Historical Review in 1972.[1] "Founding Fathers" has been widely republished. I nevertheless regret its overemphasis on antislavery accomplishment. My changed title reflects my partial disenchantment. I am grateful to the American Historical Review for permission to republish some of the previous essay in this much-altered form.

When I wrote the original essay, historians were increasingly scoffing that the Founding Fathers ignored the Declaration of Independence's antislavery imperatives.[2] That denunciation has continued to swell despite my countervailing emphasis, indeed partly because of my overstated argument.[3] My original essay, as David Brion Davis pointed out, too much conflated Thomas Jefferson

and the Founding Fathers.[4] The essay also erroneously portrayed the Founding Fathers as pragmatic reformers, eager to assault slavery whenever political realities permitted. They were in truth skittish abolitionists, chary of pouncing on antislavery opportunity. The Founding Fathers freed some slaves but erected obstacles against freeing others. They also sometimes moved past those obstacles for crass rather than ideological reasons. Thus historians who dismissed the Founding Fathers as antislavery reformers could easily dismiss my argument.

I have come to be more unhappy about the historians who appropriated "Founding Fathers." They have used my contention that the Founding Fathers chipped away at slavery to support their contention that the Declaration of Independence inspired a true American social revolution.[5] I find that argument unpersuasive, even about the white male minority. The notion is still less persuasive about African Americans and about other members of the nonwhite and nonmale majority, which means that the contention mischaracterizes American society writ large. Neither women nor African Americans nor Native Ameri-

cans conceived that the American Revolution revolutionized their lives. Their position is relevant if we are to widen American history beyond Anglo-Saxon males, to write the story of a multicultural civilization.

Some historians answer that the majority's definition of a proper social revolution is irrelevant for judging the American Revolution, since only the white male minority had the power to define the event and the society. Such positions tend to narrow American history into solely a history of the white male power structure. But in the specific case of slavery, the elite's standard for judgment widens perspectives. Wealthy revolutionaries' criterion, no less than poorer Americans' criterion and posterity's criterion, required a proper American Revolution to include the slaves. By that universal yardstick, the Founding Fathers achieved no social revolution.

The Founding Fathers instead set us on our nonrevolutionary social history. Despite their dismay at slavery, America's worst multicultural dislocation, they both timidly reformed and established towering bulwarks against reform, not least because many of them *preferred a monoracial America. I have revised this essay to include more of the bulwarks against antislavery, in company with those who think the Founding Fathers did nothing to further abolition. But I hope the revision will yield more tolerance for my continued belief, and latter-day slaveholders' worried conviction, that the Founding Fathers also did a most nonrevolutionary something to weaken slaveholders' defenses. For without that ambivalent perspective on the nation's founders, we can understand neither the subsequent meandering road toward emancipation nor America's persistently nonradical road toward a radically new multicultural social order, based on the ethics of the Declaration of Independence.*

The American Revolutionaries intended to achieve a political revolution. They brilliantly succeeded. They split the British Empire, mightiest of the world's powers. They destroyed monarchical government in what became the United States. They recast the nature of republican ideology and structure with the federal Constitution of 1787. Over the next generation, their revolution helped undermine their own aristocratic conception of republicanism, leading to Andrew Jackson's very different egalitarian republicanism.

With a single exception, the men of 1776 intended no parallel revolution in the culture's social institutions. The Founders had no desire to confiscate property from the rich and give it to the poor. They gave no thought to appropriating familial power from males and giving it to females, or seizing land from whites and returning it to Native Americans. They embraced the entire colonial white male system of social power—except for slave holders' despotism over slaves. That they would abolish. To judge them by their standards, posterity must ask whether this, their sole desired social revolution, was secured.

The Founding Fathers partially lived up to their revolutionary imperative: They barred the African slave trade from American ports; they banned slavery from midwestern territories; they dis-

solved the institution in northern states; and they diluted slavery in the Border South. Yet the Founding Fathers also backed away from their revolutionary imperative: They delayed emancipation in the North; they left antislavery half accomplished in the Border South; they rejected abolition in the Middle South; and they expanded slaveholder power in the Lower South. These retreats both inhibited final emancipation where slavery had been damaged and augmented slave holders' resources where slavery had been untouched. The advances and retreats set off both an antislavery process and a proslavery counteroffensive. Slavery would eventually be abolished, partly because the Founding Fathers shackled the slaveholders. But emancipation would be so long delayed—partly because the Founders rearmed the slavocracy—that the slavery issue would epitomize the social nonradicalism of the American Revolution.

1

Since every generation rewrites history, most historians achieve only fading influence. One twentieth-century American historical insight, however, seems unlikely to fade. In his multivolume history of slavery as a recognized problem, David Brion Davis demonstrated that throughout most of history, humankind failed to recognize any problem in slavery.[6] Then around the time of the American Revolution, Americans suddenly, almost universally, saw the institution as a distressing problem. Davis showed that throughout the Western world, a changed Enlightenment mentality and a changing industrial order helped revolutionize sensibility about slavery. The American political revolution quickened the pace of ideological revolution. Slavery, as the world's most antirepublican social system, seemed particularly hypocritical in the world's most republican nation. Most American Revolutionaries called King George's enslavement of colonists and whites' enslavement of blacks parallel tyrannies. "Let us either cease to enslave our fellow-men," wrote the New England cleric Nathaniel Niles,

"or else let us cease to complain of those that would enslave us."[7]

Yet the Founding Fathers' awareness of slavery as a problem never deepened into the perception that slavery's foundations were a problem. A slaveholder's claim to slaves was first of all founded on property rights; and the men of 1776 never conceived of redistributing private property or private power to ensure that all men (or women!) were created equal. They believed that governments, to secure slaves' natural right to liberty, must pay slaveholders to surrender the natural right to property. That conviction put a forbidding price tag on emancipation.

The price escalated because these discoverers of slavery as a problem (and nondiscoverers of maldistributed property as a problem) also failed to see that other foundation of slavery, racism, as problematic.[8] Thomas Jefferson, like most of his countrymen, suspected that blacks were created different, inferior in intellectual talents and excessive in sexual ardency. Jefferson also worried that freed blacks would precipitate racial warfare. He shrank from abolition, as did most Americans who lived amidst significant concentrations of slaves, unless the freedmen could be resettled outside the republic.[9]

That race removal condition, like the condition that seized property required compensation, placed roadblocks before emancipation. To colonize blacks in foreign lands would have added 25 percent to the already heavy cost of compensated abolition. To coerce a million enslaved humans to leave a republic as a condition for ending coercive slavery could also seem to be a dubious step toward government by consent.

The Founding Fathers' conditional aspiration to free black slaves furthermore had to compete with their unconditional aspiration to build white republics. It was no contest. The American Revolutionaries appreciated all the problems in establishing free government; but that appreciation energized them, inspired them, led to sustained bursts of imaginative remedies. In contrast, these propertied racists exaggerated all the problems in freeing blacks; and that exaggeration paralyzed them, turned them into procrastinators, led to infrequent stabs at limited reforms.

The inhibitions built into the conditional antislavery mentality could be seen even in the Virginia abolitionist who scorned the supposedly necessary conditions. Edward Coles, James Madison's occasional secretary, intruded on Thomas Jefferson's mailbox with demands that the ex-President crusade for emancipation without waiting for slaveholder opposition to relent. Coles himself acted on antislavery imperatives without waiting for action on deportation imperatives. He migrated with his Virginia slaves to almost entirely free-soil Illinois, manumitted all of them, gave each family a 160-acre farm, and provided for the education of those who were underage. After that rare demonstration of how to turn conditional antislavery into unconditional freedom, Coles advised his ex-slaves to return to Africa! The black race, said Coles, might never prosper in the bigoted white republic. That message, coming from that messenger, well conveyed the national mentality that rendered an antislavery revolution impossible.[10]

2

In conditionally antislavery post-Revolutionary America, the more blacks in a local area, the less possibility of emancipation. Where blacks formed a high percentage of the labor force, as in the original Middle South states of North Carolina and Virginia (35 percent enslaved in 1790) and in the original Lower South states of Georgia and South Carolina (41 percent enslaved in 1970), whites' economic aspirations and race phobias overwhelmed conditional antislavery.[11] In contrast, where blacks were less dense and the slavebased economy was noncrucial, as in the original northern states (all under 5 percent enslaved in 1790) and in the original Border South states of Delaware and Maryland (25 percent enslaved in 1790), the inhibiting conditions for antislavery could be overcome—but after revealing difficulties.

In northern states, the sparse numbers of blacks made slavery seem especially unimportant, both economically and racially, to the huge majority of nonslaveholders. The low percentage of blacks, however, made abolition equally unimportant, economically and racially, to most northern citizens. For the Founders to secure emancipation in the North, an unimportant set of economic/racial antislavery imperatives and a conditional strategy for solving the newly perceived slavery problem had to supplement each other, for neither tepid crass motives nor a compromised ideological awakening could, by itself, overwhelm a vigorous proslavery minority.[12]

That vigor will come as a shock to those who think slavery was peculiar to the South. Yet northern slaveholders fought long and hard to save the institution in temperate climes. Although neither slavery nor emancipation significantly influenced the northern economy, the ownership of humans vitally influenced northern slaveholders' cash flow. Slaveholders made money using slavery up North, and they could always sell slaves for several hundred dollars down South. These crass motives of a few could never have held back an ideological surge of the many had a disinterested majority passionately believed that illegitimate property in humans must be unconditionally seized. But since northern nonslaveholders conceded that this morally suspect property had legal sanction, the struggle for emancipation in the North was long a stalemate.

The only exception was far northward, in New Hampshire, Vermont, and Massachusetts. In those upper parts of New England, the extreme paucity of blacks, a few hundred in each state, led to the phenomenon conspicuously absent elsewhere: total abolition, achieved with revolutionary swiftness, soon after the Revolution. But in the more southerly New England states of Connecticut and Rhode Island, and in the mid-Atlantic states of Pennsylvania, New Jersey, and New York, where percentages of blacks were in the 1 to 5 percent range, emancipation came exceedingly gradually, with antirevolutionary evasions.

Blacks' creeping path to northern freedom commenced in Pennsylvania in 1780, where the Western Hemisphere's first so-called post-nati emancipation law was passed.[13] Post-nati abolition meant freedom for only those born after the law was enacted and only many years after their birth. The formula enabled liberty-loving property holders to split the difference between property rights and human rights. A post-nati law required that no then-held slave property be seized. Only a property not yet on earth was to be freed, and only on some distant day. Accordingly, under the Pennsylvania formula, emancipation would eventually arrive only for slaves thereafter born and only when they reached twenty-eight years of age. Slaveholders thus could keep their previously born slaves forever and their future-born slaves throughout the best years for physical labor. That compromised emancipation was the best a conditional abolition mentality could secure, even in a northern Quaker state where only 2.4 percent of the population was enslaved.

Connecticut and Rhode Island passed post-nati edicts soon after Pennsylvania set the precedent. New York and New Jersey, the northern states with the most slaves, delayed decades longer. New York slaveholders managed to stave off laws freeing the future-born until 1799, and New Jersey slaveholders, until 1804. So it took a quarter century after the revolution for these northern states to enact post-nati antislavery—in decrees that would free no one for another quarter century.

Slaves themselves injected a little revolutionary speed into this nonrevolutionary process. Everywhere in the Americas, slaves sensed when mastery was waning and shrewdly stepped up their resistance, especially by running away. An increase of fugitive slaves often led to informal bargains between northern masters and slaves. Many northern slaveholders promised their slaves liberty sooner than post-nati laws required if slaves provided good service in the interim. Thus did perpetual servitude sometimes shade gradually into fixed-time servitude and more gradually still into wage labor, with masters retaining years of forced labor and slaves gaining liberty at a snail's pace. In 1817, New York's legislature declared that the weakening system must end by 1827.[14]

Although New Jersey and Pennsylvania never followed suit, by 1840 only a few slaves remained in the North. By 1860, thirteen New Jersey slaves were the last vestige of northern slavery.

For thousands of northern slaves, however, the incremental post-nati process led not to postponed freedom in the North but to perpetual servitude in the South. When New York and New Jersey masters faced state laws that would free slaves on a future date, they could beat the deadline. They could sell a victimized black to a state down south, which had no post-nati law. One historian estimates that as many as two-thirds of New York slaves may never have been freed.[15]

Despite this reactionary outcome for some northern slaves and the long delay in liberation of others, the post-nati tradition might still be seen as a quasi-revolutionary movement if it had spread to the South. But every southern state rejected post-nati conceptions, even Delaware, and even when President Abraham Lincoln offered extra federal inducements in 1861. Instead of state-imposed gradual reform, the two original Border South states, Delaware and Maryland, experimented with an even less revolutionary process: voluntary manumission by individual masters. Delaware, which contained 9,000 slaves and 4,000 free blacks in 1790, contained 1,800 slaves and 20,000 free blacks in 1860. Maryland, with 103,000 slaves and 8,000 free blacks in 1790, contained 87,000 slaves and 84,000 free blacks in 1860. The two states' proportions of black freedmen to black slaves came to exceed those of Brazil and Cuba, countries that supposedly had a monopoly on Western Hemisphere voluntary emancipation.

Just as fugitive slaves accelerated post-nati emancipation in Pennsylvania, New York, and New Jersey, so the threat of runaways sometimes speeded manumissions in Delaware and Maryland. Especially in border cities such as Baltimore and Wilmington, masters could profitably agree to liberate slaves at some future date if good labor was thereby secured before manumission. A hard-working slave for seven years was a bargain compared to a slave who might run

away the next day, especially since the slavemaster as republican, upon offering a favorite bondsman future freedom, won himself a good conscience as well as a better short-term worker. This combination of altruism and greed, however, ultimately lost the slaveholder a long-term slave. That result, portending a day when no slaves would remain in northern Maryland, was deplored in southern Maryland tobacco belts, where manumission slowed and blacks usually remained enslaved.[16]

The Maryland-Delaware never-completed manumission movement failed to spread south of the Border South, just as the long-delayed northern post-nati movement never spread south of the mid-Atlantic. True, in Virginia, George Washington freed all his many slaves. But that uncharacteristically extensive Middle South manumission came at a characteristic time. President Washington profited from his slaves while living and then freed them in his last will and testament. President Thomas Jefferson freed a more characteristic proportion of his many Middle South slaves—10 percent. Meanwhile, Jefferson's luxurious life-style piled up huge debts, which prevented the rest of his slaves from being manumitted even after his death.

South of Virginia, Jefferson's 10 percent manumission rate exceeded the norm. A master who worked huge gangs of slaves in the pestilential Georgia and South Carolina lowlands rarely freed his bondsmen before or after he died. By 1830, only 2 percent of the South Carolina/Georgia blacks were free, compared to 8.5 percent of the Virginia/North Carolina blacks and 39 percent of the Maryland/Delaware blacks. The revolutionary U.S. sensibility about slavery had, with nonrevolutionary speed, emancipated the North over a half century and compromised slavery in the original two Border South states. But the institution remained stubbornly persistent in the Border South and largely intact in the Middle South; and Lower South states had been left unharmed, defiant, and determined to confine the Founding Fathers' only desired social revolution to the American locales with the lowest percentages of slaves.

National considerations of slavery in the Age of the Founding Fathers repeated the pattern of the various states' considerations. During national debates on slavery, many South Carolina and Georgia Revolutionary leaders denounced the new conception that slavery was a problem. Their arguments included every element of the later proslavery polemic: that the Bible sanctioned slavery, that blacks needed a master, that antislavery invited social chaos. They warned that they would not join or continue in an antislavery Union. They sought to retain the option of reopening the African slave trade. In the first Congress after the Constitution was ratified, they demanded that Congress never debate abolition, even if silence meant that representatives must gag their constituents' antislavery petitions.[17]

The Georgians and South Carolinians achieved congressional silence, even though other Southerners and all Northerners winced at such antirepublican intransigence. North of South Carolina, almost every Founding Father called slavery a deplorable problem, an evil necessary only until the conditions for abolition could be secured. The conditions included perpetuating the Union (and thus appeasing the Lower South), protecting property rights (and thus not seizing presently owned slave property), and removing freed blacks (and thus keeping blacks enslaved until they could be deported). The first step in removing blacks from the United States was to stop Africans from coming, and the last step was to deport those already in the nation. In between, conditional antislavery steps were more debatable, and the Upper South's position changed.

The change involved whether slavery should be allowed to spread from old states to new territories. In the eighteenth century, Virginians presumed, to the displeasure of South Carolinians and Georgians, that the evil should be barred from new territories. In 1784, Thomas Jefferson's proposed Southwest Ordinance would have banned slavery from Alabama and Mississippi Territories after 1800. The bill would theoretically have prevented much of the nineteenth-century Cotton Kingdom from importing slaves. The proposal lost in the Continental Congress by a single vote, that of a New Jerseyite who lay ill at home. "The fate of millions unborn," Jefferson later wrote, was "hanging on the tongue of one man, and heaven was silent in that awful moment."[18]

The bill, however, would not necessarily have been awful for future Mississippi and Alabama cotton planters. Jefferson's bill would have allowed planters in these areas to import slaves until 1800. The proposed delay in banning imports into Mississippi and Alabama stemmed from the same mentality, North and South, that delayed emancipation in Pennsylvania, New York, and New Jersey for decades. In Mississippi and Alabama, delay would have likely killed antislavery. Eli Whitney invented the cotton gin in 1793. By 1800, thousands of slaves would likely have been picking cotton in these southwestern areas. Then the property-respecting Founding Fathers probably would not have passed the administrative laws to confiscate Mississippi and Alabama slaves, since the conditional antislavery mentality always backed away from seizing slaves who were legally on the ground. Probabilities aside, the certainty about the proposed Southwestern Ordinance of 1784 remains. The Founding Fathers defeated its antislavery provisions. Nationally no less than locally, they preserved slavery in Lower South climes.

They also retained their perfect record, nationally no less than locally, in very gradually removing slavery from northern habitats. Just as state legislators abolished slavery in northern states, with nonrevolutionary slowness, so congressmen prevented the institution from spreading into the nation's Northwest Territories, with yet more nonradical caution. Although the Continental Congress removed Jefferson's antislavery provisions from the Southwest Ordinance of 1784, congressmen attached antislavery clauses to the Northwest Ordinance of 1787. Slavery was declared barred from the area of the future states of Illinois, Indiana, Michigan, Wisconsin, and Ohio. Antislavery consciousness helped inspire the ban, as did capitalistic consciousness. Upper South tobacco planters in the Continental Congress explicitly declared that they did not wish rival tobacco planters to develop the Northwest.[19]

The history of the Northwest Ordinance exemplified not only the usual combination of selfishness and selflessness, always present whenever the Founders passed an antislavery reform, but also the usual limited and slow antislavery action whenever conditional antislavery scored a triumph. Just as northern post-nati laws freed slaves born in the future, so the national Northwest Ordinance barred the *future* spread of slavery into the Midwest. But had the Northwest Ordinance emancipated the few slaves who presently lived in the area? Only if congressmen passed a supplemental law providing administrative mechanisms to seize present property. That a property-protecting Congress, led by James Madison, conspicuously failed to do, just as property-protecting northern legislatures usually freed only future-born slaves. Congressmen's failure to enforce seizure of the few midwestern slaves indicates again the probability that they would have shunned mechanisms to confiscate the many slaves in Alabama and Mississippi in 1800 had the Southwest Ordinance of 1784 passed.

The few midwestern slaveholders, their human property intact, proceeded to demonstrate, as did New York slaveholders, that slavery could be profitably used on northern farms. Slaveholding farmers soon found allies in midwestern land speculators, who thought more farmers would come to the prairies if more slaves could be brought along. These land speculators, led by the future president William Henry Harrison of Indiana, repeatedly petitioned Congress in the early nineteenth century to repeal the Northwest Ordinance's prohibition on slave imports. But though congressmen would not confiscate present slave property, they refused to remove the ban on future slaves.

Although frustrated, a few stubborn Illinois slaveholders imported black so-called indentured servants who were slaves in all but name. Once again, Congress did nothing to remove these de facto slaves, despite the de jure declaration of the Northwest Ordinance. So when Illinois entered the Union in 1818, Congress had massively discouraged slavery but had not totally ended it. The congressional discouragement kept the number of indentured black servants in Illinois to about nine hundred, compared to the over ten thousand slaves in neighboring Missouri Territory, where Congress had not barred slavery. But those nine hundred victims of the loopholes in the Northwest Ordinance kept the reality of slavery alive in the Midwest until Illinois was admitted to the Union and Congress no longer had jurisdiction over the midwestern labor system.

Then slaveholders sought to make Illinois an official slave state. In 1824, a historic battle occurred in the prairies over a statewide referendum on legalizing slavery. The leader of Illinois's antislavery forces was none other than now-Governor Edward Coles, that ex-Virginian who had moved northward to free his slaves. Coles emphasized that slavery was antithetical to republicanism, while some of his compatriots pointed out that enforced servitude was antithetical to free laborers' economic interests. Once again, as in the Baltimore masters' decisions to manumit slaves and in the congressional decision to ban slavery from the Midwest, economic and moral motives fused. The fusion of selfish and unselfish antislavery sentiments secured 58 percent of Illinois electorate. That too-close-for-comfort margin indicated how much conditional antislavery congressmen had risked when they failed to close those indentured servant loopholes. But in the Midwest as in the North, the new vision of slavery as a problem had finally helped secure abolition—half a century after the American Revolution.

4

While the Founding Fathers belatedly contained slavery from expanding into the Midwest, Thomas Jefferson and his fellow Virginians ultimately abandoned the principle of containment. In 1819–20, when Northerners sought to impose post-nati antislavery on the proposed new slave state of Missouri, Jefferson called the containment of slavery wrong. Slaves should not be restricted to old areas, he explained, for whites would never free thickly concentrated slaves. Only if slaves were thinly spread over new areas would racist whites free them.[20]

Given many Founding Fathers' conviction that emancipation must be conditional on the removal of concentrations of blacks, their latter-day argument that slaves should be diffusely scattered made more sense than their earlier argument that slaves must be prevented from diffusing. Still, the Upper South's retreat from containment of slavery illuminates the forbidding power of that race removal condition. If Upper South Founding Fathers had opted for diffusion of blacks rather than containment in 1787, as they did in 1819–20, even the diluted antislavery provision in the Northwest Ordinance probably would not have passed. Then the already almost-triumphant Illinois slaveholders probably would have prevailed, and slavery would have had a permanent toehold in the North. On the subject of the expansion of slavery into new areas, as in the matter of the abolition of slavery in old states, the Founding Fathers had suffered a total loss in the South, had scored a difficult victory in the North, and had everywhere displayed the tentativeness of so conditional a reform mentality.

5

To posterity, the Virginians' switch from containing slavery in old American areas to diffusing slavery over new American areas adds up to a sellout of antislavery. The Thomas Jeffersons, however, considered the question of whether slavery should be contained or diffused in America to be a relatively minor matter. The major issues were whether blacks should be prevented from coming to America and whether slaves should be deported from America. On these matters, conditional antislavery men never wavered.

In the letter Jefferson wrote at the time of the Missouri Controversy in which he first urged diffusion of blacks within America, he repeated that blacks should eventually be diffused outside the white

republic. Four years later, in his final statement on antislavery, Jefferson stressed again his persistent conditional antislavery solution. His "reflections on the subject" of emancipation, Jefferson wrote a northern Federalist, had not changed for "five and forty years." He would emancipate the "afterborn" and deport them at "a proper age," with the federal government selling federal lands to pay for the deportations. Federal emancipation/colonization raises "some constitutional scruples," conceded this advocate of strict construction of the government's constitutional powers. "But a liberal construction of the Constitution," he affirmed, may go "the whole length."[21]

Jefferson's "whole length" required not only federal funding but also an organization that would resettle blacks outside the United States. That need found fruition in the Upper South's favorite conditional antislavery institution, the American Colonization Society, founded in 1817.[22] William Lloyd Garrison would soon denounce the society as not antislavery at all. But to Jefferson's entire Virginia generation, and to most mainstream Americans in all parts of the country in the 1817–60 period, the American Colonization Society was the best hope to secure an altogether liberated (and lily-white) American populace.

The only significant southern opponent of the society concurred that colonization of blacks could undermine slavery. South Carolinians doubted that the American Colonization Society would remove millions of blacks to its Liberian colony. (The society, in fact, rarely resettled a thousand in one year and only ten thousand in forty-five years.) But South Carolina extremists conceded that an Upper South-North national majority coalition could be rallied for colonization. They also realized that once Congress voted for an emancipation plan, whatever the absurdity of the scheme, abolition might be near. Capitalists would never invest in the property. Slaves would sense that liberation was imminent. Only a suicidal slaveholding class, warned the Carolinians, would take such a chance. Carolinians threatened to secede if Congress so much as discussed the heresy. So con-

gressional colonization discussion halted in the late 1820s, just as South Carolina's disunion threats had halted antislavery discussions in the First Congress.[23]

A few historians have pronounced these South Carolinians to be but bluffers, cynical blusterers who never meant to carry out their early disunion threats.[24] The charge, based solely on the opinion of the few Founding Fathers who wished to defy the Carolinians, does not ring true. Many South Carolina coastal planters lived among 8:1 concentrations of blacks to whites, a racial concentration unheard of elsewhere. The Carolinians farmed expensive miasmic swamplands, unlike the cheaper, healthier slaveholding areas everywhere else. Unless black slaves could be forced to endure the pestilential Carolina jungle, the lushest area for entrepreneurial profits in North America would become economically useless. So enormous a percentage of blacks might also be racially dangerous if freed. South Carolinians' special stake in slavery engendered understandable worry when Northerners and Southerners called slavery an evil that must be removed.

So South Carolinians threatened disunion. Posterity cannot say whether they would have had the nerve to secede if an early national Congress had enacted, for example, Jefferson's conditional antislavery plan of using federal land proceeds to deport slaves. South Carolinians might have early found, as they later discovered, that their nerves were not up to the requirements of bringing off a revolution against every other state. But though they might not have been able to carry out their threats, that hardly means they were bluffing. Their threats were credible because these sincere warriors intended to act, if the nation defied their non-bluff.

Still, the larger point is that so conditional an antislavery mentality was not equipped to test South Carolinians' capacity to carry out their threats, any more than that mentality's compromised worldview was equipped to seize presently owned property from recalcitrant slaveholders. The master spirit of the age was a passion to build white republics, not an inclination to deport black slaves; and South Carolinians threatened to splinter the Union unless congressmen ceased to talk of deporting blacks. The Founding Fathers' priorities prevailed. South Carolina's threats effectively shut off congressional speculation about removing slaves from America. That left only the other major conditional antislavery aspiration still viable: shutting off the flow of Africans to America.

6

South Carolinians long opposed closure of the African slave trade, too. But their opposition to stopping future slaves from traveling to America was mild compared to their opposition to deporting slaves from America. Like the northern slaveholders who could accept emancipation if they had fifty more years to use slaves, South Carolinians could accept the end of the African slave trade if they had twenty more years to import Africans.

Their potential interest in more African imports first surfaced at the beginning of the American national experience. When drafting the Declaration of Independence and cataloging King George's sins, Thomas Jefferson proposed condemning the tyrant for supposedly foisting Africans on his allegedly slavery-hating colonies. South Carolinians bridled at the language. Jefferson deleted the draft paragraph. Although Jefferson was not present at the 1787 Philadelphia Constitutional Convention, history repeated itself. When northern and Upper South delegates proposed that Congress be empowered to end the African slave trade immediately, South Carolinians warned that they would then refuse to join the Union. The issue was compromised. Congress was given authority to close the overseas trade only after 1807. South Carolinians had a guaranteed twenty-year-long opportunity to import African slaves.

In the early nineteenth century, with the emerging Cotton Kingdom avid for more slaves, Carolinians seized their expiring opportunity. In 1803, the state officially opened its ports for the importation of Africans. Some 40,000 Africans landed in the next four years. Assuming the normal course of black natural increase in the Old South, these latest arrivals in the land of liberty multiplied to 150,000 slaves by 1860, or almost 4 percent of the southern total.

Jefferson was President at the moment when Congress could shutter South Carolina's twenty-year window of opportunity. "I congratulate you, fellow-citizens," Jefferson wrote in his annual message of December 2, 1806, "on the approach of the period when you may interpose your authority constitutionally" to stop Americans "from all further participation in those violations of human rights which have been so long continued on the unoffending inhabitants of Africa, and which the morality, the reputation, and the best interests of our country have long been eager to proscribe.[25] Closure of the African slave trade could not take effect until January 1, 1808, conceded Jefferson. Yet the reform, if passed in 1807, could ensure that no extra African could legally land in a U.S. port. In 1807 Congress enacted Jefferson's proposal.

Prompt enactment came in part because almost all Americans beyond South Carolina shared Jefferson's ideological distaste for slavery. The African slave trade seemed especially loathsome to most white republicans. But neither the loathing nor the enactment came wholly because of disinterested republican ideology. Jefferson and fellow racists hated the African slave trade partly because it brought more *blacks* to America. So too South Carolina planters were now willing to acquiesce in the prohibition partly because they considered their forty thousand imports to be enough so-called African barbarians. So too Upper South slave sellers could gain more dollars for their slaves if Cotton South purchasers could buy no more blacks from Africa. With the closure of the African slave trade—as with the Northwest Ordinance and as with the abolition of northern slavery and as with the manumission of Baltimore slaves—republican selflessness came entwined with racist selfishness; and no historian can say whether the beautiful or the ugly contributed the stronger strand.

The closure of the African slave trade emerges in the textbooks as a nonevent, worthy of no more than a sentence. Whole books have been written on the Founding Fathers and slavery without a word devoted to the reform.[26] Yet this law was the jewel of the Founding Fathers' antislavery effort, and no viable assessment of that effort can ignore this far-reaching accomplishment. The federal closure's impact reached as far as Africa. Brazil and Cuba imported over 1.5 million Africans between 1815 and 1860, largely to stock sugar and coffee plantations.[27] Slaveholders in the United States could have productively paid the then-prevailing price for at least that many black imports to stock southwestern sugar and cotton plantations.

The effect of the closure of the African slave trade also reached deep into the slaves' huts and the masters' Big Houses. If the South had contained a million newly landed "raw Africans," as Southerners called those human folk, southern slaveholders would have deployed more savage terror and less caring paternalism to control the strangers. The contest between the United States, where the nineteenth-century overseas slave trade was closed, and Cuba and Brazil, where it was wide open, makes the point. Wherever Latin Americans imported cheap Africans, they drove down slave life expectancies. In the United States, alone among the large nineteenth-century slavocracies, slaves naturally increased in numbers, thanks to less fearful, more kindly masters and to more acculturated, more irreplaceable blacks.

The closure of the African trade also changed the demographical configuration of the South and the nation, to the detriment of slaveholders' political power. When white immigrants shunned the Slave South and voyaged to the free-labor North, the South could not import Africans to compensate. The North grew faster in population, faster in labor supply, faster in industrialization, faster in the ability to seize agricultural territories such as Kansas, and faster in the ability to control congressional majorities. Worse, after African slave trade closure, the Cotton South could race after the free-labor North only by draining slaves from the Border South. The combination of manumissions and African slave trade closure doubly hindered slavery in the most geographically northern slave states. In 1790 almost 20 percent of

American slaves had lived in this Border South tier. By 1860 the figure was down to 11 percent. On the other hand, in 1790 the Lower South states had 21 percent of American slaves, but by 1860, the figure was up to 59 percent. From 1830 to 1860 the percentage of slaves in the total population declined in Delaware from 4 to 1 percent; in Maryland from 23 to 13 percent; in Kentucky from 24 to 19 percent; in Missouri from 18 to 10 percent; and in the counties that would become West Virginia from 10 to 5 percent. By 1860 Delaware, Maryland, Missouri, and the area that would become West Virginia had a lower percentage of slaves than New York had possessed at the time of the Revolution, and Kentucky did not have a much higher percentage. The goal of abolition had become almost as practicable in these border states as it had been in New York in 1776, twenty-five years before the state passed a post-nati law and fifty years before the New York slave was freed. Had no Civil War occurred, fifty years after 1860 is a good estimate for when the last Border South slave might have been freed. Then slavery would have remained in only eleven of the fifteen slave states.

To sum up the antislavery accomplishments in the first American age that considered slavery a problem: When the Founding Fathers were growing up, slavery existed throughout Great Britain's North American colonies. The African slave trade was open. Even in the North, as John Jay of New York reported, "very few ... doubted the propriety and rectitude" of slavery.[28] When the Founders left the national stage, slavery had been abolished in the North, kept out of the Midwest, and placed on the defensive in the South. A conditional antislavery mentality, looking for ways to ease slavery and blacks out of the country, prevailed everywhere except in the Lower South. If the Founders had done none of this—if slavery had continued in the North and expanded into the Northwest; if a million Africans had been imported to strengthen slavery in the Lower South, to retain it in New York and Illinois, to spread it to Kansas, and to preserve it in the Border South; if no free black population had developed in Delaware and Maryland; if no conditional antislavery ideology had left Southerners on shaky moral grounds; if, in short, Jefferson and his contemporaries had lifted not one antislavery finger—everything would have been different and far less worrisome for the Lower South slavocracy.

7

But the Founding Fathers also inadvertently empowered a worried Low South to wage its coming struggle. "Inadvertent" is the word, for most American Revolutionaries did not wish to strengthen an intransigent slavocracy, any more than they wished to delay African slave trade closure or to silence congressional consideration of colonization. The problem, again, was that these architects of republicanism cared more about building white republics than about securing antislavery. So opportunities to consolidate a republican Union counted for much and the side effects on slavery counted for little—when side effects on slavery where even noticed.

Thus at the Constitutional Convention, Lower South slaveholders, by threatening not to join the Union unless their power was strengthened, secured another Union-saving compromise. Slaves were to be counted as three-fifths of a white man, when the national House of Representatives was apportioned. This constitutional clause gave Southerners around 20 percent more congressmen than their white numbers justified. Since the numbers of members in the president-electing electoral college were based on the numbers of congressmen, the South also gained 20 percent more power over the choice of chief executive. An unappetizing number illustrates the point. The South received one extra congressman and presidential elector throughout the antebellum years as a result of South Carolina's 1803–07 importation of Africans.

The Founding Fathers also augmented Lower South territory. In 1803, Thomas Jefferson's Louisiana Purchase from France added the areas of Louisiana, Arkansas, and Missouri to the Union. In 1819, James Monroe's treaty with Spain secured the areas of Florida, Southern Alabama, and Southern Mississippi. A desire to protect slavery was only marginally involved in the Florida purchase and not at all involved in the Louisiana Purchase. Presidents Jefferson and Monroe primarily sought to protect national frontiers. But they were so determined to bolster national power and gave so little thought to the consequences for slaveholder power that their calculations about blacks could not offset their diplomatic imperatives. Their successful diplomacy yielded territories already containing slaves. Then their antislavery mentality was too conditional to conceive of confiscating slave property. The net result: The Founding Fathers contributed four new slave states and parts of two others to the eventual fifteen slave states in the Union. That increased the South's power in the U.S. Senate 27 percent and the Lower South's economic power enormously.

If the Founding Fathers had done none of this—if they had not awarded the South the extra congressmen and presidential electors garnered from the three-fifths clause; if they had not allowed South Carolina to import forty thousand more Africans; if they had not acquired Florida, Louisiana, Arkansas, Missouri, southern Mississippi, and southern Alabama; if in short they had restricted the slavocracy to its pre-1787 power and possessions—the situation would have been far bleaker for the Cotton Kingdom. Indeed, without the Founding Fathers' bolstering of slaveholder power, their antislavery reforms, however guarded, might have been lethal. As it was, the American Revolutionaries made the slave system stronger in the South, where it was already strongest, and weaker in the North, where it was weakest. That contradictory amalgam of increased slaveholder vulnerabilities and increased slaveholder armor established the pattern for everything that was to come.

8

In the 1820–60 period, and on the 1861–65 battlefields, the slaveholders fought their added vulnerabilities with their added power. By 1860, the slaveholders had fifteen states against the North's sixteen. But if the four Border South states fell away, the North's margin would widen to twenty against eleven. Then all sorts of dangers would loom for a once-national institution, which in the wake of the Founding Fathers was slowly becoming more defensively and peculiarly southern.

Southern proslavery campaigns, ideological and political, could be summed up as one long campaign to reverse the Founding Fathers' conditional antislavery drift. The conditional antislavery ideology, declaring emancipation desirable *if* blacks could be removed and *if* the Union could be preserved, persisted in the North and the Upper South throughout the antebellum period. That predominant national apologetic attitude toward slavery, Lower South zealots persistently feared, could inspire a national political movement aimed at removing blacks and slaves from the nation unless the Lower South deterred it.

Deterrence began with a determined proslavery campaign aimed at showing Southerners that slavery was no problem after all. In its extreme manifestations in the 1850s, proslavery visionaries, led by Virginia's George Fitzhugh, called wage slavery the unrecognized problem. The impolitic implication (although Fitzhugh disavowed it): Even white wage earners should be enslaved.[29] Proslavery polemicists more commonly called freedom for blacks the unrecognized problem. The common message: Black slaves should never be freed to starve as free workers in or out of America.

While proslavery intellectuals took aim at the Founding Fathers' revolutionary awareness that slavery was a problem, proslavery politicians sought to counter the waning of slavery in the Border South. With the Fugitive Slave Law of 1850, particularly aimed at stopping border slaves from fleeing to permanent liberty in the North, and the Kansas-Nebraska Act of 1854, originally urged by its southern advocates to protect slavery in Missouri, Southerners endeavored to fortify the border regime which the Fathers had somewhat weakened. So too the most dramatic (although unsuccessful) Lower South political movement of the 1850s, the

campaign to reopen the African slave trade, sought to reverse the Fathers' greatest debilitation of the slavocracy.

The minority's persistent proslavery campaigns and frequent congressional victories eventually convinced most Northerners that appeasement of a slaveholding minority damaged rather than saved white men's highest priority: majority rule in a white men's republic. That determination to rescue majority rule from the Slavepower minority underrode Abraham Lincoln's election in 1860; and with Lincoln's election came the secession of the Lower South minority. Secessionists feared not least that the President-elect might build that long-feared North-Upper South movement to end slavery by deporting blacks, especially from the compromised Border South.

The ensuing Civil War would prove that latter-day Southerners had been right to worry about slavery's incremental erosion in the borderlands. The four Border South states would fight for the Union, tipping the balance of power against the Confederacy. Abraham Lincoln would allegedly say that though he hoped to have God on his side, he *had* to have Kentucky. He would retain his native Kentucky and all the borderlands, including his adopted Illinois, which the Founders had at long last emancipated.

He would also obtain, against his initial objections, black soldiers, who would again sense an opportunity to read themselves into the Declaration of Independence. Just as fugitive slaves had pushed reluctant Pennsylvania, New York, and Maryland slaveholders into faster manumissions, so fugitive blacks should push a reluctant Great Emancipator to let them in his army and thereby make his victory theirs. Black soldiers would help win the war, secure emancipation, and thus finally defeat the slaveholders' long attempt to reverse the Founding Fathers' conditional antislavery drift.

To omit the Fathers' guarded contributions to America's drift toward the Civil War and emancipation in the name of condemning them as hypocrites is to miss the tortuous way black freedom came to the United States. But to omit the Fathers' contributions to Lower

South proslavery power in the name of calling them social revolutionaries is to deny the very meaning of the word *revolution.*

9

More broadly and more significantly, the American Revolutionaries' stance on blacks illuminated their ambivalent approach to the one truly radical social implication of the Revolution. As the historian Jack P. Greene has brilliantly shown, nothing was radical about the Declaration's affirmation of an American right to life, liberty, and the pursuit of happiness, so long as only white males' pursuits counted as American.[30] Whatever the poverty in urban slums and tenants' shacks, American colonials had long since developed a radically modern social order, dedicated to white males' pursuit of happiness and rooted in unprecedented capitalist opportunity. The Revolution, while expanding political opportunity and political mobility, only a little further widened an economic doorway already unprecedentedly open—but labeled "white males only."

For the others who peopled America—the women, the Native Americans, the blacks, in short, the majority—opportunity was closed. To include these dispossessed groups in the American Revolution—to open up a world where all men and women were at liberty to pursue their happiness—was the Declaration's truly radical social implication. No such color-blind, ethnically blind, gender-blind social order had ever existed, not on these shores, not anywhere else.

The Founding Fathers caught an uneasy glimpse of this potential social revolution. Despite their obsession with white republics and white property, they recognized that the Declaration applied to blacks, too. But their racism led them to take a step backward from the revolutionary promise of the Declaration of Independence. Most of them were no advocates of an egalitarian multicultural society *in* America. The Virginia Dynasty especially would extend quality to black Americans by moving them *out* of America. That reactionary black-removal foundation of antislavery statecraft, peculiar among all the New World slavocracies to these North Americans, did not a progressive social revolution portend.

Thomas Jefferson had captured the nonradicalism of the American Revolution in one of the great American phrases. "We have the wolf by the ears," he wrote at the time of the Missouri Controversy, "and we can neither hold him, nor safely let him go."[31] The Founding Fathers had more wolves by the ears than Jefferson had in mind: blacks, slaves, their own antislavery hopes, their implication, that *all* people must be included in the Declaration of Independence. They propounded those ideals, but they quailed before their own creation. Someday, the ideals may prevail and Americans may cease to recoil from the Declaration's implications. But it would not happen to the Founders, not with revolutionary speed, not to men who equipped a nation to hang on to slavery's slippery ears for almost a century.

Notes

1. William W. Freehling, "The Founding Fathers and Slavery," *American Historical Review, 77* (1972): 81–93.
2. See, for example, Robert McColley, *Slavery and Jeffersonian Virginia* (Urbana, Ill., 1964); Donald L. Robinson, *Slavery in the Structure of American Politics, 1765–1820* (New York, 1971); William Cohen, "Thomas Jefferson and the Problem of Slavery," *Journal of American History,* 56 (1969): 503–26.
3. Later writers have also extended the blame for failure to emancipate to encompass Northerners as well as Southerners. See, for example, Larry E. Tise, *Proslavery: A History of the Defense of Slavery in America, 1701–1840* (Athens, Ga., 1987), and Gary B. Nash, *Race and Revolution* (Madison, Wisc., 1990).
4. David Brion Davis, *The Problem of Slavery in the Age of Revolution, 177–1823* (Ithaca, N.Y., 1975), 168.
5. Most recently and notably in Gordon S. Wood, *The Radicalism of the American Revolution* (New York, 1992), 186–87, 401 *n* 43. For an estimate of this matter very close to my own,

6. David Brion Davis, *The Problem of Slavery in Western Culture* (Ithaca, N.Y., 1966), and Davis, *The Problem of Slavery in the Age of Revolution.*
7. Quoted in ibid., 292.
8. A phenomenon splendidly illustrated in Winthrop D. Jordan, *White over Black: American Attitudes toward the Negro, 1550–1812* (Chapel Hill, N.C., 1968).
9. For further discussion of Jefferson's conditional antislavery position, see William W. Freehling, *The Road to Disunion,* Vol. 1, *Secessionists at Bay, 1776–1854* (New York, 1990), 123–31. For further discussion of the black-removal condition, see below, ch. 7.
10. For an excellent discussion of this episode, see Drew R. McCoy, *The Last of the Fathers: James Madison and the Republican Legacy* (New York, 1989), 310–16.
11. All demographic statistics in this essay derive from *The Statistics of the Population of the United Sates,* comp. Francis A. Walker (Washington, D.C., 1872), 11–74, and U.S. Bureau of the Census, *A Century of Population Growth; From the First Census of the United States to the Twelfth, 1790–1900* (Washington, D.C., 1909).
12. The classic study of emancipation in the North is Arthur Zilversmit, *The First Emancipation: The Abolition of Slavery in the North* (Chicago, 1967).
13. For an excellent discussion of the Pennsylvania episode, see Gary B. Nash and Jean R. Soderlund, *Freedom by Degrees: Emancipation and Its Aftermath in Pennsylvania* (New York, 1991).
14. For a fine recent study of the New York phase, see Shane White, *Somewhat More Independent: the End of Slavery in New York City, 1770–1810* (Athens, Ga., 1991).
15. Claudia Dale Golden, "The Economics of Emancipation," *Journal of Economic History, 33* (1973): 70.
16. Torrey Stephen Whitman, "Slavery, Manumission, and Free Black Workers in Early National Baltimore," Ph.D. diss., Johns Hopkins University, 1993, expertly develops these themes. On the broader Maryland milieu, see Barbara J. Fields, *Slavery and Freedom on the Middle Ground: Maryland during the Nineteenth Century* (New Haven, Conn., 1985).
17. Joseph C. Burke, "The Pro-Slavery Argument in the First Congress," *Duquesne Review, 16* (1969): 3–15; Howard Ohline, "Slavery, Economics, and Congressional Politics," *Journal of Southern History,* 46 (1980): 335–60; Richard Newman, "The First Gag Rule," forthcoming. I am grateful to Mr. Newman for allowing me to use his excellent essay before its publication.

18. Quoted in Merrill D. Peterson, *Thomas Jefferson and the New Nation: A Biography* (New York, 1970), 283.
19. William Grayson to James Monroe, August 8, 1787, in *Letters of Members of the Continental Congress,* ed. Edmund C. Burnett, 8 vols. (Washington, D.C., 1921–36), 8:631–33. The following account of the Northwest Ordinance and its Illinois aftermath has been much influenced by the salutary notes of cynicism in Peter Onuf's fine *Statehood and Union: A History of the Northwest Ordinance* (Indianapolis, Ind., 1987) and in Paul Finkelman's several illuminating essays, especially "Slavery and the Northwest Ordinance: A Study in Ambiguity," *Journal of the Early Republic, 6* (1986): 343–70, and "Evading the Ordinance: The Persistence of Bondage in Indiana and Illinois," *Journal of the Early Republic, 9* (1989): 21–51. But for a cautionary note, see David Brion Davis's judicious "The Significance of Excluding Slavery from the Old Northwest in 1787," *Indiana Magazine of History,* 84 (1988); 75–89.
20. Jefferson to John Holmes, April 22, 1820, in *The Writings of Thomas Jefferson,* ed. Paul Leicester Ford, 10 vols. (New York, 1892–99), 10:157–58.
21. Jefferson to Jared Sparks, February 24, 1824, ibid., 10:289–92.
22. Phillip J. Staudenraus, *The African Colonization Movement, 1816–1865* (New York, 1961).
23. the theme is discussed at length in William W. Freehling, *Prelude to Civil War: The Nullification Controversy in South Carolina, 1816–1836* (New York, 1966).
24. See, for example, Paul Finkelman's otherwise illuminating "Slavery and the Constitutional Convention: Making a Covenant with Death," in *Beyond Confederation: Origins of the Constitution and National Identity,* ed. Richard Beeman et al. (Chapel Hill, N.C., 1987), 188–225.
25. A *Compilation of the Messages and Papers of the Presidents,* comp. James D. Richardson, 10 vols. (Washington, D.C., 1900), 1:408.
26. See, for example, Nash, *Race and Revolution.*
27. David Eltis, *Economic Growth and the Ending of the Transatlantic Slave Trade* (New York, 1987).
28. John Jay to the English Anti-Slavery Society, [1788], in *The Correspondence and Public Papers of John Jay,* ed. Henry P. Johnston, 4 vols. (New York, 1890–93), 3:342.
29. See below, pp. 98–100.
30. Jack P. Greene, *Pursuits of Happiness: The Social Development of Early Modern British Colonies and the Formation of American Culture* (Chapel Hill, N.C., 1988).
31. Jefferson to John Holmes, April 22, 1820, in *Jefferson's Writings,* ed. Ford, 10:157–58.

"Us Colored Women Had To Go Through A Plenty": Sexual Exploitation of African-American Slave Women

Thelma Jennings

Southern slaves were "the happiest, and, in some sense the freest people in the world," wrote George Fitzhugh, Virginia proslavery defender. He claimed bondwomen did "little hard work" and were "protected from the despotism of their husbands by their masters." In her famous diary, Mary Chesnut noted that the female slaves "take life easily. Marrying is the amusement of their life." Many antebellum southerners thought the female slaves were sensuous and promiscuous and cited the "easy chastity" of the bondwomen. Since associations were made between promiscuity and reproduction, the desired increase of the slave population seemed to be evidence of the bondwoman's passion. A slaveowner in northern Mississippi told Fredrick Law Olmsted that slaves "breed faster than white folks, a 'mazin' sight, you know; they begin younger," and, he added, "they don't very often wait to be married."[1]

Bondwomen's perception of the slave experience is in marked contrast to the slaveowners'. In her remarkable autobiography, Linda Brent, a mulatto female slave, noted, "Slavery is terrible for men; but it is far more terrible for women. Superadded to the burden common to all, *they* have wrongs, and sufferings, and mortifications peculiarly their own."[2] Female bondage was worse than male bondage because the female slave was both a *woman* and a *slave* in a patriarchal

From the *Journal of Women's History,* Winter 1990, pp. 45-74. © 1990 by Indiana University Press. Reprinted by permission.

regime where males and females were unequal, whether white or black.

Because they were slaves, African-American women were affected by the rule of the patriarch in more ways and to a greater degree than the white women in the Big House. The size of the food allotment, brutal whippings, slave sales, and numerous other variables influenced the bondwoman's view of the patriarchy. Yet because she was a woman, her view, like that of the white woman, was also gender related. According to Anne Firor Scott, the most widespread source of discontent among white women centered around their inability "to control their own fertility."[3] On the other hand, the bondwoman's entire sex life was subject to the desires of her owner.

This essay will, therefore, deal only with the bondwomen's perspective from the viewpoint of gender, using twentieth-century interviews with female ex-slaves who were at least twelve or thirteen years of age at the time of emancipation. Of the 514 women in this category, 205, or almost forty percent, made comments of this nature. Undoubtedly, the reluctance of ex-bondwomen to discuss such private matters, especially with white men and women, accounts for the fact that the number was not larger.[4] A sample of fifty-eight male slave interviews in the same category was made for comparison; twenty-seven, or 46.55 percent, made gender-related comments. Likewise, a sample of contemporary testimony for both women and men was used. Compared to the Works Progress Administration narratives, contemporary testimony offers a great deal less evidence of sexual exploitation. The men outnumber the women even more than in the WPA narratives.[5]

Female bondage was more severe than male bondage because these women had to bear children and cope with sexual abuse in addition to doing the work assigned to them, work that was often similar in type and quantity to that of male slaves. When it was profitable to exploit women as if they were men in the work force, slaveholders regarded female slaves, in effect, as genderless. But when they could be exploited in ways designed only for women, they were exclusively female—subordinate and unequal to all men. Bondwomen realized the white patriarch had the *power* to force them to mate with whomever he chose, to reproduce or suffer the consequences, to limit the time spent with their children, and even to sell them and their children.

From the beginning of adolescence, females were subject to their master's desire for them to reproduce because increasing the number of slaves meant profits to him. Intervention in the process of procreation, either through subtle or forceful means, became an integral part of the sexual exploitation of bondwomen. Numerous women testified that all owners wanted slaves to have a goodly number of children.[6] Mollie Dawson said marriage only meant "raisin' mo' darkies," something a woman had to do. A North Carolina slaveowner told the newlywed couples that "their duty was to have a houseful of chilluns for him." Jane Simpson's first master only bought two slaves, but he eventually had between fifty and a hundred as "dey raised chillun on his plantation worse than flies." Referring to her marriage, Lizzie Grant remarked, "Maser made me marry him as we were going to raise him some more slaves. Maser said it was cheaper to raise slaves than it was to buy them." She said her master never cared for the slaves' feelings.[7]

Demographic constraints could influence mate selection. Presumably, slaves on very large plantations had more latitude if the sex ratio was about equal. On small holdings or where the sex ratio was unequal, a slave man was often forced to look for a prospective wife on another plantation. Or a slave woman might seek the master's consent for marriage to a young man on another plantation because there was little or no choice on her own. As a rule, masters wanted their slaves to marry someone on the same farm or plantation. In areas where small land units prevailed, however, slaveholders had little choice except to give their consent for an abroad marriage. Since the children remained with the mother, a small slave owner with more women than men could add to his labor force by permitting abroad marriages. An increase in labor meant an increase in land use, and, thus, small farmers could become large planters. Probably, in most abroad marriages, the slaves chose their own mates. Susan Snow of Mississippi claimed all the adult slaves on her plantation were married to persons on another plantation. Camilla Jackson of Georgia said her master required his slaves to select someone on his friends' plantations. In neither case did the master choose the mates for the slaves.[8]

Generally speaking, slaveowners dictated the rules governing slave unions. Whether the woman was allowed to mate with a man who chose her or had one forced upon her by the master was crucial. Phobe Henderson vowed that her master had nothing to do with bringing Phobe and her husband together. She guessed that God did it since they fell in love. There seemed to be no trouble in Caroline Malloy getting the man of her choice.[9] Ellen Rogers' master had selected a man for her, but she loved another, whereupon her owner whipped Ellen to "bre'k me up from lovin'" him. Regardless of how hard she was whipped and slashed, Ellen would not "eben look at dat uder man," and "at las' dey 'low me hab my way for once and I git de man I want." Ellen's master, like some other slaveowners, finally chose not to antagonize her and produce a recalcitrant, sullen worker.[10]

In most cases of this type, the bull whip would cause the female slave to accept the man her master had chosen. Deep resentment is obvious in the words of Mary Gaffney, whose mate was thrust upon her. "I just hated the man I married," Mary told the interviewer, "but it was what Maser said do." At first she refused to accept the man, but, after receiving a whipping, she relented. Though Rose Williams' master treated his slaves well, he forced Rose to live with an African-American against her desires. She always held this against him. Rose's master told her to live with Rufus, a man she considered a bully. At first, Rose resisted and went to her mistress who explained the master's wishes. "Yous am de portly gal and Rufus am de portly man," Missus told Rose. "De massa wants 'you-uns for to bring forth portly chillen." Rose remained adamant until her master told her, "Woman, I'se pay big money for yous an' I'se done dat fo' de cause I'se wants yous to raise me chilluns. I'se put you to live wid Rufus fo' dat pu'pose. Now if yous don't want to be whupped at the stake, yous do w'at I'se want." After the war, Rose never married. "One 'sperience am 'nough fo' dis nigger," she explained. "Aftah w'at I'se do fo' de Marster, I'se never want any truck wid any man." An old Tennessee bondwoman expressed it this way, "He'd make 'em marry who he wanted 'em to marry. You couldn't marry who you wanted to." This is not to say the master usually chose a female's mate, for most often some young male selected his partner and then asked the master if she could become his wife.[11]

Interference with sexual activities in such a direct manner as in the case of Rose and Rufus constituted slave breeding by some slaveowners. Considerable controversy exists among historians on the nature and extent of slave breeding. U. B. Phillips attempted to disprove the abolitionist contention that many slaveowners systematically bred slaves for the market and asserted that it was "extremely doubtful that any appreciable number" attempted directly to hasten an increase in their slaves. Yet, he added, slaveowners everywhere were interested in the "multiplication" of their bondmen. In *The Peculiar Institution*, Kenneth Stampp included a fairly extensive discussion of slave breeding in his chapter on slave trading. Many slaveholders considered prolific African-American women an economic asset and encouraged them to have children as rapidly as possible. Though rewards for additional babies

were sometimes given, few owners overtly interfered with normal sexual activity. The increase was calculated as profit either as the result of sales or expanded operations. Almost two decades later, Richard Sutch defined slave breeding rather broadly as any practice of a slaveowner "intended to cause the fertility of the slave population to be higher than it would have been in the absence of such interference." Sutch claimed slave breeders in the border states and states along the Atlantic coast increased their profits by marketing young adult slaves to the southwestern slave states.[12]

Both Stampp's and Sutch's discussions of slave breeding are strictly economic in focus—an increase in *quantity* for *profits*. No mention is made of *quality* or the improvement of the species; there is no hint at the practice of eugenics. In his quantitative analysis of the slave narratives, Paul Escott briefly discusses the interference of masters with the sexual activities of slaves. He enumerates several different types of slave breeding: rewards to good breeders or sale of barren women, directed pairings often between "fine and stout" individuals, the use of stock men, and the elimination of "runty" males as fathers. Most of these types of slave breeding represent a crude form of eugenics. Though Escott cites a few examples in such cases, he does not include an explicit discussion of the eugenics of slave breeding. In fact, he does not mention the word eugenics. Robert W. Fogel and Stanley Engerman in their controversial study, *Time on the Cross,* attempt to show that slave breeding was a "myth." They contend that planters avoided direct interference in the sexual activities of slaves and attempted to influence fertility patterns through positive economic incentives. Although most of the evidence in their book is invalid or highly questionable, they are the only historians who have dealt at length with "eugenic manipulation." According to Fogel and Engerman, "the main thrust of economic incentives generated" by slavery acted "against eugenic manipulation and against sexual abuse."[13]

Eugene Genovese concluded that forced marriages affected perhaps one out of ten slave unions and caused considerable protest among the bondmen since most masters allowed them to select their own partners. Only a few historians believe that slave breeding was a common practice. In his classic study, *From Slavery to Freedom,* John Hope Franklin contends that females were frequently forced into "cohabitation and pregnancy" by their masters. Jacqueline Jones goes a step further and states that the "Masters frequently practiced a form of eugenics by withholding their permission for certain marriages and arranging others." According to Bell Hooks, considerable evidence substantiates the notion that slave breeding was a "widespread and common practice."[14]

When we turn our attention to the female interviewees in this study, we note that only twenty-five (4.86 percent) commented on slave breeding as outlined by Escott. However, six of the fifty-eight male interviewees (10.34 percent) in the sample made such comments. Only one slave (male) in the contemporary sample noted slave breeding. What is quite significant is that six of the twenty-five women and four of the six men made remarks that specifically indicated "eugenic manipulation." Evidence from the narratives, therefore, shows that slave breeding was not a myth; it did occur throughout the South and was not confined to any one region or state. Moreover, slaveowners on both large and small holdings engaged in breeding. Sometimes the slaves lived on the same plantation; at other times, they belonged to different owners.

A minority of slaveowners was interested in improvement of the species as well as an increase in the number of slaves. This type of sexual exploitation, regardless of the extent, caused both physical and mental anguish for the female slaves. It may have even caused greater humiliation than concubinage with a white man since marriage was long term and concubinage might not be. Moreover, concubinage might offer such compensations as better housing and food and a certain status. Undoubtedly, some women did not oppose a liaison with a white man, given their circumstances, whereas all female slaves abhorred breeding. Because of the awareness on the part of many black women that they could be mated indiscriminately like livestock to increase the quantity and improve the quality of the work force, they viewed the patriarch as a cruel and greedy master who had no regard for their feelings as human beings.

Some bondwomen revealed bitter resentment in very frank, pathetic terms. Katie Darling said her master would pick out "a po'tly man and a po'tly gal" and just "put 'em together because what he wanted was the stock." Slave weddings on Annie Row's place were compared to "de weddin' 'tween de cows and de bull" because "dey wants bigger niggers an' dey mates to suits demse'ves." In discussing the mating of men and women on her plantation, Polly Shine said "this never suited us much but we had to do just like our Masers made us, as we could not do any other way." Refusals would only result in whippings and "mean" treatment. A Missouri woman declared that her master and two brothers-in-law bred slaves like stock to sell. African-American men had three or four wives, "as many as dey could bear chillun by." Her grandmother, who became "stone blind"

after her first child's birth, was kept for breeding. Men and women were "just mixed up" to obtain a "certain kind or breed of chillun" to suit the white folks. After discussing similar practices, an elderly Tennessee woman remarked, "You see dey raised de chilluns ter make money on jes lak we raise pigs ter sell." All of these examples indicate a crude form of eugenics that placed human chattels on the same level as animals.[15]

Slave breeding made it very difficult for couples to establish stable family relationships. Describing the cruelty of her master, Louisa Everett said he mated slaves indiscriminately without any regard for family unions. If the master thought a certain man and woman might have strong, healthy offspring, he forced them to have sexual relations even though they were married to other slaves. In case either one showed any reluctance, the master would make the couple consummate this relation in his presence. A Texas bondwoman, Rose Pollard, remarked, "Half of us young negroes didn't know who our fathers were." She claimed slaveowners did not allow the slave children to become attached to their parents. Rose, however, did know the identity of her father and spoke of a happy family until slave sales caused separation. Comparing slaves to cattle, Mary Young declared, "We never hardly knew who our father was." After pointing out the fact that slaves could not be legally married, Millie Williams continued, "No, sah, dey jus put 'em together lak dey do cattle and hoss's. Shuck's nobody knows who der father waz."[16]

When masters used "stock men," identification of the father could prove to be impossible, as a North Carolina woman pointed out. "I specks dat I doan know who my pappy wuz, maybe de stock nigger on de plantation." On Mary Ingram's plantation, the master made the decision on who could and could not get married. "Him select de po'tly and p'lific women, and' de po'tly man, and use sich for de breeder an' de father ob de women's chilluns." The women selected were not allowed to marry and "de womens have nothin' to says 'bout de 'rangement." The old African-American advised the young girls that there was no use in refusing because they would only get a rawhide whipping and still have to submit. Freedom came in time to save Mary "f'om much ob sich 'sperience. I'se been selected." Mollie Dawson explained that "if de woman wouldn't has de man dat picks you dey would takes you ter a big stout high husky nigger somewhere and leaves you a few days jest lak de do stock now'days and you bettah begins raisin' chilluns too."[17] Two male slaves in the WPA sample gave supporting evidence to the use of "stock men." One slave man told his interviewer that his father had several women, besides his mother, by whom he had children. Another said his master would not allow him to have just one woman. He had about fifteen women and probably over a hundred children.[18]

Penalties and rewards were important factors in slave breeding. Lulu Wilson claimed her father, a free African-American, was run off her plantation because the owner thought he was too old for breeding. Her mother "took" with another man, and they must have "pleased the white folks who wanted niggers to breed like livestock, 'cause she birthed nineteen chillen." A North Carolina woman said runty males were not allowed to father children as "dey operate on dem lak dey does de male hog so's dat dey can't have little runty chilluns." This systematic castration was an extreme eugenic practice. According to a Tennessee woman, a healthy male could just take a woman after telling his master he wanted her, but a "scrubby man" was not allowed to mate with the females. Polly Cancer related that her master told a small slave who started courting her "to git coz he didn't want no runts on his place." If a slave woman did not have children, "dey would works you ter death, dey say you no count and dey soon sells you. On the other hand, a good breeder often received rewards or a reduction in her work load. Martha Jackson explained that her aunt was mostly spared whippings because she was a "breeder woman en brought in chillun ev'y twelve mont's jes' lak a cow bringing in a calf. En she say dat whut make er mo' val'able to her Ole Marster." He ordered that auntie was not to be put under any strain, while the other women worked very hard. Another bondwoman claimed the breeders made the other slaves wait on them until after their babies were born.[19]

In the narratives, two male ex-slaves gave further evidence that some slaveholders practiced a crude form of eugenics. According to Bill Simms, "If a man was a big, strong man, neighboring plantation owners would ask him to come over and see his gals, hoping that he might want to marry one of them, but if a Negro was a small man he was not cared for as a husband." In his description of a slave sale, Jordon Smith noted the prospective buyer's inspection of slave women in order to purchase a young, well-built female. Then the buyer would select a "strong, young nigger boy about the same age and buy him." When they all arrived home, the master would say to them, "I want you two to stay together. I want young niggers."[20]

According to a Georgia interviewee, "a good breedin' woman sho did fetch de money." An old ex-bondman, nearing the century mark, said he heard a breeding woman bid off for fifteen hundred dollars in Memphis. "They always brought

good money." Fannie Moore related, "De breed woman always bring more money den de rest, even de men." When a good breeder was put on the block, she was surrounded by her children to show how fast she could have them. "Tain't no use to say anything, 'cause if she do she just get whipped." Fannie claimed a breeder woman never knew how many children she had. Yet Tempie Durham boasted of her achievement. "I was worth a heap to Marse George kase I had so many chillen. De more chillen a slave have de more dey was worth." Only one other woman on the plantation had more children than Tempie, but "her children was sickly an' mine was muley strong. Dey never was sick." It is relatively easy to explain the difference in viewpoint between the two North Carolina bondwomen. Apparently, Tempie's husband was the only man in her life, and the couple had a satisfactory marriage that continued after freedom. Fortunately, she had a master who did not subject his slaves to "breeding" with brutality and threats; instead, he encouraged stable families of parents who loved each other and produced many additional slaves for him.[21] Whether female slaves were subjected to breeding or not, they were expected to bear many children regardless of their own feelings.

In her excellent study of female slaves in the plantation South, Deborah Gray White shows the importance of marriage and the family in the slave community. The cavalier and often callous attitude of the master toward slave unions conflicted with the solemnity of the marriage ceremony for the slaves, regardless of where it occurred. Another historian states that bondmen "went to great lengths to have the marriage solemnized 'officially.' "[22] Knowing this, we can better understand the emotional attitude of the bondwoman toward a master who so often said his consent was all that was necessary. This was especially disturbing if the couple had asked for a preacher. Betty Simmons, who had married the man her master gave her, remarked, "Dey marry in dem times by de word of de marster." Male slaves in the WPA interviews also testified that the master's permission and marriage "by de massa's word" were what counted. Robert Shepherd declared, "Us knowed better dan to ask de gal when us wanted to get married. Us just told our marster." A Louisiana slave woman expressed the helplessness of the slave couple in a forthright, sorrowful manner: "They needed no witness to sign, for he was king and Lord; just you live together and do as he said or take the bull whip's lashes over your head." No one could have expressed the reality of the patriarchy for both male and female slaves any better. As Bertram Wyatt-Brown has stated, when it came to patriarchs, southern white men were "the genuine article, and intended to remain so eternally."[23]

Since in reality the master's consent was all that was necessary from the white viewpoint, a slave couple *did* often "just live together." Jane Johnson claimed no slave knew what courting, "dat fancy thing," was, as "us just natchally lives together; men and women mates lak de animals out dere." A young man paid no attention to love but "just 'sires de woman they wants, dat's all." On her plantation, Lizzie Jones said slaves were not married by Bible or law. They just took up with each other and then asked the master to let them marry. If they were old enough (at least age twenty), Master would say to the young man, "Take her and go on home." Bondwomen blamed the white people for forcing a behavior that many of them characterized as similar to that of animals. They expressed their deep feelings about what the southern patriarch forced them to do. As Annie Boyd said, "De white folks made niggers carry on like brutes."[24]

One thing that distinguished a "good master" from a bad one in the slaves' eyes was his attitude toward marriage. It is impossible to determine how many couples had their marriage solemnized "officially" by a preacher or the master himself or how many simply jumped the broom. It is clear, however, that bondwomen who had a big wedding with a minister spoke with pride of the event. Lou Williams recalled, "I'se had a 'spectable weddin' cause Miss she say I was her nursemaid. De preacher he reads and I was all dressed up in white clothes and sech a supper we never had." Lou claimed she had the best white folks in the state of Maryland. Tempie Durham, dressed in white, was married on the front porch of the Big House by the black preacher of the plantation church. Tempie also spoke highly of her master and mistress. When interviewed in her early nineties, Nancy King related that she was married in a church two miles off the place by a white preacher. Her owners were "good" to their slaves and "didn' disfigure" them as some were known to do. These examples and others in the narratives indicate that a respectable wedding by a minister, black or white, definitely affected an ex-bondwoman's view of the patriarch, who often was described as a "good" master.[25]

Apparently, some bondwomen regarded a marriage ceremony at which the master read out of the Bible or from a piece of paper somewhat better than the most common broomstick ceremonies. Describing her master as "a mighty fine man," Virginia Bell said there was no broom jumping for marriage on her plantation. The master read, probably from the Bible, to the couple after supper. Then he told them to go to their quarters but to be ready for work the next morning. After relating the story of her parents' marriage by the master, a young woman commented, "Course a nigger was jes' a slave an' dey had to do what de white folks told 'em to so I guess dat way of marryin' was 'bout as good as any." Yet she expressed a common sentiment that could apply to any marriage ceremony; that is, the bondwoman realized she had to accept what was offered, even a broomstick ceremony. Having suffered much under bondage, Jenny Procter, when asked about marriage, answered, "Weddin's? Ugh um! We jes' steps over de broom and we's married."[26]

Since slaveowners tried every conceivable way to encourage or force their female slaves to have children, it would seem logical that pregnant women would have received the proper care during pregnancy and childbirth, and immediately thereafter. In fact, the nature and quality of attention a pregnant woman received varied. Interviews with ex-bondwomen reveal that, although many pregnant women were well cared for, almost as many were neglected, and a large number were actually physically abused. Inasmuch as bondwomen were well aware that "they were cogs in the plantation regime's reproductive machine,"[27] the treatment they received during pregnancy and childbirth certainly affected their view of the patriarchy.

Whether for black or white, the importance of prenatal care was not well understood; and, for both, childbirth was a dangerous procedure. Slaveowners faced a conflict of interests. They deplored the loss of time granted to a pregnant field worker, yet they faced the possibility of the loss of both mother and child if she were forced to work too long and too hard. The two objectives, immediate profits and long-term economic considerations, therefore, clashed at times. In their eagerness for profits, most slaveowners apparently agreed with the Mississippi planter who declared that "labor is conducive to health; a healthy woman will rear most children." Though they were aware to some extent that very hard work was not beneficial, they placed the blame for the loss of slave babies on their mothers, who were often accused of smothering their infants. Slaveowners also sometimes blamed the pregnant bondwomen for miscarriages that increased during the cotton boom years.[28]

According to a South Carolina woman, pregnant women on her place were taken out of the field and put in the carding and spinning room "just befo' de time." Martha Colquitt reported that owners took especially good care of slave mothers and babies. A special house was provided, and a granny woman delivered the babies. "If she found a mammy in a bad fix she would ax Mist'ess to send for Dr. Davenport." On some plantations, other old slave women assisted in taking care of the mothers and babies. Sometimes the white mistress helped a slave woman with the birthing. Bondwomen knew the real reason many masters provided good care at delivery. Fanny Hodges explained that good midwives were used at slave babies' births as "dat was good money." Polly Cancer thought that good care was provided because her master did not want any runts. It is apparent, then, that bondwomen believed proper care was based on selfish motives instead of the master's concern for his female slaves as human beings.[29]

In some instances, the period of "confinement" was as long as four to six weeks, and some women had lighter work loads for a longer period. But Betty Simmons thought a month was too short. "Iffen us hab a baby us was on'y 'low to stay in de house for one mont', carding and spinning." When the baby was one month old, the women were sent back to the field to do heavy work. Mary Ann Patterson said her master did not like for women to lift too much. If a woman had a child and no husband, her master had a man chop wood for her. Lula Walker reported that she received "de bes'" treatment all the time. "If de massa had a good sow that wuz a givin' birth to a lot of pigs ev'y year, you don't think he goin' to take a stick an' beat her do you? . . . I neber had a han' laid on me. Not one." Yet she also said, "I hadda work powerful hard. I worked like a man. I warn't no house nigger. I hoed, plowed, ditched, split rails an' anything else dat needed to be did." But she added, "Good, hard work neber hurt nobody." She never mentioned a "confinement" period. Actually, "de bes'" treatment referred mainly to a lack of whippings and lighter field work, such as hoeing, for short periods of time.[30]

Bondwomen who complained of improper care and neglect during pregnancy and childbirth were sensitive to the fact that the desire for profits caused the slaveowner to squeeze every bit of work he could from female slaves at the same time that he expected them to reproduce as much as humanly possible. "In de days of slavery woman was jus' given time 'nough to deliver dere babies," declared Susan Hamlin to her black interviewer. "Dey deliver dere babies 'bout eight in the mornin' an' twelve had to be back to work." According to Louisa Everett expectant mothers worked in the fields until they felt their labor pains, and it was not uncommon for babies to be born in the fields. A Missouri woman told her interviewer that on her plantation one of the slave women had a baby out in the field about eleven in the morning. The doctor went to the field to care for her. She was sick a long time because she got too hot before the child was born. After this happened, "the boss" was a better man. Jennie Webb's mother worked in the fields up to the day that Jenny was born. In fact, her mother gave birth between the fields and the cabins. She was then carried to the house on a horse.[31] Two WPA male interviewees gave similar evidence. James Lucas, a Mississippi slave, related, "I was born in a cotton field in cotton pickin' time, an' de womens fixed my mammy up so she didn't hardly lose no time at all." Another male slave testified that "lots of chillen was borned on a straw pile in the [wheat] field. . . . I seed that with my own eyes." After the birthing, the master sent the mother and baby to the house.[32]

For some bondwomen, the "confinement" period was very short. Ophelia Whitley said she had known women to leave the field, go have a baby, and be back at work the next day, but this did not happen often. They usually did light work for a week or two. Some owners, however, allowed mothers only two or three days after childbirth, and then they were forced to work in the field or do other work. Two weeks after childbirth, some female slaves returned to the field to hoe all day.[33] Lizzie Williams remembered that her mother had to wash standing in sleet and knee-deep snow when her baby was only three days old. She became ill and almost died. "Dats de only time dey ever was a doctor at any us nigger houses." Three days after Hannah Jones' grandmother's first baby was born, the owners made her get up and make tucked shirts for their son who was going away to college. The slave woman was a fine seamstress, but because she was "sick and weak," some of the stitches were crooked. The white mistress ordered the overseer to take the bondwoman and beat her, but the doctor examined her and said there was no use beating her—she was "stone blind."

Overseers and drivers were responsible for much of the physical abuse of pregnant women, but masters were also guilty at times. Without some explanation, such abuse is incomprehensible. The basic reason—immediate profits—that accounts for long hours of overwork also explains the use of violent methods to achieve a productive work force. Masters often suspected bondwomen of shamming and feigning illness. They became impatient with the slower work of pregnant women. In their eagerness for a bumper crop, they were determined to discipline pregnant women, as well as other workers, who failed to do the work expected of them. Undoubtedly, the patriarchal desire to show authority also accounts for some of the physical abuse: Moreover, there was unfortunately a trace of sadism in some slaveowners, as well as overseers and drivers, which was directed against the weaker members of the slave community—pregnant women, children, and the elderly. Thwarted in their desires to discipline a strong male, these slaveowners punished the pregnant women who fell behind with their work. Driven by impulse, masters in a fit of anger also punished pregnant women without ever thinking of the dangerous consequences for them and their unborn children.[34]

Pregnant women were whipped, sometimes unmercifully, to make them work faster, On Mother Ann Clark's plantation, the bullwhip was frequently used. "When women were with child they'd dig a hole in the groun' and put their stomach in the hole, and then beat 'em." Lizzie Williams explained that this method was used to punish a pregnant woman in order to keep from hurting the unborn child. On Lydia Jefferson's sugar plantation, the overseers stripped the women naked, as well as the men, and whipped them. Pregnant women were forced to lie face down in the specially dug hole in the ground. Lydia and her twin sister, Lucy, were raised in their master's house because their mother died at their birth, the result of such a whipping by a "nigger driver" a few days before the twins were born. The owners knew little of what went on in the fields since they left the bossing to the overseers.[35]

Other interviewees reported the death of pregnant women as a result of whippings of some type. Lucindy Shaw told how the overseer whipped a pregnant woman to death. An old slave man then dug a hole and rolled her in it for burial along with the baby she had birthed. On the next plantation from where Henrietta King lived, Lucy was in childbirth and was so sick she could not go to the field. The white family thought "her time was way off" and she was trying to get out of work. Finally, the overseer went to her cabin and dragged her out. "He laid huh 'cross uh big tebaccy barrell an' he tuk his rawhide an' whupt huh somepin' terrible." The woman dragged herself back to her cabin and the next day she gave birth to a baby girl. Henrietta claimed the child's back "was streaked wid raid marks all criss cross lak." Lucy died the next day.[36]

Given the pressure to reproduce for the master's profit at a time when childbirth was dangerous and children could be sold at the master's whim, we can readily understand why bondwomen would have reason to practice birth control and abortion and to induce miscarriages. Such practices maybe seen as a form of passive resistance, depriving owners of what they demanded from bondwomen. Deborah White has pointed out that it is almost impossible to determine whether slave women engaged in such practices.[37] The women selected for this study reveal little about this aspect of their private lives. Four, however, expressed their feelings. One woman was alloted to a man in Missouri, but her husband remained in Kentucky where he was alloted to another. In her mind, the bondwoman vowed that she would never marry again to have children. She, therefore, married a man who was too sick to be a father. Forced by her master to marry a man she hated, Mary Gaffney at first refused to let him touch her, but he told the master who then whipped Mary. That night, then, she let her husband have his way. "Maser was going to raise him a lot more slaves, but still I cheated Maser." Mary had no babies, and her owner wondered what was wrong. She said she chewed cotton roots and was careful not to let her master catch her. After freedom, Mary had five children. Anna Lee claimed that female slaves had started chewing cotton roots to keep from having babies. If slavery had lasted much longer, there would have been only old ones left as we had done quit breeding." Another Texas woman said women could cause a miscarriage by taking calomel, turpentine, and indigo.[38]

Two women, however, noted that cruel treatment and heavy work were sometimes linked to miscarriages. A Tennessee ex-slave said the master on an adjoining plantation, who was "a devil on earth," would kick pregnant women and cause them to miscarry. According to Lizzie Williams, pregnant women would sometimes be plowing and hit a stump, which caused the plow to jump and hurt the child and cause a miscarriage. She exclaimed, "such a whippin' as dey would get!" The owners blamed the women.[39]

Soon after giving birth, most slave mothers usually had to trust the care of their babies to someone else in order to return to the fields. From that time on, the contact they had with their children during the day was limited by the rule of the patriarch who did not consider their maternal needs and feelings, his primary motive being profit. In most cases, an old slave woman took care of the babies and small children. Larger plantations had nurseries and hospitals; smaller places used an old slave woman's house. Young slave girls also cared for the children.[40] The image of patriarchal society with happy, contented slaves dims when we read the words of Elvira Boles, who had to work very hard. "Don' evvy thing but split rails. I've cut timber—evvy thing a man could do." But she hated to leave her baby when working. "I'd leave mah baby cryin' in the yard and I'd be cryin', but I couldn't stay." As Louisa Everett pointed out, slave women had no time for their own children. Sometimes they were further deprived of what little time they did have by being forced to care for white children. Rachel Sullivan told her interviewer that as a young girl she took care of some black children while their mother served as wet nurse for a white woman. What this slave woman must have felt one can only imagine.[41]

Interviews with former bondwomen indicate that, as a rule, mothers were allowed to come from the field two times a day to nurse their babies, although on some plantations they could come more often. Jane Robinson explained, "When a mother was sent to attend to her baby, she had a certain time to stay; if she stayed over that time she was whipped." Moreover, she only came when she was told to do so. Teshan Young's mother was whipped once because she came on her own initiative to nurse. After a long, hard day's work, mothers finally got their children back.[42]

On some plantations, or when work was some distance from the quarters, mothers carried their children with them to the field. July Halfen's mother put her babies on an old piece of quilt in the fence corner while she hoed or plowed. When they cried, she would look around to see if the overseer was in sight; if not, she would stop and nurse. Bringing infants to the field, however, could have tragic consequences. In one instance, an eagle dipped down and picked one up and flew away with it. Another mother was forced to tie her smallest child to a tree limb to keep the ants and bugs from getting on it. Mothers also sometimes carried their sick babies in baskets to the field to take care of them.[43]

According to Leslie Owens, "the lack of real consideration of childbearing slaves carried over to their infants," and there was a high slave infant mortality rate. Many children became ill or died due to improper care suckling by overheated mothers, irregular feedings, filthy food, and poor hygiene. Yet other historians have pointed to the concern and solicitation that many planters had for slave children.[44]

Unfortunately, none of the interviewees in this study who were mothers spoke of child care, but we do have comments from female slaves who related experiences as children or as caretakers. Their remarks are significant because they reveal the real reasons for proper care when given and the helplessness of bondwomen in situations involving their own children. Encouraged or pressured into having many children, bondwomen were further exploited by being deprived of much of the nurturing of their offspring. Manda Edmondson, who was brought up on a plantation with many other children, told her interviewer, "Yo' see dey would want de slaves to raise big families so's to have mo' of 'em to wuk, so de chillen wuz cared fer to grow up an' be useful." An Alabama slave, who claimed her master raised slaves to sell, said children received good care because her master expected them to bring a profit. As a young slave girl, Teshan Young took care of the slave children in the nursery while their mothers were in the field. She said her master fed the children well in bowls similar to a trough. Sometimes Teshan received a whipping for letting the children hurt themselves since her master was "particular" about the children. He said, "Gib dem a good staht an' dey makes strong niggers." Lina Hunter, who helped Granny Rose take care of the slave children on her plantation, explained that the children ate out of wooden trays that looked like pig troughs, but she never commented on the quantity or quality of the food except to say that slaves in general had plenty of something to eat. Moreover, Lina noted that the children didn't work until they were age twelve to fourteen and considered big enough to go to the fields. Undoubtedly, what disturbed slave mothers the most was seeing the patriarch whip their children. Caroline Hunter said her mother stood by many days and watched the master beat her children until they bled, and she could not open her mouth. She expressed a common sentiment when she noted, "During slavery it seemed lak yo' chillun b'long to ev'ybody but you."[45]

Male slaves in the WPA sample testified that, as a rule, slave children received fairly good care. Richard Jones declared, "All de chillens in de quarter was well fed, clothed, housed, and doctored until dey was strong and well developed younguns." A Georgia male recalled that his master had warned the old woman who took care of him and other children that "she better fix us plenty to eat and give it to us on time."[46]

In all probability, slave infants and children did receive fairly good physical care as measured by the standards of the time. After all, it was in the owners' best interests to see that they developed into strong, healthy adults to be used as workers and breeders or to be sold. It must be noted that knowledge of such things as diet, sanitation, and medical treatment was very limited. House flies, for example, were a menace to the whites as well as the slaves. Moreover, owners often seemed more concerned about unborn children than pregnant women. The former represented future investment. For the highest return, the labor of pregnant women and nursing mothers should, however, be utilized in the present, while they were making their contribution to the future. This also explains why owners were careful in regulating nursing periods.

Bondwomen were not only forced to live with males of their own race but were also forced to have sexual relations with white men. Kenneth Stampp has noted that it is impossible "to measure the extent of miscegenation with precision." Interracial sexual contacts were not the "rare aberrations" of a small group of debased whites but a frequent occurrence that involved whites of all social and cultural levels. After completing his quantitative study of the slave narratives, Paul Escott observed, "Although no one will ever be able to quantify the amount of interracial sex in the Old South, it is apparent that it occurred often enough to produce substantial numbers of mulatto children." In his recent study of miscegenation, Joel Williamson notes that the upper South was the "heartland" for mulattoes. During the decade of the 1850s, mulatto slavery increased in numbers more than three times that of black slavery throughout the South. Publicly, whites were increasingly disturbed about mulattoes being free, and slavery was rapidly becoming whiter as whites enslaved mulattoes.[47]

Leslie Owens believes that planters' desires, not those of slaves, were responsible for this increase in the mulatto population, though some females willingly mixed their blood with that of white males. As Deborah White has argued, "Although not all white male–black female relationships were exploitative, most began that way, and most continued that way." Many slave women were forced to choose between miscegenation and "the worst experiences that slavery had to offer."[48] Indeed, evidence from the slave narratives supports the view that most relationships were exploitative.

White women thought they suffered most from interracial sex in the slave quarters. Their writings, as well as legal documents, reveal their pain and tragedy. Some white and undoubtedly many black men were also hurt by miscegenation. But after all the attempts have been made to determine the effects of interracial sex on southern society, "one can hardly escape the conclusion that the principal victims" were the bondwomen who were directly involved. Miscegenation under slavery was "above all an indignity" to the female slaves.[49]

Of the 514 female slaves selected for this study, sixty-three, or 12.26 percent commented on interracial sex. Twenty-two of this number (35 percent) were directly involved; that is, their fathers were white men and/or they had given birth to one or more mulatto children.[50] The number was probably much higher. Escott has shown that the sex and race of the interviewer influenced the frequency of all ex-slaves' revelations concerning miscegenation. It is reasonable to believe that some freedwomen were reticent, except with a

black woman interviewer. According to both white and black sources, *forced* interracial sex was much more frequent than slave breeding.[51] In only one instance did an interviewee state that some bondwomen were not forced. She told her Fisk University interviewer that "all the colored women didn't have to have white men, some did it because they wanted to and some were forced. They had a horror of going to Mississippi and they would do anything to keep from it."[52]

Regardless of the number involved, the freedwomen clearly indicate, as did white women, that crossing the racial barrier was a source of discontent. The difference, however, was that the bondwomen were the victims. Only slave breeding could compare with forced interracial sex in the extent of pain and humiliation they caused. Although male slaves were subjected to forced sex as stock men, in the case of miscegenation, only the bondwomen could be subjected to the white man's passion. It was a mortification "peculiarly their own." Rose Maddox said, "I can tell you that a white man laid a nigger gal whenever he wanted her. Seems like some of them had a plumb craving for the other color. Leastways they wanted to start themselves out on the nigger women." In referring to a nearby slaveholder, a Tennessee exslave told her Fisk University interviewer, "He forced nearly every decent slave woman he had. Williamson County is full of half white children he got by his slaves." After describing an incident in which she had fought off a white man (not her master) and scratched his face, Fanny Berry explained, "some slaves would be beat up so, when dey resisted, an' sometimes if you 'belled [rebelled] de overseer would kill you. Us colored women had to go through a plenty, I tell you." Fannie claimed, however, that "I wuz one slave dat de poor white man had his match."[53]

Some bondwomen indicated that there was little or no mixing of the races on their plantation. An elderly Mississippi bondwoman declared her master allowed "no ugly living" or no white man to go into the slave quarters. When asked if her master ever sold slaves, Rachel Sullivan, a bondwoman on South Carolina Governor Francis Pickens' plantation, replied, "No'm—not less dey did wrong." Then she related that three women had children by the overseer, and "massa" put them on the block. "No ma'm he wouldn't tolerate dat. He say you keep de race pure. Lawdy, he made us lib right in dem time." Her master sent the overseer "down to de low place."[54]

However, thirty-six of the interviewees who commented on miscegenation, or 57 percent, noted that the master himself was guilty of interracial sex. As Lizzie Williams noted, "Many de pore niggah women hab chillun for de massa dat is iffen de massa a mean man. Dey jes' tell de niggahs whut to do and dey know better den de fuss." After reiterating for the third time that she was not going to tell her interviewer all she knew, an old woman almost one hundred years old observed, "Old Massa done so much wrongness I couldn't tell yer all of it. Slave girl Betty Lily always had good clothes an' all the privileges. She was a favorite of his'n. But cain't tell all! God's got all!"[55]

Moreover, nine of the sixty-three interviewees who commented on interracial sex claimed the master or his son as father (14.28 percent). None treated their paternity as unusual. Alice Marshall explained that her mother was "a very light woman who never got beat" and was "kinda favorite wid de white folks." When asked about her father, Alice replied, "Well, I reckon I oughter not to tell dat, but it ain' my shame. 'Twas ole massa. . . . He's my father. Chile, dat was ev'y day happenin's in dem days." The perspective of these bondwomen fathered by their masters was typical of other female slaves. Some voiced no personal complaint. An elderly Kentucky woman reported, "I'se was never once treated as a slave cause my massa was my very own Daddy." Pricilla Owens stated that her master-father treated her "fairly well." In two instances, "young massa" was the father of the female slaves, whose mistresses were apparently widows. Both of them became house servants and received good treatment while they remained with their respective owners. In referring to her "white blood" one declared, "Lawd, it's been to my sorrow many a time cause de chillen useter chase me around and holler 'Ole yellow nigger!' Dey didn't treat me very good either." She told the interviewer she had prayed for freedom with the rest of the female slaves.[56]

Other female slaves fathered by the master expressed unhappiness and even bitterness. Referring to her master-father as "the ol' devil," Ruth Allen declared, "My mammy didn' have any more to say about what they did with her than the rest of the slaves in them days." The slaveowner kept Ruth and her mother until Ruth was about three years old, when the family saw she was going to be prettier than the master's children by his own wife. Then he sold Ruth and her mother. The master-father of Amy Patterson ran a kind of agency through which he collected slaves and yearly sold them to dealers or hired them out to other people. He promised Amy's mother he would never sell their mulatto child, but later he decided to sell all his slaves and move to another place. At first he refused to sell his daughter, but he finally sold Amy to her mother's new master because of the grief of mother and daughter.

Amy's stinging remark, disguised as a question, was "when a father can sell his own child, humiliate his own daughter by auctioning her on the slave block, what good could be expected where such practices were allowed?" Elvira Boles' first mistress did not want her on the place since she was the master's child, Elvira was auctioned to a neighbor planter, who later became the father of her oldest child. Elvira was beautiful and almost white, with long hair. She commented that, "Iffen dey had a pretty girl dey would take 'em and I'se one of 'em."[57]

Some bondwomen, however, occasionally resisted their masters' efforts but with limited success. When a Georgia slave refused her young master, he pretended she had done something and beat her, but she fought back. His mother became angry and sent the bondwoman to the courthouse to be whipped for fighting her son. The slave was beaten so unmercifully that she could not sit down. Instead of being carried home, she was put in the Negro Traders Office and sold two days later. After two unsuccessful attempts to subdue her, the master of Diana Gaskins took her to Norfolk and put her on the auction block, but Diana begged a nearby planter to buy her, and he agreed, bringing her back to the same neighborhood. Her former master could do nothing. In another instance, the slave cook, Sukie, actually fought off her master who was always trying "to make her his gal." After making him break loose, she gave him a shove and pushed "his hindparts" down in a hot pot of soap, which burned him "near to death." He got up and ran from the kitchen, not daring to yell. A few days later, he sold Sukie to a "nigger trader." But "Marse never did bother slave gals no mo'."[58]

Ten other interviewees said their fathers were white, but only three of them knew his identity—an overseer, a white northern doctor, and a Quaker. What may be surprising are the few specific indictments against overseers for interracial sex. Lydia Jefferson related that the overseer on her place took advantage of young slave girls. "And dere wasn't any purity for de young girls in de slave quarters, 'cause de overseer was always sending for de young girls to be with 'em." Another bondwoman noted only one overseer "spoiled" a slave girl on her place. After the overseer said something to Martha Bradley "he had no bizness to say," she knocked him down with the hoe and ran to the bushes. The master came and began whipping her, but he stopped when Martha explained what had happened.[59]

In only one instance did a freedwoman report that some masters who had children by their female slaves actually freed their offspring. Another bondwoman, however, said that many mulattoes were sent North. Harriett Robinson told the interviewer that her mulatto sister had three children by her master's son. "We never seen her no more after her last child was born. I found out, though, that she was in Canada." It is true that in a few instances mulatto children were well cared for and received better treatment than black children. Mary Thompson explained that, "Some of de slaves—like a seamstress—would have children by de Marster . . . and nobody had bettah bothaw dem chillun! Dey was taken good care of." Occasionally, mulatto children were even taught to read. Sylvia Cannon's remarks are significant in this case. She said whites never helped the blacks to read and write. They taught the "yellow chillun," but if they caught the "black chillun wid a book, dey nearly 'bout kill us. Dey was sho better to dem yellow chillun den de black chillun dat be on de plantation." Sylvia, who was not a mulatto, clearly felt degraded by this discrimination. A former slave on a large North Carolina plantation related that one of the slave children, Emily, looked like "a white gal" and "was treated just like she was white." Her father, a family man, paid "no more attention to her dan de rest of de niggers. But de missy she was good to her" and taught her to read.[60]

By far, the most serious indictment of the patriarchy was the sale of mulatto children and/or their mothers. Instances of such sales have already been mentioned. Other horrible accounts are found in the narratives. One bondwoman reported that her master's father sold his own "half-breed" children down the river to Louisiana plantations where the work was so severe that the slaves soon died. In another case, the slave woman herself was sold to Georgia away from her three-month-old baby because the baby's father was the young master. A jealous mistress was sometimes the cause of such sales. One woman told her Fisk University interviewer that her master was mean to the slave women even though "he was going with them. If his wife find it out he would have to sell her. He'd sell his own children by slave women just like he would sell any others" because he was "making money."[61]

How could a white father ignore his own flesh and blood and even sell his offspring? The first reason is the ideology of race. Children with even a drop of African blood were not considered members of the white family. Only offspring of a man with his white wife were family and legitimate heirs to carry on his name. Moreover, some white men did not feel responsible for the mulatto children they fathered since, according to their justification, the black, promiscuous Jezebel had

initiated the sexual relationship. Sex and race were further intertwined with capital. Slave offspring could increase the labor force or add money to the master's pockets if he sold them.

Five freedmen in the WPA sample of fifty-eight (8.62 percent) commented on interracial sex. Their remarks are quite similar to those of the black women. A North Carolina bondman claimed "plenty" of the female slaves had children by white men because they "knew better than to not do what he say." The white women seldom knew because the white men would not tell and the black women were afraid to. "So they just go on hopin' that things won't be that way always." John Finnley related, however, that one bondwoman hit her master with a hoe" 'cause he try 'fere with her and she try stop him." In return for her audacity, the female slave received 500 lashes, the "worst whipping" John ever witnessed. A Georgia male reported that when a "yellow" child was old enough to do chore work, the master-father would sell him or her. "No difference was it his own flesh and blood—if the price was right!" Yet another stated that his master willed his black concubine and their children a house, some land, and a little money.[62]

When we turn our attention to contemporary testimony, four autobiographical accounts should be noted. Linda Brent, a mulatto and the great-granddaughter of a South Carolina planter, ran away in order to escape the sexual exploitation of her master, Dr. Flint. Shortly after her birth, Louisa Picquet and her young mulatto mother were sold because Louisa resembled her white half-sister. Louisa's mother bore children for their new master, a Georgia cotton planter, but Louisa managed to resist his attempts to coerce her to join the ranks of his select consorts. Later, she was sold again and became the concubine of her new owner, who was separated from his wife. This man promised to treat her well if she behaved, but, if not, he would whip her almost to death. Elizabeth Keckley, confidante of Mary Todd Lincoln, believed that her mother's master was her father. When she was about eighteen, Elizabeth was placed with a white man in North Carolina by whom she bore a son. Ellen Craft's first master was her father, and her mother was his slave. In addition to Ellen Craft's interview, John Blassingame also included in his *Slave Testimony* the interview of an old black woman identified only as Granny, who had five children by her master. "I didn't want him, but I couldn't do nothin'," she testified. Granny would ask her master, "What do yer want of a woman all cut ter pieces like I is?"[63]

Only six contemporary male slaves in Blassingame's *Slave Testimony* commented on interracial

Table 1

Sexual Exploitation–Female Slaves (N = 514)

	Number	Percentage
Made Gender Related Comments	205	39.88
Commented on Slave Breeding	25	4.86
Commented on Interracial Sex	63	12.26

Table 2

Sexual Exploitation–Male Slaves (N = 58)

	Number	Percentage
Made Gender Related Comments	27	46.55
Commented on Slave Breeding	6	10.34
Commented on Interracial Sex	5	8.62

Table 3

Interracial Sex–Female Slaves (N = 63)

	Number	Percentage
Female Was Directly Involved	22	34.92
Noted Masters Were Guilty	36	57.14
Claimed Master or His Son as Father	9	14.28

sex; three of them were part white. Alexander Kenner said his father, a prominent white man, had seven children by his slave mother before marrying a white woman. A South Carolina slave testified that there was "a good deal" of interracial sex among the unmarried young white men who "often kept one girl steady and sometimes two on different places." And even married white men were known to leave their own places to have sexual relations with female slaves. J. W. Lindsay claimed a few slaveowners thought "a good deal" of their mulatto children and their slave "mistresses." Some sent their children to the North and some to Oberlin College. Because she refused to live with her new owner, Lewis Hayden's mother was violently punished and even sent to prison. The bondwoman practically lost her mind before her master finally sold her.[64]

Female bondage was not only different from male bondage, it was more severe as a result of sexual exploitation. Twentieth-century interviews and contemporary autobiographies of black women narrate sexual abuse and sufferings "peculiarly their own." Male slave testimony confirms the bondwomen's perspective. Throughout the South, slaveowners required bondwomen to reproduce for their profit in addition to working as long and often as hard as male slaves. The master's attitude, often insensitive and cavalier, was deeply disturbing on such matters as choice of mates, marriage, pregnancy, and child care. Some bondwomen were even subjected to breeding. Moveover, they knew they could become victims of the white man's sexual desires any time. Anne Firor Scott has described the resulting "widespread discontent" among white women; bondwomen responded in different ways, depending on temperament and circumstances. Most acquiesced in an effort to prevent themselves or family members from being beaten or sold. Others reacted violently but with little success, which caused greater pain, such as whippings and sale. Many of them seethed with resentment and bitterness, which perhaps they passed on to their children. Undoubtedly, they experienced both mental anguish and physical pain as a result of the selfish desires of the white patriarch, but they just went "on hopin' that things" wouldn't "be that way always."

NOTES

[1]George Fitzhugh, *Cannibals All! or Slaves Without Masters* (Cambridge, Mass.: Harvard University Press, 1960, orig. pub. 1859), 18; C. Vann Woodward, ed., *Mary Chestnut's Civil War* (New Haven, Conn.: Yale University Press, 1981), 168; Deborah Gray White, *Ar'n't I a Woman? Female Slaves in the Plantation South* (New York: W. W. Norton and Co., 1985), 28–46. White discusses the Jezebel image of black women. For other analyses of the Jezebel complex see: Bell Hooks, *Ain't I a Woman: Black Women and Feminism* (Boston: South End Press, 1981), 52; Angela Y. Davis, *Women, Race and Class* (New York: Random House, 1981) 176–77; Gerda Lerner, ed., *Black Women in White America: A Documentary History* (New York: Random House, 1972), 163–64; Winthrop D. Jordan, *White over Black: American Attitudes Toward the Negro, 1550–1812* (Chapel Hill: University of North Carolina Press, 1968), 150–51; Elizabeth Fox-Genovese, *Within the Plantation Household: Black and White Women of the Old South* (Chapel Hill: University of North Carolina Press, 1988), 292; Mary Frances Berry and John W. Blassingame, *Long Memory: The Black Experience in America* (New York: Oxford University Press, 1982), 115–16. Chancellor William Harper, "Harper's Memoir on

Slavery," *De Bow's Review of the Southern and Western States, 1850* (New York: AMS Press, Inc., 1967), 499; Frederick Law Olmsted, *A Journey in the Back Country, 1853–1854* (New York: Burt Franklin, 1970, orig. pub. 1860), 153. For a discussion of slave illegitimacy, see Herbert G. Gutman, *The Black Family in Slavery and Freedom, 1750–1925* (New York: Random House, Inc., 1976), 73–75, 78–79.

[2]Linda Brent, *Incidents in the Life of a Slave Girl,* ed. by L. Maria Child (New York: Harcourt Brace Jovanovich, 1973, orig. pub. 1861), 79.

[3]Anne Firor Scott, *Making the Invisible Woman Visible* (Urbana and Chicago: University of Illinois Press, 1984), 178.

[4]George P. Rawick, ed. *The American Slave: A Composite Autobiography,* 41 vols., Series 1, Supplement Series 1 and 2 (Westport, Conn.: Greenwood Press, 1972, 1977, 1979); Charles L. Perdue, Jr., Thomas E. Borden, and Robert K. Phillips, eds., *Weevils in the Wheat: Interviews with Virginia Ex-Slaves* (Charlottesville: University Press of Virginia, 1976); John B. Cade, "Out of the Mouths of Ex-Slaves," *Journal of Negro History* 20 (July 1935): 294–337.

Restriction to female ex-slaves was based on the desire to let the women speak for themselves. To my knowledge, no one has done a study on slave women using primarily the female narratives as primary source material, although Deborah Gray White relied heavily on WPA interviews with female ex-slaves in her recent work, *Ar'n't I a Woman?* On p. 24 White notes, "I found them the richest, indeed almost the only black female source dealing with female slavery."

The idea for age restriction originated with Norman Yetman, *Life Under the "Peculiar Institution:" Selections from the Slave Narrative Collection* (New York: Holt, Rinehart and Winston, Inc., 1970), 5. As Yetman points out, the quality of the narratives of older ex-slaves is generally better than those of younger ones. My primary reason for age restriction is that interviews of older ex-slaves are based to a much greater extent on first-hand experience. Sometimes an interviewee's age is not given; in such a case, content of the narrative had to provide a basis for judgement. In this category, a few narratives had to be eliminated because of poor quality—brevity, senility of interviewee, and so on. Likewise, two interviewees who were age eleven in 1865 were included because of the exceptional quality of the narratives.

For a discussion of how differences in sex and race of interviewer affected responses of the informants, see John W. Blassingame, ed., *Slave Testimony: Two Centuries of Letters, Speeches, Interviews and Autobiographies* (Baton Rouge: Louisiana State University Press, 1977), lii.

[5]The sample of twentieth-century male ex-slave interviews are those included in Yetman, *Life Under the "Peculiar Institution."* For contemporary testimony, see: Brent, *Life of a Slave Girl*; Blassingame, *Slave Testimony*; Bert James Loewenberg and Ruth Bogin, eds., *Black Women in Nineteenth-Century American Life* (University Park and London: The Pennsylvania State University Press, 1976); Elizabeth Keckley, *Behind the Scenes; or Thirty Years a Slave and Four Years in the White House* (New York: G. W. Carlton, 1868); Henry Bibb, *Narrative of the Life and Adventures of Henry Bibb, an American Slave* (New York: By the author, 1850); John Anderson, *The Story of the Life of John Anderson, the Fugitive Slave* (Freeport, New York: Books for Libraries Press, 1971, orig. pub. 1863); Frederick Douglass, *Life and Times of Frederick Douglass* (London: Collier-Macmillan, 1962, orig. pub. 1892).

[6]White, *Ar'n't I a Woman?,* 97–99; White notes that historians differ on the average age of a slave woman at first birth.

She places it in the nineteenth year, about two years earlier than white women. In this connection, see James Trussel and Richard Steckel, "The Age of Slaves at Menarche and Their First Birth," *Journal of Interdisciplinary History* 8 (Winter 1978) 8: 477–505. Trussel and Steckel concluded that menarche occurred at age fifteen, and a slave woman's age at first birth was 20.6 years. She did not bear children at the earliest possible age (504). Ada Isabell Suggs claimed girls were forced into maternity at puberty. Rawick, *The American Slave,* Indiana 6: 190. Hereafter, references from the Rawick series will be cited only by state or title, volume, and page, preceded by supplement number when applicable.

[7]The term marriage is used in this study with the understanding that slaves were not allowed to marry legally. Texas, Supplement 2, 4: 1122; North Carolina, 15: 32; Missouri, 11: 314; Texas, Supplement 2, 5: 1556.

[8]Alan Kulikoff, *Tobacco and Slaves: The Development of Southern Cultures in the Chesapeake, 1680–1800* (Chapel Hill: University of North Carolina Press, 1986), 64–76; Gutman, *Black Family in Slavery and Freedom,* 131–35, 170–71. Kulikoff and Gutman discuss how large plantations came into being. Mississippi, Supplement 1, 10: 2012; Georgia 12: 296. For examples of restrictions against abroad marriages, see Texas, Supplement 2, 6: 2124; Georgia, 12: 142, and for opposition to abroad marriages, see Mississippi 7: 172.

The narratives contain numerous accounts of dances, corn shuckings and other celebrations, religious meetings, visitations, and so on where young slave men and women on neighboring plantations could meet and be attracted to one another. Then they would try to talk the respective owners into an abroad marriage. In some cases, however, bondmen preferred an abroad marriage because they would not have to see their wives whipped when they could not protect them. See Bibb, *Life and Adventures,* 42; Anderson, *Life of Anderson,* 129. Some slaves could also have sought abroad marriages because of the African-American culture's ban on marriage between cousins. See Gutman, *Black Family in Slavery and Freedom,* 88–93.

[9]Texas, Supplement 2, 5: 1704; Georgia, Supplement 1, 4: 413. For other good examples of courting in the narratives, female and male, see: Perdue, et al., *Weevils in the Wheat,* 122, 316; *God Struck Me Dead* 19: 204; Georgia, Supplement 1, 4: 456; Georgia 12(1) 164–66; *Unwritten History of Slavery,* 18: 132; Texas, Supplement 2, 7: 2467, 2470; Florida, 17: 147. Many authorities indicate the male initiated the selection and courting. Blassingame's discussion in this regard is the best-known. He states that young slave men pursued their black women with "a reckless abandon," which their white masters often envied. See John W. Blassingame, *The Slave Community: Plantation Life in the Antebellum South* (New York: Oxford University Press, 1979), 156–61. See also Jacqueline Jones, *Labor of Love, Labor of Sorrow: Black Women, Work, and the Family from Slavery to the Present* (New York, Basic Books, Inc., 1985), 33–34; White, *Ar'n't I a Woman?,* 142–48. See also 97, 98, 104 for comments on courtship practices and Eugene D. Genovese, *Roll Jordan, Roll: The World the Slaves Made* (New York: Pantheon Books, 1974), 468–71; Leslie Howard Owens, *This Species of Property: Slave Life and Culture in the Old South* (New York: Oxford University Press, 1976), 195–97.

[10]Texas, Supplement 2, 8: 3360.

[11]Texas, Supplement 2, 5: 1453; Texas, Supplement 2, 10: 4120–23; *God Struck Me Dead,* 19, 202; Mississippi, Supplement 1, 10: 2113–14; Ohio 16: 105; Cade, "Out of the Mouths," 303; Texas, Supplement 2, 9: 3765.

[12]Ulrich B. Phillips, *American Negro Slavery* (Baton Rouge: Louisiana State University Press, 1969, orig. pub. 1918), 361–62; Kenneth Stampp, *The Peculiar Institution* (New York: Vintage Books, 1956), 245–51; Richard Sutch, "The Breeding of Slaves for Sale and the Westward Expansion of Slavery, 1850–1860" in Stanley L. Engerman and Eugene D. Genovese, eds., *Race and Slavery in the Western Hemisphere: Quantitative Studies* (Princeton: Princeton University Press, 1975), 173–210.

[13]Paul D. Escott, *Slavery Remembered: A Record of Twentieth-Century Slave Narratives* (Chapel Hill: The University of North Carolina Press, 1979), 43–45. Escott concluded such practices were "rare," but numbers could not "suggest the suffering and degradation they caused," and reticence probably caused some underreporting (45). Robert W. Fogel and Stanley L. Engerman, *Time on the Cross: The Economics of American Negro Slavery* (Boston: Little, Brown and Co., 1974), 78–86, direct quote, 85. Fogel and Engerman found the slave woman's age at first birth to be 22.5, indicating she did not bear children as soon as she was physiologically capable. This finding bolstered their claim that slaveowners did not engage in systematic or widespread breeding.

[14]Genovese, *Roll, Jordan, Roll, 464;* John Hope Franklin, *From Slavery to Freedom: A History of Negro Americans* (New York: Alfred A. Knopf, 1967), 204; Jones, *Labor of Love, Labor of Sorrow,* 34–35; Hooks, *Ain't I a Woman,* 39.

[15]Texas, Supplement 2, 4: 1050; Texas, Supplement 2, 8: 3369, 3515; Missouri, 11: 214–216; Tennessee, 16: 78.

[16]Florida, 17: 127; Texas, Supplement 2, 8: 3118; Texas, Supplement 2, 10: 4315, 4110.

[17]North Carolina, 14: 31; Texas, Supplement 2, 5: 1848; Texas, Supplement 2, 4: 1122.

[18]Yetman, *Life Under the "Peculiar Institution,"* 34–35, 92.

[19]Texas, Supplement 2, 10: 4191–92; North Carolina, 14: 31; *Unwritten History of Slavery,* 18: 300; Mississippi, Supplement 1, 7: 350; Texas, Supplement 2, 4: 1122; Alabama, 6: 222; Georgia, 12(2): 260.

[20]Yetman, *Life Under the "Peculiar Institution,"* 277, 288. An example of breeding to increase the number of slaves is found in Douglass, *Life and Times of Douglass,* 123–24. A poor white man bought one female slave, "a breeder," which was all he could afford. Then he locked her up every night with the hired man. There was great joy when she gave birth to twins.

[21](2)Georgia: 260; Yetman, *Life Under the "Peculiar Institution,"* 27, North Carolina, 15: 131–32; Fannie Moore also claimed many slave men and women married their own brothers and sisters, North Carolina, 14: 288. Escott states that frequently forced marriages broke up after emancipation. See Escott, *Slavery Remembered,* 44. See also Leon Litwack, *Been in the Storm so Long: The Aftermath of Slavery* (New York: Alfred A. Knopf, 1980), 234, 242 for his discussion of separations and reunions.

[22]White, *Ar'n't I a Woman?,* 105; Owens, *This Species of Property,* 193.

[23]Texas, Supplement 2, 9: 3540; Yetman, *Life Under the "Peculiar Institution",* 39, 80, 268; Cade, "Out of the Mouths," 305; Bertram Wyatt-Brown, *Southern Honor: Ethics and Behavior in the Old South* (New York: Oxford University Press, 1982), 226.

[24]South Carolina, 3(3): 49–50; Texas, Supplement 2, 6: 2124; Georgia, Supplement 1, 4: 456; Kentucky, 16: 59.

[25]Texas Supplement 2, 10: 4099; North Carolina, 14: 286–87; Texas, Supplement 2, 6: 2219.

[26]Texas, Supplement 2, 2: 246; Texas, Supplement 2, 4: 1286; Texas, 5(3): 212. Jumping the broomstick was the most common irregular slave marriage ritual, which transformed a "free" slave union into a legitimate slave marriage. Sometimes the ceremony accompanied a conventional Christian ritual and involved the owners. Ex-slaves rarely defined the function of this ritual, and its meaning remains obscure. See Gutman, *Black Family in Slavery and Freedom,* 275–77, 282–84.

[27]White *Ar'n't I a Woman?,* 103.

[28]Catherine Clinton, *The Plantation Mistress: Women's World in the Old South* (New York: Pantheon Books, 1982), 151–55; Olmstead, *Journey in the Back Country,* 59 direct quote; Jones, *Labor of Love, Labor of Sorrow,* 19; White, *Ar'n't I a Woman?,* 88–89; Todd L. Savitt, *Medicine and Slavery: The Diseases and Health Care of Blacks in Antebellum Virginia* (Urbana: University of Illinois Press, 1978), 115–20; Michael P. Johnson, "Smothered Slave Infants: Were Slave Mothers at Fault?" *Journal of Southern History* 47 (November 1981): 493–520. Johnson and Savitt believe that "crib death" or Sudden Infant Death Syndrome was probably responsible for the majority of slave infant deaths. Both of them, as well as Jones and White, tend to link overwork and improper prenatal care to SIDS. However, the cause of SIDS is still unknown, in spite of increased research. SIDS occurs among families of all social and economic levels and at about the same rate across races, nations, social classes, and areas of the United States, although variations associated with these factors have sometimes been noted. The babies of doctors and nurses have even been victims. See Robert B. McCall, "Sudden Infant Death," *Parents Magazine* 56 (October 1981): 112; Millard Bass, Richard E. Kravath, and Leonard Glass, "Death Scene Investigation in Sudden Infant Death," *New England Journal of Medicine,* 315 (10 July 1986): 100–05; Jeffrey R. M. Kunz and Asher J. Finkel, eds., *American Medical Association Family Medical Guide* (New York: Random House, Inc., 1987), 663.

[29]South Carolina, 3(3): 3; Georgia 12(1): 246; Arkansas Supplement 2, 1: 85; Mississippi, Supplement 1, 10: 2336; Mississippi, Supplement 1, 8: 1026; Mississippi, Supplement 1, 7: 350.

[30]Texas, Supplement 2, 9: 3541; Texas, 4(2): 43; Texas, Supplement 2, 8: 3023; Alabama, Supplement 1, 1: 432.

[31]South Carolina, 2(2): 236; Florida, 17: 129; Missouri, Supplement 1, 2: 139; Mississippi, Supplement 1, 10: 2250.

[32]Yetman, *Life Under the "Peculiar Institution,"* 217, 288.

[33]North Carolina, 15: 373; Indiana, 6: 166; Mississippi, Supplement 1, 10: 2336; Missouri, 11: 215; Arkansas 8(2): 15.

[34]See Wyatt-Brown, *Southern Honor,* 149–74 for his discussion of childrearing of white males to account for their fits of anger.

[35]Texas, Supplement 2, 10: 4100; Texas 4(1): 224; Mississippi, Supplement 1, 10: 2337; Texas, Supplement 2, 6: 1939, 1943.

[36]Mississippi, Supplement 1, 10: 1927; Perdue, et al., *Weevils in the Wheat,* 190.

[37]White *Ar'n't I a Woman?,* 84–86. See also Gutman, *Black Family in Slavery and Freedom,* 80–82. Gutman cites medical reports of such practices, notably one given by a physician in Murfreesboro, Tennessee, and the response it provoked from other doctors. See Linda Gordon, *Woman's Body, Woman's Right: A Social History of Birth Control in America* (New York: Grossman Publishers, 1976) for her discussion of pre-modern birth control.

[38]Missouri, 11: 126; Texas, Supplement 2, 5: 1453; Texas, Supplement 2, 6; 2284; Texas, Supplement 2, 6: 2299.

[39]*God Struck Me Dead,* 19: 215; Mississippi, Supplement 1, 10: 2337.

[40]Owens, *This Species of Property,* 40; *White, Ar'n't I a Woman?,* 112–14; Charles S. Snydnor, *Slavery in Mississippi* (Baton Rouge: Louisiana State University Press, 1933), 64–65. In the narratives, there are numerous examples of old women and young slave girls caring for the babies during the day.

[41]Texas, Supplement 2, 2: 337; Florida, 17: 129; Georgia, 13(4): 226.

[42]Cade, "Out of the Mouths of Ex-Slaves," 321; Texas, Supplement 2, 10: 4318. See also Arkansas, Supplement 2, 1: 81–82; Texas, Supplement 2, 6:2169; Texas, Supplement 2, 2: 288; Georgia 12(2): 255; Texas, Supplement 2, 9: 3541.

[43]Mississippi, Supplement 1, 8: 899–900; Texas, 4(2): 16; Texas 4(2): 72; Alabama, Supplement 1, 1: 99; Texas, Supplement 2, 10: 4100.

[44]Owens, *This Species of Property,* 41, 199–209; Genovese, *Roll, Jordan, Roll,* 509–19; Blassingame, *The Slave Community,* 179–91; Willie Lee Rose, *Slavery and Freedom,* edited by William W. Freehling (New York: Oxford University Press, 1982), 37–48.

[45]Mississippi, Supplement 1, 7: 675; Alabama, 6: 90; Texas, Supplement 2, 10: 4318; Georgia, 12(2): 255, 259, 269; Perdue, et al., *Weevils in the Wheat,* 150. The female narratives reveal the bondwomen's love for their children.

[46]Yetman, *Life Under the "Peculiar Institution,"* 192, 264.

[47]Stampp, *Peculiar Institution,* 350–51; Escott, *Slavery Remembered,* 46; Joel Williamson, *New People: Miscegenation and Mulattoes in the United States* (New York: New York University Press, 1984, orig. pub., 1980), 14, 25–26, 41, 63–65. More authors, those in other disciplines as well as history, have written about miscegenation or rape than any other form of sexual exploitation of African-American slave women. See especially Wyatt-Brown, *Southern Honor,* 307–24 for his discussion of slave wenching. Because of the intrastate migration of the bondwomen in this study before and after emancipation, it is impossible to determine any regional or state differences in miscegenation. There are also other variables, as previously mentioned.

[48]Owens, *This Species of Property,*. 211; White, *Ar'n't I a Woman?,* 34. Angela Y. Davis argues that rape of slave women was not an expression of white men's sexual urges, but was a weapon of domination and repression whose goal was to destroy slave women's will to resist—to demoralize the women and even their men. See Davis, *Women, Race and Class,* 23–24.

[49]Scott, *Making the Invisible Woman Visible,* 180–81; Anne Firor Scott, *The Southern Lady: From Pedestal to Politics; 1830–1930* (Chicago: The University of Chicago Press, 1970), 19, 52–53; Clinton, *The Plantation Mistress,* 199–222. On p. 222, Clinton notes that "ante-bellum patriarchs simultaneously emasculated male slaves, dehumanized female slaves, and desexualized their own wives. Catherine Clinton, "Caught in the Web of the Big House: Women and Slavery" in Walter J. Fraser, Jr., R. Frank Saunders, Jr., and Jan L. Wakelyn, eds., *The Web of Southern Social Relations: Women, Family, and Education* (Athens: The University of Georgia Press, 1985), 19–34. Stampp discusses the effects of miscegenation on all groups of southern society in *Peculiar Institution,* 353–61, direct quotes, 360–61.

Slave men suffered terrible humiliation and felt powerless to aid and protect their womenfolk, as in other cases of sexual abuse of women. But I agree with Stampp and Clinton that black women suffered most of all groups. See also Genovese, *Roll, Jordan, Roll,* 413–31 for a good overall discussion of miscegenation.

[50]These figures are not an attempt to quantify the extent of interracial sex in the antebellum South, as I agree with Stampp, Escott, Clinton, and others that this is impossible. The figures simply represent the number of female ex-slaves who had strong enough feelings about miscegenation to discuss it. In this way, these statistics help us to understand the bondwoman's view of the patriarchy on this matter.

[51]Escott, *Slavery Remembered,* 193. A good example of reticence is found in the narrative of Mary Colbert, Georgia, 12(1): 213–25. Interviewed by a white woman who described her as "almost white" with hair that was "quite straight," Mary never admitted that she was a mulatto, nor did she say her parents were mulattoes. She related that her father died when she was small and mentioned the name of the slave who was said to be her father. Mary had even considered writing her autobiography, but she gave up the idea because it would be a large task and she "would have to tell too much." Mary's master was probably her father. Escott's study (46) showed that 12.26 percent of the bondwomen commented on interracial sex compared to 4.86 percent on slave breeding.

[52]*Unwritten History of Slavery,* 18: 2.

[53]Texas, Supplement 2, 7: 2531; *God Struck Me Dead,* 19: 216; Perdue, et al., *Weevils in the Wheat,* 36.

[54]Mississippi, Supplement 1, 8: 1244; Georgia, 13(4): 227.

[55]North Carolina, 15: 297; Perdue, et al., *Weevils in the Wheat,* 273–74, 277. Bondwomen were aware that the master's liaisons with slave women often caused trouble between the master and his wife. See South Carolina 2(1): 150; North Carolina. 15: 308; Texas, Supplement 2, 8: 3292–94.

[56]Perdue, et al., *Weevils in the Wheat,* 202; Kentucky, 16: 60–61; Cade, "Out of the Mouths," 316; Georgia. 13(4): 298; Mississippi, Supplement 1, 7: 782–83, 785.

[57]Minnesota, Supplement 1, 2: 101–02; Indiana, 6: 150–51; Texas, Supplement 2, 2: 336–38.

[58]Georgia, 13(4): 293; Perdue, et al., *Weevils in the Wheat,* 257, 48–49.

[59]Arkansas, Supplement 2, 1: 68; Perdue, et al., *Weevils in the Wheat,* 255; *Unwritten History of Slavery,* 18: 277; Texas, Supplement 2, 6: 1943; Alabama, 6: 46.

[60]Texas, Supplement 2, 2: 141; Alabama, 6: 221; Oklahoma, 7: 273; Texas, Supplement 2, 9: 3863; South Carolina, 2(1): 192; North Carolina, 15: 396–97. For an instance where some mulatto women had children by their fathers or brothers, see North Carolina, 14: 219–20.

[61]Texas, Supplement 2, 2: 141; Indiana, 6: 50; Perdue, et al., *Weevils in the Wheat,* 199, 201; *Unwritten History of Slavery,* 18: 298.

[62]Yetman, *Life Under the "Peculiar Institution,"* 232, 37, 124, 308.

[63]Brent, *Life of a Slave Girl,* ix, x, 31–32; Loewenberg and Bogin, *Black Women,* 54–69, 70, 104–23; Keckley, *Behind the Scenes,* 38; Blassingame, *Slave Testimony,* 268–74, 539–40.

[64]Blassingame, *Slave Testimony,* 392, 382, 400–01, 695–96. See also 128, 703–05.

NEGRO CRAFTSMANSHIP IN EARLY AMERICA

Leonard Price Stavisky

&**M**ANY Americans continue to harbor ideas of racial hierarchies by believing that the Negro is incapable of performing a series of skilled operations. There are still those who persist in picturing him as the "plantation darky" capable only of work in the cotton fields. Nevertheless, it remains an indisputable fact that Negro labor is gradually changing from agriculture to industry. According to one recent tabulation, the number of Negro tradesmen in the United States totals more than 135,000.[1] This trend is not of recent origin. As early as 1783 a German physician, touring the United States, was astonished to find that "the gentlemen in the country have among their negroes as the Russian nobility among the serfs, the most necessary handicrafts-men, cobblers, tailors, carpenters, smiths, and the like whose work they command at the smallest possible price or for nothing almost. There is hardly any trade or craft," he observed, "which has not been learned and is not carried on by negroes."[2]

The presence of Negro craftsmanship during the first years of political independence from Britain would seem to suggest that this tradition had its origin prior to the advent of the American Revolution. Indeed, there is reason to believe that Negro workers engaged in the crafts while still on the continent of Africa. In the Sudan, almost one thousand years ago, cotton was already being woven. Long before England established colonies in the Western Hemisphere, primitive tanning, weaving, and toolmaking were practiced by the natives of Lake Tchad and Timbuctoo. As one author maintains, "the decorative character manifested in the handicrafts of the black races of Africa is of surpassing character. . . . The native hand derives the maximum of expression from the few elements afforded by the soil."[3]

While African Negroes may have had some experience in the manual arts and crafts, this had little direct influence upon American handiwork. The severance of relations with the African continent resulted in a loss of these traditional skills among the later generations of transplanted Negroes. During the early years of American slavery, little thought was given to the possibility of converting imported "savages" into artisans. Slaves were brought to America for agricultural purposes and in most instances were used for no other work. Among the planter class there were those who felt that craftsmanship did nothing more than replace the stock which it consumed and hence was less productive than agriculture.[4] Still others feared that industrialization would bring the slave into contact with free workers and provide access to tools needed for fashioning weapons, thus increasing the danger of insurrection.[5] These factors, together with the hostility of white artisans to slave competition[6] and the widespread belief that black men were inferior in mind and body[7] served as ample justification for restricting the Negro to predominantly agricultural service.

On the other hand, the steady decline in the price of colonial tobacco, the mainstay of Southern agrarianism, weakened the arguments of its advocates. The handicrafts, even if they created products only commensurate with the value of the materials originally expended, as the planters had maintained, were not completely unproductive. Manufacturing, unlike agriculture, was independent of seasonal weather fluctuations and seemed more conducive to specialization, thereby affording greater opportunity for improvement.[8] Even Thomas Jefferson, the champion of agrarian America, eventually recognized industrialism as one of the major pillars of our prosperity and urged a policy which would plant the manufacturer and husbandman side by side and establish "at the door of every one that exchange of mutual labors and comforts, which we have hitherto sought in distant regions."[9]

Unquestionably the strongest argument for the use of Negro artisans was a scarcity of labor. During most of the colonial period, in spite of constant demand for the products of skilled craftsmanship, the supply of workers who had mastered the trades was generally inadequate. The province of South Carolina in 1731 had only one potter, while Connecticut, the following year, had not enough capmakers to manufacture one half the hats worn by the inhabitants. Writing of New Hampshire, Jeremy Belknap deplored the "want of experienced and industrious workmen."[10] Peter Purry, of Neufchâtel, while advising European emigrants about to depart for the Southern colonies, emphasized the need for tradesmen. Those desirous of going as servants, he remarked, should be carpenters or good laborers. Without referring specifically to the shortage of tailors, Puny notified each to take with him at least three or four good shirts and a suit of clothes.[11] In a similar vein Benjamin Franklin called attention to the "continued demand for artisans of all the necessary and useful kinds to supply those cultivators of the earth with houses and with furniture and utensils of the grosser sorts, which cannot so well be brought from Europe."[12]

This situation gave the few established tradesmen excellent bargaining powers. In many communities the price of labor rose steadily, occasionally becoming almost prohibitive. In New York at the beginning of the eighteenth century the "high wages of the labourer" seriously hampered the production of naval stores.[13] To add to the difficulties facing the colonial employer, virgin land was available at reasonable rates. As late as 1779 Dr. Hewit reported that the "artificer and tradesman, after having labored for a few years at their respective employments, and purchased a few negroes, commonly retreat to the country, and settle tracts of uncultivated land.[14] Masters tried to import European workers, but the results were often unsatisfactory. Indentured servants, just as domestic tradesmen, were attracted by the prospects of cheap land. Leaving before their contracts had expired, these men had little difficulty disappearing into the mass of free citizens.[15] As a last resort employers turned to their final source of potential industrial labor—Negro slaves.

The employment of slave mechanics, it was commonly agreed, would restrain the rapid turnover in manpower and counteract the excessive wage demands of free workers. In scattered instances American Negroes began working at the trades only a few years after the introduction of slavery. By 1649 one Virginia planter had forty colored helpers whom he instructed in spinning, weaving, and shoemaking. With only about three hundred Negroes in the entire colony, this meant that approximately one out of every seven was receiving instruction in the crafts.[16] Five years later Richard Johnson, a mulatto carpenter, was granted one hundred acres of land in Northampton County, Virginia.[17] In old New Amsterdam Negroes were required to build roads and fortifications, while in 1676 Colonel Richard Morris employed sixty to seventy slaves at his New Jersey iron mill and plantation.[18] However, in spite of these early evidences, it was not until the eighteenth century that Negro craftsmanship became a factor of some importance in American economy.

Skilled Negro labor, in one form or another, was present in every province of colonial America,[19] although in no large area did craftsmanship constitute the predominant form of Negro service. The North employed its black inhabitants as household domestics and unskilled laborers, while in the South their capability as field hands overshadowed many attempts to use them extensively for other purposes. Probably the largest proportion of Negro artisans was to be found in the middle provinces, whose flourishing towns served to encourage the development of the trades, and where Negroes could become assistants to established tradesmen. In New York, Philadelphia, and Baltimore, Negroes worked as bakers, brewers, bricklayers, butchers, carpenters, cooks, coopers, distillers, goldsmiths, plasterers, shoemakers, silversmiths, and weavers.[20] Even in the towns of New England, where the number of black inhabitants was always small, Negroes were assimilated into industry. Reflecting the commercial trends of the coastal region, many engaged in various phases of shipbuilding. At a Boston slave auction in October, 1751, five "strong hearty stout Negro men, most of them Tradesmen, such as Caulkers, Sailmakers, etc.," were offered for sale, while in Newport and Providence, Rhode Island, slave workers gave service as anchor makers, mast builders, rope makers, and spinners.[21]

Occupying a unique role in the development of Negro craftsmanship were the Southern colonies. In this region, agriculture dominated the economy, and domestic manufacturing was conceived as ancillary to the traditional agrarian system. On many plantations, slaves, although primarily engaged in planting, found it necessary to have some mechanical knowledge in order to attend to any serious emergency that might arise. From these beginnings emerged a corps of slave artisans whose work was identified with the prevailing agrarian economy and upon whose skills the planters began to depend with increasing frequency. Probably the first trade in which the Southern Negro received instruction was coopering. In preparing the crop for market, large numbers of casks were required, and slaves were therefore taught to cut, bend, and hoop staves into the required shapes. Before the end of the colonial period, one writer insists, every large estate in the rice belt of South Carolina had its own coopering shop. Workers were also needed to construct the small boats on which the shipment was transported to market, while others were given training in the navigation of these vessels, hence the development of Negro ship carpenters and pilots. It is safe to assume that anyone who could not work at the trades himself and did not have slaves who understood these tasks, often found living in the South rather difficult.[22]

With the passage of time the relationship between agriculture and the crafts became even closer. Added numbers of Southern slaves were taught to practice the trades, thus partially relieving dependence upon Europe and the Northern provinces. Often the children of the household servants were encouraged to sew and embroider. Planters also built looms and put their slaves to work at making cloth. George Washington, like countless other slaveowners, had a weaving house on his estate, employing a white supervisor and five Negro girls, who together supplied the clothing for many persons living in the vicinity. Even the medium-sized plantation was equipped with spinning wheel and weaving loom, in this way ensuring the profitable use of valuable labor at times when the selling price of tobacco fell below production expenditures.[23]

On the other hand, some of the larger plantations became almost economic units in themselves, having at their disposal sufficient men and equipment to continue operating irrespective of conditions outside. During the most pressing days of the American Revolution, when the British were dangerously near and supplies were virtually unobtainable, many plantations escaped privation because of facilities installed during peacetime. On the plantation of George Mason, for example, were slave "carpenters, coopers, sawyers, blacksmiths, tanners, curriers, shoemakers, spinners, weavers and knitters, and even a distiller." His forest land furnished wood for the carpenters and coopers; his cattle provided skins for the tanners, curriers, and shoemakers; his sheep and his cotton fields supplied the spinners and weavers, while his fruit trees were used by the distillers.[24] John Dixon of Williamsburg, Virginia, owned a host of slave handicraftsmen, including blacksmiths, carpenters, barbers, shoemakers, and plasterers. On another plantation were "several pairs of sawyers, two coopers, two or three indifferent house-carpenters and a ship-carpenter and caulker." The estate of William Byrd of Westover, a mere 43,000 acres, had two hundred and twenty Negroes, "many of them being Tradesmen," who were assessed at 7,000 pounds. According to Philip V. Fithian, Robert Carter operated textile factories, mills, bakeries, salt works, smiths' shops, and iron forges. Carter's slave labor supply, at one time numbering more than five hundred, included one Negro whom the master would not sell for five hundred pounds. Such plantations, having at their disposal extensive working forces, mines, transportation facilities, shops, mills, and tools, seemingly approximated many of the features of modern "vertical" trusts in controlling every aspect of their own production and distribution.[25]

The individual worker followed a similar pattern. Almost invariably he was responsible for the production of a single item from its first to its last stage. Division of labor during the colonial period was largely non-existent, and therefore each craftsman was expected to plan, construct, and ornament his own product. Furthermore, every trade carried a very broad implication. Regardless of his occupation the slave artisan usually had to know various other crafts related to his own. Thus the Negro blacksmith often could perform every phase in the production of iron, including the skilled art of fashioning tools, while the carpenter was simultaneously a cabinetmaker, wood turner, builder, coffin and pattern maker, architect, contractor, wheelwright, sawyer, and cooper.[26] To accomplish this required more than an average amount of intelligence and ability. Several slave craftsmen were described as being "very artful," "very sensible," or "ingenious," while a few even mastered two or more foreign languages. In the relatively short period of three months, one Southern planter was able to train thirty Negroes to produce a weekly total of one hundred and twenty yards of cotton and woolen cloth. Two Negro Workers in South Carolina were each capable of producing two pairs of shoes per day. Another shoemaker in the same province attended to his master's shop alone for a period of nine years, while in New York an aged shopkeeper pleaded with a court to commute the sentence of a convicted slave blacksmith so that the Negro could continue to support him.[27]

In some instances Negro artisans gained a limited measure of recognition because of their workmanship. Slave craftsmen at Andover, New Jersey, produced superior iron wares which were eventually accepted for high quality on the basis of brand name alone.[28] Even in the "artistic" crafts Negro workers managed to leave their imprint. Serving as pipe carvers, upholsterers, tool and instrument makers, and manufacturers of cabinets, chairs, and other types of furniture, many performed skillfully for their employers. In Boston Thomas Fleet, a printer, kept in his shop three colored helpers who worked at setting type and cutting wooden blocks. One of these printers was responsible for engraving all the pictures found in the publications of his master. As a young man Gilbert Stuart, the Republic's first great portrait painter, derived great pleasure from observing the work of Neptune Thurston, a New England slave cooper, who sketched portraits on the heads of the casks in his master's shop. According to J. A. Porter, our only contemporary likeness of Negro poetess Phillis Wheatley, a rough copperplate engraving, was probably the work of a slave.[29]

In other fields of artistic craftsmanship Negro labor was likewise represented. The luxuriously built Southern mansions, notably Jefferson's dwelling at Monticello, as well as the decorative hand-wrought grills and balconies found in the older quarters of New Orleans and Charleston, still attest to the quality of eighteenth century slave labor.[30] One of the original surveyors of our nation's capital at Washington, Benjamin Banneker, the Negro astronomer and mathematician whose contributions evoked praise from Jefferson,[31] once experimented as an amateur handicraftsman. In the province of Maryland in the year 1762 Banneker is reported to have constructed the first clock ever made in America. A factor even more astonishing to his neighbors was that the builder had undertaken the task without ever having seen a clock before. Using a small watch as his model, wood as his raw material, and a pocket knife as his tool, he meticulously assembled a machine which remained in perfect operation for over two decades.[32] Employed at allied occupations in some of the larger towns were Negro goldsmiths, jewelers, and silversmiths. William Ball of Philadelphia, a prominent white silversmith and jeweler, used several Negro assistants. In his Front Street shop, next to the London Coffee House, Ball manufactured "gold and silver in all its branches." In 1778 he was temporarily plagued by a labor shortage, for "three Negro men, viz., Tom, by trade a silversmith," left his shop and deserted to the British army.[33] Probably the most famous Maryland craftsman of his day, William Faris of Annapolis, whose many undertakings brought him into the realm of the silversmith, cabinetmaker, jeweler, and clockmaker, also relied on the services of slave helpers. After 1770 Faris became so well established that, unlike other shopkeepers, he found it unnecessary to advertise. Nevertheless, as one biographer maintains: "An appraisal of William Faris' ability as a working silversmith is difficult, as it is impossible to distinguish between the work of his own hand and the silver made in the shop by his workmen."[34]

In some instances such skills as the Negro acquired while in a state of slavery later became a source of employment when he was free. Recognizing this fact, masters, when preparing statements of manumission, often provided that these former servants should be permitted to leave with their tools.[35] On the other hand, the situation confronting the freedman was not always enviable. Thrust into a different environment, deprived of all the protective influence of a master, confronted by the hostility of established white tradesmen, and subjected to almost as many legal restrictions as a slave,[36] the liberated Negro worker encountered great difficulty in trying to assimilate himself into the mass of free citizens. To add to these obstacles, he frequently discovered that much of the instruction which he had received as a slave, especially if he had been trained on a plantation, was elementary in nature and not of the highest standards.[37] It is not surprising that many freedmen either abandoned the crafts or lapsed into a state of servitude.[38] Thus a combination of white prejudice, original inexperience, and a lack of opportunity for improvement served as limiting factors in the early development of skilled Negro craftsmanship in America.

NOTES

1. Gordon B. Hancock, "The Changing Status of Negro Labor," *Southern Workman*, LX (August, 1931), 352–53; U.S. Dept. of Commerce, Bureau of the Census, *Sixteenth Census of the United States: 1940* (Washington, 1943), III, 88.

2. Johann D. Schoepf, *Travels in the Confederation, 1783–1784*, ed. by Alfred J. Morrison (Philadelphia, 1911), II, 221.

3. George S. Schuyler, "Craftsmen in the Blue Grass," *Crisis*, XLVII (May, 1940), 158; Giles B. Jackson and D. Webster Davis, *The Industrial History of the Negro Race in the United States* (Richmond, 1908), p. 13; W. E. B. Du Bois, *The Negro American Artisan* (Atlanta, 1912), pp. 25–26; P. G. LePage, "Arts and Crafts of the Negro," *International Studio*, LXXVIII (March, 1924), 477–78.

4. Alexander Hamilton, *Works*, ed. by John C. Hamilton (New York, 1851), III, 219; Adam Smith, *The Wealth of Nations*, ed. by Edwin Cannan (New York, 1937), pp. 631–33.

5. Several of the slaves implicated in the New York "Negro conspiracy" of 1741, which allegedly had as its objective the burning of the city and the murder of its inhabitants, were artisans. Even the preliminary meetings were held at the homes of white tradesmen whom the Negroes probably met while at work. Daniel Horsemanden, *The New York Conspiracy, or a History of the Negro Plot* (New York, 1810), *passim*. Aptheker makes reference to this conspiracy as well as to an abortive Virginia plot involving a slave blacksmith who used his skill to fashion three hundred spears for the intended insurrection. Herbert Aptheker, *American Negro Slave Revolts* (New York, 1943), pp. 114–15, 192–93, 211.

6. The term "white artisan," as used here, applies primarily to the "journeyman" class rather than to the "master" craftsman, who himself may have employed slave assistants. Such protests by white workers against the competition of slave labor usually were presented in the form of petitions to the colonial authorities. Richard B. Morris, *Government and Labor in Early America* (New York, 1946), p. 185 n.; Morris, "Labor and Mercantilism," in *The Era of the American Revolution* (New York, 1939), pp. 79–80; Marcus W. Jernegan, *Laboring and Dependent Classes in Colonial America, 1607–1783* (Chicago, 1931), pp. 20–21; John F. Watson, *Annals of Philadelphia and Pennsylvania in the Olden Times* (Philadelphia, 1844), 1, 97–98; Cheesman A. Herrick, *White Servitude in Pennsylvania* (Philadelphia, 1926), p. 28; Papers of Daniel Horsemanden (MSS.), pp. 175–76 in the library of the New York Historical Society; Samuel D. McKee, *Labor in Colonial New York* (New York, 1935), p. 127. For a statement by a colonial office reiterating the grievances of local artisans, see Charles Z. Lincoln, ed., *Messages from the Governors* (Albany, 1909), 1, 260.

7. Perhaps typical of the eighteenth century Virginia gentry, Colonel George Mason maintained that slavery discouraged the arts and crafts, for it prevented the importation of white laborers "who really enrich and strengthen a country." George Livermore, *The Opinions of the Founders of the Republic on Negroes as Slaves, Citizens, and Soldiers* (Boston, 1863), p. 56. Similar opinions may be found in Thomas Jefferson, *Writings*, ed. by H. A. Washington (New York, 1863), VIII, 386; William Byrd to Lord Egmont, July 12, 1736, *American Historical Review*, I (October, 1895), 89; Lorenzo D. Turner, "Anti-Slavery Sentiment in American Literature," *Journal of Negro History*, XIV (October, 1929), 386.

8. Robert Beverly, *The History of Virginia* (London, 1722), p. 255; Jernegan, *Laboring and Dependent Classes*, p. 8; Jernegan, "Slavery and the Beginnings of Industrialism in the American Colonies," *American Historical Review*, XXV (January, 1920), 222; Hamilton, III, 198–201.

9. Jefferson's Tammany Society speech, Feb. 29, 1808, in Saul K. Padover, ed., *The Complete Jefferson* (New York, 1943), pp. 529–30.

10. J. P. Purry, "A Description of the Province of South Carolina, Drawn up at Charles Town, in September, 1731," in Peter Farce, ed., *Tracts and Other Papers* (Washington, D.C., 1836–46), II, no. XI, 14; Governor and Company of Connecticut to the Board of Trade, October, 1732, in Mary K. Talcott, ed., "The Talcott Papers," Connecticut Historical Society, *Collections*, IV (Hartford, 1892), 263; Works Project Administration, Federal Writers' Program, *New Hampshire: A Guide to the Granite State* (Boston, 1938), p. 37.

11. "Artificers are so scarce at present," Purry observed, "that all sorts of work is very dear; Taylors, Shoemakers, Smiths &c. would be particularly acceptable." Purry, *op. cit.*, pp. 7, 14.

12. Benjamin Franklin, *Works*, ed. by Jared Sparks (Boston, 1836–40), II, 471–72.

13. Robert Livingston to the Lords of Trade, May 13, 1701, in E. B. O'Callaghan, ed., *Documents Relative to the Colonial History of the State of New York* (Albany, 1856–87), IV, 875.

14. Bartholomew R. Carroll, ed., *Historical Collections of South Carolina* (New York, 1846), I, 377. Also consult Benjamin Franklin, *Observations concerning the Increase of Mankind, Peopling of Countries*, etc. (Boston, 1755), p. 4; Governor William Franklin to the Earl of Hillsborough, June 14, 1768, quoted in Publications of the Colonial Society of Massachusetts, VI, *Transactions, 1899, 1900* (Boston, 1904), 360; Albert C. Myers, ed., *Narratives of Early Pennsylvania, West New Jersey, and Delaware, 1630–1707* (New York, 1912), p. 328.

15. E. B. O'Callaghan, *Documentary History of the State of New York* (Albany, 1849–51), I, 499; Philip A. Bruce, *Economic History of Virginia in the Seventeenth Century* (New York, 1896), II, 413. In addition one could not be certain of the quality of work of imported help. Occasionally inexperienced laborers successfully misrepresented themselves as skilled artisans in order to gain passage to the Western Hemisphere. Even those indentured immigrants who were potentially capable, many colonial employers insisted, viewed America as a land of relaxation, thus performing half-hearted service and refusing to toil for as many hours as they had been accustomed to in Europe. *A Complete Revisal of All the Acts of Assembly of the Province of North Carolina* (New Bern, 1773), p. 79; B. Franklin, *Works*, ed. by John Bigelow (New York, 1905), III, 101; Stella H. Sutherland, *Population Distribution in Colonial America* (New York, 1936), p. 216.

16. "Raymond B. Pinchbeck, *The Virginia Negro Artisan and Tradesman* (Richmond, 1926), p. 15; Evarts B. Greene and Virginia D. Harrington, *American Population before the Federal Census of 1790* (New York, 1932), p. 136.

17. Pinchbeck, p. 23.

18. George E. Haynes, *The Negro at Work in New York City* (New York, 1912), p. 66; O'Callaghan, *Docs. Rel. to Col. Hist. of New York*, I, 499, II, 474, III, 307; Marion T. Wright, "New Jersey Laws and the Negro," *Journal of Negro History*, XXVIII (April, 1943), 161.

19. Slavery was prohibited in the colony of Georgia before 1750, and hence the development of Negro craftsmanship in that region was somewhat retarded.

20. For examples of Negro craftsmanship in the middle colonies consult: "Eighteenth Century Slaves as Advertised by Their Masters," *Jour. Negro Hist.*, I (April, 1916), 179, 194, 203; *Archives of the State of New Jersey*, 1st series, XX (1898), 8, 263, XXVIII (1916), 48; *Archives of Maryland*, XXVIII (1908), 43; O'Callaghan, *Docs. Rel. New York*, IV, 875, V, 444, 460; *Papers of the Lloyd Family of the Manor of Queens Village, Lloyd's Neck, Long Island, New York, 1654–1826* (New York Historical Society, Collections, LIX, LX, 1927), I, 261, 560; Harry B. Yoshpe, ed., "Record of Slave Manumissions in New York during the Colonial and Early National Periods," *Jour. Negro Hist.*, XXV (January, 1941), 89; Rita S. Gottesman, ed., *The Arts and Crafts in New York, 1726–1776* (New York Hist. Soc., Collections, LXIX, 1938), pp. 48, 140; Alfred C. Prime, ed., *The Arts and Crafts in Philadelphia, Maryland, and South Carolina, 1721–1800* (Philadelphia, 1929–32), I, 48; Prime, *Colonial Craftsmen of Pennsylvania* (Philadelphia, 1925), p. 3; Mrs. A. C. Prime, ed., *Three Centuries of Historic Silver* (Philadelphia, 1938), pp. 52–53; New York *Mercury*, Mar. 1, 1756, Aug. 30, 1756, Dec. 9, 1765; New York *Gazette*, July 6–13; 1730, Aug. 27–Sept. 3, 1733; March 24–31, 1735; New York *Weekly Post-Boy*, Apr. 3, 1749; *Pennsylvania Gazette*, Mar. 21, 1737, Apr. 21, 1761, Aug. 6, 1777; *Pennsylvania Packet*, May 1, 1784.

21. Boston *Post-Boy*, June 22, 1752, in Elizabeth Donnan, ed., *Documents Illustrative of the History of the Slave Trade to America* (Washington, 1930–35), III, 66; Lorenzo J. Greene, "The New England Negro as Seen in Advertisements for Runaway Slaves," *Jour. Negro Hist.*, XXIX (April, 1944), 139; H. Gardner to C. Chaplin, Dec. 23, 1774, *The Commerce of Rhode Island, 1726–1800* (Massachusetts Historical Society, *Collections*, 7th series, IX, X 1914–15), I, 523; Newport *Mercury*, Apr. 27, 1772; Boston *News-Letter*, Jan. 29, 1748, in George F. Dow, ed., *The Arts and Crafts in New England, 1704–1775* (Topsfield, Mass., 1927), p. 197. For other examples of New England Negro tradesmen consult: Boston *Independent Chronicle and the Universal Advertiser*, Jan. 16, 1777; "Advertisements from the Records of Middle-sex County, Virginia, March 5, 1677–78," *William and Mary College Quarterly*, VI (October, 1897), 117; "Eighteenth Century Slaves Advertised," *Jour. Negro Hist.*, I, 165; *Boston News-Letter and Evening Post*, July 11, 1746, in Donnan, III, 66; Providence *Gazette*, July 28, 1770, reprinted in William D. Johnston, *Slavery in Rhode Island, 1755–1776* (Providence, 1894),

p. 28; also newspaper extracts in Dow, pp. 62, 187, 188, 189, 195, 197, 202, 304.

22. W.P.A., Federal Writers' Program, *The Negro in Virginia* (New York, 1940), p. 47; Edward McCrady, *The History of South Carolina under the Royal Government, 1719–1776* (New York, 1899), p. 387; J. Urmstone to the Secretary of the Society for Propagating the Gospel, July 7, 1711, in Ulrich B. Phillips, ed., *Plantation and Frontier Documents* (Cleveland, 1910), II, 272

23. J. Hector St. Jean de Crèvecoeur, *Sketches of Eighteenth Century America*, ed. by Henry L. Bourdin, et al. (New Haven, 1925), p. 143; Jesse W. Parkhurst, "The Role of the Black Mammy in the Plantation Household," *Jour. Negro Hist.,* XXIII (July 1938), 358; Julia C. Spruill, *Women's Life and Work in the Southern Colonies* (Chapel Hill, 1938), p. 75; Frances Little, *Early American Textiles* (New York, 1931), p. 31. As an illustration of the extent of household manufacturing, during the year 1768 George Washington's slave weavers produced more than 1,355 yards of cloth. One of Washington's neighbors, Robert Carter, apparently abandoned the use of white textile workers after once trying Negro labor, although the change may have been influenced by a shortage of white artisans during the American Revolution. Phillips, II, 315, 324–25.

24. From the MS. Recollections of George Mason, quoted in Thomas J. Wertenbaker, *Patrician and Plebian in Virginia* (Charlottesville, 1912), p. 50.

25. *South Carolina Gazette,* Jan. 2, 1749, Sep. 19, 1751, reprinted in Thomas J. Wertenbaker, *The Old South* (New York, 1942), pp. 230, 231; William Byrd, *The Secret Diary of William Byrd of Westover, 1709–1712,* ed. by Louis B. Wright and Marion Tinling (Richmond, 1941), p. 186; *Another Secret Diary of William Byrd of Westover, 1739–1741,* ed. by Maude H. Woodfin and Marion Tinling (Richmond, 1942), pp. 324, 323; Philip V. Fithian, *Journal and Letters of Philip Vickers Fithian, 1773–1774: A Plantation Tutor of the Old Dominion,* ed. by Hunter Farish (Williamsburg, 1945), pp. xi, 173; Du Bois, *Negro American Artisan,* p. 35; Hugh Jones, *The Present State of Virginia* (London, 1724), pp. 44, 60, 131, 135, in Sabin's *Reprints,* 1865.

26. Pinchbeck, p. 14; Charles B. Bradley, *Design in the Industrial Arts* (Peoria, Ill., 1946), p. 26; W. E. B. Du Bois, *The Negro Artisan* (Atlanta, 1902), pp. 17, 33; Philip A. Bruce, *The Social Life of Virginia in the Seventeenth Century* (Lynchburg, 1929), p. 120.

27. "Eighteenth Century Slaves Advertised," *Jour. Negro Hist.,* I, 186, 187, 196, 197; Broadus Mitchell, *The Rise of Cotton Mills in the South* (Baltimore, 1921), p. 13; *South Carolina Gazette,* Jan. 14, 1764, May 24, 1768, reprinted in Jernegan, "Slavery and Industrialism," *Am. Hist. Rev.,* XXV, 234; E. B. O'Callaghan, ed., *Calendar of Historical Manuscripts in the Office of the Secretary of State, Albany, New York* (Albany, 1856–66), Part II, 444.

28. New York *Gazette and Weekly Mercury,* Mar. 1, 1773; *Pennsylvania Gazette,* June 29, 1774; William Allen, *Extracts from Chief Justice William Allen's Letter Book,* ed. by Lewis B. Walker (Pottsville, 1897), p. 70; Charles S. Boyer, *Early Forges and Furnaces in New Jersey* (Philadelphia, 1931), p. 28.

29. *New York Gazette,* Mar. 24–31, 1735; New York *Gazette* or *Weekly Post-Boy,* Jan. 6 1763; Gottesman, pp. 140, 317; Boston *Gazette,* Jan. 27–Feb. 3, 1728; Boston *News Letter,* Apr. 8–15, 1742; Dow, pp. 195, 272; *South Carolina and American General Gazette,* June 3, 1771; Prime, *Arts and Crafts in Philadelphia,* I, 167; James A. Porter, *Modern Negro Art* (New York, 1943), pp. 15, 16, 18.

30. Charles S. Johnson, *The Negro in American Civilization* (New York, 1930), p. 11; W.P.A., Writers' Program, *Virginia: A Guide to the Old Dominion* (New York, 1940), p. 77; Albert H. Sonn, *Early American Wrought Iron* (New York, 1928), III, 7–8; J. A. Porter, "Four Problems in the History of Negro Art," *Jour. Negro Hist.,* XXVII (January, 1942), 13–14; Alain Locke, *Negro Art, Past and Present* (Washington, 1936), p. 15; Locke, *The Negro in Art* (Washington, 1940), p. 8; Schuyler, in *Crisis,* XLVII, 158.

31. Writing to Banneker on August 30, 1791, Jefferson declared: "No body wishes more than I do to see such proofs as you exhibit, that nature has given to our black brethren, talents equal to those of the other colors of men, and that a want of them is owing merely to the degraded condition of their existence both in Africa and America." Thomas Jefferson, *Writings,* ed. by P. L. Ford (New York, 1892–99), V, 377.

32. Carter G. Woodson, *The Education of the Negro Prior to 1861* (New York, 1915), p. 91; Henry E. Baker, "Benjamin Banneker, the Negro Mathematician and Astronomer," *Jour. Negro Hist.,* III (April, 1918), 105–107, 111; "Benjamin Banneker, the Negro Astronomer," *Atlantic Monthly,* XI (January, 1863), 81, 82–83; Du Bois, *Negro Artisan,* p. 29; Robert Fortenbaugh, "The Learned Negro," *Jour. Negro Hist.,* XIV (April, 1929), 239–42.

33. Boston *Gazette,* Nov. 14, 1752, in Dow, p. 62; New York *Mercury,* Aug. 30, 1756; New York *Gazette or Weekly Post-Boy,* Feb. 23, 1764, in Gottesman, p. 48; *Pennsylvania Gazette,* Aug. 6, 1777; *Pennsylvania Packet,* Oct. 12, 1772, Sept. 1, 1778, May 1, 1784, in Prime, *Arts and Crafts in Philadelphia,* I, 43–46, 78–79. A less honorable form of the silversmith trade was practiced by those Negroes who stole household plate, stripped off the precious metal, and then sold it to an equally unscrupulous dealer. Governor Hunt of New York to the Lords of Trade, Nov. 14, 1710, in O'Callaghan, *Docs. Rel. to New York,* IV, 187; *South Carolina Gazette,* Feb. 22, 1752, Mar. 9, 1752, in Prime, *Arts and Crafts in Philadelphia,* I, 93, 102.

34. Of one of his Negro workers, by trade a silversmith, jeweler, and lapidary, Faris once said: "There are few if any better workmen in America." Jacob H. Pleasants and Howard Sill, *Maryland Silversmiths: 1715–1830* (Baltimore, 1930), pp. 257–58, 266; *Maryland Gazette,* Nov. 8, 1759, Dec. 4, 1760, Aug. 25, 1763, Aug. 2, 1764, Jan. 4, 1770, in Prime, *Arts and Crafts in Philadelphia,* I, 241–42.

35. *Abstracts of Wills on File in the Surrogate's Office of New York, 1665–1784* (New York Hist. Soc., Collections, XXV–XXXVI, 1892–1903]), V, 42; James M. Wright, *The Free Negro in Maryland, 1634–1860* (New York, 1921), pp. 154–55 n.

36. In order to keep the number of manumissions at a minimum, many colonies called for proof that the servant had served meritoriously and required that the master file a complete report and post a bond guaranteeing that the Negro would not become a liability on the community. Furthermore, the freedman was generally prohibited by law from having any dealings with slaves. In some cases the free Negro was compelled to repair the public highways for a specific period each year without receiving remuneration for his labor. Finally, at the discretion of the colonial authorities, adult freedmen who neglected to work or who did not pay their taxes, as well as emancipated minors, could be bound out for service to local employers. Walter Clark, ed., *The State Records of North Carolina* (Goldsboro, 1895–1906), XXIV, 221; W. W. Hening, ed., *The Statutes at Large, Being a Collection of all the Laws of Virginia* (Philadelphia, 1823), VI, 112; Charles Z. Lincoln, et al., eds., *The Colonial Laws of New York from the Year 1664 to the Revolution* (Albany, 1894–96), II, 683; *Acts and Laws of His Majesty's Province of the Massachusetts Bay in New England* (Boston, 1726), p. 176; *Acts and Resolves of the Province of Massachusetts Bay* (Boston, 1869–1924), I, 519; J. H. Trumbull and C. J. Hoadley, eds., *The Public Records of the State of Connecticut, 1776–1780* (Hartford, 1894–95), I, 415–16; Pinchbeck, pp. 20–21; James T. Mitchell and Henry Flanders, eds., *The Statutes at Large of Pennsylvania from 1682–1801* (Harrisburg, 1896–1908), IV, 62–63; B. W. Leigh and W. W. Hening, eds., *The Revised Code of the Laws of Virginia* (Richmond, 1819), I, 434–35; "Court Records Pertaining to Negro Education in Virginia in the Eighteenth Century," *Virginia Magazine of History and Biography,* II (April, 1895), 429.

37. As the Reverend Hugh Jones of Virginia was quick to observe, the work of slave craftsmen was not always "the aptest or nicest." Plantation artisans had been readily used for minor tasks, but owners did not have complete confidence in the ability of their slaves to handle operations of a more technical nature. It is interesting to note that certain masters, including William Byrd, went to great expense to secure the services of foreign artisans in spite of the availability of Negroes who had been trained in the crafts. Jones, p. 36; Du Bois, *Negro Artisans,* p. 13.

38. Edward R. Turner, *The Negro in Pennsylvania: Slavery-Servitude-Freedom, 1639–1861* (Washington, 1911), pp. 89–91.

SLAVE REVOLTS AND RESISTANCE

American Slave Insurrections Before 1861

HARVEY WISH

A GRAPHIC ILLUSTRATION of the cyclic fears of Negro uprisings during the 1830's is afforded by the remarks of several whites of Mississippi in 1859 to Frederick L. Olmsted:

> Where I used to live (Alabama) I remember when I was a boy—must ha' been about twenty years ago—folks was dreadful frightened about the niggers. I remember they built pens in the woods where they could hide and Christmas time they went and got into the pens, fraid the niggers was risin'.[1]

The speaker's wife added her recollection to this comment:

> I remember the same time where we was in South Carolina, we had all our things put up in bags so we could tote 'em if we heard they was comin' our way.[2]

Slave outbreaks and plots appeared both North and South during the Colonial period. Sometimes the white indentured servants made common cause with the Negroes against their masters. This was the case in 1663 when a plot of white servants and Negroes was betrayed in Gloucester County, Virginia.[3] The eastern counties of Virginia, where the Negroes were rapidly outnumbering the whites, suffered from repeated scares in 1687, 1709, 1710, 1722, 1723, and 1730.[4] A patrol system was set up in 1726 in parts of the state and later extended. Attempts were made here as elsewhere to check the importation of slaves by high duties.

Two important slave plots, one a serious insurrection, disturbed the peace of New York City in 1712 and 1741. In revenge for ill-treatment by their masters, twenty-three Negroes rose on April 6, 1712, to slaughter the whites and killed nine before they were overwhelmed by a superior force. The retaliation showed an unusual barbarous strain on the part of the whites. Twenty-one Negroes were executed, some were burnt, others hanged, and one broken on the wheel.[5] In 1741 another plot was reported in New York involving both whites and blacks. A white, Hewson (or Hughson), was accused of providing the Negroes with weapons. He and his family were executed; likewise, a Catholic priest was hanged as an accomplice. Thirteen Negro leader were burnt alive, eighteen hanged, and eighty transported.[6] Popular fears of further insurrections led the New York Assembly to impose a prohibitive tax on the importation of Negroes. This tax, however, was later rescinded by order of the British Commissioner for Trade and Plantations.[7]

The situation in colonial South Carolina was worse than in her sister states. Long before rice and indigo had given way to King Cotton, the early development of the plantation system had yielded bumper crops of slave uprisings and plots. An insurrection, resulting in the deaths of three whites, is reported for May 6, 1720.[8] Ten years later an elaborate plot was discovered in St. John's Parish by a Negro servant of Major Cordes. This plan was aimed at Charleston, an attack that was to inaugurate a widespread war upon the planters. Under the pretense

---

[1]Frederick Law Olmsted, *A Journey in the Back Country* (New York, 1860), 203

[2]*Ibid.*

[3]Ulrich B. Phillips, *American Negro Slavery* (New York, 1918), 472.

[4]William P. Palmer, ed., *Calendar of Virginia State Papers* (Richmond, 1875), I(1652–1781), 129–130; also James Curtis Ballagh, *A History of Slavery in Virginia* (Baltimore, 1902), 79–80; also Coffin, *Principal Slave Insurrections*, 11.

[5]Letter of Governor Robert Hunter to the Lords of Trade in E. B. O'Callaghan, ed., *Documents Relative to the Colonial History of the State of New York* (Albany, 1855), V (1707–1733), 341–2.

[6]*Gentleman's Magazine*, XI (1741), 441.

[7]Elizabeth Donnan, ed., *Documents Illustrative of the Slave Trade to America* (Washington, 1930–35), III, 409. (Hereafter: D.S.T.) Joshua Coffin also reports plots and actual outbreaks in other slaveholding areas in the Northern Colonies. East Boston is said to have experienced a minor uprising in 1638. In 1723, a series of incendiary fires in Boston led the selectmen to suspect a slave plot and the militia was ordered to police the slaves. Another plot was reported in Burlington, Pennsylvania, during 1734. Coffin, *Principal Slave Insurrections*, 10, 11, 12.

[8]Coffin, *Principal Slave Insurrections*, 11.

From the *Journal of Negro History*, July 1937, pp. 35–45. © 1937 by the Association for the Study of African-American Life and History, Inc. Reprinted by permission.

of conducting a "dancing bout" in the city and in St. Paul's Parish the Negroes gathered together ready to seize the available arms for the attack. At this point the militia descended upon the blacks and killed the greater number, leaving few to escape.[9]

Owing partly to Spanish intrigues the same decade in South Carolina witnessed many more uprisings. An outbreak is reported for November, 1738.[10] The following year, on September 9, the Stono uprising created panic throughout the southeast. About twenty Angola Negroes assembled at Stono under their captain, Tommy, and marched toward Spanish territory, beating drums and endeavoring to attract other slaves. Several whites were killed and a number of houses burnt or plundered. As the "army" paused in a field to dance and sing they were overtaken by the militia and cut down in a pitched battle.[11] The following year an insurrection broke out in Berkeley County.[12] Charleston was threatened repeatedly by slave plots.[13] These reports are confirmed officially in the petition of the South Carolina Assembly to the King on July 26, 1740. Among the grievances of 1739 the Assembly complained of:

> . . . an insurrection of our slaves in which many of the inhabitants were murdered in a barbarous and cruel manner; and that no sooner quelled than another protected in Charles Town, and a third lately in the very heart of the Settlements, but happily discovered in time enough to be prevented.[14]

Repercussions of slave uprisings in South Carolina sometime affected Georgia as well. This was particularly true in 1738.[15] In 1739 a plot was discovered in Prince George County.[16] To many slaves St. Augustine on Spanish soil seemed a welcome refuge from their masters.

Indications of many other insurrections in the American Colonies may be inferred from the nature of early patrol laws: The South Carolina law of 1704 for example contains a reference in its preamble to recent uprisings in that Colony.[17] In the British and French possessions to the south, particularly in the West Indies, affairs were much worse and put the planter of the North in constant fear of importing rebellious slaves and the contagion of revolt.

In considering the insurrections of the national period, it is at once evident that abolitionist propaganda played a relatively minor role despite the charges of southern politicians after 1831. The genealogy of revolt extends much further back than the organized efforts of anti-slavery advocates. It is true, however, that white men played an important role in many Negro uprisings, frequently furnishing arms, and even leadership, as well as inspiration.[18] The motives for such assistance varied from philanthropy to unadulterated self-interest. As might be expected, insurrections tended to occur where King Cotton and his allies were most firmly entrenched and the great plantation system established.

Slave unrest seems to have been far greater in Virginia rather than in the states of the Lower South. Conspiracies like those of Gabriel in 1800 and Nat Turner in 1831 attained national notoriety. The Gabriel plot was developed in the greatest secrecy upon the plantation of a harsh slave-master, Thomas Prosser, several miles from Richmond. Under the leadership of a young slave, Gabriel, and inspired by the examples of San Domingo and the emancipation of the ancient Israelites from Egypt, some eleven hundred slaves had taken an oath to fight for their liberty. Plans were drawn for the seizure of an arsenal and several other strategic buildings of Richmond which would precede a general slaughter of all hostile whites. After the initial successes, it was expected that fifty thousand Negroes would join the standard of revolt. Beyond this point, the arrangements were hazy.[19] A faithful slave however exposed the plot and Governor James Monroe took rapid measures to secure the cooperation of the local authorities and the federal cavalry. Bloodshed was averted by an unprecedented cloudburst on the day set for the conspiracy and the utter demoralization of the undisciplined "army." . . .

Between Gabriel's abortive plot and the Nat Turner uprising, several more incidents occurred which disturbed the sleep of Virginians. In January, 1802, Governor Monroe received word of a plot in Nottaway County. Several Negroes suspected of participation were executed.[20] That same year came disclosures of a projected slave uprising in Goochland County aided by eight or ten white men.[21] Several plots were reported in 1808 and 1809 necessitating almost continuous patrol service.[22] The war of 1812 intensified the apprehensions of servile re-

[9]Edward Clifford Holland, *A Refutation of the Calumnies Circulated Against the Southern and Western Slates Respecting the Institution and Existence of Slavery* (Charleston, 1822), 68–69, 81.

[10]Ralph Betts Flander, *Plantation Slavery in Georgia* (Chapel Hill, 1933), 24.

[11]*Gentleman's Magazine*, X (1740), 127–8.

[12]See the Constable's bill in the *Magazine of American History*, XXV (1891), 85–6.

[13]Edward McGrady, *The History of South Carolina Under the Royal Government* (1719–1776), (New York, 1899), 5.

[14]Appendix to Holland, *A Refutation of the Calumnies*, —, 71. Another plot of December 17, 1765, is mentioned in *D.S.T.*, IV, 415.

[15]Flanders, *Plantation Slavery in Georgia*, 24; similarly, South Carolina's slave plots sometimes required the assistance of North Carolina as in the scare of 1766. William L. Saunders, ed., *Colonial Records of North Carolina* (Raleigh, 1890), VIII (1769–1771), 559.

[16]Jeffrey R. Brackett, *The Negro in Maryland* (Baltimore, 1889), 93.

[17]H. M. Henry, *The Police Control of the Slave in South Carolina* (Vanderbilt University, 1914), 30.

[18]One aspect of this subject is discussed in James Hugo Johnston's article, "The Participation of White Men in Virginia Negro Insurrections," *Journal of Negro History*, XVI (1931), 158–167.

[19]Details of the Gabriel Plot are in the *Calendar of Virginia State Papers*, X (1808–1835), 140–173, et passim; T. W. Higginson, "Gabriel's Defeat," *The Atlantic Monthly*, X (1862), 337–345; Robert R. Howison, *A History of Virginia* (Richmond, 1848), II, 390–3.

[20]Hamilton, ed., *Writings of James Monroe*, III, 328–9.

[21]James H. Johnston, "The Participation of White Men in Virginia Negro Insurrections," 161.

[22]*Calendar of Virginia State Papers*, X (1808–1835), 31, 62.

volt. Petitions for troops and arms came during the summer of 1814 from Caroline County and Lynchburg.[23] Regiments were called out during the war in anticipation of insurrections along the tidewater area. During the spring of 1816 confessions were wrung from slaves concerning an attack upon Fredericksburg and Richmond. The inspiration for this enterprise was attributed to a white military officer, George Boxley. The latter claimed to be the recipient of divine revelations and the instrument of "omnipotence" although he denied any intention of leading an insurrection. His relatives declared that he was insane, but his neighbors in a complaint to the governor showed serious misgivings on this point:

"On many occasions he has declared that the distinction between the rich and the poor was too great; that offices were given to wealth than to merit; and seemed to be an advocate for a more leveling system of Government. For many years he has avowed his disapprobation of the slavery of the Negroes and wished they were free."[24]

Boxley was arrested but escaped. About thirty Negroes were sentenced to death or deportation in consequence.

The years preceding the Nat Turner insurrection brought further news of plots discovered. During the middle of July, 1829, the governor received requests for aid from the counties of Mathews, Gloucester, the Isle of Wight and adjacent counties.[25] The ease with which "confessions" were obtained under duress casts doubt upon the reality of such outbreaks, but the reports are indicative of the ever-present fear of attack.

Nat Turner's insurrection of August 21, 1831, at Southampton, seventy miles from Richmond, raised fears of a general servile war to their highest point. The contemporary accounts of the young slave, Nat, tend to overemphasize his leanings toward mysticism and under-state the background of unrest.[26] . . .

Rumors of slave plots continued to disturb Virginia up to the era of emancipation. During 1856, the state, in common with other slaveholding states, shared in the general feeling that a widespread conspiracy, set for December 25, was maturing. Requests for aid came to the Governor from the counties of Fauquier, King and Queen, Culpeper, and Rappahannock; and particularly from the towns of Lynchburg, Petersburg, and Gordons-

ville.[27] As for John Brown's visionary deed at Harper's Ferry in the autumn of 1859, the aftermath can be easily imagined. The spectre of a general insurrection again haunted the minds of the white citizenry and large patrols were kept in constant service to prevent Negro meetings of all types.[28]

Maryland and North Carolina, although more fortunate than their slave-ridden neighbor, did not escape unscathed. The news of Nat Turner and John Brown brought panic to the other states. In Maryland, baseless rumors of conspiracies, rather than actual outbreaks, seemed to be the rule. In 1845 a plot was "disclosed" in Charles County, Maryland, and a number of Negroes were subsequently sold out of the state.[29] Ten years later there was general excitement over alleged uprisings in Dorchester, Talbot and Prince George's Counties. Resolutions were adopted at the time by various citizens asking that slaveholders keep their servants at home.[30] The reaction to John Brown's raid of 1859 was more intense than had ever before been experienced over insurrections in Maryland. The newspapers for days were full of nothing else but the Harper's Ferry incident. Large patrols were called out everywhere and talk was general of a concerted uprising of all the slaves in Maryland and Virginia. A martial atmosphere prevailed.[31]

In 1802 an insurrection was reported in Bertie County, North Carolina, necessitating an elaborate patrol system.[32] A decade later, another outbreak in Rockingham County was narrowly averted,[33] and in 1816 further plots were discovered at Tarboro, New Bern, Camden and Hillsboro.[34] Several minor disturbances occurred in 1821 among the slaves of Bladen, Carteret, Jones, and Onslow Counties.[35] On October 6, 1831, a Georgia newspaper reported an extensive slave conspiracy in North Carolina

[23]*Ibid.*, 367, 388.

[24]*Calendar of Virginia State Papers*, X, 433–6.

[25]*Ibid.*, 567–9.

[26]Thomas Gray, ed., *Nat Turner's Confession* (Richmond, 1832); Samuel Warner, ed., *The Authentic and Impartial Narrative of The Tragical Scene of the Twenty Second of August, 1831*, New York, 1831 (A collection of accounts by eye witnesses); and William Sidney Drewry, *Slave Insurrections in Virginia, 1830–1865* (Washington, 1900), *passim*. The immediate results of the Nat Turner affair are summarized in John W. Cromwell's "The Aftermath of Nat Turner's Insurrection," *The Journal of Negro History*, V (1920), 208–234.

[27]*Calendar of Virginia State Papers*, XI (1836–1869), 50. Other rumors of unrest during 1856 came from the towns of Williamsburgh and Alexandria, and from Montgomery County. See Laura A. White, "The South in the 1850's as seen by British Consuls," *The Journal of Southern History*, I (1935), 44.

[28]Brackett, *The Negro in Maryland*, 97–99.

[29]Brackett, *The Negro in Maryland*, 96.

[30]*Ibid.*, 97.

[31]*Ibid.*, 97–99.

[32]John Spencer Bassett, *Slavery in the State of North Carolina*, Johns Hopkins University Studies in Historical and Political Science, XVII (Baltimore, 1899), 332. The nature of North Carolina laws during 1777–1788 regarding insurrections indicates the keen fears entertained of slave uprisings. One preamble of 1777 begins " . . . Whereas the evil and pernicious practice of freeing slaves in this State, ought at this alarming and critical time to be guarded against by every friend and well-wisher to his country . . ." This idea is repeated in the insurrection laws of 1778 and 1788. Walter Clark, ed., *The State Records of North Carolina* (Goldsboro, N.C., 1905), XXIV (1777–1788), 14, 221, 964. The laws regulating manumission were made increasingly stringent for fear of creating a dangerous class of free Negroes.

[33]*Calendar of Virginia State Papers*, X (1808–1835), 120–2.

[34]A. H. Gordon, "The Struggle of the Negro Slaves for Physical Freedom," *Journal of Negro History*, XIII (1928), 22–35.

[35]Hugh T. Lefler, ed., *North Carolina History Told by Contemporaries* (Chapel Hill, 1934), 265.

with ramifications in the eastern counties of Duplin, Sampson, Wayne, New Hanover, Lenoir, Cumberland, and Bladen.[36]

Slave plots in South Carolina during the national period seem to have been abortive for the most part, but several of the projects could easily have been uprisings of the first magnitude. During November, 1797, slave trials in Charleston disclosed a plot to burn the city. Two Negroes were hanged and three deported.[37] The Camden plot of June, 1816, was a very serious affair and envisaged a concerted attempt to burn the town and massacre its inhabitants. A favorite slave reported the plot to his master, Colonel Chesnut, who thereupon informed Governor Williams. Six of the slave leaders were executed and patrol measures were strengthened.[38]

The outstanding threat of insurrection in the State was the Denmark Vesey plot of 1822.... The leader, Denmark, was a free Negro of Charleston, a native of St. Thomas in the West Indies, who had purchased his freedom in 1800 from the proceeds of a lottery prize and had since worked in the city as a carpenter. He desired to emulate the Negro leader of St. Domingo and win the freedom of his people. Preaching that conditions had become intolerable for the slave, he urged a war against the slave-holder. A white man was to purchase guns and powder for his proposed army; Charleston was to be captured and burnt, the shipping of the town seized and all would sail away for the West Indies to freedom. Again a "faithful slave"—or spy—exposed the plot and severe reprisals were instituted. Thirty-five Negroes were executed and thirty-seven sold out of the state.

Because of the number of free Negroes involved, the Legislature passed an act preventing such persons from entering the state. To avoid, as far as possible, the contagion of abolitionist and kindred ideas, the purchase of slaves was forbidden from the West Indies, Mexico, South America, Europe, and the states north of Maryland. Slaves, who had resided in these forbidden areas, were likewise denied entrance into South Carolina. A Charleston editor, Benjamin Elliot, penned a sharp reply to the Northern accusations of cruelty, by pointing out that New York in the insurrection of 1741 had executed thirty-five and deported eighty-five. He demanded that the Federal Government act under its power to suppress insurrection. In July, 1829, another plot was reported in Georgetown County and in 1831, the year of Nat Turner's attack, one in Laurens County.

Georgia, like South Carolina, was able to avert the worst consequences of repeated slave plots. One was reported in Greene County in 1810,[39] a plan to destroy Atlanta came to light in May, 1819,[40] during 1831, disquieting rumors came from Milledgeville and Laurens County[41] four years later, a plot for a general uprising on the Coast was disclosed;[42] in 1851 another plot in Atlanta was reported;[43] and in 1860, similar reports came from Crawford and Brooks Counties.[44]

Florida experienced an uprising in March, 1820, along Talbot Island which was put down by a detachment of federal troops.[45] Another was reported in December, 1856, in Jacksonville.[46] Alabama discovered a plot in January, 1837, believed to have been instigated by a free Negro, M'Donald.[47] Mississippi seems to have been the central area of a widespread slave plot in July, 1835, threatening the entire Cotton Kingdom. Far-reaching plans of revolt had been drawn up by a white, John A. Murrell, who enjoyed a reputation as a Negro kidnapper and land pirate. Ten or fifteen Negroes and a number of whites were hanged for participation in the plot.[48]

Next to Virginia, Louisiana had the greatest difficulty among the southern states in coping with repeated attempts at insurrection. Governor Claiborne of the Mississippi Territory received frequent letters concerning plots in various parts of Louisiana. In 1804, New Orleans seems to have been threatened.[49] Several months later another alarm came from the plantations at Pointe Coupee.[50] In 1805, the attempt of a Frenchman to teach the doctrine of equality to slaves, led to general fears of an uprising.[51]

An actual outbreak occurred in January, 1811. Beginning from a plantation in the parish of St. John the Baptist, about thirty-six miles above New Orleans, a concerted slave uprising spread along the Mississippi. The Negroes formed disciplined companies to march upon New Orleans to the beating of drums. Their force,

---

[36]Milledgeville (Georgia) *Federal Union*, October 6, 1831, quoted in *ibid.*; The repercussion of the Nat Turner insurrection at Murfreesboro, Hertford County, has been graphically described by an eye witness. "It was court week and most of our men were twelve miles away at Winton. Fear was seen in every face, women pale and terror stricken, children crying for protection, men tearful and full of foreboding, but determined to be ready for the worst." Quoted from the Baltimore *Gazette*, November 16, 1831, by Stephen B. Weeks, "The Slave Insurrection in Virginia." *American Magazine of History*, XXV (1891), 456.
[37]H. M. Henry, *The Police Patrol of the Slave in South Carolina*, 150.
[38]Holland, *A Refutation of the Calumnies*, 75.
[39]Flanders, *Plantation Slavery in Georgia*, 274.
[40]*Niles Register*, XVI (1819), 213.
[41]Flanders, *Plantation Slavery in Georgia*, 274.
[42]*Niles Register*, XLIX (1935–6), 172.
[43]Flanders, *Plantation Slavery in Georgia*, 275; Georgia suffered in common with the other southern states during the scare of 1856; White, "The South in the 1850's as Seen by British Consuls," 43.
[44]Flanders, *Plantation Slavery in Georgia*, 275–6, 186. The abolitionists were accused of organizing the slave plots of the thirties and thereafter. One New England abolitionist, Kitchel, who opened a school for Negroes in Tarversville, Twigg County, Georgia, in 1835, was driven out of the community because he was said to have incited the slaves to revolt. *Ibid.*, 275.
[45]Helen H. Catterall, ed., *Judicial Cases Concerning American Slavery and the Negro* (Washington, 1926), III, 327 (Hereafter: J.C.N.).
[46]James Stirling, *Letters from the Slave States* (London, 1857), 299.
[47]*J.C.N.*, III, 141. Alabama had two rumors of slave plots reported in 1860; White, "The South in the 1850's as Seen by British Consuls," 47.
[48]*Niles Register*, XLIX (1835–6), 119; also Elizur Wight, ed., *Quarterly Anti-Slavery Magazine* (New York, 1837), II, 104–11.
[49]Dunbar, Rowland, ed., *Official Letter Book of W. C. C. Claiborne* (Jackson, 1917), II (1801–1816), 337–8.
[50]*Ibid.*, III (1804–1806), 6.
[51]*Ibid.*, 187.

estimated to include from 180 to 500 persons, was defeated in a pitched battle with the troops.[52] According to one historian many of those executed were decapitated and their heads placed on poles along the river as an example to others.[53]

Another uprising took place in the same area in March, 1829, causing great alarm before it was suppressed. Two leaders were hanged.[54] Other plots were reported in 1835, 1837, 1840, 1841 and 1842.[55] An uprising occurred in August, 1856, at New Iberia.[56]

The situation in Tennessee, Kentucky, and Texas may be briefly summarized. In Tennessee, plots were disclosed during 1831, 1856, and 1857.[57] Kentucky, in December, 1856, hanged several ringleaders of an attempted insurrection at Hopkinsville, in which a white man was involved.[58] That same year, two Negroes were punished by being whipped to death in Texas for an alleged conspiracy at Columbus, Colorado County.[59]

Owing to the nature of such a study any claim to an exhaustive treatment would be mere pretense. An analysis of slave patrol history alone would suggest the existence of far more conspiracies and outbreaks than those already mentioned. It is clear however that *ante-bellum* society of the South suffered from a larger degree of domestic insecurity than the conventional view would indicate. No doubt many Negroes made the required adjustments to slavery, but the romantic picture of careless abandon and contentment fails to be convincing. The struggle of the Negro for his liberty, beginning with those dark days on the slaveship, was far from sporadic in nature, but an ever-recurrent battle waged everywhere with desperate courage against the bonds of his master.

---

[52]*Ibid.*, V (1809–1811), 93–142.
[53]Francois Xavier Martin, *The History of Louisiana* (New Orleans, 1829), II, 300–301. During the fall of the following year another plot was reported. *J.C.N.*, III, 449.
[54]*Niles Register*, XXVI (1829), 53.
[55]*Ibid.*, LIII (1931–8), 129; LX (1841), 368; LXIII (1842–3), 212.
[56]V. Alton Moody, *Slavery on the Louisiana Sugar Plantations* (Univ. of Michigan Press, 1924), 41; also Phillips, *American Negro Slavery*, 486. *J.C.N.*, III, 648.
[57]Caleb P. Patterson, *The Negro in Tennessee*, Univ. of Texas Bulletin No. 225 (Austin, February 1, 1922), 49; *J.C.N.*, II, 565–69; Stirling, *Letters from the Slave States*, 294.
[58]*J.C.N.*, 299.
[59]Frederick Law Olmsted, *A Journey Through Texas* (New York, 1857), 513–4; Stirling, *Letters from the Slave States*, 300.

Unit 4

Unit Selections

Key Points to Consider

❖ What role did external forces play in the abolitionist movement?

❖ What forms of protests were utilized by slaves to challenge the institution of slavery?

❖ Why were white Union officers fearful of black solidiers?

❖ What role did African Americans serve in the cause of the Confederacy?

 **Links** **www.dushkin.com/online/**

These sites are annotated on pages 4 and 5.

International threats, in 1791, helped fuel the fires of the abolitionist movement outside of the continental U.S. In a violent slave rebellion, France lost an estimated 50,000 soldiers. When threatened by an invasion by both Spain and Britain, France chose to end slavery in San Domingo and Haiti.

On September 19, 1839, the district court in Connecticut opened proceedings on the *Amistad* and the trial of 53 captive slaves. The trial, pitting greed against morality, was at once reduced to issues regarding property rights. Ultimately the Supreme Court, moved by the eloquence of John Quincy Adams and Roger S. Baldwin, declared that Cinqué (whose real name was Singbe Pieh) and 52 other Africans had indeed been kidnapped.

The efforts of blacks in securing their own freedom prior to emancipation is often downplayed. By 1862, Wayne Durrill notes, slaves significantly increased their protests against the "peculiar institution" and its rules. In several notable cases the status, expectations, and conditions of servitude were often the product of arbitration between planters and slaves. Slaves registered their discontent either by joining up with the Union army, disrupting of the plantation system, or simply escaping.

Abraham Lincoln, on March 4, 1861, under the threat of rebellion and assassination, was inaugurated. During this period of crisis, he consistently strove to find a way to preserve the Union and avoid a civil war. Thus, while Lincoln considered slavery a retrograde institution, he was not concerned with ending it. Lincoln could even be classified as an apologist in that he "conceded that the peculiar institution, in the states where it already existed, was protected by the Constitution." It would take a civil war to remove this cancer in the body politic.

As the Civil War unfolded, the existence of slaves and ex-slaves increasingly became entangled with that of the Union and Confederate forces. While the Civil War put all relationships to the test, it also afforded greater freedom and much firmer legal grounds for establishing families. Archival records created by agencies of the government, especially the Army and the Freedmen's Bureau, provide a rich source of information regarding family formation and permanence of ex-slaves.

Labor shortages created by the Civil War forced the federal government to enlist large numbers of blacks in both the navy and the army. Frequently, inexperienced and unenlightened white military officers, fearful of black soldiers, relied upon acts of barbarism to control them. As one might expect, black soldiers responded in kind and also through mutiny. The potential of blacks to mutiny caused many to question their reliability.

Although the War Department officially sanctioned the use of blacks in combat roles, many people, like Abraham Lincoln, had strong reservations against utilizing blacks in military capacities. Others, such as Major General David Hunter, actively recruited escaping slaves and looked upon them as essential to the military effort.

Few historians have documented the role played by free blacks and slaves in the Confederate war effort. Craig Renner observes that most blacks served the Confederate cause in unofficial capacities, posing several problems for the South. Southern political and military leaders, much like their Union counterparts, could not agree on whether or not blacks should be enlisted in the army. Whether for patriotic or pragmatic reasons, a considerable body of information documents the significant contributions made by these black Confederates.

The question of patriotism, courage, and duty was answered in 1863 by Sergeant William H. Carney. Carney was one of over 100,000 black troops who served in about 140 all-black regiments for the Union cause. As a member of the all-black Company C of the 54th Massachusetts Infantry he led a charge against intense musketry and cannon fire in the assault on Fort Wagner. For his courage and valor he was awarded the Medal of Honor.

"All we want is make us free!"

An 1839 mutiny aboard a Spanish ship in Cuban waters raised basic questions about freedom and slavery in the United States

By Howard Jones

Around 4:00 A.M. on July 2, 1839, Joseph Cinqué led a slave mutiny on board the Spanish schooner *Amistad* some 20 miles off northern Cuba. The revolt set off a remarkable series of events and became the basis of a court case that ultimately reached the U.S. Supreme Court. The civil rights issues involved in the affair made it the most famous case to appear in American courts before the landmark Dred Scott decision of 1857.

The saga began two months earlier when slave trade merchants captured Cinqué, a 26-year-old man from Mende, Sierra Leone, and hundreds of others from different West African tribes. The captives were then taken to the Caribbean, with up to 500 of them chained hand and foot, on board the Portuguese slaver *Teçora*. After a nightmarish voyage in which approximately a third of the captives died, the journey ended with the clandestine, nighttime entry of

THE NEW HAVEN COLONY HISTORICAL SOCIETY

Sengbe Pieh—given the name Joseph Cinqué in Cuba—who is depicted in a painting by Nathaniel Jocelyn.

the ship into Cuba—in violation of the Anglo-Spanish treaties of 1817 and 1835 that made the African slave trade a capital crime. Slavery itself was legal in Cuba, meaning that once smuggled

ashore, the captives became "slaves" suitable for auction at the Havana barracoons.

In Havana, two Spaniards, José Ruiz and Pedro Montes, bought 53 of the Africans—including Cinqué and four children, three of them girls—and chartered the *Amistad*. The ship, named after the Spanish word for friendship, was a small black schooner built in Baltimore for the coastal slave trade. It was to transport its human cargo 300 miles to two plantations on another part of Cuba at Puerto Principe.

The spark for the mutiny was provided by Celestino, the *Amistad*'s mulatto cook. In a cruel jest, he drew his hand past his throat and pointed to barrels of beef, indicating to Cinqué that, on reaching Puerto Principe, the 53 black captives aboard would be killed and eaten. Stunned by this revelation, Cinqué found a nail to pick the locks on the captives' chains and made a strike for freedom.

In the small, hot, and humid room beneath the Senate chamber, [John Quincy] Adams challenged the Court to grant liberty on the basis of natural rights doctrines found in the Declaration of Independence.

ALL: NEW HAVEN COLONY HISTORICAL SOCIETY

In this painting by an unknown artist (above, left), the badly weather-beaten schooner Amistad is at anchor in Long Island Sound, while several of the mutineers head for shore in search of provisions. In two of a series of murals painted in 1939 by Hale Woodruff (above, right) for the Amistad centennial, the Africans are depicted during the pre-dawn revolt and on their return home, almost three years later.

On their third night at sea, Cinqué and a fellow captive named Grabeau freed their comrades and searched the dark hold for weapons. They found them in boxes: sugar cane knives with machete-like blades, two feet in length, attached to inch-thick steel handles. Weapons in hand, Cinqué and his cohorts stormed the shadowy, pitching deck and, in a brief and bloody struggle that led to the death of one of their own, killed the cook and captain and severely wounded Ruiz and Montes. Two sailors who were aboard disappeared in the melee and were probably drowned in a desperate attempt to swim the long distance to shore. Grabeau convinced Cinqué to spare the lives of the two Spaniards, since only they possessed the navigational skills necessary to sail the *Amistad* to Africa. Instead of making it home, however, the former cap-

tives eventually ended up off the coast of New York.

Cinqué, the acknowledged leader of the mutineers, recalled that the slave ship that he and the others had traveled on during their passage from Africa to Cuba had sailed away from the rising sun; therefore to return home, he ordered Montes, who had once been a sea captain, to sail the *Amistad* into the sun. The two Spaniards deceived their captors by sailing back and forth in the Caribbean Sea, toward the sun during the day and, by the stars, back toward Havana at night, hoping for rescue by British anti-slave-trade patrol vessels.

When that failed, Ruiz and Montes took the schooner on a long and erratic trek northward up the Atlantic coast.

Some 60 days after the mutiny, under a hot afternoon sun in late August 1839, Lieutenant Commander Thomas Gedney

of the USS *Washington* sighted the vessel just off Long Island, where several of the schooner's inhabitants were on shore bartering for food. He immediately dispatched an armed party who captured the men ashore and then boarded the vessel. They found a shocking sight: cargo strewn all over the deck; perhaps 50 men nearly starved and destitute, their skeletal bodies naked or barely clothed in rags; a black corpse lying in decay on the deck, its face frozen as if in terror; another black with a maniacal gaze in his eyes; and two wounded Spaniards in the hold who claimed to be the owners of the Africans who, as slaves, had mutinied and murdered the ship's captain.

Gedney seized the vessel and cargo and reported the shocking episode to authorities in New London, Connecticut. Only 43 of the Africans were still alive,

Margru was one of the three female captives on board the Amistad. After her return home, she was educated at the American mission school and sent back to the United States to study. She then returned to Africa, where she became principal of the mission's school.

including the four children. In addition to the one killed during the mutiny, nine had died of disease and exposure or from consuming medicine on board in an effort to quench their thirst.

The affair might have come to a quiet end at this point had it not been for a group of abolitionists. Evangelical Christians led by Lewis Tappan, a prominent New York businessman, Joshua Leavitt, a lawyer and journalist who edited the *Emancipator* in New York, and Simeon Jocelyn, a Congregational minister in New Haven, Connecticut, learned of the *Amistad's* arrival and decided to publicize the incident to expose the brutalities of slavery and the slave trade. Through evangelical arguments, appeals to higher law and "moral suasion," Tappan and his colleagues hoped to launch a massive assault on slavery.

The *Amistad* incident, Tappan happily proclaimed, was a "providential occurrence." In his view slavery was a deep moral wrong and not subject to compromise. Both those who advocated its practice and those who quietly condoned it by inaction deserved condemnation. Slavery was a sin, he declared, because it obstructed a person's free will inherent by birth, therefore constituting

a rebellion against God. Slavery was also, Tappan wrote to his brother, "the worm at the root of the tree of Liberty. Unless killed the tree will die."

Tappan first organized the "Amistad Committee" to coordinate efforts on behalf of the captives, who had been moved to the New Haven jail. Tappan preached impromptu sermons to the mutineers, who were impressed by his sincerity though unable to understand his language. He wrote detailed newspaper accounts of their daily activities in jail, always careful to emphasize their humanity and civilized backgrounds for a fascinated public, many of whom had never seen a black person. And he secured the services of Josiah Gibbs, a professor of religion and linguistics at Yale College, who searched the docks of New York for native Africans capable of translating Cinqué's Mende language. Gibbs eventually discovered two Africans familiar with Mende—James Covey from Sierra Leone and Charles Pratt from Mende itself. At last the *Amistad* mutineers could tell their side of the story.

Meanwhile, Ruiz and Montes had initiated trial proceedings seeking return of their "property." They had also secured their government's support under Pinckney's Treaty of 1795, which stipulated the return of merchandise lost for reasons beyond human control. To fend off what many observers feared would be a "judicial massacre," the abolitionists hired attorney Roger S. Baldwin of Connecticut, who had a reputation as an eloquent defender of the weak and downtrodden.

Baldwin intended to prove that the captives were "kidnapped Africans," illegally taken from their homeland and imported into Cuba and thus entitled to resist their captors by any means necessary. He argued that the ownership papers carried by Ruiz and Montes were fraudulent and that the blacks were not slaves indigenous to Cuba. He and his defense team first filed a claim for the *Amistad* and cargo as the Africans' property in preparation for charging the Spaniards with piracy. Then they filed suit for the captives' freedom on the grounds of humanity and justice: slavery violated natural law, providing its victims with the inherent right of self-defense.

The case then entered the world of politics. It posed such a serious problem for President Martin Van Buren that he decided to intervene. A public dispute over slavery would divide his Democratic party, which rested on a tenuous North-South alliance, and could cost him reelection to the presidency in 1840. Working through his secretary of state, slaveholder John Forsyth from Georgia, Van Buren sought to quietly solve the problem by complying with Spanish demands.

Van Buren also faced serious diplomatic issues. Failure to return the Africans to their owners would be a violation of Pinckney's Treaty with Spain. In addition, revealing Spain's infringement of treaties against the African slave trade could provide the British, who were pioneers in the crusade against slavery, with a pretext for intervening in Cuba, which was a long-time American interest.

The White House position was transparently weak. Officials refused to question the validity of the certificates of ownership, which had assigned Spanish names to each of the captives even though none of them spoke that language. Presidential spokesmen blandly asserted that the captives had been slaves in Cuba, despite the fact that the

Grabeau, drawn here from life by William H. Townsend in 1839, had been a blacksmith in his Mende homeland before he was seized by slave dealers and sent to Cuba for sale on the slave market.

international slave trade had been outlawed some 20 years earlier and the children were no more than nine years old and spoke an African dialect.

The court proceedings opened on September 19, 1839, amid a carnival atmosphere in the state capitol building in Hartford, Connecticut. To some observers, Cinqué was a black folk hero; to others he was a barbarian who deserved execution for murder. Poet William Cullen Bryant extolled Cinqué's virtues, numerous Americans sympathized with the "noble savages," and pseudo-scientists concluded that the shape of Cinqués skull suggested leadership, intelligence, and nobility. The New York *Morning Herald,* however, derided the "poor Africans," "who have nothing to do, but eat, drink, and turn somersaults."

To establish the mutineers as human beings rather than property, Baldwin sought a writ of habeas corpus aimed at freeing them unless the prosecution filed charges of murder. Issuance of the writ would recognize the Africans as persons with natural rights and thus undermine the claim by both the Spanish and American governments that the captives were property. If the prosecution brought charges, the Africans would have the right of self-defense against unlawful captivity; if it filed no charges, they would go free. In the meantime, the abolitionists could explore in open court the entire range of human and property rights relating to slavery. As Leavitt later told the General Antislavery Convention in London, the purpose of the writ was "to test their right to personality."

Despite Baldwin's impassioned pleas for justice, the public's openly expressed sympathy for the captives, and the prosecution's ill-advised attempt to use the four black children as witnesses against their own countrymen, Associate Justice Smith Thompson of the U.S. Supreme Court denied the writ. Thompson was a strong-willed judge who opposed slavery, but he even more ardently supported the laws of the land. Under those laws, he declared, slaves were property.

He could not simply assert that the Africans were human beings and grant freedom on the basis of natural rights. Only the law could dispense justice, and the law did not authorize their freedom. It was up to the district court to decide whether the mutineers were slaves and, therefore, property.

Prospects before the district court in Connecticut were equally dismal. The presiding judge was Andrew T. Judson, a well-known white supremacist and staunch opponent of abolition. Baldwin attempted to move the case to the free state of New York on the grounds that Gedney had seized the Africans in that state's waters and not on the high seas. He hoped, if successful, to prove that they were already free upon entering New York and that the Van Buren administration was actually trying to enslave them. But Baldwin's effort failed; the confrontation with Judson was unavoidable.

Judson's verdict in the case only appeared preordained; as a politically ambitious man, he had to find a middle ground. Whereas many Americans wanted the captives freed, the White House pressured him to send them back to Cuba. Cinqué himself drew great sympathy by recounting his capture in Mende and then graphically illustrating the horrors of the journey from Africa by sitting on the floor with hands and feet pulled together to show how the captives had been "packed" into the hot and unsanitary hold of the slave vessel.

The Spanish government further confused matters by declaring that the Africans were both property and persons. In addition to calling for their return as property under Pinckney's Treaty, it demanded their surrender as "slaves who are assassins." The real concern of the Spanish government became clear when its minister to the United States, Pedro Alcántara de Argaiz, proclaimed that "The public vengeance of the African Slave Traders in Cuba had not been satisfied." If the mutineers went unpunished, he feared, slave rebellions would erupt all over Cuba.

Argaiz's demands led the Van Buren administration to adopt measures that constituted an obstruction of justice. To facilitate the Africans' rapid departure to Cuba after an expected guilty verdict, Argaiz convinced the White House to dispatch an American naval vessel to New Haven to transport them out of the country *before* they could exercise the constitutional right of appeal. By agreeing to this, the president had authorized executive interference in the judicial process that violated the due-process guarantees contained in the Constitution.

Judson finally reached what he thought was a politically safe decision. On January 13, 1840, he ruled that the Africans had been kidnapped, and, offering no sound legal justification, ordered their return to Africa, hoping to appease the president by removing them from the United States. Six long months after the mutiny, it appeared that the captives were going home.

But the ordeal was not over. The White House was stunned by the decision: Judson had ignored the "great [and] important political bearing" of the case, complained the president's son, John Van Buren. The Van Buren administration immediately filed an appeal with the circuit court. The court upheld the decision, however, meaning that the case would now go before the U.S. Supreme Court, where five of the justices, including Chief Justice Roger Taney, were southerners who were or had been slaveowners.

Meanwhile, the Africans had become a public spectacle. Curious townspeople and visitors watched them exercise daily on the New Haven green, while many others paid the jailer for a peek at the foreigners in their cells. Some of the most poignant newspaper stories came from professors and students from Yale College and the Theological Seminary who instructed the captives in English and Christianity. But the most compelling attraction was Cinqué. In his mid-twenties, he was taller than most Mende people, married with three children, and, according to the contemporary portrait by New England abolitionist Nathaniel Jocelyn, majestic, lightly bronzed, and strikingly handsome. Then there were the children, including Kale, who learned enough English to become the spokesperson for the group.

The supreme court began hearing arguments on February 22, 1841. Van Buren had already lost the election, partly and somewhat ironically because his *Amistad* policy was so blatantly pro-South that it alienated northern Democrats. The abolitionists wanted someone of national stature to join Baldwin in the defense and finally persuaded former President John Quincy Adams to take the case even though he was 73 years old, nearly deaf, and had been absent from the courtroom for three decades. Now a congressman from Massachusetts, Adams was irascible and hard-nosed, politically independent, and self-righteous to the point of martyrdom. He was fervently antislavery though not an abolitionist, and had been advising Baldwin on the case since its inception. His effort became a personal crusade when the young Kale wrote him a witty and touching letter, which appeared in the *Emancipator* and concluded with the ringing words, "All we want is make us free."

Baldwin opened the defense before the Supreme Court with another lengthy appeal to natural law then gave way to Adams, who delivered an emotional eight-hour argument that stretched over two days. In the small, hot, and humid room beneath the Senate chamber, Adams challenged the Court to grant liberty on the basis of natural rights doctrines found in the Declaration of Independence. Pointing to a copy of the document mounted on a huge pillar, he proclaimed that, "I know of no other law that reaches the case of my clients, but the law of Nature and of Nature's God on which our fathers placed our own national existence." The Africans, he proclaimed, were victims of a monstrous conspiracy led by the executive branch in Washington that denied their rights as human beings.

Adams and Baldwin were eloquent in their pleas for justice based on higher principles. As Justice Joseph Story wrote to his wife, Adams's argument was "extraordinary . . . for its power, for its bitter sarcasm, and its dealing with topics far beyond the records and points of discussion."

On March 9, Story read a decision that could not have surprised those who knew anything about the man. An eminent scholar and jurist, Story was rigidly conservative and strongly nationalistic, but he was as sensitive to an individual's rights as he was a strict adherent to the law. Although he found slavery repugnant and contrary to Christian morality, he supported the laws protecting its existence and opposed the abolitionists as threats to ordered society. Property rights, he believed, were the basis of civilization.

Even so, Story handed down a decision that freed the mutineers on the grounds argued by the defense. The ownership papers were fraudulent, making the captives "kidnapped Africans" who had the inherent right of self-

The court proceedings shown above in the Woodruff mural panel, "Trial of the Captive Slaves," proved to be long and tumultuous.

defense in accordance with the "eternal principles of justice." Furthermore, Story reversed Judson's decision ordering the captives' return to Africa because there was no American legislation authorizing such an act. The outcome drew Leavitt's caustic remark that Van Buren's executive order attempting to return the Africans to Cuba as slaves should be "engraved on his tomb, to rot only with his memory."

The abolitionists pronounced the decision a milestone in their long and bitter fight against the "peculiar institution." To them, and to the interested public, Story's "eternal principles of justice" were the same as those advocated by Adams. Although Story had focused on self-defense, the victorious abolitionists broadened the meaning of his words to condemn the immorality of slavery. They reprinted thousands of copies of the defense argument in pamphlet form, hoping to awaken a larger segment of the public to the sordid and inhumane char-

acter of slavery and the slave trade. In the highest public forum in the land, the abolitionists had brought national attention to a great social injustice. For the first and only time in history, African blacks seized by slave dealers and brought to the New World won their freedom in American courts.

The final chapter in the saga was the captives' return to Africa. The abolitionists first sought damage compensation for them, but even Adams had to agree with Baldwin that, despite months of captivity because bail had been denied, the "regular" judicial process had detained the Africans, and liability for false imprisonment hinged only on whether the officials' acts were "*malicious* and without probable *cause*." To achieve equity Adams suggested that the federal government finance the captives' return to Africa. But President John Tyler, himself a Virginia slaveholder, refused on the grounds that, as Judge Story had ruled, no law authorized such action.

To charter a vessel for the long trip to Sierra Leone, the abolitionists raised money from private donations, public exhibitions of the Africans, and contributions from the Union Missionary' Society, which black Americans had formed in Hartford to found a Christian mission in Africa. On November 25, 1841, the remaining 35 *Amistad* captives, accompanied by James Covey and five missionaries, departed from New York for Africa on a small sailing vessel named the *Gentleman*. The British governor of Sierra Leone welcomed them the following January—almost three years after their initial incarceration by slave traders.

The aftermath of the *Amistad* affair is hazy. One of the girls, Margru, returned to the United States and entered Oberlin College, in Ohio, to prepare for mission work among her people. She was educated at the expense of the American Missionary Association (AMA), established in 1846 as an outgrowth of the Amistad Committee and the first of

NEW HAVEN COLONY HISTORICAL SOCIETY

This letter to Lewis Tappan from John Quincy Adams was in response to the gift of a Bible that had been sent to Adams by Cinqué and his comrades after they had been freed by the court and allowed to return home.

Kaw-Mende before his death around 1879. No conclusive evidence has surfaced to determine whether Cinqué was reunited with his wife and three children, and for that same reason there is no justification for the oft-made assertion that he himself engaged in the slave trade.

The importance of the *Amistad* case lies in the act that Cinqué and his fellow captives, in collaboration with white abolitionists, had won their freedom and thereby encouraged others to continue the struggle. Positive law had come into conflict with natural law, exposing the great need to change the Constitution and American laws in compliance with the moral principles underlying the Declaration of Independence. In that sense the incident contributed to the fight against slavery by helping to lay the basis for its abolition through the Thirteenth Amendment to the Constitution in 1865.

Howard Jones is University Research Professor and Chair of the Department of History at the University of Alabama. He is the author of numerous books, including Mutiny on the Amistad: The Saga of a Slave Revolt and Its Impact on American Abolition, Law, and Diplomacy, *published by Oxford University Press.*

its kind in Africa. Cinqué returned to his home, where tribal wars had scattered or perhaps killed his family. Some scholars insist that he remained in Africa, working for some time as an interpreter at the AMA mission in

The long road
to abolition

by Nelly Schmidt

The eradication of slavery in North America and the West Indies proceeded at snail's pace. Even the leaders of the French Revolution dragged their feet.

■ Some words are historically loaded. "The abolition of slavery" is of course a convenient phrase, but historical authenticity requires us to choose terms more faithful to reality. The process the Americas went through in the nineteenth century and are still going through today, may be more accurately described as the destruction of the system of slavery. It was a slow process, beginning with the ending of slavery in San Domingo/Haiti in August-September 1793.

The crucial importance of resistance movements by slaves themselves in triggering this process is just beginning to be realized. The case of San Domingo/Haiti is a typical example of this: a slave revolt that turned out to be impossible to curb was what triggered the abolitionist movement there in 1791.

In response to Spanish and British threats to invade the island, Sonthonax, the civil com- missioner assigned to the colony by the revolutionary government in Paris, decided on 29 August 1793 to end slavery in the north, and this measure was extended to the west and south of the colony in September and October of the same year. The measure was confirmed on 4 February 1794 (16 pluviôse of the year II) by the Convention, which decreed that "all men without distinction of colour domiciled in the colonies are French citizens, and shall enjoy all the rights guaranteed by the Constitution". The 1795 Constitution even specified that "the French colonies are an integral part of the Republic and are subject to the same constitutional law", and provided for their accession to the status of departments.

This assimilationist legislation, however, never came into force. In 1802, the legislative body declared itself in favour of reintroducing slavery. On 17 May the Consulate, taking the view that "illusions of liberty and equality have been spread to these remote lands" (i.e. France's American colonies), where "the difference between civilized and uncivilized men" was too "striking", passed a decree providing that "In the colonies restored to France under the Treaty of Amiens dated the 6th germinal of the year X, slavery shall be maintained in accordance with pre-1798 laws and regulations".

The opposition aroused by the coming into force of this decree obliged Napoleon Bonaparte to dispatch military expeditions to Guadeloupe and San Domingo. The colonial war that raged

> Though Marster was a Mef'dis' preacher, he whip his slaves, an' den drap pitch an'tuppentine on dem from a bu'nin' to'ch.
>
> Marster preach to de white folks Sunday mo'nin'. Den, at night, all de marsters roun' dat country sen' dey slaves, an' he preach to us. He had two fav'rit tex'es he uster preach from to de slaves. One was, "Serv'nts, obey your marsters". He didn' say much 'bout de Marster in Hebben, but allus tole us to obey our earthly marsters. De other tex' was "Thou shalt not steal". He preach dat over an' over, to de niggers. Dey couldn' read deir Bibles, so dey hatter b'llebe jis' what he say.
>
> Since I's got to readin' an' studyin', I see some of de chu'ches is wrong, an' de preachers don' preach jis' like de Bible say.
>
> *Jack White*
> *slave*

Reprinted with permission from the *Unesco Courier*, October 1994, pp. 20-24.

77

in these two islands ended with the reintroduction of slavery in Guadeloupe. In San Domingo one of the great leaders of the insurrection, Toussaint Louverture, was captured and imprisoned in France, at Fort-de-Joux in the Jura, where he died in April 1803. But the French troops sent to impose the reintroduction of slavery were defeated, and the independence of the colony (under its old Amerindian name of Haiti) was finally proclaimed on 1 January 1804.

> When Dr. Cannon found out dat his carriage driver had larned to read and write while he was takin' de doctor's chillun to and f'om school, he had dat nigger's thumbs cut off, and put another boy to doin' de drivin' in his place.
>
> *Tom Hawkins*
> *slave*

The British practise "the right of search"

Emancipation in the British colonies which followed thirty years later was likewise largely the result of the long rebellion by the slaves of Jamaica (1831–1832). As early as 1780 a humanitarian trend had emerged in England, one of its supporters being a young M.P. of aristocratic origin, William Wilberforce: in 1807 he persuaded the House of Commons to prohibit the transatlantic slave trade. From that date onwards, and then after the 1815 Congress of Vienna (which drew up a European agreement on ending the slave trade), Britain was to lead a campaign for the inspection of slave-ships, which were pronounced illegal.

Well-established net- works of illicit slave trade had grown up from the coasts of Africa to Brazil, the United States, Cuba and the French colonies of Guadeloupe and Martinique. Propaganda against this trade—though not against the system of slavery itself—developed particularly in London, where numerous leaflets circulated in several languages. One of them entitled *The cry of the Africans against their European oppressors, or a look at the murderous commerce known as the slave trade*, by Thomas Clarkson, which appeared in 1822, contained the famous cross-sections of the slave-ship *Brookes*. The "right of search" practised by British transatlantic vessels aroused lively controversy. France and the United States in particular grudgingly accepted the role of policemen of the seas first performed by the British.

> My moster would put slaves in a calaboose at night to be shipped de next morning. He always limited de lashes to five hundred. After whipping dem, he would rub pepper and salt on deir backs, where whipped, and lay dem before de fire until blistered, and den take a cat, and make him claw de blisters, to burst dem.
>
> *Robert Burns*
> *slave*

A proliferation of petitions and the creation of a society for the abolition of the slave trade eventually brought about an investigation by the Crown. But it was not until 1823 that an Anti-Slavery Society was founded in London.

In 1831 the Crown manumitted slaves within its own lands, and on 28 August 1833 the King approved an Act voted by Parliament emancipating slaves in the British West Indies, Guyana and British Honduras (now Belize). This Act gave the planters generous compensation, and set a time-limit of four-to-six years for the complete liberation of slaves employed in farming and domestic work. They were subject to compulsory unpaid apprenticeship under their masters, limited to four years because of the difficulty of enforcing such a system. Only children under six and adults over sixty were declared free in August 1834.

The new citizens of the Republic

Little attempt is usually made to situate the beginnings and the accelaration of abolitionist processes in the context of the resistance by slaves themselves to the system of slavery. By and large, European abolitionist move- ments remained very timid. In Paris a decision to abolish slavery was not on the agenda of the Société francaise pour l'abolition del l'esclavage, founded in 1834 and modelled on the British Anti-Slavery Society. Nor did it form part of the programme of the provisional government that came to power after the revolutionary days of February 1848. But Victor Schoelcher, who had travelled in the French colonies and had set himself up as the apostle of the abolition of slavery, managed to persuade the Minister of the Navy and the Colonies that a general uprising was imminent if the *status quo* were maintained; he got the government to accept the principle of abolition in the French colonies. It was only at this price that law and order, and work on the sugar-cane plantations, could be maintained. He was appointed Under-Secretary of State for the Colonies and

Chairman of the Commission for the Abolition of Slavery, which on 27 April got the new government to sign a decree providing for immediate emancipation. This instrument was modelled on the British precedent, and granted slave-owning colonists compensation; but its original feature was that it made the "new freedmen" citizens empowered to elect their representatives to the National Assembly in Paris by universal suffrage.

The introduction of this decree in the French colonies—where rebel slaves had already forced the governors to proclaim liberty even before the text arrived from Paris—caused riots in the Danish colonies of the Virgin Islands (St. Croix, St. John and St. Thomas), where in July 1848 Governor Von Scholten had urgently to promulgate an emancipation decree drawn up by King Christian VIII's government. In 1864 a similar decree was brought into force in the Dutch colonies.

A different kind of emancipation of slaves was to be seen in the United States and the Spanish colonies, in the context of armed conflicts. This was the case in Latin America in the days of Bolivar, and also in Cuba starting with the Ten Years' War, between 1868 and 1878. Slaves were promised their freedom in return for enlisting in the armies being raised against Spain. The Moret law (from the name of the Spanish Minister for the Colonies) was passed by the Cortes in 1870 and brought into force in Puerto Rico in 1873, and then progressively in Cuba in 1880 and 1886.

In the United States slavery was not so much a colonial as a national problem. The northern states, where industrialization had come relatively early and progressed relatively quickly, were exposed to effective propaganda from the Quakers and other Protestant sects. Indeed, the Quakers were the only white group to plead the cause of emancipation of the negroes in England's North American colonies before the War of Independence. As early as 1688 the Quaker community in Pennsylvania had protested against "the business of buying and keeping blacks".

In 1755 the principles set forth in the Declaration of Independence were injected into the debate on slavery. During the war the negro slaves of New England intensified their anti-slavery activities and produced a stream of petitions. They claimed to be following the example of the oppressed colonists "in their present glorious struggles for freedom". Vermont, by prohibiting bondage in its 1777 Constitution, took the lead among the northern states which proclaimed the ending of slavery. The same step was taken by Massachusetts and New Hampshire, while Pennsylvania, Rhode Island and Connecticut opted for gradual emancipation.

> No siree, I never did learn how to read and write. I just hold to the end of the pencil so the white man can sign my name.
>
> *Eli Davison*
> *slave*

> Old Missus and young Missus told the little slave children that the stork brought the white babies to their mothers, but that the slave children were all hatched out from buzzards' eggs. And we believed it was true.
>
> *Katie Sutton*
> *slave*

> I recollect seein' one biscuit crust, one mornin'. Dey throwed it out to de dogs, an' I beat de dog to it.
>
> *Alex McCinney*
> *slave*

Disappointed hopes

In 1830 the movement acquired fresh impetus. William Lloyd Garrison founded the newspaper *The Liberator*. In 1845 Frederick Douglass, a fugitive arrived from the south, published his famous autobiography and settled in Washington, where he made a career in journalism and diplomacy. Harriet Tubman helped to organize the clandestine departure of slaves from the south to the north and Canada via the "underground railroad". In 1848 the Free Soil Society and then in 1854 the Republican Party (whose candidate Abraham Lincoln was elected President of the United States in 1860) included in their manifestoes the ending of slavery throughout the country. The end of the War of Secession in 1865 made it possible in any event to enshrine abolition in the Thirteenth Amendment to the United States Constitution.

After Puerto Rico in 1873 and Cuba in 1886, it remained for Brazil in 1888 to promulgate the last slave emancipation decree in the Americas—having received the largest number of captives from the illicit slave trade in the nineteenth century.

Each decree was followed by an often lengthy period of transition to other ways of regulating labour and social relations. In the Caribbean, agreements were very soon concluded between the European governments and various agencies in Africa, India, Indonesia and China for the importation of underpaid contract (indentured) labour. With the arrival of several hundred thousand of these coolies, recruited from among the most deprived peoples, the "new freedmen" inevitably found themselves excluded from the labour market: the central administrations had fixed their wages at four times those of the new immigrants.

While the Second Republic in France gave freedmen in its colonies citizenship rights, this was not the case elsewhere. In the British West Indies, for instance, decentralization of power by the Colonial Office allowed the local planters' assemblies to institute a means-tested suffrage which disenfranchised the slaves recently freed from their period of apprenticeship. In the United States, when the Thirteenth Amendment to the Constitution, officially ending slavery in all the states of the Union, was approved, the Ku Klux Klan came into being in Tennessee in December 1865. The southern states adopted a policy of discrimination and racial segregation similar to apartheid, and it was to take another century to bring this to an end.

The quotations from the testimony of slaves that accompany this article are taken from *Bullwhip Days*, edited by James Mellon © 1988 Grove/Atlantic, New York.

NELLY SCHMIDT
is a French historian who is engaged in research at France's National Centre for Scientific Research (CNRS). She is the author of *Victor Schoelcher* and *La suppression de l'esclavage aux Caraïbes, Une perspective comparative*, both published in 1994.

The Struggle for Black Freedom before Emancipation

Wayne K. Durrill

Wayne K. Durrill teaches American history at the University of Cincinnati.

The Civil War has recently become a hot ticket. The movie, *Glory,* the PBS series "The Civil War" by Ken Burns, and James McPherson's recent Pulitzer Prize-winning account of the conflict have all dramatized the continuing relevance of the war as a defining experience for a people and a nation. These stories, however, have often neglected an important part of that defining experience: the role of black people in securing their own emancipation. Most accounts of war date emancipation from Lincoln's famous proclamation and the military campaigns that followed. Even *Glory,* which traces the heroic deeds of black soldiers from Massachusetts, portrays slaves in the lowcountry of South Carolina as incompetent and ineffectual, persons who simply waited for Northern free black liberators to march South and rescue them from bondage.

However, even this relatively enlightened view of the role of black people in their own emancipation is historically inaccurate. As Ira Berlin and his colleagues have shown in their monumental multi-volume series, *Freedom: A Documentary History of Emancipation,* slaves throughout the South squeezed freedom in dribs and drabs from their own local situation as opportunities arose in wartime. In Kentucky, where blacks re-

mained in bondage until after the Civil War, slaves fled to Tennessee where they could join the Union army as laborers and later as soldiers, and thereby free themselves and sometimes their families. Others stayed home, testing the limits of servitude in a volatile and dangerous situation, always with an eye toward establishing claims to property and place, as well as to their own humanity. These black struggles for freedom within slavery are sometimes difficult to visualize. Indeed, they seem to be a contradiction in terms. Yet they did occur, and with an intensity and regularity that historians have only just begun to uncover. As an example of such struggle, let us examine the story of how one group of North Carolina slaves redefined the rules of slavery in the crisis of war so as to create for themselves a larger space in which to carry on a life separate from their white masters.

In September of 1861, after the fall of federal forces off Hatteras Island on North Carolina's Outer Banks, Major General John Wool, Union commander of the island, reported that "negro slaves" were "almost daily arriving at this post from the interior." They came in small groups, many traveling over one hundred miles from the counties bordering the Albemarle Sound. At Columbia, on the eastern edge of the Sound and about five miles from William Pettigrew's plantation, a certain planter had

brought his slaves to town for "safe-keeping." The militia had already mustered there and the town had a jail if he needed it. But shortly after their arrival, thirteen of the man's slaves quietly stole a boat and sailed for Hatteras, setting in motion a chain of events that quickly spread through counties all around the Sound. One planter complained that news of the escape had spread among slaves in the area, and he reasoned, "We may look for others to leave soon." In response, slave owners throughout the Sound region began to move to the upcountry, taking with them as many of their slaves as they could support on the land available to them.

William Pettigrew, one of the richest planters in Washington County, North Carolina, grasped the crisis early on and resolved to remove his slaves before planting began the following spring. On 4 March 1862, the planter arranged for twenty-five Confederate cavalrymen to descend upon Magnolia plantation. The move took the slaves by surprise, and all were captured. That day, men, women, and children were loaded onto wagons guarded by armed troopers, and began a long journey upcountry. After a nine-day forced march, Pettigrew and the slaves came to Haywood, a small crossroads community about fifty miles west of Raleigh where the planter had located a small farm for sale. He purchased the farm as his base camp in the upcountry, but it was too small to support any but a handful of his slaves. The others he drove on foot fifty miles further west where he leased out eighty-seven of them in nineteen groups to fifteen different planters.

The exchange of slaves for promissory notes, however, signified more than simply a purchase of labor. It included a broader transfer of power from one planter to another. For this reason, William Pettigrew insisted that persons who hired his slaves provide them with certain goods in the coming year, mostly food, clothing, and shoes. The planter might have provided the goods himself and factored the cost into his asking price. But he did not. Instead, he included in the contract detailed directions specifying what each slave should receive. In doing so, Pettigrew ensured that his slaves' new master would become the sole source of some crucial goods for them, thus giving the new master enormous leverage over the hired-out slaves. By his actions, Pettigrew produced not merely new employers for his slaves, but new masters.

Such contracts, however, did not settle all questions of a planter's dominance and a slave's submission in the upcountry. Planters and slaves, in fact, had always created their own mutual expectations, in part by contesting the rules by which they lived. Before the war, this had not been a conflict among equals, to be sure. Instead, the struggle between planter and slave presumed an unequal resolution; the master would rule and the slave submit. But in 1862, the relations between planters and slaves had changed dramatically, even in the upcountry. Many of the Pettigrew slaves worked for new masters who might or might not be skilled in managing human property. Would these men have the wherewithal to nail the meat-house door shut, call in the slave patrol, or face down a personal challenge? No one knew. But William Pettigrew's slaves were determined to find out.

Mary Jane, for example, decided early on to see just what kind of master she had been assigned. William Pettigrew had hired her out as a cook to a planter named George Foushee, along with a slave named Dick Lake, his wife

Jenny, and their five children. Mary Jane complained "mostly of colick" during her first three weeks at Foushee's place. In that period, she rendered "very little service" in the planter's view. According to Foushee, "She don't seem to be very bad off, just sick enough to keep her from work." The planter further wondered if "a good deal of it is deception." To find out, Foushee asked Dick Lake about her, and the slave's answer confirmed the planter's suspicions. According to Lake, Mary Jane had "never done much the year she was in a family way." Mary Jane had a history of probing the limits of her master's power.

Similarly, Jenny took advantage of the change of masters to renew work rules she had known at Magnolia plantation. She had just borne a child and informed Foushee that she had "never been required to do any work until her child was eight weeks old." She also objected to Foushee's plan to put her to work in the fields. At Magnolia she always had labored as a cook and now complained that she "could not work out."

When members of the slave family initiated the same contest that took place on the Foushee plantation, Caveness could not comprehend their actions for what they were.

Mary Jane, Jenny, and their fellow slaves did not wish simply to avoid work by refusing to labor for their masters. Most, in fact, worked steadily and with a will. In late March, a friend of William Pettigrew's who saw some of the planter's slaves "most every Sunday" in church, reported them at work and "well satisfied" with their new circumstances. Therefore, the action taken by Mary Jane and Jenny must be inter-

preted as having some more specific purpose. Mary Jane had succeeded in making pregnancy a privileged status at their old plantation. Here, she renewed the rule by making a public event of her refusal to work while pregnant. Similarly, she served notice upon George Foushee that Pettigrew slaves could not be required to work when ill, no matter how slight the planter thought evidence of any malady appeared. Jenny, for her part, sought to reinforce two rules. The first would give women a special status when pregnant. The second would renew a longstanding division between housework and fieldwork that served as the basis for some very important and very sharp distinctions among the Pettigrew slaves themselves.

George Foushee understood all of this on a practical level. Doubtless, he could never admit publicly, or perhaps even to himself, that Mary Jane and Jenny's actions constituted a challenge to the local rules that governed relations between masters and slaves. But Foushee did have the presence of mind to remain calm. He reported by letter to William Pettigrew the two slaves' failure to work diligently. But Foushee did not propose that either he or Pettigrew take any action. The planter concluded his account of Mary Jane's behavior by saying simply, "I hope she will be better hereafter."

Mary Jane did become better. After she had made her point, she returned to work as usual. Other planters, however, did not fully appreciate the give-and-take that an exercise of a master's power required, particularly when the power of masters had been so undermined by Union military activity on the North Carolina coast. Or perhaps some planters sensed in small challenges larger issues that George Foushee had overlooked.

A. E. Caveness is a case in point. Caveness had hired one slave family from William Pettigrew—Jack, his pregnant wife, Venus, and their six young children. The children must have been young because the entire family hired out for twenty-five dollars, less than the cost of hiring a single prime male field hand. Caveness got a good deal more than he bargained for, however, when he paid his pittance to William Pettigrew. When members of the slave family initiated the same contest that took place on the Foushee plantation, Caveness could not comprehend their actions for what they were. In his view, the slaves attempted to "over-run" him. Finally, in a fit of ill-temper, the planter whipped the oldest child, a gal named Sarah, for what he considered her "laziness and disobedience."

The girl's parents objected violently to this. They "made a great ado about it," according to one account, so much so that Caveness felt compelled to "take Venus in hand." At that point, Venus "started off" down the plantation road and, as she walked, turned to the planter and told him off. What exactly she uttered that day remained a matter of dispute. Caveness claimed that she shouted, I am "going to the Yankees." Doubtless, she had no such intention—if she even spoke these words. Venus and her family had just made the nine-day trek from the coast on foot. She well knew that she needed food and extra clothing for such a journey, that Confederate troops blanketed eastern North Carolina and would demand a pass from her, and that William Pettigrew would hire a slave catcher to find her long before she reached federal lines. Later, Venus's husband claimed that she had said no such thing. By the slave's account, Venus told Caveness that she intended to walk to the plantation of William Campbell, Pettigrew's friend, presumably to lodge a complaint against her new master for his actions. Whatever the exact words, Venus had made her point in producing this small drama—pubicly and loudly She feared no man, planter or otherwise, and if she chose to oppose that man, she would make her claim a matter of public debate.

Caveness "ordered her to come back," but Venus refused and continued walking down the road. The planter then got his whip and followed her. Some distance from the house, he finally caught up with her. Again, Caveness commanded Venus to return to the plantation. Once more, the slave refused and voiced her intention to leave. At that point, the planter lost all patience and good sense. Caveness began to whip Venus, at which time Jack, who evidently had followed the two, "got in between them." The planter then "fell to

work on Jack, and drove both slaves back to the house."

But Venus had succeeded in her purpose even as she and her husband bore the lashes of the planter's whip. Caveness complained that "the fuss might have been heard all over the neighborhood." If he hoped to exercise any power over Pettigrew's slaves, Caveness now would have to submit to the scrutiny of his neighbors, both black and white. Each side in this conflict would mobilize its supporters. The battle between master and slave over who would rule the family, and particularly the children of Venus and Jack, became a public controversy.

In one sense, the customary rights of slaves acting within the rules of paternalism had been renewed. Yet, there was more to the story than a restoration of peaceable relations between masters and slaves.

The next day, Caveness traveled to William Campbell's plantation, where he hoped to make his case to the county's planters. To Campbell, he gave an account of the basic facts in the matter. But Caveness made no attempt to justify his actions. Instead he simply announced a solution. He demanded that Campbell, who had been charged with managing William Pettigrew's interest in Chatham and Moore counties, write to the slaves' owner seeking "permission to conquer them." If Pettigrew refused to grant him such authority, Caveness demanded that their master "take them away." By this ultimatum, Caveness cast the conflict in terms of fundamental is-

sues—in this case, the interest of planters in dominating their slaves. Essentially, Caveness argued that all planters must stand with him, no matter what the specifics of this case, in order to preserve their power over slaves as a whole.

Meanwhile, Venus and Jack also made their opinions known throughout the neighborhood. The couple communicated their interpretation of the conflict to slaves belonging to William Campbell who, in turn, approached their master after Caveness returned home. They told Campbell that Caveness had "not been good "to Pettigrew's slaves. They argued that Caveness was "a man of bad temper," and he acted "very ill" to Jack and his family. In particular Campbell's slaves charged that Caveness had refused to give Jack and his family "enough to eat," even though he had "plenty of meat and bread" to sell to other persons in the neighborhood.

During the next two weeks, Jack and Venus appealed directly to William Campbell. When Campbell visited the family, Jack accused Caveness of abusing them "without any just cause." To support the charge, the slave pointed out that recently Caveness had "knocked Edith [his youngest child] down with a handspike." The blow cut the little girl "severely on the head." And "since the first difficulty with Venus," Caveness had "knocked [her also] down with a chair." That piece of viciousness caused Venus to miscarry. On 10 June, she was reported "very bad off." Moreover, after he struck Venus, Caveness "threatened to kill her if she did not get up and go to work," according to Jack's account.

Jack therefore requested that Campbell write to William Pettigrew in order to give the planter the slaves' version of events. In the letter, Jack argued that he and his family had "worked harder" that spring than they had "ever worked in their lives," but Caveness could not be satisfied. Therefore, he implored William Pettigrew to remove them from Caveness's plantation. Jack declared his family "willing to live anywhere," even "on half feed," as long as they would "not be abused." We "did not want to put you to any trouble," Jack told his master, "but we can not stand it."

In the end, Jack and his wife prevailed. Their story had a ring of truth that even Caveness himself made no attempt to deny. Moreover, Caveness's poor reputation in the area precluded his attempt to mobilize planter opinion in his cause. Campbell considered Caveness "very hard to please" and "a very passionate man." Finally, Caveness did not help his own case when he admitted to Campbell that if he had carried his gun along, he would have "killed some of them."

But all of this might have come to nothing if Venus had not made the dispute a public event. By mobilizing local opinion, both black and white, Jack and Venus forged a means by which the Pettigrew slaves could shape their own destiny, at least in some small part. William Campbell considered his slave's version of events "only negro news" and therefore, "only to be used as such." Yet, he recommended to William Pettigrew that Jack and his family be removed from Caveness' plantation to a place where they would be "well cared for." "If Caveness is not willing to keep them and treat them humanely as other negroes are treated in this part of the country," wrote Campbell, "I should take them away."

In one sense, the customary rights of slaves acting within the rules of paternalism had been renewed. Yet, there was more to the story than a restoration of peaceable relations between masters and slaves. The abuse by Caveness of Venus and her children provided an unprecedented opportunity to challenge a slaveholder. Caveness had made certain guarantees to Pettigrew—physical safety and an adequate subsistence for the slaves—that he failed to fulfill. And ironically, by insisting on Pettigrew's rights in his property, Venus advanced her own claim as a human being. Indeed, she used those double-edged claims to turn Caveness's own class against him; she forced Pettigrew and others to recognize not only her right to safety and subsistence but also her right to be heard and recognized as a person. In doing so, Venus and Jack and all the other Pettigrew slaves participated in a much larger defining moment, the self-emancipation of America's slaves in the crucible of the Civil War.

THE JACKSONVILLE MUTINY

B. Kevin Bennett

AT 1200 HOURS on December 1, 1865, six soldiers from the 3d United States Colored Troops (USCT) were led from the guardhouse at Fort Clinch, Fernandina, Florida, and executed by a firing squad drawn from white troops at the garrison. The six soldiers, privates David Craig, Joseph Green, James Allen, Jacob Plowden, Joseph Nathaniel, and Thomas Howard, were executed for mutiny, the last servicemen in the American armed forces to be executed for this offense.[1] Inasmuch as the Civil War period marked the first time in American history that blacks served in the military in appreciable numbers, the Jacksonville Mutiny is a tragic but instructive beginning milestone from which the progress of the black soldier within the military justice system can be measured.

As a result of large scale operations and resultant massive casualties, the Civil War created a manpower crisis, which in turn led to the enlistment of large numbers of blacks into the Federal military and naval services. Free blacks served in a limited capacity in the Revolution and War of 1812, their participation limited by the relatively small number of free blacks (and by the prejudices of society). The Civil War, however, was the first real opportunity for blacks to join organized military units and to strike a blow for the freedom and status of their race. Recruitment for the military was spurred on by the exhortations of black leaders like Frederick Douglass, who declared, "let the black man get upon his person the brass letters U.S., an eagle on his button, and a musket on his shoulder and bullets in his pocket, and there is no power on earth which can deny that he has earned the right of citizenship." In

---

[1] In 1882, three Indian Scouts (Sgt. Jim Dandy, Corp. Skippy, and Sgt. Dead Shot), who were attached to the 6th U.S. Cavalry, were executed on the charge of mutiny. These individuals were in an auxiliary status as scouts, and the offense for which they were convicted should have been charged as murder. These scouts joined with a party of hostile Indians in a firefight that resulted in the death of an officer and six soldiers. See General Court Martial Order 12 of 1882.

From *Civil War History*, Vol. 38, No. 1, 1992, pp. 39-50. © 1992 by The Kent State University Press. Reprinted by permission.

response, blacks turned out in large numbers. By the end of the war, over two hundred thousand had joined the Union army and navy.[2]

One of the earliest units formed was the 3d USCT, which was organized at Camp William Penn near Philadelphia in July 1863. Comprised of escaped slaves and freedmen from the various northern states, it was, like all black units, officered by whites.[3] After a brief period of basic training, the regiment embarked in August 1863 for Morris Island, South Carolina, where it served in the trenches before Fort Wagner (a campaign recently made famous by the movie *Glory*). Having suffered substantial casualties during this campaign, the regiment was transferred in February 1864 to Jacksonville, Florida, which was occupied by Union forces. From then until the end of the war the men served on outpost duty, continually fighting skirmishes and mounting raids and expeditions into the Confederate-held interior of the state. After the cessation of hostilities, the regiment continued to be stationed in Florida on occupation duty. Assigned the unenviable chore of trying to reestablish and uphold federal authority in a hostile environment, the soldiers of the 3d USCT found the duty marked with endless hours of boredom and frustration. In the absence of the excitement and challenge of combat, many of the soldiers turned to alcohol and chafed under the continuing restrictions of military discipline.

Commanding the regiment was twenty-three-year-old Lt. Col. John L. Brower, a native of New York City. Unlike most white officers assigned to black regiments, Brower had no previous enlisted military experience when he obtained a direct commission as a captain in August 1863. Rather, it appears that he obtained his commission through political connections. Brower had only recently been promoted, assuming command on September 12, 1865, when the former regimental commander, Colonel Bardwell, was promoted to the position of military district commander.[4] Unfortunately for the enlisted rank and file, it appears that in addition to his inexperience, Brower was something of a martinet. Despite the fact that the 3d USCT had served honorably as a combat regiment and was shortly due to muster out, Brower was determined not to slacken military dis-

cipline. While strictness and control were necessary to keep troops in line during battle, this inflexible discipline only served to exacerbate an already strained relationship between most of the officers and the enlisted men of the 3d USCT. Indications of this discontent was evidenced in a "letter to the editor" from a black soldier to a black religious publication. Decrying the contemptuous and callous treatment of black laundresses and camp followers by white officers of the 3d USCT, he noted, "We have a set of officers here who apparently think that their commissions are licenses to debauch and mingle with deluded freewomen under cover of darkness. The conduct of these officers is such that their presence among us is loathsome in the extreme."[5]

For their part, the officers were concerned about the growing insubordination and drunkenness of troops. While willing to serve in black regiments despite the negative connotations attached to such an assignment, the officers were by and large a cross section of the society from which they were drawn. While they may have desired the abolition of slavery and respected the fighting qualities of their black troops, rare indeed was the individual officer untainted by some form of racism. From letters and journals it seems that most white officers considered blacks just one step removed from barbarism. As recent descendants of primitive peoples, black soldiers, so their officers felt, lacked self-control and discipline. "The Negro is very fanciful and instable in disposition," stated one officer. White officers greatly feared that their troops could go wild and riot at any time.[6] Just as the fear of brutal violence in slave revolts terrified Southerners, so too it made the Northern white officers uneasy with the possibility of armed mutiny. One officer in a black regiment wrote his wife, "I do not believe we can keep the Negroes from murdering everything they come to once they have been exposed to battle."[7] Additionally, it seems that some officers were at a loss on how to teach and administer discipline to their troops. As one enlightened regimental commander pointed out, "Inexperienced officers often assumed that because these men had been slaves before enlistment, they would bear to be treated as such afterwards. Experience proved to the contrary. Any punishment re-

sembling that meted out by overseers caused irreparable damage."[8] Given the volatile environment that existed within the regiment, it did not require much for the long-simmering discontent to explode into confrontation. The incident providing the spark occurred on Sunday, October 29, 1865, two days before the regiment was to be mustered out.

From the testimony recorded in various court-martial transcripts, it appears that during the midmorning hours of Sunday, October 29, an unnamed black soldier was apprehended while attempting to pilfer molasses from the unit kitchen. The arresting officer was Lieutenant Greybill, who was acting as Officer of the Day. Greybill then undertook to punish the soldier by having him tied up by his thumbs in the open regimental parade ground.[9] When the prisoner resisted the efforts of Greybill and Lieutenant Brown (the regimental adjutant) to tie him up, Brower arrived on the scene and the prisoner was bound "after some difficulty."[10]

During the time that the prisoner was being strung up, a crowd of enlisted men gathered and threatened to free him. Pvt. Jacob Plowden, a forty-four-year-old former slave from Tennessee, began "talking loudly" and disputed the authority of the officers to punish a man by tying him up by the thumbs. Plowden, who was alleged to "have been considerably in his liquor," stated, "it was a damn shame for a man to be tied up like that, white soldiers were not tied up that way nor other colored soldiers, only in our regiment." He further announced that "there was not going to be any more of it, that he would die on the spot but he would be damned if he wasn't the man to cut him down."[11] Plowden was not alone in his attempts to incite the crowd. Pvt. Jonathan Miller began moving among the crowed, shouting "Let's take him down, we are not going to have any more of tying men up by the thumbs."[12]

According to an eyewitness account by another officer, a group of about 35 unarmed enlisted men started advancing toward the three officers and the prisoner. Pvt. Richard Lee was in the lead, telling the crowd to "Come on, the man has been hanging there long enough." Brower, standing by the side of the prisoner, waited until the group was within 15 feet. Drawing his revolver, he fired into the crowd. Two of the shots struck Pvt. Joseph Green in the elbow and side, and he

[2] Steven A. Channing, *Confederate Ordeal* (New York: Time-Life Books, 1984), 145.

[3] Late in the war, several blacks were commissioned as officers to serve in black regiments. Additionally, several regiments of free blacks raised early in the war by General Butler and Sen. Jim Lane were officered by blacks. These officers, however, were replaced with whites.

[4] Military Service Record, John L. Brower, National Archives, Washington, D.C. (hereafter cited as NA).

[5] RHB to the editor, *A. M. E. The Christian Recorder,* August 6, 1864.

[6] Joseph Glatthaar, *Forged in Battle: The Civil War Alliance of Black Soldiers and White Officers* (New York: Free Press, 1989), 84.

[7] Ibid., 86.

[8] Thomas W. Higginson, *Army Life in a Black Regiment* (Williamstown, Mass.:

Corner House, 1971), 259.

[9] The punishment of tying up by the thumbs, while not prohibited, was looked upon with great disfavor by most commanders. A number of departmental commanders had banned the practice at the time of the incident. The punishment called for the offender to be stripped to the waist and strung up by the thumbs for several hours so that only his toes were touching the ground. This obviously was a painful punishment that could easily result in dislocated thumbs.

[10] Transcript of General Court-Martial of Pvt. Richard Lee, 001477, Record Group 153, NA.

[11] Transcript of General Court-Martial of Pvt. Jacob Plowden, ibid.

[12] Transcript of General Court-Martial of Pvt. Jonathan Miller, ibid.

fell wounded in the parade ground. Pandemonium broke loose, and the crowd retreated with a number of soldiers yelling "Go get your guns, let's shoot the Son of a Bitch."[13]

While a number of the soldiers dispersed after the firing—some 15 to 20 did, in fact, get their weapons and return to the parade area where they opened fire on Brower and other officers—Greybill departed the camp to obtain assistance from the town, several shots whistling close behind him.[14] The adjutant, Lieutenant Brown, mounted his horse and proceeded to the section of camp where Company K was located. There he attempted to have the company fall in so as to quell the mutiny. As the company was forming, several of the armed mutineers, Privates Harley, Howard, and Nathaniel, also arrived in the area. Several shots were fired at Brown whereon several soldiers forcibly subdued Nathaniel and Howard and took their muskets away. The company by this time was gathering about Brown, querying him as to what was going on. During this confusion Harley took Brown's service revolver from its holster and attempted to take him prisoner. In a matter of minutes, however, the noncommissioned officers of Company K had restored order in that area.[15]

At the time this was occurring, Lieutenant Fenno came out from his quarters to investigate the firing. He was quickly surrounded by several enlisted men whom he attempted to question. He met with curses and "improper language" from Pvt. Calvin Dowrey. Fenno responded by drawing his saber and slashing Dowrey on the left arm, slightly wounding him. While Fenno's attention was distracted by several other soldiers, Dowrey returned with a fence rail and walloped Fenno on the right side of the head. While Fenno was attempting to pick himself off the ground, another unknown soldier forced him down again into the dirt with a buttstroke of his musket. The soldier with the musket then disappeared into the crowd, and several soldiers took the fence rail away from Dowrey.[16]

Meanwhile, a fairly brisk firefight took place at the regimental parade ground between Brower and several of the mutineers. The gunfire abruptly ended after an estimated 30–40 shots when Brower's finger was shot off. Pvt. Richard Lee, one of the original instigators, yet one who had not taken up arms, rushed over to Brower and, with the help of several others, escorted him

to the relative safety of the cookhouse. Several of the mutineers followed close behind, notably Pvt. James Allen, who yelled, "Let me at him, let me shoot the son of a bitch."[17] Lee tried to ward the pursuers off, warning them to "stop their damn foolishness."[18] As Brower was seeking refuge in the cookhouse, Captain Walrath arrived with a number of troops, who disarmed the mutineers and quelled the disturbance. Brower then left the cookhouse and started for town, aided by several enlisted soldiers. A number of mutineers who had not been apprehended followed a short distance behind, shouting threats and insults. The mutiny had pretty much spent its force at this point, although Allen did take Captain Parker prisoner, tying him up in the officer's tent. Colonel Bardwell, the former regimental commander, arrived as the mutiny was winding down. Inasmuch as Bardwell was well respected by the troops, he was able to settle the situation, obtain aid for the wounded, and effect the immediate release of Parker.[19] With respect to the immediate cause of the mutiny, it appears that Pvt. James Thomas took advantage of the confusion and worked furiously to release the prisoner; however, just when he had succeeded in cutting the post down he was apprehended at gunpoint by Captain Barker.[20]

As was to be expected, fifteen of the suspected mutineers were confined, and charges drafted and preferred against them. With a speed that would please many a modern day prosecutor, a convening order was issued on October 30, 1865, with the court-martial scheduled to convene on October 31, 1865. The proceedings were a general court-martial, composed of seven officers headed by the provost marshal of the 3d USCT, Maj. Sherman Conant.[21] The accused were all offered but declined the assistance of counsel and proceeded to trial representing themselves. The separate trials began on October 31, 1865, and ran until November 3.

By the time of the Civil War, three kinds of court-martial had evolved in the army: general, regimental, and garrison. Of those, only a general court-martial could try officers and capital cases, impose sentences of death, dishonorable discharge from the service, forfeiture of more than three months pay, or any lengthy period of imprisonment.[22] A general court-martial could be convened only by the president, the secretary of war (acting under the order of the president), a general officer commanding an army, or a

colonel commanding a separate department. Exceptions made during the Civil War allowed the commander of a division or separate brigade (as was true in this case) to appoint such a court.[23]

Of the fifteen soldiers who were to stand trial, fourteen were charged with mutiny, a violation of Article 22, Articles of War. Mutiny was defined as the unlawful resistance or opposition to superior military authority, with a deliberate purpose to subvert the same or to eject that authority from office.[24] The remaining accused, Pvt. Archibald Roberts, was charged with a violation of Article 99, conduct prejudicial to the good order and military discipline. Roberts did not take part in the actual mutiny but afterwards was overheard to say, "Lt. Colonel Brower, the God-Damned Son of a Bitch, he shot my cousin. Where is he, let me see him."[25]

The maximum punishment for mutiny in time of war, rebellion, or insurrection was death by shooting. Unfortunately for the accused, Florida was still considered to be in a state of rebellion, notwithstanding that the last organized Confederate forces had surrendered in May 1865. Since a state of rebellion was considered to exist, the court-martial that was convened had the authority to assess a death penalty, and this "state of rebellion" status also limited the amount of appellate review that would be afforded to any soldier sentenced to death. In times of peace any death sentence was required to be transmitted to the secretary of war, who would review it and present it to the president for his consideration along with his recommendation.[26] If a state of war or rebellion existed, the division or department commander had the power to confirm and execute sentences of death. He could, if he so desired, suspend the execution of a death sentence so as to allow review by the president and the condemned an opportunity to petition for clemency. This suspension and review process was not required while a "state of rebellion" existed.[27]

In regard to the composition of the court-martial, black troops were afforded one advantage in that they were usually tried by officers assigned to black regiments. Although not specifically required by regulations, the practice was first instituted by Maj. Gen. Benjamin F. Butler to shield the black troops from abuse and prejudice.[28] While this was obviously a prudent safeguard for the black troops in general, it was of dubious value in a mutiny case such as this where

[13] Ibid.
[14] Transcript of General Court-Martial of Pvt. Thomas Howard, ibid.
[15] Transcript of General Court-Martial of Pvt. Joseph Nathaniel, ibid.
[16] Transcript of General Court-Martial of Pvt. Calvin Dowrey, ibid.
[17] Transcript of General Court-Martial of Pvt. James Allen, ibid.
[18] Transcript of General Court-Martial of Pvt. Richard Lee, ibid.
[19] Transcript of General Court-Martial of Pvt. Joseph Green, ibid.
[20] Transcript of General Court-Martial of Pvt. James Thomas, ibid.
[21] Special Order 189, District of East Florida, 1st Separate Brigade, Oct. 30, 1865, ibid.
[22] Du Chanel, *How Soldiers Were Tried*, Civil War Times Illustrated, Feb. 1969, p. 11.
[23] William Winthrop, *Military Law and Precedents* (Washington, D.C.: GPO, 1868), 79.
[24] Ibid., 578.
[25] General Court-Martial Transcript of Pvt. Archibald Roberts, 001477, RG 153, NA.
[26] Du Chanel, *How Soldiers Were Tried*, 12.
[27] Winthrop, *Military Law and Precedents*, Article 65, p. 618.
[28] Glatthaar, *Forged in Battle*, 199.

the prosecution witnesses were for the most part officers from the same regiment.

The trial procedure for general court-martials and utilized in the Jacksonville cases was as follows: first, the judge advocate read the order assembling the court and asked the accused if he had any objections to being tried by any member of the court. Following the negative response received in each case, the judge advocate administered the oath to each member of the court, and the president administered the oath to the judge advocate. The judge advocate then read the charges, the general nature of the offense, and the specifications. The accused would then enter his plea of guilty or not guilty. The witnesses for the prosecution were then sworn in and questioned by the judge advocate, the court, and the accused. After all its witnesses had testified and were cross-examined, the prosecution rested its case. Then the defense witnesses and the accused were sworn in, questioned, and cross-examined. Before the court was closed, the accused had the opportunity to make a statement, either oral or in writing. This statement, though not considered evidence, could be considered by the court in its deliberations. After "having maturely deliberated upon the evidence adduced," the court announced its findings, and, if the accused was found guilty, the sentence. Decisions on guilt required only a simple majority; a sentence of death, however, needed a two-thirds majority. The summarized transcript was authenticated by the judge advocate who would then forward the court record to the officer having authority to confirm the sentence.[29]

Once commenced, the Jacksonville trials were carried out with great dispatch. The longest appears to have been four hours in length, the shortest, one hour. Starting with four court-martials on October 31, three were held on November 1, three on November 2, and five on November 3. Twenty-two witnesses provided testimony in the various court-martials, the most appearances being logged by Lieutenant Brown, the prosecution's star witness. Indeed, Brown seems to have possessed an uncanny ability to remember the faces and mutinous acts of quite a number of individuals. From the testimony offered it appeared that he was most eager to provide damning evidence against the various accused. Particularly in the case of Pvt. Joseph Nathaniel, his questionable testimony that Nathaniel fired upon him cost Allen any chance of escaping the death penalty. The defense strategy, to the extent that

there was one, was first to show that a soldier had not taken up arms. If that fact was beyond controverting, then it was crucial to show that he had not fired at the white officers during the mutiny. This act clearly was the dividing line between a death sentence and a lengthy prison term. In his testimony, Brown swore that a shot that had whistled over his head came from Nathaniel's weapon. The two black noncommissioned officers who had apprehended Nathaniel and taken his weapon testified that they had not witnessed Nathaniel discharging his musket. Further, they checked his musket for signs of firing and found it capped and loaded.[30] Despite the obviously exculpatory nature of this evidence, the court-martial panel either discounted or disregarded it and found Nathaniel guilty of firing at Brown.

Another troubling feature of Brown's and several other officers' testimony was the issue of Lt. Colonel Brower firing into the unarmed group of soldiers. During the first few court-martials, all the officers including Brown testified that Brower had fired into the crowd and that the soldiers were unarmed at the time. On the second day of the proceedings, however, Brown asserted that Brower had fired warning shots into the air. Perhaps realizing the inconsistency of this testimony with the wounds suffered by Private Green, both Brown and Greybill later claimed that the crowd was armed at the time Brower opened fire.[31]

Curious also was the part played by Brower in the court-martials. He testified in only one, that of Pvt. Joseph Green. Brower did not testify about the events leading up to the mutiny, nor did he discuss the specifics of his actions or the mutiny. He testified that Green advanced upon him with a musket and that he had fired to disable Green. Green disputed that account, claiming that he had not taken up arms until after he was shot.[32] Shortly after testifying, Brower was mustered out and quickly shipped back home to New York City. In light of this, one cannot help but wonder what transpired between Brower and his superiors in the two days between the mutiny and his mustering out. Considering his incredible overreaction by opening fire combined with his allowing punishments that, while not specifically prohibited, were looked upon with great disfavor, one has to suspect that the command was anxious to be rid of an embarrassment.

Given the expedited nature of the proceedings and the sentences handed down, one might readily conclude that the trials were nothing more than "kangaroo courts."

Notwithstanding the brevity of the trials and the fact that the accused were not represented by counsel, it appears that the president, Major Conant, endeavored to ensure each accused a full and fair hearing. Conant, a former noncommissioned officer with the 39th Massachusetts Volunteers, consistently asked questions of the various witnesses in an effort to ascertain facts and resolve inconsistencies. Unfortunately, the same balanced approach was lacking from the judge advocate, Lieutenant Knight. Procedurally, he was required to assist the accused in eliciting favorable testimony when they were not represented by counsel, but his questions were leading and seemed designed to elicit only incriminating evidence.[33]

When the last court-martial had adjourned on November 3, thirteen of the accused had been found guilty of mutiny. Another, Private Roberts, was convicted of conduct prejudicial to good order. Only one accused, Pvt. Theodore Waters, was acquitted of the charge of mutiny. Privates Plowden, Craig, Allen, Howard, Green, and Nathaniel were sentenced to execution by shooting. Private Dowrey received a sentence of fifteen years at hard labor with Privates Morie and Harley receiving ten years. A sentence of two years at hard labor was adjudged against Privates Lee (both Richard and Alexander), Miller, and Thomas. Roberts received a relatively light sentence of two months' confinement. All received dishonorable discharges and total forfeiture of pay.[34]

Upon the conclusion of the trials, the mission of mustering out the remainder of the regiment was completed. The court record was authenticated and forwarded for review on November 10 to the department commander, Maj. Gen. John Foster.[35] In reviewing the records, Foster declined to exercise any leniency, approving each finding of guilty and adjudging sentence. Interestingly, Foster disapproved the findings of not guilty with respect to Private Waters, noting on the record that there was insufficient evidence![36] Foster set the execution date for December 1, 1865, between the hours of noon and 2 P.M. and further designated the place of imprisonment as Fort Jefferson, located on Dry Tortugas Island in the Florida Keys.[37]

The court records of the proceedings were apparently forwarded to the Bureau of Military Justice in Washington, D.C. on November 13, 1865, but no actual legal review of the cases appears to have taken place until after the executions. This was evidenced by the troubling case of Pvt. David Craig, one of the soldiers sentenced to death. Contained

[29] Winthrop, *Military Law and Precedents,* Article 65, p. 618.

[30] Transcript of General Court-Martial of Pvt. Joseph Nathaniel, 001477, RG 153, NA.

[31] Transcript of General Court-Martial of Pvt. Sam Harley, 001477, RG 153, NA.

[32] Transcript of General Court-Martial of Pvt. Joseph Green, ibid.

[33] Winthrop, *Military Law and Precedents,* Article 35, p. 592.

[34] General Orders 39, Dept. of Florida, Nov. 13, 1865, 001477, RG 153, NA.

[35] Foster had earlier risen to prominence as an officer in the besieged garrison of Fort Sumter in April 1861.

[36] Transcript of General Court-Martial of Pvt. Thomas Waters, 001477, RG 153, NA.

[37] This was the same infamous prison where the alleged Lincoln conspirators, Dr. Samuel Mudd and Michael O'Laughlin, were incarcerated.

with Craig's service file is a letter from his foster father H. C. Marehand, dated December 10, 1865, to U.S. Sen. Edgar Cowan (Pa.) requesting that the sentence of execution be suspended pending a review and investigation of the case. Craig, a twenty-one-year-old laborer from Pennsylvania, had been raised by Marehand. The letter indicated that Marehand had received correspondence the previous day from Craig indicating his dilemma and proclaiming his innocence in that "he [Craig] had been excused to take the guns from some of the mutineers and then was arrested."[38] In response to the congressional inquiry, a telegraph was sent to General Foster to suspend the sentence and to transmit the record for review. Unfortunately the telegraph and suspension were too late as the executions had been carried out nine days earlier. Foster replied by telegraph on December 16 informing the War Department of the execution and the fact that the court records had been forwarded on November 13. There is an additional handwritten notation on the telegraph: "Senator Cowan informed, Dec 20."[39] Apart from the question of the late delivery of Craig's letter and the belated legal review is the mystery of what happened to the record of Craig's court-marital. Among all the records arising from the Jacksonville Mutiny, his record alone has either been lost or destroyed.

Fortunately for the imprisoned soldiers the legal process did not end with the deaths of their six comrades. In December 1865, a review of the court-martial records was accomplished by the judge advocate general of the army, Joseph Holt. Although his review was limited to strictly procedural matters, a further review on the merits was conducted by the Bureau of Military Justice in late 1866, which resulted in the prison sentences of the surviving mutineers being commuted. Pvt. Jonathan Miller was released in November 1866, and the others, Privates Calvin Dowrey, Morie, Harley, Thomas, and Alexander Lee, were discharged in January 1867. Pvt. Richard Lee had previously died from typhoid fever.[40]

From that point the lives of the participants in the mutiny slip into obscurity. Of the officers, there remains no further record of Lt. Col. Brower as he failed to file for a pension. Lieutenant Brown returned to Indiana, married, and died in 1912.[41] Major Conant left active duty immediately after the trials. Interested in promoting the welfare of newly freed blacks, he accepted a position with the Freedman's Bureau in Florida. He later returned to New England and died in Connecticut in 1924.[42] Of the black mutineers who survived prison, even less is known. Having been dishonorably discharged they were ineligible to apply for a military pension, thus no recorded information is available. About the only postscript is a letter contained within the file of Pvt. Jacob Plowden. Dated in 1878, it was written by his brother on behalf of Plowden's minor son Jesse, attempting to collect any arrears in pay due Plowden.

In light of the severe sentences handed down, it appears that the court-martial failed to consider as mitigating the egregious actions of the commanding officer. By his condoning the use of a disreputable and inflammatory punishment and in imprudently firing into a group of unarmed soldiers, he essentially provoked an armed mutiny from what appeared to be insubordination. While it is perhaps too easy to criticize the commander's actions, less drastic methods could have been used to quell the initial disturbance. Nor were the harsh sentences meted out that unusual in the context of the black soldier in the Civil War. While blacks comprised 9 percent of the total manpower in the Union Army, they accounted for just under 80 percent of the soldiers executed for the offense of mutiny during the Civil War period.[43] Based upon this statistical data, the appearance of disproportionate punishment and racial bias in mutiny cases is clearly suggested. Additionally, one has to question the fairness of these court-martials given their composition, the absence of defense counsel, and the rapid fashion in which they were tried and the sentences carried out. While the concept of due process was not well defined, even by the minimal standards of the time, an element of fairness was lacking.

In reviewing the transcripts and the testimony offered, however, there seems to be little doubt that Privates Plowden, Green, Howard, and Allen were among the group of soldiers that took up arms and fired upon their officers. Additionally there was no dispute that Privates Nathaniel, Morie, and Alexander Lee took up arms; however, there was considerable evidence that they did not fire their weapons. In the case of Lee, which was the shortest court-martial, the accused merely proffered that he had been drunk during the mutiny and did not remember a thing. With respect to the cases of privates Harley, Dowrey, Richard Lee, Miller, and Thomas, the court was probably justified in finding them guilty of mutiny for their various acts in inciting, assisting, and attempting to free the prisoner. Likewise there was no dispute that Roberts had uttered the disrespectful language about Brower in public hearing and was guilty of conduct prejudicial to good order. Therefore, with the exception of the unusual case of Craig, it seems likely that the findings of guilty on the charges of mutiny were supported by the evidence.

The Jacksonville Mutiny was a tragedy. Black soldiers had achieved remarkable gains through their noteworthy participation in the Civil War, not the least of which was the end of slavery. Their gains in the administration of military justice was less evident.

[38] H. C. Marehand to Sen. Edgar Cowan, Dec. 10, 1865, Military Service Record of Pvt. David Craig, NA.
[39] Gen. John Foster to Col. J. A. Hardie, Dec. 16, 1865, Military Service Record of Pvt. David Craig, NA.
[40] Monthly Returns from Fort Jefferson, Florida, File 10-27-1, Returns from Army Posts (National Archives Microfilm Publication M617, Roll 542), NA.
[41] Military Service Records, Cyrus W. Brown, NA.
[42] Military Service Records, Sherman Conant, NA.
[43] Robert I. Alotta, *Civil War Justice: Union Army Executions under Lincoln* (Shippensburg, Penn.: White Mane, 1989), 26.

The image of the American Civil War as a 'white man's fight' became the national norm almost as soon as the last shot was fired. **Susan-Mary Grant** looks at the experience and legacy of the conflict for black Americans.

PRIDE AND PREJUDICE IN THE AMERICAN CIVIL WAR

... You can say of the colored man, we too have borne our share of the burden. We too have suffered and died in defence of that starry banner which floats only over free men. ... I feel assured that the name of the colored soldier will stand out in bold relief among the heroes of this war. ...

(Henry S. Harmon, 3rd United States Colored Infantry, October 1863)

Far better the slow blaze of Learning's light,
The cool and quiet of her dearer fane,
Than this hot terror of a hopeless fight,
This cold endurance of the final pain,
Since thou and those who with thee died for right
Have died, the Present teaches, but in vain!

(Paul Laurence Dunbar, 'Robert Gould Shaw.')

In 1897, over thirty years after the end of the American Civil War, a very special monument to that war was erected opposite the Statehouse in Boston. Designed by the Irish-born sculptor Augustus Saint-Gaudens, it depicted in profile the figure of Robert Gould Shaw, the twenty-five-year-old white officer of the North's showcase black regiment, the Massachusetts 54th, leading his men through Boston on their way to South Carolina in 1863. An unusual piece of sculpture, Saint-Gaudens had worked hard to avoid representing the black troops in any kind of stereotypical manner, portraying them instead as noble patriot soldiers of the American nation. Both in its novelty and in its sentiment the monument remains impressive according to the art critic Robert Hughes, 'the most intensely felt image of military commemoration made by an American.'

However, the Saint-Gaudens monument in no way reflected the general mood of the American people towards those black troops who had fought in the conflict, as the poet Paul Laurence Dunbar's response to Shaw's sacrifice reveals. Between 1863, when Henry Harmon expressed his optimism about history's treatment of the black soldier, and 1897, the American nation had all but forgotten that black troops had ever played a role in the Civil War. Both Saint-Gaudens and Dunbar were working at a time when segregation was beginning to bite in the South with the 'Jim Crow' Laws, but the exclusion of black troops from the national memory of the Civil War began long before the 1890s. In the Grand Review of the Armed Forces which followed the cessation of hostilities very few blacks were represented. Relegated to the end of the procession in 'pitch and shovel' brigades or intended only as a form of comic relief, neither the free black soldier nor the former slave was accorded his deserved role in this poignant national pageant. Rather than a war fought for liberty, in which the role of the African-American soldier was pivotal, the image of the American Civil War as a 'white man's fight' became the norm almost as soon as the last shot was fired.

The relationship between the black soldier and the 'land of the free' has always been ambiguous. The involvement of black troops in America's wars from colonial times onwards followed a depressing pattern. Encouraged to enlist in times of crisis, the African-American soldier's services were clearly unwelcome in time of peace. Despite this, the link between fighting and freedom for African-Americans was forged in the earliest days of the American nation, and once forged proved resilient. During the colonial era, South Carolina enacted legislation that offered freedom to slaves in return for their military services. By the conclusion of the American Revolution military service was regarded as a valid and successful method of achieving freedom for the slave, as well as an important expression of patriotism and loyalty to the nation.

It was unsurprising, therefore, that when hostilities commenced between North and South in 1861 blacks throughout the North, and some in the South too, sought to enlist. However, free blacks who responded to Abraham Lincoln's call for 75,000 volunteers found that

This article first appeared in *History Today*, September 1998, pp. 41-48. © 1998 by History Today, Ltd. Reprinted by permission.

their services were not required by a North in which slavery had been abolished but racist assumptions still prevailed. Instead they were told that the war was a 'white man's fight,' and offered no role for them. The notable black leader, Frederick Douglass, himself an escaped slave, summed the matter up:

> Colored men were good enough to fight under Washington. They are not good enough to fight under McClellan. They were good enough to fight under Andrew Jackson. They are not good enough to fight under Gen. Halleck. They were good enough to help win American independence but they are not good enough to help preserve that independence against treason and rebellion.

Douglass further recognised that unless the issues of arming free blacks and of freeing the slaves were addressed, the Union stood slim chance of success. The Union, however, showed little sign of heeding his warnings. In the early months of the conflict the *National Intelligencer* reinforced the view that the war 'has no direct relation to slavery. It is a war for the restoration of the Union under the existing constitution.' Yet under the pressures of conflict it became increasingly difficult to maintain such a limited policy. This was particularly true for those generals in the field who found themselves having to deal with both the free black population and a growing number of slaves who, dislocated by the war, were making their way to Union lines. Whilst the Federal Government prevaricated on the question of arming blacks for a variety of mainly political reasons, the Union generals found themselves faced with a problem that required immediate resolution. Consequently, the first moves towards both arming blacks and freeing slaves during the American Civil War came not from Washington but from the front line.

Initial steps in this direction proved clumsy, though an important precedent as far as the slaves were concerned was set early on in the conflict. In 1861 Benjamin A. Butler, in charge of Fortress Monroe in Virginia, declared that all slaves who escaped to Union lines were 'contraband of war' and refused to uphold the terms of the Fugitive Slave Law, which bound him to return to their owners. Butler's policy did not have much of an impact on attitudes in Washington, but it did reinforce the views of those who felt that slavery was of great military use to the Confederacy and ought to be attacked on those grounds alone. In Missouri in 1861, John C. Fremont, commander of the Department of the West, declared all slaves owned by Confederate sympathisers to be free. Lincoln insisted that Fremont modify his announcement to bring it into line with the 1861 Confiscation Act, which removed slaves only from those actively engaged in hostilities against the Union.

In late March 1862, Major General David Hunter, commander of the Department of the South, emancipated all slaves held in Georgia, South Carolina and Florida, and forced as many escaped male slaves as he could find into military service. Not only was Hunter's announcement rejected by Lincoln, but the aggressive manner in which he went about recruiting blacks for the Union army served only to alienate the very people he was attempting to help. Thomas Wentworth Higginson, the white officer in charge of what became the First South Carolina Volunteers, was in no doubt that the suspicion his troops expressed towards the Federal Government was the natural legacy of bitter distrust bequeathed by the abortive regiment of General Hunter.' More successful were the efforts of Jim Lane in Kansas. A former US Senator and a brigadier general in the Union army, Lane chose simply to ignore the War Department and raised a black regiment, the First Kansas Colored Volunteers, in 1862. This regiment was finally recognised the following year, by which time it had already seen active service against the Confederacy.

Although the War Department sanctioned the recruitment of black troops in August 1862, black regiments were not properly raised until after Lincoln's Emancipation Proclamation of January 1st, 1863. The decision came at a time when the war was not going well for the Union, and coincided with the first draft in the North. In some ways this helped. Racist objections to the arming of blacks could easily, if cynically, be countered on the grounds that it was better that a black soldier die than a white one. As John M. Broomall, Congressman from Pennsylvania noted:

> I have never found the most *shaky* constituent of mine, who, when he was drafted, refused to let the blackest negro in the district go as a substitute for him.

Abraham Lincoln acknowledged such sentiments in his famous letter to James Conkling, written in August, 1863, in which he defended his emancipation decision. 'You say you will not fight to free negroes. Some of them seem willing to fight for you,' Lincoln noted, 'but no matter. . . . I thought that whatever Negroes could be got to do as soldiers leaves just so much less for white soldiers to do, in saving the Union'. He concluded:

> . . . there will be some black men who can remember that, with silent tongue and clenched teeth, and steady eye, and well-poised bayonet, they have helped mankind on to this great consummation; while, I fear, there will be some white ones unable to forget that, with malignant heart, and deceitful speech, they have strove to hinder it.

For many blacks, Lincoln's latter point was the important one. They were initially confident that their acceptance, however reluctantly granted, by the Union army offered them the opportunity both of short-term military glory and longer-term acceptance into the nation as a whole. As Frederick Douglass put it:

> Once let the black man get upon his person the brass letters US, let him get an eagle on his button, and a musket on his shoulder and bullets in his pocket, and there is no power on earth which can deny that he has earned the right to citizenship in the United States.

Corporal James Henry Gooding, a former seaman and volunteer in the Massachusetts 54th, anticipated that 'if the colored man proves to be as good a soldier as it is confidently expected he will, there is a permanent field of employment opened to him, with all the chances of promotion in his favor.' The First Arkansas Colored Regiment had an equally optimistic view of the future. They gleefully marched into battle singing, to the tune of 'John Brown's Body':

> We have done with hoeing cotton, we have done with hoeing corn,
> We are colored Yankee soldiers, now, as sure as you are born;
> When the masters hear us yelling, they'll think it's Gabriel's horn,
> As it went sounding on.

They will have to pay us wages, the
wages of their sin,
They will have to bow their foreheads
to their colored kith and kin,
They will have to give us house-room,
or the roof shall tumble in!
As we go marching on.

Not everyone shared such optimism.
One black New Yorker argued that it
would be foolish for blacks to heed the
Union's call to arms since the race had
no reason 'to fight under the flag which
gives us no protection.' Initially, this
pessimistic view appeared to be the
more realistic. The white response to the
raising of black regiments was far from
positive, and inspired a backlash against
the whole idea of emancipation. Notwithstanding racist arguments in favour
of blacks rather than whites being killed,
most whites did not believe that blacks
would make effective soldiers, seeing
them as cannon fodder at best. Attitudes
began to change only with the battlefield
successes of several of the black regiments. Even before its official recognition by the War Department, Jim Lane's
black regiment had performed well in
Missouri, prompting one journalist to
write that it was 'useless to talk any
more about negro courage. The men
fought like tigers, each and every one
of them.' Skirmishes between Thomas
Wentworth Higginson's First South
Carolina and the rebels, and between
Benjamin Butler's Second Louisiana
Native Guards and Confederate cavalry
and infantry regiments were equally decisive in terms of proving that the black
troops could and would fight, but did
little to alter the northern public's perception of the black regiments. The first
major engagement for those came in the
spring of 1863, with an assault on Port
Hudson on the Mississippi in Louisiana.
The assault itself was misconceived, and
the Union army suffered a defeat, but
for the black troops who had fought
there Port Hudson proved a turning
point of sorts. One lieutenant reported
that his company had fought bravely,
adding 'they are mostly contrabands,
and I must say I entertained some fears
as to their pluck. But I have none now'.
The New York *Times* was similarly impressed:

Those black soldiers had never before
been in any severe engagement. They
were comparatively raw troops, and
were yet subjected to the most awful
ordeal that even veterans ever have to

experience—the charging upon fortifications through the crash of belching
batteries. The men, white or black,
who will not flinch from that will
flinch from nothing. It is no longer
possible to doubt the bravery and
steadiness of the colored race, when
rightly led.

If further proof were required that the
black soldier had potential, one of the
Civil War's most bloody engagements,
the battle of Milliken's Bend, fought
shortly after the Port Hudson defeat,
provided it. Here, too, raw black recruits
found themselves facing substantial
Confederate forces. In the black units
engaged, casualties ran to 35 per cent
and for the Ninth Louisiana Infantry
alone casualties reached 45 per cent.
The cost was high but, as at Port Hudson, white commanders declared themselves impressed with the behaviour
under fire of the black troops. Charles
A. Dana, the Assistant Secretary of War,
concluded that:

The sentiment in regard to the employment of negro troops has been
revolutionized by the bravery of the
blacks in the recent Battle of
Miliken's Bend. Prominent officers,
who used in private to sneer at the
idea, are now heartily in favor of it.

At the same time as black soldiers
were proving their valour on the Mississippi at Port Hudson and Milliken's
Bend, the North's most famous black
regiment, the Massachusetts 54th, was
preparing to set off for its first major
campaign and a place in the history
books. Fort Wagner, on the northern
tip of Morris Island in South Carolina,
was the main defence both for Charleston and for Battery Gregg which
overlooked the entrance to Charleston
Harbour. The taking of the fort would
have been a significant prize for the
Union forces, enabling them to attack
Fort Sumter and hopefully Charleston
itself. Originally, the plan had been to
use the 54th in a minor supporting
role, but its commander, Robert Gould
Shaw, recognised the importance of
being seen to take an active part in the
forthcoming engagement and cam-
paigned vigorously for his regiment to
be given a more prominent place in the
attack. He was successful, and the
54th received orders to head the attack
on the fort on July 18th, 1863.

As with Port Hudson, the attack on
Fort Wagner, one of the most heavily defended of the Confederate forts, was
doomed to failure, and the Union forces
sustained heavy casualties. The Massachusetts 54th lost over half its men, including Shaw who was shot through the
heart as he took the parapet of the fort.
His troops held the ground he had
reached for barely an hour. Yet in the
more general battle against racism Fort
Wagner, like Port Hudson, was a significant success. The New York *Tribune* reminded its readers that:

If this Massachusetts Fifty-fourth had
faltered when its trial came, two hundred thousand colored troops for
whom it was a pioneer would never
have been put into the field. . . . But
it did not falter. It made Fort Wagner
such a name to the colored race as
Bunker Hill has been for ninety years
to the white Yankees. . . . To this Massachusetts 54th was set the stupen-
dous task to convince the white race
that colored troops would fight,—and
not only that they would fight, but that
they could be made, in every sense of
the word, soldiers.

Thanks in part to the bravery of the
Massachusetts 54th, therefore, by the
end of 1863 the Union army had recruited some 50,000 African-Americans—both free blacks and former
slaves—to its ranks. By the end of the
war this number had risen to around
186,000, of which 134,111 were recruited in the slave states. African-
American troops comprised 10 per cent
of the total Union fighting force, and
some 3,000 of them died on the battlefield plus many more in the prisoner of
war camps, if they made it that far.
Overall, one third of all African-Americans who fought were casualties of the
Civil War.

The propaganda success of the assaults on Port Hudson, Milliken's Bend
and Fort Wagner were, however, only
part of the story as far as the African-
American troops were concerned. The
fact that blacks had shown that they
could fight in no way diminished the
prejudice they experienced in the Union
army. Nor did it resolve the crux of the
issue which was that the war, for many
of the black troops, was in essence a
very different conflict from that experienced by the whites. In purely practical
terms, the conditions experienced by African-American troops were far inferior

to those experienced by some white ones. It is important not to overstate this, however. By the time the black regiments were raised and sent into the field the Civil War had been going on for almost two years. Fresh recruits, therefore, of whatever colour, found themselves facing a rebel army with much more combat experience. At Milliken's Bend, for example, the most experienced officers had been in uniform for less than a month. Even worse, some of the black troops had received only two days of target practice prior to the battle, and in a war where fast reloading was crucial for survival they simply lacked the necessary skill.

The African-American regiments also received a greater proportion of fatigue duty than many of the white regiments, thereby denying them essential fighting experience. The quality of weapons distributed to them was also not always on a par with those the white regiments received, although again it is important to bear in mind that adequate weaponry was a problem for many regiments, both black and white. Medical care for the black regiments was equally inadequate, and a particular problem given the high rate of combat casualties in these regiments. Many of the black troops, being relatively new to the field, had little immunity to the diseases that infected the camps, and the problem was compounded by a white assumption that blacks were not as susceptible to disease as whites. Finding surgeons to work with black troops was also difficult. Again, racism alone does not account for this. By 1863 there was a general shortage of physicians in the Union army, and those that could put up with the rigours of camp life had long ago been snapped up by regiments formed earlier in the war.

Unfortunately, deliberately prejudicial policies compounded the more general problems that the African-American regiments faced after 1863. Most obviously, blacks were never promoted on a par with whites. Benjamin Butler, in mustering in the Louisiana regiments, had created a mixed officer class. Jim Lane in Kansas did likewise, and since he was acting against orders anyway he never troubled himself to defend his actions. However, when Governor Andrew sought to appoint black officers to the Massachusetts 54th and 55th, he was told that white officers only would be accepted. Similarly, when Jim Lane's

Kansas regiments were officially recognised, its black officers were not. In the South, Nathaniel Prentiss Banks, on taking over from Butler, promptly set about removing all the black officers, usually by forcing them to resign. In many cases the argument used to defend such blatant racism was that blacks lacked the necessary literacy skills and knowledge to cope with high command. In many cases, particularly as far as the contraband regiments were concerned, there was an element of truth to the charge. The white officers were no more capable in this regard than the blacks: the only difference was that the white officers were not being put under the microscope to the same extent. By the conclusion of the war only one in 2,000 black troops had achieved officer rank, and these mostly by the indirect route of becoming either chaplains or physicians.

Of all the discriminatory policies to impact on the African-American regiments, however, the most damning related to pay. At the outset there was no indication that the War Department intended to pay black troops less than whites. When Governor Andrew was granted permission to raise the Massachusetts 54th, he was instructed to offer $13 per month, plus rations and clothing, along with a bounty of $50 for signing up and $100 on mustering out. However in June 1863, the War Department decided that black troops were entitled to only $10 per month, of which $3 should be deducted for clothing. The reasoning was that the raising of black regiments came under the Militia Act of 1862, which specified the lower rate of pay on the grounds that it was intended for noncombatants.

The matter prompted an angry backlash from black troops and many of the officers. Governor Andrew, embarrassed at the turn of events, offered to make up the difference out of his own pocket, but the 54th would not let him. There was a principle at stake. As one black volunteer put it:

Now it seems strange to me that we do not receive the same pay and rations as the white soldiers. Do we not fill the same ranks? Do we not cover the same space of ground? Do we not take up the same length of ground in a graveyard that others do? The ball does not miss the black man and strike the white, nor the white and strike the black.

Corporal John B. Payne, of the Massachusetts 55th, declared his unwillingness 'to fight for anything less than the white man fights for'. The issue of pay went beyond prejudice alone. It represented the crux of the problem for those black regiments who fought in the Civil War, and threw into sharp focus many of the inconsistencies and contradictions that lay at the heart of Union war aims. The Union had, from the outset, been faced with two distinct yet linked problems: the role of the free black and the future of the slave. Equality and emancipation were not synonymous, yet one could not be addressed without affecting the other. The question over the citizenship right of free northern blacks went hand in hand with the larger and more troubling question of slavery—for many the root cause of the conflict. Northern blacks were well aware of this and, unlike northern whites, could not and would not avoid the wider implication of the conflict. Many blacks saw the Civil War as a battle for emancipation long before it became apparent that Lincoln shared this view and far ahead of a northern public who regarded it as a war for the restoration of the Union as it had been, with slavery intact. Frederick Douglass, for one, was of the opinion that the future of the American Republican experiment itself rested on the triumph of the black soldier and the freed slave. For Douglass, the evil of slavery had corrupted the white man as much as it had degraded the slave, and the Civil War was an opportunity not just to end the institution but to rededicate the nation to the principles set out in the Declaration of Independence. Freedom for both white and black depended not just on a Union victory but on complete reassessment of the national ideal. As he summed it up to a Boston audience in 1862:

My friends, the destiny of the colored American, however this mighty war shall terminate, is the destiny of America. We shall never leave you. The allotments of Providence seem to make the black man of America the open book out of which the American people are to learn lessons of wisdom, power, and goodness—more sublime and glorious than any yet attained by the nations of the old or the new world. Over the bleeding back of the American bondsman we shall learn mercy. In the very extreme difference of color and feature of the negro and the Anglo-Saxon, shall be learned the highest ideas of sacredness of man and the fullness and protection of human brotherhood.

Ultimately, the problem facing both African-American soldiers and their spokesmen in the North was that their vision of the meaning of the Civil War clashed with that of the majority of whites. For blacks, the Civil War offered an opportunity not just to end slavery, but to redefine American national ideals. Their determination to fight in the face of hostility and prejudice left their dedication to these ideals in no doubt whatsoever. In this regard, their experience of the Civil War gave them a far more expansive, optimistic and demanding vision of the nation's future than it did many whites. As George Stephens of the Massachusetts 54th noted 'this land must be consecrated to freedom, and we are today the only class of people in the country who are earnestly on the side of freedom'. This was not a message that whites wished to hear.

Ultimately, the nation as a whole chose to ignore both the sacrifice of the black regiments and the implications of their involvement in America's greatest national crisis. As North and South came together over an increasingly selective interpretation of what the Civil War had been about, the opportunity to reconstruct the nation on a new basis of equality was thrown away. On Memorial Day 1871, speaking at the Tomb of the Unknown Soldier at Arlington, Frederick Douglass lamented the call 'in the name of patriotism to forget the merits of this fearful struggle, and to remember with equal admiration those who struck at the nation's life, and those who struck to save it.' In the end, the need to find some common ground between North and South encouraged the growth of a patriotism that rejected the pride of those black troops who had fought and died for the nation.

On May 31st, 1997, a hundred years after the Saint-Gaudens monument was first unveiled, a re-dedication ceremony was held at the site. The day included an historical reenactment of Shaw's troops leaving for the South and a speech by General Colin Powell in which he drew parallels between the Union's decision to raise black regiments during the Civil War and the contemporary army's leading role in the fight for racial equality in America today. Despite Powell's words, the many thousands of books written on the American Civil War to date and the cinematic success of the Hollywood film about the Massachusetts 54th, *Glory,* the war continues to be regarded by many as a white man's war. The overt racism of 1897 has dissipated, yet the significance of the black soldier in America's bloodiest conflict continues to be downplayed.

FOR FURTHER READING:

Ira Berlin, et al., *Slaves No More: Three Essays on Emancipation and the Civil War* (Cambridge University Press, 1992); Joseph T. Glatthaar, *Forged in Battle: The Civil War Alliance of Black Soldiers and White Officers* (Penguin/Meridian Books, 1991); Hondon B. Hargrove, *Black Union Soldiers in the Civil War* (McFarland, 1988); James G. Hollandsworth, Jr., *The Louisiana Native Guards: The Black Military Experience During the Civil War* (Louisiana State University Press, 1995); Ervin L. Jordan, Jr., *Black Confederates and Afro-Yankees in Civil War Virginia* (University Press of Virginia, 1995); Edwin S. Redkey (ed.), *A Grand Army of Black Men: Letters from African-American Soldiers in the Union Army, 1861–1865* (Cambridge University Press, 1992).

Susan-Mary Grant is a lecturer in history at the University of Newcastle upon Tyne. She is the author of The American Civil War *(UCL Press, forthcoming).*

FORGOTTEN REBELS

Blacks Who Served the Confederacy

Craig J. Renner

Rick Ford, twenty-six, learned about the Civil War exploits of his great-great-grandfather, John J. Jenkins, from his great-grandmother.

"He was at the Battle of Gettysburg," Ford remembers. "He would tell her about it when she was a child. He would break out in a sweat, get tears in his eyes when he talked about it."

Since then, he has spent a great deal of time trying to confirm through military records his ancestor's service in the war. "The only unit I can document him being with is the First Maryland regiment," Ford says. The only thing he knows for sure is that Jenkins left his home in Charles County in southern Maryland, crossed the Potomac River that separates the Free State from Virginia (and, at that time, Union and rebel states), and was mustered into Confederate service around Petersburg in 1862. Ford has extensively searched through rosters of Virginia soldiers and has found enlistment records, though incomplete, for several soldiers with the name John Jenkins.

Ford isn't sure which one is his relative, though, in part because of a complicating factor in his search: John Jenkins was a free black man,

"and the [Virginia Confederate enlistment] records don't give any indication if a soldier was black or white," says Ford.

A unique and often overlooked story in American history is the role free blacks and slaves played in the Confederate war effort. A wealth of historical and anecdotal records suggests that blacks' support of the lost cause was considerable, though not overwhelming, and that their motivations were sometimes patriotic, more often pragmatic. The question of whether to use blacks as armed soldiers divided the rebel cause for most of the war. It remains a controversial issue 130 years later, even as a few historians—and an increasing number of African Americans like Rick Ford—try to assess the meaning of this forgotten factor in history.

Minority within a minority

Determining the exact number of blacks who served with or assisted rebel forces is impossible. Ervin L. Jordan, Jr., of the University of Virginia, who has extensively studied the history of black Confederates, has estimated that approximately 15 percent of

slaves and 25 percent of free blacks in secessionist Virginia supported the Confederacy.

In many cases, they enlisted and fought. At the Battle of Antietam in 1862, over three hundred fully armed and uniformed blacks were observed to be under the command of Gen. Stonewall Jackson. Describing black soldiers that he directed, Gen. Nathan Bedford Forrest stated that "finer Confederates did not live." But in the large majority of cases, they provided unarmed civilian labor for the rebel army by building fortifications, serving as cooks, and performing the countless other tasks necessary to fielding an army. Those who could provide skilled labor, such as blacksmiths, were often put into service as well.

That should not be surprising, says Ed Smith, a history professor at American University in Washington, D.C., and another leading scholar in this field.

"Support is the better part of any military," remarks Smith. "For every guy out there shooting a gun, there's another eight or ten backing him up. If your support lines aren't right, you're wasting the lives of brave men, because you didn't prepare for the situation correctly." For com-

JULIO ZANGRONIZ/ZANGRONIZ PHOTOGRAPHY

Rick Ford *(right)* and his half brother, Kevin Craig, participate as Confederates in a living history presentation in Cedar Creek, Virginia.

Smith. "The only people who traveled extensively in the antebellum South were the wealthy and their servants. So they would pick up a tremendous amount of knowledge through association." He points out that Jedediah Hotchkiss, the cartographer for and close adviser of Stonewall Jackson, was black.

To illustrate his point, Smith recounts the story of Robert Smalls of South Carolina, a black man who became a congressman from the Palmetto State during Reconstruction.

"He [Smalls] was a very good seaman. On one occasion, he stole a ship out of a South Carolina harbor and was able to navigate it into open water," says Smith. "When Robert E. Lee learned of this, he was outraged. Lee knew that this meant that the South was vulnerable to naval attack by the Union." This was particularly true of areas of Virginia that could be reached via the various inlets of the Chesapeake Bay.

Still, for most of the war, blacks who served in Confederate units did so in an unofficial capacity; rebel political leaders and army officers, like their Union counterparts, were split on the question of whether to enlist blacks in the Southern army.

In his book, *Black Confederates and Afro-Yankees in Civil War Virginia*, Jordan notes that Gen. Patrick Cleburne argued that ending slavery and arming blacks would gain Britain's support and transform the Confederate effort into one seeking independence for all Southerners. Contrarily, the feelings of those who opposed the idea were best summarized by a wealthy Georgian, Howell Cobb: "If slaves will make good soldiers, our whole theory of slavery is wrong."

In March 1865, facing massive shortages of manpower and almost certain defeat, the Confederate Congress finally authorized the raising of 300,000 troops "irrespective of color." The directive also stipulated that no slave would be forced to

manders on both sides, he points out, conscripting blacks became a military necessity.

Smith also believes that blacks provided another aspect critical to military success: knowledge of the terrain of the South, especially Virginia's Shenandoah Valley.

"Many slaves, especially those connected to a wealthy household, had a far better understanding of the South than most whites," contends

COURTESY OF THE MUSEUM OF THE CONFEDERACY, RICHMOND, VIRGINIA

Above: Jefferson Shields, Stonewall Jackson's cook, displays his rebel medals in a photo taken after the war. Several blacks served in the Confederate leader's inner circle. *Above right:* J.B. White and John Terrill of the Sixth Tennessee Cavalry.

fight and all would be given their freedom upon being honorably discharged. Notably, however, it did not include any provisions for the freedom of a slave's family and failed to draw the British government into supporting the rebellion.

But in some respects, the debate that tied up the Confederate Congress had already been decided in the field, argues Smith. Most rebel units were state militias, he notes. And since the secessionist ideal the units fought for was based on the concept of states' rights, "these states reserved the right to do pretty much whatever they wanted. And they were not going to let a bunch of politicians in Richmond tell them the composition of their units." As a result, blacks served as individuals, as servants with masters who had enlisted, and in predominantly or all-black units as early as 1861, and they were present as Confederates at all the major battles of the war.

Pragmatic patriots

In examining the role of blacks in the Confederacy, the question immediately arises: Why would blacks defend a society in which they were being enslaved? Most at least privately agreed with the feeling of one slave, who is reputed to have said during the debate over whether to officially arm blacks, "Just give us the guns, and you'll see what side we point them at."

The motivation of black rebels was explained by historian Benjamin Quarles. He said that free blacks "had a sense of community responsibility which impelled them to throw their lot with their neighbor," despite their personal dislike of slavery.

Historian Smith agrees. "The assumption is that all blacks were slaves and all slaves were mistreated, so therefore somebody who fought for the Confederacy had to

be out of his mind," argues Smith. But he contends that blacks in the South fought for the Confederacy out of feelings of patriotism, loyalty, friendship: "all the reasons you would fight for your country.

"To make this story true, you have to downplay the coercion," he contends. "They weren't sure how it would turn out for them, so they took a chance. People don't take chances today. That kind of commitment of blind faith, hoping that the future will reward us or our sacrifice, is no longer the American way."

To buttress this point, Smith points out that over five thousand blacks served in the Continental Army during the Revolutionary War, though they had no more rights or liberty than blacks in the South during the Civil War. Moreover, in doing so, the soldiers in the War for Independence rejected an offer of immediate freedom made by the king of England. "If you can fight

97

for the independence of the colonies without any guarantee you would benefit from it," argues Smith, "then it shouldn't surprise you that blacks could fight for the independence of the South."

Jordan believes that motivations have to be examined on a case-by-case basis. Some were genuinely patriotic; most, he feels, were more pragmatic. Free blacks "stood to lose an awful lot," he observes. Jordan asserts that they remained loyal to the Confederacy to protect their property interests (some free blacks owned land, and a few owned slaves), join what they thought was the winning side, or deter a victorious South from taking away their freedom.

According to Jordan, free blacks in the South often had their loyalty tested by Confederate soldiers dressed in Union garb. "Some had a customary response when asked who they supported," Jordan recounts. "They'd say, 'I'm on God's side,' and leave it at that."

Ford's search has not revealed what inspired his great-great-grandfather to leave home and cross the Potomac River, but he suspects Jenkins got caught up in the antifederal fervor that swept southern Maryland when the war broke out. "I have no idea [why he joined]; I wish I knew. The majority of people in southern Maryland had a nasty idea toward anything that wore blue. I assume he did, too."

Monumental skirmish

Regardless of the number and motivations of blacks who remained loyal to the Confederacy, the issue of acknowledging their service remains as controversial today as it was for rebels during the war.

Greg Eanes is a Gulf War veteran, journalist, and member of the Sons of Confederate Veterans (SCV) chapter in Nottoway County, Virginia, about fifty miles south-west of Richmond.

After reading a book on Virginia's black Confederates by James Brewer,

Eanes, who is white, realized that many Afro-Virginian Confederates came from Nottoway County. During the Civil War, the town of Burkeville in particular was a main rail junction serving rebel forces in Petersburg.

In 1993, at the behest of the local SCV chapter, Eanes initiated an effort to build a monument honoring Nottoway blacks who had served the lost cause. Eanes saw the project not just as an educational endeavor that would put the Confederacy in what he feels is its proper historical perspective but as a measure allowing the county to move ahead and overcome past racial differences.

"History should not be a divisive thing," says Eanes. "These men served their country. They deserve to be recognized."

Initially, his plans for the monument went smoothly. In August 1993, his request to erect a statue memorializing the soldiers was unanimously approved by the Nottoway County commissioners, including two African Americans.

But resistance to the proposed monument grew quickly after the head of the county chapter of the NAACP opposed the memorial. And emotions quickly began to rise. One local critic referred to Eanes and SCV members as "neo-Nazis" and equated the memorial with Jews being forced to commemorate the Holocaust.

It was just the kind of reaction Eanes and the SCV feared. "The feedback in the county [to the monument] was mixed," he remarks. "But some who opposed it also opposed the way we were being treated."

THE ELLEN S. BROCKENBROUGH LIBRARY, THE MUSEUM OF THE CONFEDERACY

Confederate surgeons with a body servant, Ben Harris, in a photo taken during the war.

In September 1993, the local elected officials responded to the controversy by establishing a commission to consider Eanes' request. Two of the five members were vocal critics of the memorial, including the critic who had called Eanes a hatemonger. In October of that year, the panel recommended that the proposal be rejected.

Though the project is now on what Eanes calls "permanent hold," he still believes the fight was worthwhile, in part because he feels it has helped launch a debate about the role blacks played in the Confederacy. "In that respect we've won, because it has created a greater awareness. Journals [in places] as far away as England have mentioned the controversy."

In recent years, local SCV chapters and the national organization have paid increasing attention to recognizing local black heritage. Some scholars in Confederate circles are

PETER HOLDEN/THE WORLD AND I

American University professor Edward Smith began studying blacks' role in the Confederacy after reviewing wartime correspondence.

skeptical about their motivations for doing so, saying that while most members, like Eanes, are genuinely trying to take the sting out of the war for blacks, others may be using Afro-Confederates as a shield to preempt black criticism of the Confederacy.

In the end, Eanes feels the Nottoway County monument controversy had some important, smaller victories. During the debate, "a black friend of mine told me, 'Even I was taught that if you saw a Confederate flag in the back window of a truck, it meant redneck.' And I said, 'Look back at what you just said. You were *taught*.' "

An untold story

While acknowledging black participation in the secessionist effort remains, in some places, a controversial subject, in academic circles it is still largely dismissed.

Smith recalls the case of a student who was researching a paper on the topic a few years ago. "She told me she had told another professor about the subject she was working on. And the professor told her, 'Dr. Smith is crazy. There weren't any blacks who fought for the Confederacy.' I told the student to look for herself," he remembers. The student, he points out, ended up writing the paper.

Smith says he is undeterred by such skepticism. He became interested in the topic while reading the letters of slaves and free blacks written during the war. "When you start plowing into the letters, you see blacks out of the stereotype you've been introduced to and begin to realize there is an untold story," he observes.

But in conversation, the frustration he feels over the lack of cover-age given the topic becomes evident. Black media outlets, Smith feels, won't talk about these Confederates "because it gives a different focus on [a] history that they have already decided is one way."

The result, he says, is confusing. "Kids are introduced to history in such a way they [don't] even begin to speculate if there is anything else out there. If you tell the average black kid that [Union generals] Grant and Sherman didn't like blacks, they would think you were crazy."

Historians, he thinks, are failing to present both sides of the controversy. "Our job is to present things people may not have access to," he states. "A lot of that may be stuff you don't like. But if you are going to be true to the profession, you have to do it. History is pretty in a lot of ways and ugly in a lot of ways, but the whole story has to be told."

COURTESY CANTON, MS., CONVENTION AND VISITOR BUREAU

A monument in Canton, Mississippi, commemorates blacks who served the Confederacy.

a snowstorm, Ford's great-grand-mother couldn't direct him to the precise burial place.

Locating the site will be difficult, says Ford. "I can't find his obituary in the county paper, and the church doesn't have any records of graves going back that far. We may never find it."

Since finding out about his heritage, Ford has participated as a Confederate in several battle reenactments and living history presentations, including one at Gettysburg. He realizes his participation is often viewed with shock by blacks, who may feel he is glorifying a nation and a cause that subjugated blacks.

"I know they feel it brings back a bad memory," he says. "But the whole reason for civil war wasn't about slaves; the main reason for separating was states' rights. Not all people are willing to accept that blacks were Confederates, but I am."

Additional Reading

Hubert Blackerby, *Blacks in Blue and Gray: Afro-American Service in the Civil War*, Portals Press, Columbia, Maryland, 1979.

James H. Brewer, *The Confederate Negro: Virginia's Craftsmen and Military Laborers, 1861–1865*, Books on Demand, Ann Arbor, Michigan; originally published by Duke University Press, Durham, North Carolina, 1969.

Ervin L. Jordan, Jr., *Black Confederates and Afro-Yankees in Civil War Virginia*, University Press of Virginia, Charlottesville, 1995.

Benjamin Quarles, *The Negro in the Civil War*, Little, Brown, Boston, 1953.

Richard Rollins, ed., *Black Southerners in Gray: Essays on Afro-Americans in Confederate Armies*, Journal of Confederate History Series, vol. 11, Southern Heritage Press, Murfreesboro, Tennessee, 1994.

Craig J. Renner is an editor of the Culture section of THE WORLD & I.

Back in southern Maryland, Rick Ford is just trying to piece together the whole story of his ancestor's service. He knows, for example, that Jenkins died in 1912 and was buried at the Holy Ghost Church in the town of Issue in southern Charles County. But the grave was never given a headstone, and because Jenkins was buried in the middle of

Gallantry under Fire

Could "colored" troops stand up to real combat? A charge at New Market Heights settled the question once and for all

John E. Aliyetti

IT WAS THE FALL OF 1864, AND THE CON-federacy was gasping for its final breaths. Earlier in the year, Lieutenant General Ulysses S. Grant had relentlessly pressed the Union Army of the Potomac against the Confederate Army of Northern Virginia in a series of battles at the Wilderness, Spotsylvania, North Anna, Cold Harbor, and the Crater at Petersburg. In August, Admiral David Farragut sailed into Mobile Bay and neutralized the last Confederate port in the Gulf of Mexico. On September 2, Union Major General William T. Sherman captured Atlanta. Virginia's precious Shenandoah Valley, the lifeblood of the Confederacy, was on its way to becoming little more than a charred wasteland.

Now, in mid-September, a deadly confrontation was about to occur, a struggle forgotten among the famous conflicts of the war, a battle that would provide a benchmark of valor, not only for the Civil War, but also for future generations of American soldiers. It was a fight that would convince some of the most stubborn skeptics that black men could rise to the call of battle as well as white men.

Major General Benjamin F. Butler, commander of the Army of the James, had convinced Grant to allow him to break out of his stalemated position in the Bermuda Hundred area, near the James River, south of Richmond, Virginia, to launch a two-pronged assault

LIBRARY OF CONGRESS

Most of the fighting in the engagement at New Market Heights was done by black regiments, including Fleetwood's 4th United States Colored Troops and the 22d U.S. Colored Troops.

From *Civil War Times Illustrated*, October 1996. © 1996 by Cowles Magazines, Inc. Reprinted through the courtesy of Cowles Magazines, Inc., publishers of *Civil War Times Illustrated*.

against key forts and possibly break through to Richmond itself. Butler's plan had Major General Edward Ord's XVIII Corps, less its 3d Division, crossing the James at Varina and attacking Fort Harrison. Major General David Bell Birney's X Corps would cross at Deep Bottom and attack the Confederate position along the New Market Road, with its main effort directed against Fort Gilmer.

The 3d Division of the XVIII Corps would lead the attack against the Confederate defense at an area along the New Market Road known as New Market Heights. For this assignment, Butler attached the division, under the command of Brigadier General Charles J. Paine, to Birney's X Corps, placing it on the left flank. The division faced a true test: the black troops who made up its nine regiments were freemen and former slaves who had never been in combat, and their commander, although a Butler favorite, had never led a division-size unit into battle.

Butler was an avowed abolitionist and was one of the first to encourage the acceptance of black men into the army. In May 1861 he had labeled a few black deserters of a Confederate labor battalion "contraband of war" and concluded that, as such, they could be "confiscated." In 1862, when he commanded the Union troops occupying New Or-

leans, he hurriedly recruited three regiments of liberated slaves from southern Louisiana and had them in the field by November of that year to face a threatened Confederate attack.

In the fall of 1864, there were more than 100,000 black troops in the Union forces in about 140 all-black regiments. At the war's end, almost 10 percent of the Yankees under arms would be black men. And while most people knew of the courage displayed by the black 54th Massachusetts Infantry the previous year at Fort Wagner, in South Carolina's Charleston Harbor, Butler sensed that some units still distrusted black regiments. In discussing his plan with Grant, he stated, "I want to convince myself, whether, under my own eye, the Negro troops will fight; and if I can take with the Negroes, a redoubt that turned Hancock's corps on a former occasion, that will settle the question."

On September 28, 1864, the 3d Division rested at Deep Bottom, Virginia, awaiting the arrival of the X Corps. Like most Union divisions, the 3d consisted of three brigades, each with three regiments. Although the strength of the regiments fluctuated daily, on this day the division had about 3,800 effectives. All the commissioned officers were white, and the enlisted men black. Colonel John H. Holman commanded the 1st Brigade, which consisted of the 1st, 22d,

and 37th United States Colored Troops (U.S.C.T.). Colonel Alonzo G. Draper led the 2d Brigade, with the 5th, 36th, and 38th U.S.C.T. The 3d Brigade, which was short one regiment (the 10th U.S.C.T. on detached duty) had Colonel Samuel A. Duncan in command of the 4th and 6th U.S.C.T. The 2d U.S.C.T. Cavalry would also take part in the action, but it was not attached to any brigade. Birney held in reserve the 7th, 8th, and 9th U.S.C.T., and the 29th Connecticut Colored Infantry, all of which had been assigned to the X Corps.

The next morning, the division was in a line of brigades, ready to commence the attack. From right to left they were Duncan's brigade (whose right flank tied in with the left flank of the X Corps' 1st Division, commanded by Brigadier General Alfred H. Terry), then Draper's brigade, and lastly, Holman's brigade. Holman's task was to keep the left flank secure. The division would advance in coordination with the general attack of the X Corps. Duncan's troops would lead, closely supported by Draper and, if necessary, some of Holman's troops.

The plan called for a swift attack against New Market Heights. Some unconfirmed accounts have the troops advancing with unloaded rifles so they would not stop to fire. The division expected to be going against inexperienced

NATIONAL ARCHIVES

At Deep Bottom, Virginia, along the James River, Federal soldiers rest at one foot of the pontoon bridge that Brigadier General Charles J. Paine crossed with his division of black regiments to reach New Market Heights.

a long time coming
The Medal of Honor

Long after the United States had declared itself independent from England, Americans still shared a general distaste for any lingering reminder of the British nobility. The thought of fancy dress uniforms decked with rows of colorful medals reminded them of the crusty aristocracy whose domination their forefathers had fought so hard to escape. So, except for one short-lived recognition program initiated by George Washington in 1782, the U.S. military never instituted a formal system of rewarding individual gallantry with medals.

At the start of the Civil War, that anti-medal bias pervaded the U.S. Army's high command. It required action by the navy to force the army to reconsider its position. When Navy Secretary Gideon Welles asked Congress to approve a medal for the navy, his request was granted, and President Abraham Lincoln signed the Navy Medal of Honor bill on December 21, 1861. Not to be outdone by the navy, the army developed its own program, and on July 12, 1862, the Army Medal of Honor bill became law. Although frequently referred to as the "Congressional Medal of Honor," the correct term is simply "Medal of Honor." Only enlisted men were eligible for the award initially, but the act was amended on March 3, 1863, to include officers.

The first black soldier to receive the medal was Sergeant William H. Carney of Company C of the 54th Massachusetts Infantry (Colored). Carney had grabbed his unit's flag after the bearer was shot down in the attack on Fort Wagner, South Carolina, on July 18, 1863. He led the advance to the wall of the fort under "intense musketry and cannon fire," and when he found himself surrounded by only dead or wounded troops, he returned to Union lines with the colors. He was wounded twice during the ordeal.

Through the course of the war, 2,438 Medals of Honor were awarded for "gallantry in action." That number seemed far too large to those scrutinizing the recognition program a few decades later. So an Army commission was formed to review

ABOVE AND BEYOND

The original army Medal of Honor. The engraving shows Minerva, the Roman goddess of wisdom and the arts, repulsing a male figure. Minerva represents the Union, and the male, the Confederacy.

the situation. On January 17, 1917, the commission ruled that many of the medals issued since the program's inception had been awarded outside the scope of the original intent. The ruling rescinded 911 of the medals, including the 864 given to all the members of one Civil War regiment.

Officially, then, the final tally of Medal of Honor winners during the Civil War was 1,200 soldiers, 310 sailors, and 17 Marines. The first medals were presented by Secretary

of War Edwin M. Stanton to six members of "Mitchel's Raiders," and the last was awarded more than 41 years after the war's end.

A total of 37 Medals of Honor were earned for gallantry during the engagement at New Market Heights, with 14 awarded to black troops. The final medal earned by a black soldier for gallantry in that battle was presented to Sergeant Major Thomas R. Hawkins, a veteran of the 6th U.S. Colored Troops, in 1870, about a month before he died.

The other 13 soldiers of the U.S. Colored Troops honored for gallantry in the battle were: Private William H. Barnes, Company D, 38th Regiment; 1st Sergeant Powhatan Beaty, Company G, 5th Regiment; 1st Sergeant James H. Bronson, Company D, 5th Regiment; Sergeant Major Christian A. Fleetwood, Company D, 4th Regiment; Private James Gardner, Company I, 36th Regiment; Sergeant James H. Harris, Company B, 38th Regiment; Sergeant Alfred B. Hilton, Company H, 4th Regiment; Sergeant Milton M. Holland, Company B, 56th Regiment; 1st Sergeant Alexander Kelly, Company F, 6th Regiment; Corporal Miles James, Company B, 36th Regiment; 1st Sergeant Robert A. Pinn, Company I, 5th Regiment; 1st Sergeant Edward Ratcliffe, Company C, 38th Regiment; and Corporal Charles Veal, Company D, 4th Regiment.

On July 9, 1918, Congress approved two "secondary medals": the Distinguished Service Cross and the Silver Star. Later, other medals were added to the so-called "Pyramid of Honor." The warrant for the Medal of Honor was clarified as "gallantry and intrepidity at the risk of life, above and beyond the call of duty." The clarification also specified that the gallant action should have been such that, if the nominee had not acted as he did, he could not have been criticized.

—John E. Aliyetti

militia, but they would soon find that the butternut-clad infantrymen defending the heights were the seasoned Texas veterans of Gregg's Brigade, under the command of Colonel Frederick S. Bass. Supporting the Texans were the 3d Richmond Howitzers; the 1st Rockbridge Artillery; and a cavalry brigade,

fighting dismounted, commanded by Brigadier General Martin W. Gary.

General Paine wanted to wait for Colonel Joseph C. Abbott's 2d Brigade of Terry's division, on his right, to move out and draw some attention from the Confederates before he committed his men, but there was no firing from that

area. In a letter to his father dated October 3, Paine wrote, "I waited a good while to hear Terry begin because I wanted him to draw some of the enemy away from me if he c'd, but after waiting a good while and not hearing from Terry I started my column. . . ." The two regiments of Duncan's brigade moved out with the three regiments of Draper's brigade close behind and slightly to the left. The troops formed a front about 400 hundred yards wide. Holman's brigade moved to cover the flank, and the 22d U.S.C.T. sent out skirmishers.

Rebel pickets began firing at the movement in their front and then fell back to a fortified line of rifle pits at the base of the heights. It was then they realized the size of the attacking force. Terry's three brigades and the rest of the X Corps finally began to advance, and the five-brigade front stretched to about 2,300 yards.

Duncan's brigade entered a ravine and came under a more intense fire. To Duncan's right, Terry's units were pinned down by an enfilade of artillery fire from the heights. In the ravine where Duncan's force struggled, men began to fall from the Texans' musket fire. "The enemy, in very heavy force, . . . were met with a terrific and galling fire," read an article in the *Richmond Enquirer* on November 22. "Texans, mounting the works, shot them like sheep." The artillery units on the heights were firing into the X Corps' lines, but the 3d Division continued to press ahead.

Casualties mounted in Duncan's brigade as it came to an abatis, a protruding line of sharpened loblolly pine. Axmen were called to the front to cut through the dense wood. As they worked, 16 cannon on the heights bombarded the stalled attackers. Many company commanders fell as they tried to rally the men. Duncan himself had been wounded four times and was down.

Paine sent Draper a message to move his brigade to the right, "as we are getting the worst of it over there." Draper's regiments now came on over the same ground Duncan's brigade had crossed. Through the dust and carnage, they surged through the first abatis only to encounter another line of obstacles the defenders had erected.

Meanwhile, except for the 22d U.S.C.T., which was still operating as skirmishers on the left flank, Holman's brigade moved in as reserve behind Draper and Duncan, but received no orders to engage. The 2d U.S.C.T. Cavalry was dismounted and deployed as skirmishers to Duncan's right. Effectively,

the division was now advancing on a one-brigade front, about 1,100 men, half of them skirmishers.

Fire poured down from a palisade of fortified rifle pits that formed the main Confederate line below the crest of the hill. Beyond the second barrier, Four Mile Creek formed a marshy area. The Federals had to wade the creek, and as they tried to reform on the other side, many commenced firing. Draper later reported the fire "made so much confusion that it was impossible to make the orders understood." Smoke and lead filled the air. A Lieutenant Bancroft of the 38th U.S.C.T. went down when a bullet passed through his hip as he slogged through the marsh. Unable to walk, he continued forward on his hands and knees, waving his sword and urging his men to follow. The leading units were now about 30 yards from the main enemy defense line, but the attacking force was in danger of collapse.

Draper tried to get his regimental commanders to rally around the colors and charge, but they and their men were falling all around him. The commander of the 5th Regiment, Lieutenant Colonel G. W. Shirtliff, fell mortally wounded. It was his third wound since the attack had begun. Elsewhere in the 5th, black soldiers rose from the ranks to replace lost junior officers. Sergeant Major Milton Holland, a 20-year-old from Austin, Texas, now led Company C; Richmond-born 1st Sergeant Powhatan Beaty commanded Company G; 1st Sergeant James Branson, a Virginia-born 19-year-old from Pennsylvania, led Company D; and 1st Sergeant Robert Pinn, an Ohio farmer, led Company I.

With disaster imminent, heroes of every rank snatched regimental colors and national standards from dying hands and led the bloodied mass into a smoking hell. Sergeant Major Christian Fleetwood of the 4th U.S.C.T. seized the national colors after a second bearer had fallen, and they ended up in the hands of Corporal Charles Veal. Corporal Miles James of the 36th U.S.C.T. was wounded so badly in the arm that the limb was immediately amputated. James, with blood from the mutilated stump soaking his tunic, kept moving forward, loading and firing with one arm.

As the momentum of Draper's attack deteriorated, the fire against his brigade roared in undiminished intensity. For 30 minutes chaos reigned on the battlefield. Then a few men from Duncan's brigade took up a yell, which caught on and swelled to a roar as the desperate force rallied to its colors. The screaming surge engulfed Draper's brigade, and with a rush, the 3d Division carried the Southerners' main line of defense. A Rebel officer mounted the parapet, and Private James Gardner of the 36th shot him down. Gardner charged the barrier and ran his bayonet through the man as the Confederate defenders fell back.

The din of cannon and musket fire to the right of the 3d Division rose in fury. Birney, aware that his flank was secure with Paine in control of the heights and with the subsequent easing of the enfilading fire against him, directed the X Corps to attack Fort Gilmer. But General Robert E. Lee, commander of the Army of Northern Virginia, was brilliant at maneuvering troops behind his own lines and managed to reinforce the defenders. Fort Gilmer held against a ferocious assault.

At the end of the battle, the Confederate line was pushed back. Ord's force captured and held Fort Harrison, subsequently renamed Fort Burnham for Brigadier General Hiram Burnham, who was killed at the head of his brigade, leading the attack. But the Richmond defense remained intact. Lee counterattacked the next day against troops armed with repeating rifles and was handed heavy casualties for his effort. He was forced to pull back and reconstruct his battered perimeter.

Butler's plan marked Grant's last serious effort to enter Richmond north of the James. The siege of Richmond continued another six months, until April 1, 1865, when Union forces broke through Lee's line at Petersburg. Eight days later Lee surrendered his army at Appomattox Court House.

By the war's end, more than 186,000 black men had served in the Union army. Their units had fought in 149 engagements and 39 major battles. During that time, 20 black men—16 soldiers and four sailors—were cited for valor and awarded the Medal of Honor. Fourteen of those medals were won on September 29, 1864, at New Market Heights, by men of General Paine's 3d Division. The 29th was truly a day of glory for the 3d Division soldiers, but they paid for that glory with the blood of hundreds of men.

Butler admitted years later that he had deliberately exposed his black units to risk far out of proportion to the value of their objective in the engagement at New Market Heights, but he had done it in order to establish confidence in their reliability. After the battle, he attempted to reward their heroic effort by ordering Tiffany's of New York to strike a solid silver medal known as the Army of the James Medal, which he later pre-sented to more than 200 of his troops. His unique recognition program, however, created much controversy, and the army forbade the soldiers to wear the medal on their uniforms.

The 3d Division's performance, however, was not controversial, as more widely accepted tokens of appreciation attest. One such token is the highway historical marker on Virginia Route 5, near New Market Road, which reads: "On 28 September 1864, elements of Maj. Gen. Benjamin F. Butler's Army of the James crossed the James river to assault the Confederate defenses of Richmond. At dawn, on 29 September, 6 regiments of the U.S. Colored Troops fought with ex-ceptional valor during their attack along New Market Road. Despite heavy casualties, they carried the earthworks and succeeded in capturing New Market Heights north of the road. Of the 16 Medals of Honor awarded to 'Negro' soldiers during the Civil War 14 were bestowed for this battle. 'The capacity of the Negro race for soldiers had then and there been fully settled forever.' "

John E. Aliyetti is a freelance writer living in Royal Oak, Maryland.

Unit 5

Key Points to Consider

❖ After reading Frederick Douglass's 1866 essay, "Reconstruction," why would you say that he was so skeptical of Congress's ability to handle reconstruction?

❖ How did Reconstruction allow for the reinstitution of white control over Southern institutions?

❖ Why was the entrance of blacks into the political arena considered one of the most revolutionary aspects of the reconstruction program?

❖ What forms of opposition did freedwomen face during and after Reconstruction?

 **Links**   **www.dushkin.com/online/**

These sites are annotated on pages 4 and 5.

While some have argued that Reconstruction represented a radical attempt to transform America, a skeptical Frederick Douglass questioned whether the Civil Rights Bill, the Freedmen's Bureau Bill, and the proposed constitutional amendments went far enough. He argued that Reconstruction should protect both whites and blacks in such a way that it would "cause Northern industry, Northern capital, and Northern civilization to flow into the South." Similarly, August Meier argues that Reconstruction was far from a genuine revolution, but a superficial process that essentially allowed for the return of white hegemony in the southern states.

The most radical aspect of the Reconstruction program, according to John Hope Franklin, was that it allowed Negroes into the "political arena." Franklin points out that many of the negative myths regarding the Reconstruction program (i.e., the subordination of the South to Negro rule or large numbers of carpetbaggers and scalawags) were primarily generated by opponents of Reconstruction.

Historians have typically failed to come to terms with the freedwomen's role in the wartime and postbellum South. Leslie Schwalm points out that freedwomen who sought the means and opportunity to live and subsist as free from white intervention as possible encountered considerable opposition.

Reconstruction and Freedom

As originally published
in *The Atlantic Monthly*

December 1866

Reconstruction

by Frederick Douglass

THE assembling of the Second Session of the Thirty-ninth Congress may very properly be made the occasion of a few earnest words on the already much-worn topic of reconstruction.

Seldom has any legislative body been the subject of a solicitude more intense, or of aspirations more sincere and ardent. There are the best of reasons for this profound interest. Questions of vast moment, left undecided by the last session of Congress, must be manfully grappled with by this. No political skirmishing will avail. The occasion demands statesmanship.

Whether the tremendous war so heroically fought and so victoriously ended shall pass into history a miserable failure, barren of permanent results,—a scandalous and shocking waste of blood and treasure,—a strife for empire, as Earl Russell characterized it, of no value to liberty or civilization,—an attempt to re-establish a Union by force, which must be the merest mockery of a Union,—an effort to bring under Federal authority States into which no loyal man from the North may safely enter, and to bring men into the national councils who deliberate with daggers and vote with revolvers, and who do not even conceal their deadly hate of the country that conquered them; or whether, on the other hand, we shall, as the rightful reward of victory over treason have a solid nation, entirely delivered from all contradictions and social antagonisms, based upon loyalty, liberty, and equality, must be determined one way or the other by the present session of Congress. The last session really did nothing which can be considered final as to these questions. The Civil Rights Bill and the Freedmen's Bureau Bill and the proposed constitutional amendments, with the amendment already adopted and recognized as the law of the land, do not reach the difficulty, and cannot, unless the whole structure of the government is changed from a government by States to something like a despotic central government, with power to control even the municipal regulations of States, and to make them conform to its own despotic will. While there remains such an idea as the right of each State to control its own local

affairs,—an idea, by the way, more deeply rooted in the minds of men of all sections of the country than perhaps any one other political idea,—no general assertion of human rights can be of any practical value. To change the character of the government at this point is neither possible nor desirable. All that is necessary to be done is to make the government consistent with itself, and render the rights of the States compatible with the sacred rights of human nature.

The arm of the Federal government is long, but it is far too short to protect the rights of individuals in the interior of distant States. They must have the power to protect themselves, or they will go unprotected, in spite of all the laws the Federal government can put upon the national statute-book.

Slavery, like all other great systems of wrong, founded in the depths of human selfishness, and existing for ages, has not neglected its own conservation. It has steadily exerted an influence upon all around it favorable to its own continuance. And today it is so strong that it could exist, not only without law, but even against law. Custom, manners, morals, religion, are all on its side everywhere in the South; and when you add the ignorance and servility of the ex-slave to the intelligence and accustomed authority of the master, you have the conditions, not out of which slavery will again grow, but under which it is impossible for the Federal government to wholly destroy it, unless the Federal government be armed with despotic power, to blot out State authority, and to station a Federal officer at every cross-road. This, of course, cannot be done, and ought not even if it could. The true way and the easiest way is to make our government entirely consistent with itself, and give to every loyal citizen the elective franchise,—a right and power which will be ever present, and will form a wall of fire for his protection.

One of the invaluable compensations of the late Rebellion is the highly instructive disclosure it made of the true source of danger to republican government. Whatever may be tolerated in monarchical and despotic governments, no republic is safe that tolerates a privileged class, or denies to any of its citizens equal rights and equal means to maintain them.

It remains now to be seen whether we have the needed courage to have that cause [for rebellion] entirely removed from the Republic. At any rate, to this grand work of national regeneration and entire purification Congress must now address itself, with full purpose that the work shall this time be thoroughly done.

If time was at first needed, Congress has now had time. All the requisite materials from which to form an intelligent judgment are now before it. Whether its members look at the origin, the progress, the termination of the war, or at the mockery of a peace now existing, they will find only one unbroken chain of argument in favor of a radical policy of reconstruction.

The people themselves demand such a reconstruction as shall put an end to the present anarchical state of things in the late rebellious States,—where frightful murders and wholesale massacres are perpetrated in the very presence of Federal soldiers. This horrible business they require shall cease. They want a reconstruction such as will protect loyal men, black and white, in their persons and property: such a one as will cause Northern industry, Northern capital, and Northern civilization to flow into the South, and make a man from New England as much at home in Carolina as elsewhere in the Republic. No Chinese wall can now be tolerated. The South must be opened to the light of law and liberty, and this session of Congress is relied upon to accomplish this important work.

The plain, common-sense way of doing this work is simply to establish in the South one law, one government, one administration of justice, one condition to the exercise of the elective franchise, for men of all races and colors alike. This great measure is sought as earnestly by loyal white men as by loyal blacks, and is needed alike by both. Let sound political prescience but take the place of an unreasoning prejudice, and this will be done.

NEGROES IN THE FIRST AND SECOND RECONSTRUCTIONS OF THE SOUTH

August Meier

"REVOLUTIONS never go backwards": so declared the editors of the first Negro daily newspaper, the New Orleans *Tribune,* late in 1864.[1] Northern troops had occupied the city and much of Louisiana as early as 1862, and the *Tribune* insisted that the logical second step, after crushing the slaveholders' rebellion, was that the national government divide their plantations among the freedmen. Washington failed to act upon this proposal, and seventy years later W. E. B. Du Bois, in assessing the reconstruction experience, perceived it as a revolution that had indeed gone backwards. It had gone backwards, he held, mainly because Congress had failed to press forward to the logical corollary of its reconstruction program; the distribution of the former slaveowners' land among the Negroes.[2] More recently, Willie Lee Rose, though starting from a different philosophy of history, arrived at rather similar conclusions. In her volume on the South Carolina Sea Island Negroes during the Civil War she describes how the military authorities divided many of the Sea Island plantations among the freedmen. President Andrew Johnson, however, returned the lands to the former owners, and Congress failed to intervene. Mrs. Rose pithily sums up this sequence of events by entitling the last chapter of her book "Revolutions May Go Backwards."[3] Nevertheless, in the face of such distinguished scholarly opinion, I would like to suggest that what occurred during reconstruction was really not a genuine revolution, not even an abortive one.

Consider the following example. In Georgia, in April, 1868, slightly a year after the passage of the Reconstruction Act of 1867, a constitution drawn up under the procedures required by Congress was ratified by the voters, and new officials were elected. The process of reconstruction was supposedly completed when, in July, the legislature ratified the Fourteenth Amendment, and military authority was withdrawn. The new state government, however, was no genuinely "radical" regime. Just six weeks later the legislature expelled its Negro members, on the grounds that Negroes, though guaranteed the right to vote, had not been specifically made eligible for office.[4]

Before they departed, one of the Negro representatives, Henry M. Turner, a minister of the African Methodist Episcopal Church, and formerly a Civil War chaplain and Freedmen's Bureau agent, delivered a ringing, sarcastic speech, defiantly expressing his vision of a democratic America. He would not, he said, behave as some of his thirty-one colored colleagues had, and attempt to retain his seat by appealing to the magnanimity of the white legislators. He would not, "fawn or cringe before any party nor stoop to beg them for my rights," like "slaves begging under the lash. I am here to defend my rights, and to hurl thunderbolts at the men who would dare to cross the threshold of my manhood. . . . I was not aware that there was in the character of the [Anglo-Saxon] race so much cowardice, . . . pusillanimity . . . [and] treachery." It was the Negroes who had "set the ball of loyalty rolling in the State of Georgia . . . and [yet] there are persons in this legislature, today, who are ready to spit their poison in my face, while

[1] New Orleans *Tribune,* Nov. 29, 1864. This paper was one of a series read at Roosevelt University in the fall of 1965, marking the centennial of reconstruction.
[2] W. E. B. Du Bois, *Black Reconstruction* (New York, 1935).
[3] Willie Lee Rose, *Rehearsal for Reconstruction: The Port Royal Experiment* (Indianapolis, 1964).
[4] Ethel Maude Christler, "The Participation of Negroes in the Government of Georgia, 1867–1870" (M.A. thesis, Atlanta University, 1932), *passim,* is the best general treatment. See also C. Mildred Thompson, *Reconstruction in Georgia, Economic, Political and Social* (New York, 1915), chaps. vii, viii, and x.

From *Civil War History,* June 1967, pp. 114-130. Reprinted by permission of the Kent State University Press. © 1967.

they themselves ... opposed the ratification of the Constitution. *They* question my right to a seat in this body."

Then, in rhetoric typical of the era, Turner stated the Negro's claims.

The great question is this. Am I a man? If I am such, I claim the rights of a man. Am I not a man because I happen to be of darker hue than honorable gentlemen around me? ... Why, sir, though we are not white, we have accomplished much. We have pioneered civilization here; we have built up your country; we have worked in your fields, and garnered your harvest, for two hundred and fifty years. And what do we ask of you in return ... ? Do we ask retaliation? We ask it not. ... but we ask you now for our RIGHTS. It is extraordinary that a race such as yours, professing gallantry, and chivalry, and education and superiority, living in a land where ringing chimes call child and sire to the Church of God—a land ... where courts of justice are presumed to exist ... can make war upon the poor defenseless black man. ...

You may expel us, gentlemen, but I firmly believe that you will someday repent it. The black man cannot protect a country, if the country doesn't protect him; and if, tomorrow, a war should arise, I would not raise a musket to defend a country where my manhood is denied. ... You may expel us ... ; but while you do it remember that there is a just God in Heaven, whose All-Seeing Eye beholds alike the acts of the oppressor and the oppressed, and who, despite the machinations of the wicked, never fails to vindicate the cause of justice.[5]

The events just described epitomize two things: the aspirations and hopes of Negroes on the one hand; and the superficial character of the reconstruction process on the other. Pressure from Congress and the state supreme court did later secure a reversal of the ban on Negro legislators, and one Georgia Negro, Jefferson Long, sat in Congress for a term. Nevertheless, southern whites actually dominated the state's government, and by 1872 the Redeemers, or Democrats, had returned to power. Thus the period of so-called Radical or Black reconstruction can scarcely be said to have existed in Georgia; and what happened in that state can hardly be called a revolution, even a revolution that later went backwards. Most writers on the history of Negroes during reconstruction have dwelt upon developments in South Carolina, Louisiana, and Mississippi, where Negroes formed a majority of the population and therefore held more high offices than elsewhere. What happened in Georgia was, however, a good deal more typical of what happened in most of the southern states during reconstruction.

The failure of congressional reconstruction, the return of the southern states to white hegemony, and the subordination and oppression of the black man were due not only to southern

white recalcitrance, but equally as much to northern indifference and to the limitations in congressional policy. Northern indifference to the Negro's welfare and the consequent inadequacies of Congress' program were deeply rooted in the historical racism of the American public. They were thus fundamentally a continuation of a cultural tradition that had not only permitted existence of slavery in the South, but had relegated free Negroes to second-class citizenship in the North.

In the opening months of the Civil War, for example, Negroes and the small band of white abolitionists had been far in advance of northern opinion in regarding the war as fundamentally a struggle for the emancipation of the slaves. From the day of the firing on Fort Sumter, Negroes had envisioned the situation as an irrepressible moral conflict between slavery and liberty, and a war for the rights of man in fulfillment of the genius of the American democratic faith. However, the President, the Congress and most of the nation at first regarded the war simply as a campaign to preserve the Union, and only slowly and reluctantly, and as a result of the exigencies of a prolonged and difficult military conflict, did the Federal government come to emancipate the slaves and enlist Negroes in the armed forces.[6] Moreover, the vast majority of northerners continued to resist the idea that Negroes should be accorded the rights of citizens. In 1863, at the thirtieth anniversary convention of the founding of the American Anti-Slavery Society, Frederick Douglass excoriated those abolitionists who felt that their work was accomplished when the slaves were freed. Negroes, along with a handful of white abolitionists, formed the vanguard of those who insisted that with emancipation the struggle for Negro freedom had only begun. To Negroes the issues were moral ones, based upon the promise of American life, upon the assumptions of the American faith that were rooted in the Declaration of Independence and the ethics of Christianity. As a conclave of Pennsylvania leaders declared in 1868: "It is America that you have to civilize, to Christianize, and compel to accept and practically apply to all men, without distinctions of color or race, the glorious principles and precepts laid down in her immortal Declaration of Independence."[7]

Long before the war had ended, northern Negro leaders had spelled out the specific program they deemed essential for the creation of a truly democratic America. In October, 1864, the race's most prominent men met in Syracuse, New York, to organize an Equal Rights League that would agitate for citizenship rights and racial equality. At that time the slaves had not yet been freed in the loyal Border States, and most of the northern states prohibited Negroes from voting, from testifying against whites in court, from serving on juries, and in some cases from attending public schools (even segregated schools). The convention delegates were critical of the fact that most northern states still refused to accord Negroes the ballot, and they even denounced the Republican party for being arrayed with the proslavery Democratic party in its support of racial prejudice. Their two chief demands were abolition and political equality. As Douglass pointed out in an address before the Massachusetts Anti-Slavery Society a few months later, Negroes wanted the suffrage ...

---

[5]Henry M. Turner, *Speech on the Eligibility of Colored Men to Seats in the Georgia Legislature ... September 3, 1868* (Augusta, 1868), *passim*.

[6]James M. McPherson, *The Negro's Civil War* (New York, 1965), chaps. ii and iii; McPherson, *The Struggle for Equality: Abolitionists and the Negro in Civil War and Reconstruction* (Princeton, 1964), chap. iii.

[7]*Proceedings of the American Anti-Slavery Society at its Third Decade ... December 3, 4, 5, 1863* (New York, 1864), pp. 110–118; *Proceedings of the Fourth Annual Meeting of the Pennsylvania State Equal Rights League ... 1868* (Philadelphia, 1868), p. 35.

because it is our right, first of all. No class of men can, without insulting their own nature, be content with any deprivation of their rights. Again, I want the elective franchise ... because ours is a peculiar government, based upon a peculiar idea, and that idea is universal suffrage. If I were in a monarchical ... or aristocratic government, where the few ruled and the many were subject, there would be no special stigma resting upon me because I did not exercise the elective franchise ... , but here, where universal suffrage ... is the fundamental idea of the Government, to rule us out is to make us an exception, to brand us with the stigma of inferiority, and to invite to our heads the missiles of those about us. ...[8]

Douglass and other Negro leaders, while addressing the nation on matters of abolition and citizenship, advocated also a program of economic and moral improvement to be undertaken by Negroes themselves. The Syracuse convention exhorted the freedmen "to shape their course toward frugality, the accumulation of property, and above all, to leave untried no amount of effort and self-denial to acquire knowledge, and to secure a vigorous moral and religious growth." To men of the nineteenth century thrift and industry and the acquisition of property—especially land—were essential parts of the good life, along with citizenship rights. Moreover, a common school education was almost a *sine qua non* for securing a comfortable livelihood. It cannot be overemphasized that along with agitation for political and civil rights, Negro leaders stressed the cultivation of middle-class morality, the pursuit of education, and the acquisition of property. To use the phraseology of the time, these things, like the ballot, were regarded as essential for elevating the race and securing its inclusion in the "body politic."

Southern Negroes espoused the same program, and in some respects were more radical than the northern ministers, editors and artisan-businessmen who predominated at Negro conventions. Representative of the point of view of articulate southern Negroes was the New Orleans *Tribune*, which in 1864 and 1865 prefigured the outlook of most Negro spokesmen during the decade after the war. This journal denounced Lincoln's plan of reconstruction and endorsed that of the congressional Radicals. Only through congressional reconstruction would Negroes "secure the full enjoyment of our rights—not as a matter of gratuitous or benevolent grant, revocable at will—but as an embodiment of the principles set forth in the Declaration of Independence."[9] Highest among these rights was that of the franchise, for it was the only means by which Negroes could protect themselves from civil and economic discrimination.[10] To those who argued that a time of preparation should elapse

before the ex-slaves were enfranchised, the *Tribune* replied: "We do not know of a single reform, in the whole course of history, that was brought about by gradual and systematic preparation. In fact, how is preparation practicable without the free exercise of the right contended for ... ? Could the white man of America be prepared to the general exercise of the franchise, unless by going to the polls and voting?" Given the opportunity, the freedmen would show a comprehension of "their own interests" and a "Devotion to the Union" that should justify their immediate enfranchisement.[11]

The *Tribune* also gave pointed attention to the question of segregation. It opposed a bill introduced in the legislature, providing for separate schools,[12] and it continually protested against the system of "star cars" for Negroes in the city until the military authorities ordered the provisional governor to end this example of discrimination.[13] The editors regarded segregation as silly, since it was due to the white man's lust that miscegenation had proceeded to the point where "it would be a pretty hard thing to find a pure ... Negro in the whole city of New Orleans, where seventy thousand persons of African descent are now residing."[14]

The journal devoted much space to economic matters, especially to the conditions under which the former slaves labored on the plantations. On this subject the *Tribune* went far beyond the thinking of most northern Negro leaders at this time, and beyond the thinking of many southern leaders as well. The editors boldly advocated what only the most radical of the Republicans and abolitionists were thinking of—the destruction of the plantation system. It criticized the United States government for not immediately confiscating and dividing the lands of the rebellious planters into five-acre lots, to be assigned to the "tillers of the soil" at a nominal price, so that the freedmen would be "thoroughly imbued with that ... praise-worthy 'Yankee' idea, *that every man should own the land he tills, and head and hands he works with.*"[15] In calling for these steps the editors hoped to accomplish a democratic revolution in the South against the power of the antebellum slaveowning aristocracy: "The division of the lands is the only means by which a new, industrious and loyal population may be made to settle in the South. Large estates will always be in the hands of an aristocracy. Small estates are the real element of democracy."[16]

Broadly speaking, the Negro elite stressed above all the importance of the franchise and civil rights. Next in order of importance, in the thinking of most of them, was the value of at least a common school education for the masses of the race. Finally, they were concerned with the economic problems of the freedmen. Most of them urged the masses to work hard, save their money, and acquire property; but some at least advocated a radical expropriation of the slaveowners' plantations and the creation, under Federal benevolence, of a numerous landowning yeoman peasantry. Such a policy would not only provide Negroes with an economic opportunity, but would supply the foundation for loyal and democratic governments in the southern states.

On the other hand, the evidence indicates that the masses had a scale of priorities that was precisely the opposite of that

---

[8]*Proceedings of the National Convention of Colored Men ... 1864* (Boston, 1864); Frederick Douglass, "What the Black Man Wants," in William D. Kelley, Wendell Phillips and Frederick Douglass, *The Equality of all Men Before the Law* (Boston, 1865), pp. 36–37.
[9]New Orleans *Tribune*, Jan. 3, 1865.
[10]*Ibid.*, Aug. 5, 1865; Sept. 13. 1864.
[11]*Ibid.*, May 4, 1865.
[12]*Ibid.*, July 26, Dec. 24, 1864; Feb. 17, 1865.
[13]*Ibid.*, Feb. 28, May 21, Aug. 10, 1865.
[14]*Ibid.*, Aug. 15, 1865.
[15]*Ibid.*, Sept. 10, Sept. 24, 1864.
[16]*Ibid.*, Sept. 15, 1865.

of the elite. Their primary interest was in land ownership. Close to this in importance for them was education. Though politics was of somewhat lesser value in their thinking, enfranchisement did initiate enthusiastic political participation on the part of the freedmen. Like the elite Negroes they displayed a profound awareness of the importance of political activity in American culture. The same is true of their interest in education. Old and young flocked to the schools opened by the northern missionaries and the Freedmen's Bureau. Especially notable were the freedmen's own efforts at self-help in education, establishing schools, hiring teachers, and erecting buildings.

Most of all, like oppressed peasants the world over, the freedmen wanted land. As Vernon Lane Wharton put it in his study of Negroes in Mississippi after the Civil War: "Their very lives were entwined with the land and its cultivation; they lived in a society where respectability was based on ownership of the soil; and to them to be free was to farm their own ground."[17] When President Andrew Johnson restored the Sea Island plantations to their former owners, he sent General O. O. Howard, head of the Freedmen's Bureau, to Edisto Island to inform the freedmen of his decision. The Negroes who crowded the church at which Howard spoke were disappointed and angry, and shouted "No, no!" to his remarks. Howard later recorded in his autobiography that one man called out from the gallery: "Why, General Howard, why do you take away our lands? You take them from us who have always been true, always true to the Government! You give them to our all-time enemies! That is not right!" The committee selected by the freedmen to meet with the representatives of the planters in order to arrange the details of the transfer of property informed Howard that they would not work for their old masters under overseers, though they were willing to *rent* the land if ownership was ruled out. The planters, however, were not interested in this kind of arrangement and after a series of indignation meetings the freedmen wrote a final appeal to the President. They insisted that it was "very oppressing ... [that] wee freemen should work for wages for our former oners." They felt it was unfair for the President to expect the freedmen to ask "for bread or shelter or Comfortable for his wife and children" from men whom they had fought against "upon the feal of battle." They had, they said, no confidence in their former masters, one of whom had declared he would refuse to sell land to freedmen, even at $100 an acre. Johnson, of course, remained unmoved, and in the end the Negroes had to capitulate.[18]

A significant number of the freedmen attempted to buy their own farms, even in the face of white reluctance to sell land to them. Travelers from the North, Freedmen's Bureau agents

and missionaries reported enthusiastically upon evidence of progress in this direction. A New England cotton planter on the Sea Islands reported the case of "a black Yankee ... [with] the energy" and eye "for his own advantage of a born New Englander." His industry and sharp dealing had put him ahead of the other on the plantation, though half of them had fenced in their own gardens and were raising vegetables for the Hilton Head market.

Linus in his half-acre has quite a little farmyard besides. With poultry-houses, pig-pens, and corn-houses, the array is very imposing. He has even a stable, for he made out some title to a horse, which was allowed; and then he begged a pair of wheels and makes a cart for his work; and not to leave the luxuries behind, he next rigs up a kind of sulky and bows to the white men from his carriage. As he keeps his table in corresponding style ... the establishment is rather expensive. So, to provide the means, he has three permanent irons in the fire, his cotton, his Hilton Head express, and his seines. ... While other families "carry" from three to seven acres of cotton, Linus says he must have fourteen. ... With a large boat which he owns, he usually makes weekly trips to Hilton Head, twenty miles distant, carrying passengers, produce and fish. ... I presume his savings since ... the capture of the island amount to four or five hundred dollars. He is all ready to buy land, and I expect to see him in ten years a tolerably rich man.[19]

Only a few with exceptional ability or luck were able to become permanent and substantial landowners. The plantation system remained intact. In fact, it may even have increased in extent. It simply changed its form. Instead of slavery, the characteristic labor arrangement became that known as sharecropping.

By the last quarter of the nineteenth century sharecropping, in combination with the crop-lien system, had become a system of gross exploitation, which reached its most extreme form in debt peonage. Here was a system in which the Negro tenant was almost at the complete mercy of the white planter. Yet, in its origins at least the sharecropping system was not something that was simply forced upon Negroes, but was in part a result of the freedmen's desire for independence, freedom and economic advancement. Much research on this subject remains to be done before the origins of sharecropping during the reconstruction period will be fully understood but recent studies suggest that what likely happened followed the general pattern outlined below.[20]

After the emancipation of the slaves and the close of the Civil War, planters generally attempted to employ Negroes as wage laborers with annual contracts. Under these contracts the freedmen were worked in gangs as they had been under slavery. In order to enforce the contractual obligation, it was common for planters to hold back part of the pay until the end of the cotton harvest. Such a system, characterized by gang labor and with its powers of coercion lodged in the planter's hands, smacked altogether too much of slavery and Negroes resisted working under it. Universally the freedmen wanted to own their own land; where this was not possible they preferred to rent land for cash if they could. But, as in the case of the Sea Islands, planters resisted such an arrangement because it did

---

[17]Vernon Lane Wharton, *The Negro in Mississippi, 1865–1890* (Chapel Hill, 1947), p. 59.
[18]Rose, *Rehearsal for Reconstruction*, pp. 353–355.
[19]Elizabeth Ware Pearson (ed.), *Letters from Port Royal* (Boston, 1906), p. 37.
[20]The ideas developed in the following discussion owe a good deal to material in Martin Abbott, "Free Land, Free Labor, and the Freedmen's Bureau," *Agricultural History*, XXX (1956), pp. 150–156; and Joel Williamson, *After Slavery: The Negro in South Carolina During Reconstruction, 1861–1877*, chaps. iii and v.

not give them as much control over the labor force as they desired. The sharecropping system thus seems to have emerged, in large part, as a sort of compromise. Under it, the tenants had their own plots, organized their own time, and were not subject to the *direct* discipline of the planters. On the other hand the system was beneficial to the planter in that it encouraged the tenant to stay on the land until the crop was harvested, and encouraged him to work hard since he kept a share of the crop. Nevertheless, as late as the 1880's it was common for planters in certain areas to complain about the sharecropping system.

Rudimentary sharecropping arrangements had appeared even before the close of the Civil War, but they received considerable impetus from the encouragement of the Freedmen's Bureau during the later 1860's. Negroes were never satisfied with the system; they always aspired to become cash renters or landowners. Moreover, what started out as a concession to the freedmen's desire for independence, quite rapidly became a system of racial repression.

The responsibility for the unsatisfactory resolution of the land question did not rest entirely with the southern whites. In large part it rested upon the actions of the northern whites. Despite the talk of confiscation, most political leaders—even many of the Radical Republicans and abolitionists—had too strong a sense of the importance of property rights to espouse confiscation of anyone's estates—even those of the rebels. In the end it was Congress and the Republicans as much as President Johnson who betrayed the freedmen on this crucial matter. The proposal was entirely too revolutionary for nineteenth-century America. The Republican leaders and the upper-and middle-class white abolitionists were for the most part simply too conservative to accept confiscation with equanimity. In fact, in their thinking, the right of an individual to his personal freedom and to his property were two closely interrelated rights, both of them founded in the values of individualism. For a similar reason there was a lack of unity among the friends of the freedmen regarding the degree to which the government should practice a paternalistic benevolence in uplifting the ex-slaves. Many thought that government assistance to the freedmen in the form of granting them land would discourage the individual initiative and independence which they hoped the freedmen, crushed down under slavery, would quickly develop.[21]

In some ways the land issue was the central or crucial issue in reconstruction as far as Negroes were concerned. As the New Orleans *Tribune* suggested, and as students as diverse as W. E. B. Du Bois and Gunnar Myrdal have maintained more

recently,[22] it can be argued that the failure to confiscate the large estates and redistribute them in small plots among the freedmen, doomed Congress' plans for political reconstruction to failure and the black men to generations of oppression. Viewed more broadly, the North's failure to grapple seriously with the land question was simply part and parcel of the whole pattern of northern indifference to the status of Negroes in American society. To put the matter baldly, most of the people in a position of political influence were not really interested in the Negroes' welfare. Only a handful of Radical Republicans had any sincere desire to make Negroes full citizens. Citizenship rights and the franchise were provided almost as a by-product of political squabbling in Washington. The civil rights bills and the Fourteenth and Fifteenth Amendments were passed reluctantly, and only as the result of long battles and many compromises. Recent research suggests that they would not have been passed at all if President Johnson and the Democrats had acted skillfully instead of pushing the moderate Republicans into accepting the proposals of the Radicals. Negro suffrage resulted mainly from the desire to protect southern white unionists and from northern fears about the disloyalty of the ex-rebels.[23]

Moreover, as noted above, at the end of the Civil War Negroes did not enjoy equal rights, even in a legal sense, in more of the North. The states of the Old Northwest rejected efforts to enfranchise Negroes within their borders, and outside of New England and New York Negroes did not obtain the franchise until after the passage of the Fifteenth Amendment. And because the Fifteenth Amendment was rejected by a number of northern states, it was ratified only with the votes of the reconstructed southern states. Jim Crow practices existed in most of the Old Northwest and the Middle Atlantic states. In Pennsylvania, for example, only a long fight led by Negro abolitionists finally secured a state law against segregation in public conveyances in 1867; and not until 1881 was school segregation abolished in that state.[24] The Fourteenth Amendment, now interpreted as making segregation unconstitutional, was actually extremely vague on the matter of Negro rights. For most congressmen, even the Radicals, granting protection to life, liberty and property, and equality before the law, meant nothing more than the right to own and dispose of property, to sue and be sued, and to testify in courts. It apparently did not imply desegregation of transportation and public accommodations—a lack rectified only with the passage, after several years' arduous agitation, of Sumner's Supplementary Civil Rights Act in 1875. This law, unfortunately, for the most part went unenforced. The Fourteenth Amendment certainly did not encompass the idea of school desegregation. All these things, however, have been read into the amendment by the Supreme Court during the last twenty years.

Whether one accepts the older view that politicians and capitalists desirous of continued Republican ascendancy brought about Negro enfranchisement in order to protect their interests, or whether one accepts the newer view that Negroes received suffrage and citizenship rights as a sort of by-product of the political factionalism in Washington and the self-defeating tactics of Johnson and the northern Democrats, one thing

---

[21]For a suggestive discussion see Kenneth Stampp, *The Era of Reconstruction* (New York, 1965), pp. 28–30.

[22]Du Bois, *Black Reconstruction, passim;* Gunnar Myrdal, *An American Dilemma* (New York, 1944), I, 244–227.

[23]I have been greatly stimulated by Eric L. McKitrick, *Andrew Johnson and Reconstruction* (Chicago, 1960); LaWanda and John H. Cox, *Politics, Principle, and Prejudice, 1865–1866* (New York, 1963), and Stampp, *The Era of Reconstruction,* though none of these authors would necessarily fully agree with conclusions stated here and elsewhere in this paper.

[24]Leslie H. Fishel, Jr., "Northern Prejudice and Negro Suffrage, 1865–1870," *Journal of Negro History,* XXXIX (1954), 8–26; McPherson, *Negro's Civil War,* pp. 255–261; McPherson, *Struggle for Equality,* chap. x.

emerges quite clearly—responsible whites in positions of influence were simply not listening to the Negroes. Negroes received their rights in the South for a few brief years during reconstruction not because of the brilliantly worded resolutions, addresses and petitions of the Negro conventions and orators, or because of the deep-rooted desires of the mass of freedmen for economic independence and dignity, but because of the activities of the northern whites, to whom the welfare of the Negroes was usually an incidental or secondary issue. What was true for the Republicans was also true in modified form for the abolitionists. James McPherson, in his recent volume, *The Struggle for Equality,* makes a good case for attributing at least a part of the development of congressional sentiment for Negro rights to the agitation of some of the old abolitionists who felt that their work was not done with the emancipation of the slaves. Yet even the abolitionists were divided, many of them asserting that once emancipated the southern freedman should be left to help themselves. Others, like the great orator, Wendell Phillips, and certain of the northern school teachers who went south after the war and made the education of the freedmen their life work, were sincerely interested in bringing citizenship rights and real equality for the Negroes. Even these idealists often had an unconscious paternalism about them. They sincerely believed in racial equality, but they also believed that they knew what was best for the Negroes. Willie Lee Rose records the shock that some of the white missionaries of the Sea Islands received when Negroes wanted to make their own decisions.[25]

There is little evidence that such people listened, at least very much, to what the Negroes were saying. Rather their views in favor of citizenship rights and, in some cases, of land for the Negroes, were not a response to Negro demands, but grew out of their own philanthropic ideals. McPherson carefully records the influence of Negro abolitionists upon the white abolitionists during the Civil War and reconstruction. But from reading his book it is clear that the only Negro whom the white abolitionists really listened to in this period was Frederick Douglass, a figure so Olympian that he commanded respect; and it does not appear that they listened even to him very much.

The granting of citizenship rights and the vote to Negroes came about not because of what the Negroes were articulating, but because of what whites, for their own various reasons, decided to do about the Negroes. Even the most advanced and liberal journals did not deem it worth their while to report what Negroes themselves were thinking and doing about their status and their future. Since the white abolitionists and Radical Republicans were not, for the most part, genuinely committed to a belief in the essential human dignity of Negroes—much as many of them verbally protested that they did—it was easy for many of them to become disillusioned with reconstruction, to accept the southern viewpoint about

corruption and black power and to wash their hands of the whole problem. This was even true of many who had once been enthusiastic about guaranteeing Negroes their citizenship rights.

It is thus clear how it was that Turner and his colored colleagues were so easily expelled from the Georgia legislature, and how it was that even though they were readmitted the following year, Georgia returned to the hands of the white supremacists in 1872. It also should be clear why congress was really ineffective in dealing with the violence perpetrated by the Ku Klux Klan and other terrorist organizations, and why it was that, one after the other, the southern states were all permitted to return to white supremacy. The fact is that neither the North as a whole, nor Congress, nor even the majority of the white abolitionists were sufficiently concerned about Negroes to protect the citizenship rights which they had guaranteed them.

These attitudes, characteristic even of the Negroes' friends, afford some insight into the role which Negroes played in southern politics during the era of congressional or black reconstruction. We can spell out the numbers and names of prominent Negro officeholders, and at first glance the list is impressive. Two Negroes, Alonzo J. Ransier and Richard H. Gleaves, served as lieutenant-governor in South Carolina; three, Oscar J. Dunn, C. C. Antoine, and P. B. S. Pinchback, held this office in Louisiana, and Pinchback served briefly as acting governor; and one, A. K. Davis, was lieutenant-governor in Mississippi. South Carolina and Mississippi had Negro speakers of the house—Robert B. Elliott and Samuel J. Lee in South Carolina, and John R. Lynch in Mississippi. William J. Whipper was an associate justice of the supreme court of South Carolina. James J. Hill served as secretary of state in Mississippi; Francis L. Cardozo held both that post and that of state treasurer in South Carolina; and Jonathan C. Gibbs was first secretary of state and superintendent of education in Florida. Three other states also had Negro superintendents of education: Mississippi, Louisiana, and Arkansas. On the national level Mississippi sent two Negroes to the Senate—Blanche K. Bruce and Hiram R. Revels; and seven states elected Negroes to the House of Representatives during reconstruction.

No one has really yet investigated the question: exactly how did the Negro politicians function in the southern reconstruction governments?[26] Probably, just as their numbers were small in proportion to the number of Negroes in the southern states, so their influence was less than their abilities or numbers warranted. After all, even the white abolitionists, the most equalitarian group in American society, did not permit their Negro colleagues in the movement to play a significant leadership role. Douglass, the only Negro of real influence in the movement, had to establish himself as an independent force outside of the two major antislavery societies. It is therefore most unlikely that the mixed bag of northerners and southerners, idealists, opportunists and adventurers that composed the southern Republican party were willing to accord Negroes a vital role.

Only three states, South Carolina, Louisiana, and Alabama, sent more than one Negro to the national House of Repre-

---

[25]McPherson, *Struggle for Equality, passim;* Rose, *Rehearsal for Reconstruction,* p. 369.
[26]For a thoughtful discussion of the Negro political leaders during reconstruction see John Hope Franklin, *Reconstruction: After the Civil War* (Chicago, 1961), pp. 86–92, 133–138.

sentatives; four others—Georgia, Mississippi, Florida, and Louisiana—were represented by one each; while three southern states—Virginia, Arkansas, and Texas—sent no Negroes at all to Congress during reconstruction. Moreover, outside of Florida, where Gibbs was superintendent of education, only Arkansas and the three states with a Negro majority in their population selected Negroes for prominent state-wide office. Even taking these three states—Mississippi, Louisiana, and South Carolina—we find that never was a Negro elected governor; that Negroes were unable to send one of their number to the United States Senate from either Louisiana or South Carolina, despite efforts to do so; and that only one of the states, South Carolina, had a Negro on its supreme court. And only in South Carolina did Negroes form a majority in the constitutional convention or even for a brief period in one house of the state legislature.

We know practically nothing of the interaction among the Negro and white politicians, but it would appear that to a remarkable extent office-holding at the highest levels tended to be a symbolic function. Each of the three states with a Negro majority had Negro lieutenant-governors—a purely honorific post. The two Negroes who served in the United States Senate were both moderates. Revels, the first one, voted Democratic consistently after reconstruction, while the other, Bruce, became a large plantation owner. In post-reconstruction Mississippi, the Bruce-Hill-Lynch triumvirate, which dominated the state's Republican party, cooperated closely with the Democrats, making a deal known as fusion, whereby a few posts would go to Negroes in those sections of the state where they were in a heavy majority, though most of the posts and all the important ones remained in white hands. A similar arrangement obtained in the black counties of coastal South Carolina.[27]

The power of the Negro politicians in these states is revealed by what happened to the school system. A nonsegregated school system was an important issue raised in a number of the state constitutional conventions. But only South Carolina and Louisiana provided for mixed schools in their constitutions. Even in these two states, in fact, the schools were administered so that there was practically no integration. Only the New Orleans school system and the University of South Carolina were integrated.[28] Neither on this issue nor on land reform were the Negro politicians able to deliver—any more than they were able to control a fair proportion of the offices.

The foregoing should not be taken as suggesting that Negro politicians were powerless. They were not. In Florida, for example, Negroes exercised a balance of power between two white factions, and under the astute leadership of the state superintendent of education, Jonathan C. Gibbs, were able to obtain certain concessions and keep Florida in the ranks of the

Radical states until 1877. In Louisiana and South Carolina the Negro majorities among the voters did exercise some power, and certain individuals, such as Robert Brown Elliott and Francis L. Cardozo, seem to have been men with a measure of influence. But not only was their influence far less than the prosouthern historians have insisted, but it was also considerably less than their numbers, education, and ability warranted. Neither southern white opportunists, nor paternalistically benevolent northern whites, were inclined to accord positions of real power to Negroes.[29]

If the states with Negro majorities experienced a relative lack of political power on the part of Negroes, it is clear why in other states Negro officeholders had even less of a role, beyond the symbolic one. Effective power stayed in the hands of the whites in all the southern states. Much of the responsibility for this situation rests with the Republicans in Congress.

As the North, the Republicans, and many of the abolitionists deserted and betrayed the southern Negroes, the visions of the equal rights conventions of the 1860's and the hopes of the rural black masses remained only hopes. Sharecropping and peonage, mob violence and disfranchisement became the order of the day. By 1877 southern Negroes were left with only the shreds of their status during the apogee of congressional reconstruction. And even these shreds were destroyed in the wave of proscriptive legislation passed at the turn of the century. Meanwhile, the Supreme Court turned the Fourteenth Amendment upside down. In 1883 it held the Civil Rights Act of 1875 unconstitutional, and thirteen years later, in 1896, it enunciated the separate-but-equal doctrine, justifying state laws requiring segregation. And two years after that, in 1898, it sustained the provisions of the Mississippi constitution of 1890 with its subterfuges that effectively emasculated the Fifteenth Amendment.

Yet these two amendments, passed during the first reconstruction, are the constitutional basis of the new or second reconstruction of the present decade. First of all they were the foundation for the NAACP court victories which, starting in 1915, had by the 1950's so undermined the legal underpinnings of the southern race system that they produced a revolution of expectations among Negroes. And that revolution in expectations is at the bottom of the civil rights revolution of the 1960's. Secondly, it is largely in these reconstruction amendments that the legislative and executive branches have found constitutional sanction for increasing federal intervention in the South.

Although tactics differ markedly from those employed during the first reconstruction, Negro demands today are remarkably similar to those made a hundred years ago—civil rights, the franchise, and economic opportunity. Like prominent Negroes then, civil rights leaders today are concerned with more than constitutional rights; and, quite remarkably, in both cases there is the conviction that the Federal government should undertake the responsibility of providing special assistance to the Negro to compensate for the past. Yet there is a striking difference in the dynamics of the two situations. A hundred years ago whites were not listening to what Negroes were saying.

---

[27] Wharton, *Negro in Mississippi*, pp. 202–203; George B. Tindall, *South Carolina Negroes, 1877–1900* (Columbia, S.C., 1952), pp. 62–64.

[28] Louis R. Harlan, "Segregation in New Orleans Public Schools During Reconstruction," *American Historical Review*, LXVII (1962), pp. 663–675; Williamson, *After Slavery*, pp. 219–223, 232.

[29] For a sharply contrasting view see Williamson, *After Slavery*, chaps. xii and xiii.

But in the 1960's Negroes, rather than whites, furnish the impetus for social change.

A century ago, as in our own day, something of a moral revolution was going on in the conscience of white America, a revolution forced by the slavery question. It is true that the causes behind that moral revolution were not themselves entirely moral. For one thing they were largely military. Northerners who expected a short war were shocked by military defeat into advocating the destruction of the slave system; and this very practical and *amoral* consideration blended inextricably with, and gave enormous stimulus to fervently moral antislavery doctrines. For the first time white northerners generally became convinced that slavery was a moral evil that had to be swept away; that the Civil War was God's punishment upon a transgressing nation that had condoned slavery for so long. But few came to believe that Negroes were inherently equal to whites.

In the 1960's again military exigencies have played their role in changing the moral climate—the country's leading role in world affairs, the Cold War, and the crucial position of colored nations in the international power system. Yet unquestionably more and more white Americans have become aware that Negroes have aspirations that should be respected. This new awareness has been manifested not only in the increasing concern for equal rights but also in the way in which whites have been paying attention to what Negroes are saying and doing.

Will the new reconstruction prove as temporary and evanescent as the old? The history of the first reconstruction suggests that revolutions—if indeed there was a revolution—can go backwards; that the white majority may grow disillusioned or just weary of idealism.[30] On the other hand, the recent changes in the attitudes of white Americans appear more deeply rooted than those of a hundred years ago. For one thing changing racial views are part of a long-term trend rooted in the New Deal period, in the moral sensitivities aroused as a result of the struggle with racist Nazi Germany, and the postwar international pressures. Moreover for the past couple of decades the northern Negro vote has been a decisive factor in many elections, and the weight of increasing numbers of registered Negro voters in the South will be felt, the current "white backlash" notwithstanding.[31]

Reforms can be reversed; revolutions may indeed go backwards. It is conceivable that the new reconstruction will be undone as was the old. Certainly, at best it will be accomplished in a halting and spasmodic manner, and every advance will be the fruit of costly and hard-fought struggles, involving compromises and even reverses along the way. Nevertheless, if one may hazard a prediction, the increasing sensitivity of whites to the Negroes' needs and demands—a growing concern for Negroes as *persons* as contrasted to concern about the *institution* of slavery—suggest that the new reconstruction is more likely to prove to be a permanent one.

[30]For sensitive discussion of such trends see C. Vann Woodward, "What Happened to the Civil Rights Movement?" *Harper's Magazine* (Jan., 1967), pp. 29–37.
[31]See, for example, Reese Cleghorn and Pat Watters, "The Impact of Negro Votes on Southern Politics," *The Reporter* (Jan. 26, 1867), pp. 24–25, 31–32.

Negro Officials
After The Civil War

BY DR. JOHN HOPE FRANKLIN

The Act of March 2, 1867, was specific about the qualifications of those who were to have a voice in the new program of reconstruction. Constitutions were to be written by delegates "to be elected by the male citizens of the state, twenty-one years old and upward, of whatever race, color, or previous condition, who have been resident in said state for one year . . . except such as may be disfranchised for participation in the rebellion or for felony at common law." It was no easy task to administer satisfactorily these provisions of the Act. The commanding generals in the Southern military districts were hard pressed to find competent and qualified registrars to enroll the electorate. They used Union army officers and Freedmen's Bureau agents; and a few of them used some Negroes. Travel into remote areas was difficult, and in some instances weeks elapsed before registrations were received, compiled, and made ready for elections.

Some of the commanding generals felt a deep responsibility to provide a little political education for those voters who had never had the experience or the opportunity to participate in politics. Several of them gave explicit instructions to registration officials to provide the freedmen with adequate information regarding their political rights. Freedmen's Bureau officers and agents engaged by the generals to work in the registration program helped the new voters understand their rights and duties. When Bureau officials had no political literature of their own to distribute, they disseminated materials prepared by the Union League, which was, as we shall see, easily the most active organization in the political education of the Negro.

When the criteria for becoming electors were applied to the people of the South, three groups qualified. One group was the vast majority of Negroes whose loyalty to the Union was unquestioned and who merely had to prove that they were not felons and had lived in the state one year. Another was the Northerners who had taken up residence in the South. If they met the residence requirements, they were enrolled. Finally, there were the native Southerners who qualified to take the "ironclad oath," and who were scrutinized with the greatest care. The rank and file among these groups was to be the center of the controversy that raged over the ensuing decade. Out of these groups were to come the leaders who bore the majority responsibility for both the good and the evils flowing from the difficult task of rebuilding the South.

The entrance of Negroes into the political arena was the most revolutionary aspect of the reconstruction program. Out of a population of approximately four million, some 700,000 qualified as voters, but the most of them were without the qualifications to participate effectively in a democracy. In this they were not unlike the large number of Americans who were enfranchised during the age of Jackson or the large number of immigrants who were being voted in herds by political bosses in New York, Boston, and other American cities at this time. They were the first to admit their deficiencies. Beverly Nash, an unlettered former slave sitting in the South Carolina convention, expressed the views of many when he said: "I believe, my friends and fellow-citizens, we are not prepared for this suffrage. But we can learn. Give a man tools and let him com-

From *Negro Digest,* November 1961, pp. 63-74. Adapted from *Reconstruction: After the Civil War.* University of Chicago Press.
© 1961 by John Hope Franklin. Reprinted by permission.

mence to use them, and in time he will learn a trade. So it is with voting. We may not understand it at the start, but in time we shall learn to do our duty."

Like Nash most of the Negroes were illiterate. A slave existence could hardly be expected to prepare one for the responsibilities of citizenship, especially when there were laws, as there were in slave states, banning the teaching of slaves. Even if Negroes were free, as were more than 200,000 in the slave states before the war, laws forbade their being taught to read and write. Indeed, when they came out of slavery many Negroes did not know their own names; many did not even have family names. It goes without saying that a considerable number had not the vaguest notion of what registering and voting meant.

None of this is surprising. It had been only two years since emancipation from a system that for more than two centuries had denied slaves most rights as human beings. And it must be remembered that in these two years the former Confederates, in power all over the South, did nothing to promote the social and political education of the former slaves. What is surprising is that there were some—and no paltry number—who in 1867 were able to assume the responsibilities of citizens and leaders.

Among South Carolina's Negro leaders was state treasurer Francis L. Cardozo, educated at Glasgow and London, who had been a minister in New Haven and, after the war, was principal of a Negro school in Charleston. Robert B. Elliott, born in Massachusetts, trained at Eton College in England, and elected to Congress in 1870, was urbane and articulate. J. J. Wright, a state supreme court justice, had studied at the University of Pennsylvania and had been a respected member of the Pennsylvania bar before moving to South Carolina after the war. Congressman James Rapier's white father sent him to school in Canada, and when he returned to his native Alabama after the war he had not only an ample formal education but a world of experience gained from travel and work in the North. Florida's secretary of state, Jonathan C. Gibbs, graduated from Dartmouth College and had been a Presbyterian minister for several years when reconstruction began. Among the Negro leaders of North Carolina James W. Hood, assistant superintendent of public instruction, and James H. Harris, an important figure in the 1868 constitutional convention, were educated, respectively, in Pennsylvania and Ohio. Many others, among them Henry M. Turner of the Georgia legislature, Hiram Revels, United States senator from Mississippi, and Richard H. Gleaves, member of Congress from South Carolina, had much more than the rudiments of a formal education when they entered upon their official duties.

Significant among Negro leaders were those who were almost wholly self-educated. Robert Smalls of South Carolina pursued his studies diligently until he had mastered the rudiments. Later he went to the United States House of Representatives. In Mississippi, John Roy Lynch regularly took time off from his duties in a photographer's studio to gaze across the alley into a white schoolroom, where he kept up with the class until he had mastered the courses taught there. When he became speaker of the Mississippi house and later a member of Congress, he relied on this earlier training. Before Jefferson Long went into Congress from Georgia, he had educated himself and had become a merchant tailor in Macon. There were numerous other self-educated Negro leaders, including John Carraway and Peyton Finley of Alabama, James O'Hara and A. H. Galloway of North Carolina, and James W. Bland and Lewis Lindsay of Virginia. From this educated element came the articulate, responsible Negroes who contributed substantially to the writing of the new constitutions and the establishment of the new governments in the former slave states.

Most of the Negro leaders were ministers. A fair number taught school. Some were employees of the Freedmen's Bureau or another federal agency. Here and there one found a Negro who had been trained in the law. There were, of course, farmers; and there were some artisans engaged in a variety of occupations. The economic interests and aspirations of the Negro leaders varied widely. It would be wrong to assume that they had no economic interests or that they had no views regarding the economic future of the South.

One of the really remarkable features of the Negro leadership was the small amount of vindictiveness in their words and their actions. There was no bully, no swagger, as they took their places in the state and federal governments traditionally occupied by the white planters of the South. The spirit of conciliation pervaded most of the public utterances the Negroes made. In his first speech in the South Carolina convention Beverly Nash asserted that the Southern white man was the "true friend of the black man." Pointing to the banner containing the words "United we stand, divided we fall," Nash said, "If you could see the scroll of the society that banner represents, you would see the white man and the black man standing with their arms locked together, as the type of friendship and union which we desire."

Negroes generally wished to see political disabilities removed from the whites. In South Carolina several Negroes presented a resolution asking Congress to remove all such disabilities, and it was passed. In Louisiana the Negroes requested that former Confederates be permitted to vote but, for the time being, not to hold office. In Alabama James T. Rapier, a Negro delegate to the constitutional convention, successfully sponsored a resolution asking Congress to remove the political disabilities of those who might aid in reconstruction. In Mississippi a Democratic paper, the Jackson Clarion, admitted that in their general conduct Negroes "have known consideration for the feelings of the whites. . . . In other words, the colored people had manifested no disposition to rule or dominate the whites, and the only Color Line which had existed, grew out of the unwise policy which had previously been pursued by the Democratic Party in its efforts to prevent the enjoyment by the newly-emancipated race of the rights and privileges to which they were entitled, under the Constitution and laws of the country." In South Carolina Beverly Nash declared that in public affairs "we must unite with our white fellow-citizens. They tell us that they have been disfranchised, yet we tell the North that we shall never let the halls of Congress be silent until we remove that disability."

Negroes attempted no revolution in the social relations of the races in the South. Francis B. Simkins in his "New Viewpoints of Southern Reconstruction" has accurately observed that "the defiance of the traditional caste division occasionally expressed in an official reception or in an act of the legislature was not reflected generally in common social relations." Negroes, as a rule, conceded to the insistence of whites that they were a race apart; and they made little or no attempt to invade social privacies. They did not even attempt to destroy white supremacy except where such supremacy rejected Negroes altogether as human beings, and there was almost nowhere any serious consideration given to providing legal approbation of interracial marriages. While Negroes sought equality as human beings, they manifested no desire to involve themselves in the purely social relations of whites as individuals or as groups. "It is false, it is a wholesale falsehood to say that we wish to force ourselves upon white people," declared the near-white P. B. S. Pinchback of Louisiana.

Nor did any considerable number of Negroes seek to effect an economic revolution in the South. Henry McNeal Turner, the fearless Negro leader who was almost universally disliked by white Georgians, did what he could to assist the whites in recovering their economic strength. In the Georgia convention he secured the passage of two resolutions that indicated a remarkable willingness to stabilize the economic life of the white community. One sought to prevent the sale of property whose owners were unable to pay their taxes; the other provided for the relief of banks. In South Carolina Negro leaders such as Robert DeLarge and Francis Cardozo supported relief measures with the full knowledge that whites would benefit as much as Negroes.

The movement of Northerners into the South after the Civil War is a part of the exciting drama of the migrations that had seen the continent populated from ocean to ocean and had taken Americans, new and old, wherever opportunity beckoned. The movement into the South was greatly stimulated by the favorable observations of scores of thousands of Union soldiers who had seen action on Southern battlefields. Some were mustered out of the army while still in the South and, despite some Southern feelings of hostility against them, decided to adopt the South as their home. Others, back in their Northern homes, waited only for the first opportunity to return to the South. By the fall of 1866, for example, more than five thousand Union soldiers had settled in Louisiana alone. The movement was also stimulated by the large number of industrialists and investors who saw in the underdeveloped South an important new economic frontier. Those committed to the view that the South's recovery from the war would be accompanied by an era of unparalleled expansion began to move into the region, bringing with them their own resources, and often the resources of others, with which to build railroads and factories and to purchase farm land and other properties.

Many federal agents—some from the Department of the Treasury, others from the Freedman's Bureau—settled in the South and called it home. Northern teachers, men and women, braved numerous indignities at the hands of hostile whites in order to teach Negroes, and they cast their lot with the South.

There were those form the North, moreover, who saw new political opportunities in the South. They hoped to use the newly enfranchised element and the problems arising out of reconstruction to achieve political power and economic gain. For them the South was a "happy hunting ground" that they could not resist. As to any frontier, there went to the South the adventurers, those who wanted to "get rich quick," and ne'er-do-wells who were fully prepared to embrace *any* cause, including Radical Reconstruction, that would benefit them.

These were the people who have been called "carpetbaggers" for the last ninety years. This opprobrious term, used as early as 1846 to describe any suspicious stranger, was applied indiscriminately to all Northerners in the South during reconstruction. It has generally implied that as a group they had nothing in the way of worldly possessions and were thoroughly unprincipled in their determination to fleece and exploit the South until their carpetbags fairly bulged with the possessions of Southerners and they were forced to acquire new coffers in which to place their ill-gotten gains. They have been described as a group at work on a grand master plan to Africanize the country. One historian described them as "gangs of itinerant adventurers, vagrant interlopers" who were "too depraved, dissolute, dishonest and degraded to get the lowest of places in the states they had just left." These descriptions fall far short of the mark. They impugn the integrity and good intentions of thousands whose motives were otherwise. Even more important, perhaps, is the fact that such descriptions show no understanding of the variety and complexity of the motives underlying the migrations and no appreciation for the economic and political relationships that grew out of such motives.

There is no evidence that even the considerable number of Negro migrants from the North were interested in "Africanizing" the country. Indeed the term was an extravagance, a flourish—like "Negro rule"—used to express disgust. The other common descriptions are equally inaccurate. As Thomas Conway pointed out a few months after the war, many Northerners, including the teacher, preacher, merchant, husbandman, mechanic, laborer, and discharged Union soldier, were ready to move South. He had persuaded Northern men to take $3,000,000 into the South to purchase land, make loans, and advances on crops. Their only fears were whether there was sufficient law and order to maintain security for their investments. But they went South, and they continued to go all during the reconstruction period. In November, 1865, Sidney Andrews observed that already several Massachusetts men were in business in Charleston; and he estimated that at least half the stores on the principal streets of the city were run by Northern men.

The careers of Captain H. S. Chamberlain and General John T. Wilder, both of Ohio, illustrate the kind of activities in which numerous so-called carpetbaggers were engaged. When Chamberlain was mustered out of the Union army in Knoxville, Tennessee, in 1865, he at once entered the iron and coal business in Knoxville and is regarded by some as the real founder of the modern iron industry south of the Ohio. In 1867 Chamberlain joined with General Wilder, later of Wilder's Lightning Brigade of Ohio, to organize the Roane Iron Company, which bought large tracts of coal and iron land and engaged extensively in the operation of coke works, iron mines, and furnaces. Together they became involved in many industrial and financial ventures, including the Dixie Portland Cement Company, the Brookside Cotton Mills of Knoxville, and the First National Bank of Chattanooga.

That all so-called carpetbaggers were not simply Radicals with no consideration for the welfare and development of the South can be seen also in the life of Willard Warner, planter, politician, and iron manufacturer. Born in Granville, Ohio, and educated at Marietta College, Warner served in the Union army and went to the Ohio senate in 1865. Two years later he moved to Alabama, and with his ample resources engaged in cotton planting for several years. He became active in Republican politics and served in the United States Senate from 1868 to 1871. Then he organized the Tecumseh Iron Company and served as president and manager until 1873. For this venture more than $100,000 was supplied by his Northern associates. Later he moved to Tennessee, where he had extensive investments and blast furnaces. The overthrow of reconstruction seems not to have affected this "carpetbagger," for as late as 1900 the Conservatives (the Democrats) in his adopted state elected him to the Tennessee legislature.

If recent historians have reviled Northerners who settled in the South after the Civil War, their Southern contemporaries were inclined to be grateful to them for their contributions to Southern development. Clinton A. Cilley, born in New Hampshire and a Harvard graduate, settled in North Carolina in 1866. After a career in law, including several years as a judge of the Lenoir Superior Court, he was called in 1900 "one of North Carolina's ablest lawyers and finest citizens." General Wilder, the iron manufacturer, was very popular among Southerners, including former Confederates. During the Spanish-American War the governor of Tennessee named the training camp near Knoxville "Camp Wilder," in honor of the carpetbagger from Ohio. Lieutenant B. H. True of the 136th New York Volunteers, who settled in Georgia in 1865, was consistently popular with his new neighbors; they not only supported his newspaper, the *Appeal and Advertiser,* but elected him, as the "celebrated farmer from Morgan County," to the State Agricultural Society.

The interest of such men and groups of men in the political future of the South was real. With so much at stake in the way of investments and with full appreciation of the economic potential of the South they could not be indifferent to the uncertain political winds that were blowing across their adopted home. Their interest transformed itself into a strong desire to attain certain specific political goals for the South. One was the achievement and maintenance of law and order. They had seen enough hostility and lawlessness in many Southern communities to cause considerable uneasiness about the safety of their investments. They wanted governments that would insure this safety; and if they could facilitate the establishment of such governments, they would certainly do so. Another was the maintenance of a close alliance between government and the business community. They had seen the importance of such an alliance in numerous developments in Washington during

the war and in the effective service that several state governments in the North had rendered the business community. Favorable banking and insurance laws, tax exemptions or rebates, land grants and other assistance to railroads were among the favors the government could and would, under certain desirable circumstances, grant to business and industry. If at all possible, Northerners would see that this was done in the South.

Finally, most Northerners in the South were convinced that their goals could best be attained through a vigorous, well-organized Republican party throughout the South. This was, after all, the party responsible for the intimate relationship between government and business on the national level and in several Northern state governments. They knew that there was little chance of luring the former Confederates into the Republican party and that the Democratic party would oppose at every turn whatever Republicans attempted to do. Southern Democrats tended to equate Republicans with abolitionists and thus to regard them as the destroyers of the South's cherished economic and social system. Northern Republicans had to look to others in the South for political support.

A Republican in the South did not have to belong to the Thaddeus Stevens–Charles Sumner wing of the party to reach the conclusion that Negro suffrage was not only desirable but imperative. For the conclusion was inescapable that the party's strength would come from Negroes and from whatever support they could secure from loyal native Southerners. They did all they could to promote the enfranchisement of the Negro and draw him into the Republican party. This did not mean, however, that the so-called carpetbaggers were interested in "Africanizing" the South. Even when they undertook to "Northernize" the South, there was no revolution in the general social relations between Negroes and whites. B. H. True, a New Yorker living in Georgia, said that he was as friendly toward the Negro as anyone, "but there is an antagonism which we all have against the race; that I cannot get rid of; I do not believe any man can." Had these Radicals been radical on social questions, they would have opposed the laws against intermarriage that were enacted during the Radical regime. They would also have stood for one system of public schools open to all races, but their infrequent expressions in favor of such a system were feeble indeed. These matters—unlike Negro suffrage—were not among their primary interests, and they gave them scant attention.

It was only natural that Northerners in the South could wield political influence and exercise power far out of proportion to their numbers. They were the best prepared to step into the vacuum created by the disfranchisement of the former Confederates. They had training and experience in political and economic matters that neither Negroes nor loyal native Southerners had. They clearly knew what their interests were and how best they could be secured. Finally they had the support of the powerful, victorious party that was in control of affairs in Washington. While their influence in the South was not always decisive or even critical, it was invariably a factor in the determination of affairs, present and future, in the Southern states.

No group of postwar Southern leaders has been reviled or castigated—or misunderstood—more than loyal native Southerners, commonly known as "scalawags." The term came in all likelihood from Scalloway, a district in the Shetland Islands where small, runty cattle and horses were bred. It was used in Western New York before the Civil War in referring to a "mean fellow, a scape grace." In the South the term was used by the opponents of reconstruction to describe those they regarded as the lowest, meanest element in society. These were the Southerners who could swear that they had never voluntarily given aid, countenance, counsel, or encouragement to persons in rebellion and had exercised or attempted to exercise the functions of no office under the Confederacy. They were largely men who had opposed secession. The votes against secession in some state legislatures, together with the known sentiment against such drastic action, indicates that a considerable number of Southerners dragged their feet or refused to have any part in the Confederate cause. Many had for years smarted under a system that gave every advantage to the planter class, to which very few of them belonged. They bitterly resented the course of action, pursued by the planter class, which had led to a war that, from their point of view, became more and more a "poor man's fight."

It is impossible to determine how many so-called scalawags were qualified to participate in reconstruction under the terms of the several acts of Congress. Likewise it is impossible to determine the extent to which those who took the "ironclad oath" were eligible to do so. After June, 1867, those who took the oath were, as President Johnson had indicated to the commanding generals, judges of their own honesty. Since the machinery as well as the personnel of registration was of questionable efficiency, it is entirely possible that many who were clearly not eligible registered anyway. There were some eligibles who refused to register, and many who were not eligible advised the loyal Southerners to have no part in the Radical regime. Others advised the eligibles to register and then defeat the Radical effort by voting against it. "If we are to wear manacles," said Governor Perry of South Carolina, "let them be put on by our tyrants, not ourselves."

But there were those in the South who counseled loyal Southerners to participate in the new reconstruction program and then to restrain any excessive or revolutionary tendencies that might militate against the best interests of the South. The fact that Negroes were to participate did not degrade white Southerners or diminish their influence unless they purposely abandoned the field to Negroes. The New Orleans Picayune told its readers that promptness in registering and voting would convince the North "that we mean to take care of our own affairs." The Savannah News gave similar advice when it declared that Georgia expected every man to do his duty and register without delay to show his reverence for his "nobel commonwealth." The Charleston Daily Courier echoed the same view: "That you should register is an imperative duty which each man owes to himself, to his community and to his state."

A curious assortment of native Southerners thus became eligible to participate in Radical Reconstruction. And the number increased as the President granted individual pardons or issued new proclamations of amnesty. It became increasingly difficult to make a distinction between the views of the loyal Southerners and the views of those whose citizenship was being restored. On political and social questions they ranged from the radicalism of James W. Hunnicut of Virginia, who stood for the full legal and social equality of Negroes and whites, to the conservatism of Milton Candler, a Georgia senator who claimed that Negroes were not citizens and therefore were not eligible to hold office. Certainly the majority of these loyal Southerners could not be described as Radicals in the sense of embracing the policies and program for Negroes set forth by the Radicals in Congress. Often they advocated segregation of Negroes and whites in educational and other institutions. Often they spoke as vigorously for the rights of the South as did any former Confederate. Their primary interest was in supporting a party that would build the South on a broader base than the plantation aristocracy of ante-bellum days. They found it expedient to do business with Negroes and so-called carpetbaggers; but often they returned to the Democratic party as it gained sufficient strength to be a factor in Southern politics.

These were the people who were called scalawags by their adversaries. They hardly deserved the name, nor did they deserve the numerous other opprobrious labels pinned on them by hostile critics. Wade Hampton called them "the mean, lousy and filthy kind that are not fit for butchers or dogs." Another called them "scaly, scabby runts in a herd of cattle." Even the historians have joined in the verbal assault on these loyal native Southerners. One describes scalawags as "vile, blatant, vindictive, unprincipled." Perhaps during the period of their ascendancy the scalawags committed many offenses against the social order; for the graft and corruption they must take at least a part of the blame. But their most serious offense was to have been loyal to the Union during the Civil War or to have declared that they had been loyal and thereby to have enjoyed full citizenship during the period of Radical Reconstruction.

It is extremely difficult to determine the strength of the three groups that dominated the South during Radical Reconstruction. There was constant fluctuation in the show of strength, particularly among the native Southerners and the Northerners living in the South. And there was constant defection, with Negroes dropping out of the picture under Ku Klux Klan or other pressures, with Northerners leaving or going over to the Conservatives, as the opponents of Radical Reconstruction were called, and with "loyal" Southerners deviating from or deserting the Radical cause altogether. The best that one can do is look at the comparative numerical strength of the three groups and draw some inferences from the observation. A likely time for such a comparison is 1867-68, when the several state conventions wrote the new constitutions required by the Reconstruction Acts.

The figures . . . illustrate several significant points. In the first place, except for South Carolina, Negroes enjoyed no numerical domination in the conventions. The only other state in which they were nearly a majority was Louisiana, where by agreement they were to constitute 50 per cent of the delegates. Thus, "Negro rule," as reconstruction has been erroneously described, had an inauspicious beginning and, indeed, was never to materialize. Second, the so-called carpetbaggers were in the minority in every state except Mississippi. Many were so preoccupied with personal undertakings, or with setting up schools and churches, that they had no time for public service. Their position, however, was adequately represented by those new settlers who did find time to serve. Finally, the native whites had a larger numerical representation in the conventions than is usually recognized. Dominating several conventions, such as those in Alabama, Georgia, and North Carolina, and having substantial numbers in others, they were prepared to play a significant part in the deliberations and in the administration of affairs in their states.

Although leadership in the South came from these three groups, at least in the early days of congressional reconstruction, it does not follow that the leaders invariably worked together in promoting a Radical program. Their motives, values, and goals were not the same and their effort to work together was often strained because of these differences. Far from entering into any conspiracy to degrade and destroy the Southern way of life, they frequently worked at cross purposes. At times the position of the Negro leaders approached that of the crusading abolitionists. Meanwhile, the so-called carpetbaggers frequently preoccupied themselves with building up the alliance between the business community and the Republican-controlled state government. All too often, moreover, the loyal Southerners talked and acted like the conservative former Confederates whom they presumably opposed. Co-operation was at best loose and irregular, forced at times only by the threat of their common destruction. It was under these circumstances that the three groups of leaders forged a program for the reconstruction of the Southern states. How such a program actually emerged is one of the fascinating chapters in American history.

Definitions

Conservative: A Statesman who is enamored of existing evils, as distinguished from the Liberal, who wishes to replace them with others.—Ambrose Bierce, *The Devil's Dictionary.*

"SWEET DREAMS OF FREEDOM":

Freedwomen's Reconstruction of Life and Labor in Lowcountry South Carolina

Leslie A. Schwalm

In his memoir of Civil War and Reconstruction, rice planter Charles Manigault offered what he regarded as some of the "leading Characteristicks of *The NEGRO, and . . . The Times,* through *which we have recently passed.*" For Manigault, those characteristics were exemplified by his former slave Peggy, who offered ample evidence of how emancipation and Confederate defeat had turned Manigault's world upside down. Manigault noted that as the war came to a close, former slaves plundered and destroyed planter homes throughout his lowcountry South Carolina neighborhood. Peggy "seized as *Her part* of the *spoils* my wife's Large & handsome Mahogany Bedstead & Mattrass & arranged it in her own Negro House *on which she slept* for some time" and in which Manigault bitterly imagined she enjoyed *"her Sweet Dreams of freedom."* Peggy also confiscated from the Manigault residence some *"Pink Ribands,* & tied in a dozen bows the woolly head of her Daughter, to the admiration of the other Negroes." Lastly, Manigault noted Peggy's response when he, joined by his son and a former overseer (and Confederate officer), came onto the farm and "immediately began to pitch the Negro Effects" into two wagons, intending to evict the freedpeople. Only Peggy ("the lady of the *Big Mahogany Bed*") tried to intervene: "placing her arms *akimbo,* said 'She would go off to the Provost Marshal in town & *stop our unlawful proceedings with their property in their own homes.*' "[1]

Peggy's appropriation of her former mistresses' furniture, her use of contraband ribbons to style her daughter's hair, and her public challenge to Manigault's authority all signaled to Manigault that Peggy was pursuing her freedom with a literal vengeance, or what Manigault described as "reckless-

From the *Journal of Women's History,* Spring 1997, pp. 9-38. © 1997 by Indiana University Press. Reprinted by permission.

ness and Ingratitude." In the actions of freed-women like Peggy, and also in the responses that she and freedwomen like her provoked from former owners and from the civilian and military agents of Reconstruction, lies one of the most underexplored dynamics of the South's transition from slavery to freedom and the subject of this essay: the influence of former slave women's defining acts of freedom on the South's transition to a free labor society.

In the last 15 years, historians have produced an impressive body of work reexamining the South's transition from slavery to freedom during and after the Civil War, work that has yielded new information and a richer understanding of the complex process, and implications, of American emancipation.[2] Yet much of this scholarship, despite its emphasis on the multifaceted involvement of former slaves in shaping the South's transition to a free society, has omitted the actions and experiences of half of the four million who passed from slavery to freedom. Too often the transition from slavery to freedom has been investigated and portrayed as though slave women did not share that experience or failed to contribute to the process; enslaved African-American women like Peggy, it would seem, had little if any specific or general influence on the shape of the path slaves forged which led from slavery to freedom.[3]

Historians' failure to come to terms with freedwomen's role in the wartime and postbellum South has not been entirely a matter of omission. Despite the dearth of research, many scholars have characterized freedwomen's role in the postbellum conflict as allegedly withdrawing and retreating from the labor force, a conclusion that relies upon the infallibility of contemporary observations by northern and southern whites, and also on census-based estimates of freedwomen's labor-force participation.[4] Even with limited evidence, scholars have freely interpreted freedwomen's motivations and expectations based on their alleged withdrawal from the paid workforce. Some posit that freedwomen gladly yielded to the demands of their husbands that they withdraw from agricultural employment, that they voluntarily collaborated with their husbands' postemancipation claims to the privileges and prerogatives of a patriarchally-ordered family and household. Others suggest that freedwomen were imitating white behavior, anxious to claim for themselves the privileges they perceived in elite white women's domesticity—not the least of which was an escape from the physical demands of field work and the demeaning labor of domestic service.[5] The work of Jacqueline Jones and Gerald

Jaynes has offered a significant departure from speculation, given their more focused investigations into the actions of freedwomen in the postwar South. Both have turned their attention to freedwomen's creative attempts to choose productive and reproductive labor in their own and their families' best interests. Yet while Jones posits that "Only at home could [freedwomen] exercise considerable control over their own lives and those of their husbands and children and impose a semblance of order on the physical world," Jaynes has persuasively argued that freedwomen's actions must be evaluated in the context of specific postwar agricultural economies, offering an important challenge to the somewhat deterministic assumption that all freedwomen acted alike.[6] The conclusion that freedwomen's refusal to work in the manner demanded or prescribed by southern or northern whites actually culminated in women's wholesale withdrawal from labor markets across the South is premature, and its acceptance as "common knowledge" has deterred closer investigation of freedwomen's influence over and participation in wartime and postbellum conflict.

With the themes of withdrawal and retreat used to characterize women's postbellum experience, freedwomen like Peggy have been easily ignored as actors on the public landscape, the landscape from which historians typically identify the "facts" of Reconstruction. Yet Peggy's actions were both "public" and, as this essay will argue, typical for lowcountry freedwomen. In the actions of freedwomen like Peggy we find clues to some of the many ways in which former slave women distinguished their freedom from their slavery—from the vengeful ransacking of their former owners' homes, to the significance of dress and hair style in claiming and asserting a new personal dignity, to "reckless" confrontations with the plantation whites who had defined the day-to-day nature of exploitation under slavery. Recent research suggests there were also other important arenas in which former slave women tried to give meaning and substance to their freedom. Sharon Holt has revealed how freedwomen's (and men's) efforts to increase their autonomy and their resources were intertwined with their desire to build, staff, and sustain schools, churches, mutual and benevolent societies, and a host of other independent institutions.[7] Elsa Barkley Brown has reminded us that when Radical Reconstruction opened the political arena to freedmen, freedwomen also brought forward their own claims to citizenship, to political meetings and rallies, to voter registration, and to the polls.[8] Work, which had been so central to women's experience of slavery, was also critical to women's definition of freedom. In lowcountry South Carolina, freed-women escalated the battle to define black free-dom when they sought autonomous control over plantation lands, when they negotiated and recon-structed plantation and domestic labor, and when they defended the new autonomy of their families and household economies from exploitation by planters and unwelcome intervention by northern agents of Reconstruction. In seeking control over their field labor on lowcountry rice plantations, women sought to distance themselves from the power and control of former slaveowning whites *outside* of the rice fields as much as *in* them.

Determined to pursue freedom on their own terms, freedwomen who sought the means and the opportunity to live and subsist as free from white intervention as possible encountered con-siderable opposition from several sources. Op-position came from white vigilantes, planters, mistresses and overseers, all anxious for the re-turn of a reliable and subordinate labor force, and from U.S. soldiers and agents of the Freedmen's Bureau who were frustrated by former slaves' un-willingness to embrace the tenets of the free labor society many Northerners envisioned for the post-war South. The letters, reports, complaints, and official responses generated by freedwomen's ob-servers and antagonists offer a rich record of freedwomen's efforts to reconstruct life and labor in lowcountry South Carolina. They also reveal that an important part of the work of defining freedom lie in freedwomen's determined efforts to reveal and disrupt the relations of power and domination that had marked their lives as en-slaved laborers in the rice fields and planter residences of lowcountry plantations.[9] When freedwomen insisted on working "in their own way and at such times as they think fit," they were articulating a politics of· Reconstruction in which women's experience of gender, race, and a history of enslavement were inseparable. They made the issue of reconstructing work their own, an integral part of their desire and intent to secure black freedom.

The women who had been held in slavery in mainland lowcountry South Carolina were situ-ated in a region marked by a specific geography, a unique African-American culture, and a particu-lar plantation setting organized around a single crop cultivated under a distinctive system of slave labor. African-American women enslaved else-where in the South were faced with a very differ-ent set of circumstances before, during, and after the Civil War. The rice-planting region of low-country South Carolina contained some of the South's largest plantations and wealthiest planters,

and before the war, some of its largest, most sta-ble, and culturally autonomous slave communi-ties.[10] On the eve of the war, rice agriculture rested squarely on the shoulders of slave women whose lives were spent in the fields and ditches that marked the distinctive lowcountry terrain. As in other advanced plantation regimes, slave women on rice plantations were a significant pro-portion of "prime" field hands. However, to para-phrase from the introduction to an anthology on slave labor in the Americas, it was the particulars of slaves' labor which "determined, in large mea-sure, the course of their lives."[11] Slave labor in the rice fields was organized under the task sys-tem, so that the work of preparing fields, and cul-tivating and processing the rice crop, was assigned to women by the task—a portion of an acre for hoeing, a certain number of linear feet for ditch-digging, a certain number of rice sheaves cut and tied. This distinguished slave women's task labor from women's dawn-to-dusk gang labor in almost every other plantation economy. The pace of task labor was set by slaves, who—with considerable effort—could often complete their tasks by mid-afternoon. For slave women, this translated into more daylight hours for the labor of raising and caring for families and for a variety of activities related to independent production.

Slave women's work in the rice fields and the elaborate residences of rice planters not only shaped their experience of slavery, but also influ-enced their wartime struggle to escape or destroy slavery. The naval blockade of southern ports and the subsequent disruption of trade, the with-drawal of white men from agriculture to military service, and demands by the Confederate military and state authorities for slave labor and slave-pro-duced goods all disrupted the long-established patterns of plantation life and labor in the low country.[12] The forced removal of lowcountry slaves to the state's more protected interior further undermined the traditional cycle of rice agricul-ture as well as the local ties which for many gen-erations had anchored lowcountry plantation production and slavery. With the occupation of Port Royal by Union forces early in the war, the threat posed by the proximity of the enemy ex-acerbated the war's domestic interruptions in South Carolina.

For lowcountry slave men and women, these wartime conditions translated into incremental disruptions of the traditions, customary rights, so-cial relations, and domestic networks that they had forged over several generations of struggle against slavery. Yet even as wartime shortages forced a deterioration in the standard of living in the slave quarters, slave women accelerated the wartime collapse of slavery by slowing plantation production, resisting the new forms of exploitation introduced during the war, and escaping lowcountry plantations in unprecedented numbers and making their way to the fleet of federal ships blockading the coast. When slave women seized the opportunities presented by the war to further weaken the institution of slavery or to secure their own freedom, it was not only slavery which they hoped to leave behind, but also the worsening conditions of life on lowcountry plantations. Long before emancipation became a part of Union policy, slave women were struggling to alter the conditions of life and labor on South Carolina plantations.

It bears stressing that war affected not only the material conditions of lowcountry slave life but also the relationships of power that were integral to slavery. As planters became increasingly unable to purchase or afford the most basic necessities; as they became subject to impressment of their plantation products and slaves; as they, their overseers, and their sons became vulnerable to conscription; and, as increasing numbers of plantation mistresses assumed unprecedented and unanticipated responsibility for plantation operations in light of the absence of husbands and sons, slaves watched the weakening of their masters' ability to dominate. Slave women not only observed, but tested and acted upon, the wartime crisis of plantation mastery. Overseers and planter families alike complained during the war of slave women disrupting the peaceful operation of their plantations, threatening to run away, and slowing the pace of work.[13] One rice plantation mistress complained early in the war of the "license" increasingly taken by slaves; they "all think this a crisis in their lives that must be taken advantage of. . . . [T]imes and slaves, have changed" since secession.[14] The weaknesses in the bedrock of slavery exposed by the war were seized upon and widened by slave women who were determined to make the war's trajectory towards emancipation irreversible.

Thousands of slave women fled lowcountry plantations during the war and made their way to the Union-occupied Sea Islands, beginning their transition from slavery to freedom under the dominion of northern missionaries, civilians, and military authorities. Unlike native Sea Islanders who staked out their own portion of plantation lands and continued to live in their slave quarters, slave women from the mainland rice plantations constituted a refugee population. They found living quarters in refugee camps, abandoned buildings, or temporary barracks, and pieced together a living from the employment they found in the Quartermaster's Department, as regimental laundresses or cooks, from the pay of their enlisted kin or husbands, or by marketing provisions to Union soldiers stationed on the islands. Yet their appreciation for the protection, schooling, and charity offered by northern military and civilian authorities did not slow women's response when the freedom offered under northern tutelage was less than what they expected. Whether this meant shaming the northern missionary women who pointedly ignored the pressing needs of young "unmarried" slave mothers, challenging military authorities who tried to prevent their entry into soldiers' camps to sell provisions or to "see and be seen," or leading groups of women to protest unacceptably low wages, these refugees from mainland slavery were hardly content to await passively the redefinition of black life and labor by others. Before the war had ended, these contraband women were already engaged in the process of defining and defending their freedom.[15]

Women's pursuit of freedom gained momentum and breadth in the immediate aftermath of the war. The final dissolution of lowcountry slavery in early 1865, coinciding with the chaotic closing weeks of war in the wake of Sherman's advance through the state, inspired newly freed slave women to attack former overseers, raid planter residences and storehouses, and confiscate or destroy planter property. From the smallest luxuries to the most expensive furnishings, freedwomen clothed themselves and their children in confiscated and previously forbidden finery "in pride of their freedom." In the aftermath of the war, former slave women's defining acts of freedom were also found in their efforts to reunite their families, separated before or during the war; in the strategies they adopted to endure calamitous material conditions and to evade violent attacks by white reactionaries and northern soldiers; and in the ways they reorganized and reallocated their agricultural, domestic, and household labor.

For most lowcountry freedpeople, women and men, land was critical to the freedom and independence they sought for themselves, their families, and their communities. Lowcountry freedpeople shared a definition of freedom as their right not simply to survive, but to work and thrive without white intervention on the land they had worked as slaves and where generations of their ancestors had lived, worked, and died.[16] On the Sea Islands and on the mainland, from Georgetown to the Savannah River, freedpeople held public meetings, organized commissions, appointed delegations, and formed paramilitary guards to protest the accelerating process of restoration under the terms of Johnsonian Reconstruction and to prevent returning white landowners from setting foot on the islands and usurping their own claims to the land.[17] As federal Reconstruction policy accelerated the restoration of so-called "abandoned lands" to white planters, freedpeople were forced either to relinquish their claims or defend them. Freedwomen figured in many of the conflicts that flared in defense of those claims. They physically forced planters or overseers off the plantation, threatened violent confrontations with bureau agents and armed guards of U.S. soldiers, and individually refused to cooperate with white landowners.[18]

Women's vigorous resistance to restoration was evident in a violent confrontation that developed on Keithfield plantation. In March 1865, former slaves had driven the white overseer off the plantation, and for the rest of the year a community of about 150 freedpeople lived on and independently worked the plantation, cultivating at least a partial crop of rice.[19] But early in 1866 Keithfield's absentee planter, a widow, asked a neighboring planter to help her retake control of Keithfield. She could not have chosen a figure more hated by local freedpeople, for this neighbor, Francis Parker, Sr., had helped carry out the ritualized public execution of recaptured fugitive slaves during the war. Adding to the potential for conflict, Parker attempted (with the approval of the local bureau agent) to install as overseer Dennis Hazel, a former slave driver.[20]

In March 1866, according to Parker and Hazel's account of the conflict, Parker sent his son and Hazel to deliver work orders to the people at Keithfield, but the men's authority was repudiated by Abram, whom the freedpeople had appointed their foreman. Parker's son threatened to bring Abram before the local provost marshal and "break him" but left the plantation before doing so. Abram called the women and men in from the field. The work gang turned their tools— "Axes hatchets hoes and poles"—into weapons, and attacked Hazel, threatening to kill him. Hazel escaped and that afternoon returned to the plantation with Parker's son and two soldiers. On their appearance, the freedpeople assaulted them with their tools and pelted them with bricks and stones. Sukey and Becky entered the fray armed with heavy clubs. Joined by Jim, they exhorted their fellow laborers to join the fight, "declaring that the time was come and they must yield their lives if necessary—that a life was lost but once, and they must try and kill" the intruders. The crowd was joined by eight or ten "infuriated women," including Charlotte Simons, Susan Lands, Clarrisa Simons, Sallie Mayzck, Quashuba and Magdalen Moultrie, who were armed with heavy clubs and hoes, and backed by four or five men. The women made a point of their particular hatred for the former slave driver Hazel by focusing their attack on him; the soldiers' efforts to defend him from their blows were "entirely ineffectual." Parker pleaded with the women to let up their attack on Hazel, promising to leave and let Freedmen's Bureau authorities settle the matter, but, as he recalled, "the mob was not to be reasoned with." The freedmen encouraged the women; "kill him, now is your time, don't let him get away." Three times, Parker called on the freedmen to "exert themselves," to stop and force back what he described as "the maddened women." The freedmen replied to Parker that he "had no business over there anyhow—that no white man could control them now they were free." Sukey and Becky then shifted their attack from Hazel to Parker. Sukey seized a hickory stick out of Parker's hands and beat him with it over his back; both she and Becky delivered a series of heavy blows to his head. One of the soldiers, "his face covered with blood" and apparently disarmed by the freedpeople, "beseeched his comrade to shoot" at the mob, but Parker insisted no shooting take place, "fearing such a measure might further madden the desperate mob." Parker and Hazel turned to make a hasty retreat, begging the men to keep the women back, but before Parker could escape he was "struck very heavily over my right eye with a club in the hands of a woman Becky—the blow bringing blood instantly, and making me stagger with blindness—[.]" He noted that "vigorous efforts to strike me again were continued by women among whom I recognized Sukey, Becky, Quashuba, Charlotte, Susan." Now fearing for his life, Parker (followed by Hazel) made the only escape he could, by jumping into the river and swimming out to their boat, "under a shower of missiles." Parker and Hazel left the soldiers to make their own escape by foot, bloodied and disarmed by the freedpeople.

Later, an armed guard of U.S. soldiers temporarily settled the incident by arresting several of the ringleaders. Three of the freedmen were charged with inciting the freedwomen to violence; five of the women served sentences in the local jail. Although the Freedmen's Bureau agent called the violence attending Keithfield's restoration "unusual," reports from across the lowcountry noted the vigor of women's participation as freedpeople resisted rice planters who attempted to reclaim their plantations and to reinstate overseers and former slave drivers. The reports confirmed the fears of Freedmen's Bureau agents who knew that freedpeople were cultivating so-called abandoned lands "in anticipation of being left to enjoy the fruits of their labors"; agents anticipated that the return of planters would inevitably lead to "serious difficulties" but seemed surprised at the role played by freedwomen.[21]

Some freedwomen faced more immediate battles when former owners remained on the plantations at the close of the war. Freedwomen's involvement in the conflicts was noted by the overseers, former owners, and white elites who were as outraged at freedwomen's purposeful violation of antebellum rituals of deference and subordination as by the actual content of their demands. Although conflict and resistance had been part of the fabric of day-to-day life under slavery, by the late summer of 1865, freedwomen were clashing with former slaveowners and other whites in a new, more public, and openly declared arena. Freedwomen like Peggy had added a new public strategy of insubordination and direct confrontation to their antebellum repertoire of evasive tactics and deceptive appearances.[22] They challenged former slaveowners' and overseers' expectations of ritualized, deferential behavior as they set out in clear terms and with definitive action how they believed life and labor should differ in freedom from their experience under slavery.

In the fall and early winter of 1865, lowcountry planters complained with growing frequency that freedpeople left the plantations without permission, refused work orders, and made threats against planters. Planters complained that freedpeople "not only will not work now, but tell you so openly & plainly. . . ."[23] They accused former slaves of being saucy, insolent, intractable, disobedient, and dangerous. Even in this general climate of conflict and resistance, men and women of the lowcountry planter class, white overseers, soldiers, and agents of the Freedmen's Bureau all complained pointedly about the insubordinate behavior of former slave women. Freedwoman Jane, who rejected work orders and slapped her white mistress, was denounced by her employers as "an audacious creature."[24] Mary Ann "boldly [and] unblushingly" confronted her former owner in the field, refused his assignment of work unrelated to the present crop, and "frequently contradicted me and spoke to me as roughly and as defiantly as if I had been the meanest old negro in the country." He was as alarmed by Mary Ann's defiant bearing towards him as by her insistence on determining for herself which work she would and would not perform.[25] Another planter characterized freedwomen as idle and insolent, vagrant, playing sick and doing no work; the driver's

wife thought she was "too fine a lady to think of doing any work," and even Eve, while admittedly "an old woman," he described as "very impertinent."[26] It was the behavior of women like these that prompted the agent on one lowcountry plantation to complain that "[t]he more kindness offered to them the more ingratitude & abuse we receive," an unwitting admission that freedwomen were challenging the facade of reciprocal relations that had masked the abusive and exploitative nature of antebellum paternalism.

Beyond their insistence on bringing radical change to their relationships with lowcountry elites, lowcountry freedwomen's reputation for insubordination was in part a consequence of the specific kinds of demands they made in postwar labor arrangements. Freedpeople needed to innovate new family economies to cope with conditions of starvation and want; they sought a balance between their ties to specific communities and plantation lands and their need for cash, or food and basic goods. After the harvest, freedmen (husbands and fathers) left the plantations in pursuit of day labor, sold firewood or fruit to passing steamers or in nearby towns, or found other temporary avenues into the cash economy. Freedwomen—often wives and mothers—remained on the plantations and assumed a frontline role in ongoing plantation battles over the shape of postemancipation labor while caring for family and tending independent crops.[27] Some families on mainland plantations managed to plant "private crops of their own," and the men "hire out now & then . . . to neighbors" while freedwomen and children remained on the plantation.[28] This strategy not only exacerbated planters' concern about securing essential postharvest labor from freedpeople, it also placed freedwomen in direct conflict with planters.

Freedwomen fueled the escalating labor conflict by their refusal to perform postharvest domestic chores for planters. Planters had customarily assigned female slaves a range of postharvest labor that included spinning and weaving, the manufacture of clothing, butchering and preserving meat, and other kinds of domestic production critical to the maintenance and support of plantation operations. That labor had eaten into the hours slavewomen might otherwise have spent with, and working for, their own families. In the fall of 1865, freedwomen who had contracted to work as field hands were no longer willing to perform "double duty" in domestic production for their employers. This included freedwoman Mary Ann, who "shewed the virago from the start"; according to her former owner, "she has refused to rake[,] fence[,] or do any work," leading him to fear that her behavior "will poison all the rest of the people of the place."[29] Freedwomen on one of the Allston plantations brought an end to the extra burden of postharvest wool production, first by killing off the plantation sheep, and then eating them. One planter's wife reported that in order to get former slaves to work even half tasks in the field, chores related to domestic production, such as spinning, had to be totally abandoned. Another planter's wife found herself reported to a local bureau agent for trying to compel female field hands to do her spinning and weaving. Even young women like sixteen-year-old Margaret Brown rejected "weaving after night" for her employer, who took her refusal as provocation enough to beat her with his bare hands and with a stick.[30]

Freedwomen's contributions to lowcountry labor conflicts did not go unnoticed or unanswered. According to bureau and military records, many freedwomen paid a dear price for the audacity of insisting on their right to define free labor on their own terms. Their experience of violence at the hands of an outraged employer was not unusual. Hagar Barnwell had been ordered by her former owner to go into the kitchen and work, but "she refused . . . as she had contracted to work in the field." When Barnwell vowed she would leave the plantation rather than work in his kitchen, the man threatened her with his pistol, stated he would kill her if not for the need to get his crop in, and then he took her to a shed and tied her up by her thumbs so that her feet barely touched the ground. Barnwell eventually escaped, but appealed to three different army officers as well as a local magistrate before she found someone willing to investigate her mistreatment.[31] In another instance, "a Woman named Sarah . . . was tied up by the thumbs" by a planter and two accomplices, as punishment for violating plantation rules; "Sarah was pregnant and . . . she was kept suspended for nearly two hours," reported the agent, and "in consequence of this brutality the birth of the child was forced." The infant "was dead when delivered" and Sarah "has not been expected to live."[32] Their refusal to withdraw from disputes over the meaning of black freedom meant that freedwomen became targets for physical attack, resulting in a record of brutality that historians of the postbellum South are only beginning to plumb.[33]

Planters and overseers were so intent on regaining control of plantation lands (and bureau and military personnel so determined that this was in the best interests of all lowcountry residents) that many failed to anticipate what freed-women soon demonstrated: Restoration was only an incremental concession, the beginning of a longer process of negotiation on lowcountry plantations.[34] Between 1865 and 1867, it was not unusual for planters, their land restored, to discover that freedpeople "were not willing to make any contracts, inasmuch as the contract system would tend to bring them into a state of slavery again."[35] Along the Santee River, a region the Georgetown bureau agent described as "in a very unsettled state," planters discovered how quickly freedpeople could render restoration a hollow victory for planters. Many planters simply found that they could not negotiate with freedpeople; "the word of the planters to the freedpeople has no weight." The apparent accidental burning of a Santee River planter residence, following restoration, dissuaded other planters from returning.[36]

The owner of two Waccamaw River plantations returned in early 1866, to discover that nearly sixty women and men, formerly his slaves, had resided on and worked the plantations in his absence, and now, "in a state of utter insubordination, refused to contract, claiming the right to remain on the places." They insisted "they will only work in their own way & at such times as they think fit, without the supervision of an agent or any white man & insist upon renting the lands, they to fix the amount to be paid us according to their notions of justice."[37] Although ultimately forced by the course of Reconstruction politics and their determined northern benefactors to relinquish control over the plantations and instead work for planters under the labor contract system, freedwomen disregarded the terms of the contracts and persisted in laboring on their own terms, while also focusing debate and open conflict on the nature of plantation labor and their new relationships to overseers, former slave drivers, employers, and former owners. The responses of military and civilian agents of Reconstruction to freedwomen's actions similarly underwent a noticeable change. In 1865, observers viewed freedpeople's resistance to restoration and contract labor primarily as a threat to the immediate peace and good order of a region still recovering from war, posing an obstacle to the military's efforts to prevent further starvation and reduce the chaos of the southern countryside. But by 1866, their continued resistance to the restoration of the lowcountry plantation economy was construed by some of the military and civilian agents of Reconstruction as a conscious and ill-informed rejection of the tenets of free labor during the crucial, first full year of freedom.[38]

Although both freedmen and freedwomen insisted on setting the terms of their labor in accordance with their own ideas about what freedom meant, it was freedwomen's refusal to work as they had under slavery that planters and northern agents of Reconstruction commented on most frequently and most bitterly. More than one planter complained to the Freedmen's Bureau that he was "forced to discharge my freedwomen for neglect and refusal to do less than reasonable tasks."[39] Planter E. B. Heyward's complaints in 1867 were typical:

> The women have got rather lazy and try your patience severely. The work progresses very slowly and they seem perfectly indifferent.... The women appear most lazy, merely because they are allowed the opportunity. They wish to stay in the house, or in the garden all the time— If you chide them, they say "Eh ch! Massa, aint I mus' mind de fowl, and look a' me young corn aint I mus' watch um." And to do this, the best hand on the place will stay at home all day and every day....

Heyward also noted that the "men are scarcely much better"; men and women both seemed to "feel bound as a slave and work under constraint, are impudent, careless and altogether very provoking." As a consequence, Heyward was cautious in his interactions with former slaves, saying "If the women get mad ... they run in their holes like Fiddlers and won't come out. I therefore never quarrel.... I avoid all difficulties, and make a kind of retreating fight." The freedwomen working on his cousin's plantation were scarcely much better; they "come out on a kind of frolic and sow and cover his rice doing it of course abominably. All the work is badly done."[40]

John DeForest, a bureau agent in upcountry South Carolina, was among the first to label freedwomen's rejection of a "prime" hand's labor and seeming withdrawal from field labor as the "evil of female loaferism." DeForest—whose memoir is often cited by historians as contemporary evidence of women's universal withdrawal from field labor—noted that "myriads of women who once earned their own living now have aspirations to be like white ladies and, instead of using the hoe, pass the days in dawdling over their trivial housework, or gossiping among their neighbors." DeForest's characterization of women's social and reproductive labor as "trivial" was undoubtedly as firmly rooted in the devaluation of (white) women's unpaid housework in the North, as in the judgment he was also making about freedwomen's unpaid labor in and connected to the support of their households. Both issues were important to the way northern and southern whites viewed the decisions freedwomen were making.

What was the extent of women's withdrawal from the lowcountry work force? Even DeForest was careful to add that he "did not mean that all women were thus idle; the larger proportion were still laboring afield, as of old; rigid necessity held them up to it." The withdrawal of some women from the waged workforce, he concluded, was gaining popularity among freedpeople just as it had "among us white men and brethren."[41] Most contemporary observers commenting on freedwomen's seeming withdrawal from field labor failed to qualify its extent, as DeForest had; planters from across the state reported that freedwomen would simply stay in their cabins if starvation did not drive them to work. Freedwomen "generally decline to work altogether and depend on their lords [husbands] for their support," reported one planter in 1866, although another nearby planter relied on a plantation labor force composed of two freedwomen to every freedman.[42]

Freedwomen's efforts to shape their labor on lowcountry rice plantations from within the contract labor system are partially documented in the surviving labor contracts filed by lowcountry planters with the Freedmen's Bureau between 1865 and 1868. Although labor contracts offer at best an incomplete record of labor arrangements in the postwar era, they do suggest some important trends in the labor force participation of men and women, trends that appear consistent with the descriptive examples from other sources provided so far.[43]

Freedwomen's enrollment on the labor contracts for Georgetown District (see Table 1) suggests that they were continuing to work in the lowcountry rice fields but increasingly rejected full-time field labor. From 1866 to 1868, freedwomen's names were consistently nearly half of those signed to the contracts—which was very close to the proportion of slave women who were working in the rice fields before the war. Nonetheless, their intent to decrease the amount of agricultural labor they performed for planters was demonstrated by contracting not as prime or full hands, but as three-quarter or half hands. In fact, according to their enrollment on the labor contracts, men as well as women insisted on working less than they had as slaves. While a significant proportion of contracting freedwomen continued to work as full hands, many insisted on working less than a full hand would. Drawing on a subset of the labor contracts (those where the workers were indicated as contracting as full or partial hands), we learn that the percentage of freedwomen contracting as full hands on Georgetown plantations had declined from nearly 69 percent

Table 1: Georgetown Labor Contracts, 1866—1868

	1866		1867		1868	
Number of contracts with rating (total number of contracts)	57 (171)		45 (88)		14 (38)	
	Women	Men	Women	Men	Women	Men
Number of rated hands (total rated and unrated)	800 (2088)	749 (2267)	812 (1461)	669 (1409)	191 (586)	161 (601)
Percentage contracting as full hands	68.75	81	54.4	81.3	34	70
Percentage contracting as 3/4 hands	11	6	16.2	6.27	31.9	18
Percentage contracting as 1/2 hands	17.75	7.87	27	9.27	29.3	11
Percentage contracting as 1/4 hands	2.5	2.8	1.9	3.1	4.7	—

of the women who contracted to work in the fields in 1866, to 34 percent in 1868. During the same years, in this same subset of all contracted hands, the percentage of freedmen contracting as full hands also declined, but at a much lower rate—from 81 percent to 70 percent.[44]

Further evidence that lowcountry freedwomen had not retreated from the battle to transform plantation labor was seen in their refusal to labor under former slave drivers and overseers, and their insistence on selecting their own foremen—regardless of the fact that most of the bureau-approved labor contracts for 1866 and 1867 gave that prerogative to their employers. Planters anticipated former slaves' refusal to work under their former overseers; as one planter warned, "I suppose there is no doubt of the ill will of the slaves to him—and in any case I do not think you could expect to renew your relations there or elsewhere *through any overseer formerly employed*— . . . the petty despot who came between you & them will never be submitted to."[45] But the refusal of southern whites to admit the specific grounds for freedpeople's hatred of former overseers—overseers' exploitation of the productive and reproductive labor of slaves, their oftentimes sexually-charged domination, coercion, and violence against slave women—was also a denial of the extent to which freedpeople now rejected the relations of domination so critical to their experience of slavery.[46] While southern white men defended the sensitivities of white women to the

wartime horrors so recently perpetrated by northern whites (southern white women "would be averse, for the present at least, to intimate social relations with those who have been . . . connected with the suffering which they have endured"), African-American women were afforded no such protection.[47] When freedwomen claimed the right to live and work free from their former tormentors, whites responded with derision. Freedwomen on El Dorado plantation secured the right to work under a foreman of their own choosing, but the plantation mistress ridiculed the fact that "the 'foreman' escorts the women with an air of gallantry" to the fields, directing their labor "in the most courteous manner," addressing them as "ladies" even as they wielded their hoes in the field.[48]

In fact, the fight against the reinstatement of antebellum overseers and slave drivers was a struggle in which freedwomen gained particular notoriety. Freedwomen explicitly challenged the power and authority of their former overseers, purposefully and publicly violating the ritualized behavior of subservience, obedience, and submission demanded from them while slaves, at the same time escalating the protracted battle over the terms and conditions of their labor. Some overseers found freedwomen's verbal attacks on their authority so sharp as to threaten "manhood and common sense." Even agents of the Freedmen's Bureau concurred, reporting that while freedmen were "tolerably civil" towards former masters, "the women, especially those advanced in age, are abusive, with remarkable aptitude at 'billingsgate,'" the vituperative verbal weaponry exercised by women in London's famous open-air fish market.[49] Edwin Tilton, 12 years the overseer on Waverly plantation, complained in January 1866 that he was "subject of the most gross abuse" by the freedwomen, formerly slaves on the plantation, who candidly expressed their feelings about his employment on the plantation. On another plantation, freedwomen rebuked the white overseer when he attempted to revoke privileges they had won in slavery, such as the right to the open range of their poultry and farm animals on the plantations; in addition, they had become fierce defenders of their right to perform their labor without his supervision. One freedwoman, he reported, "has used very [sic] abusive and somewhat threatening language to me for shooting hogs in the field," and a second freedwoman "has ordered me out of her task, saying if I come in her task again she would put me in the ditch." When the same overseer tried to take a seat in a boat being used to transport seed rice, one of the freedwomen demanded to know, as he reported, "who told me to sit down in the boat." Daunted by freedwomen's determined efforts to undermine his authority on the plantation, this particular overseer appealed for the support of an armed guard from local military authorities.[50]

Freedwomen's repudiation of the legitimacy of overseers' authority may have been prompted by reasons beyond their outrage at their experiences of exploitation; freedwomen may also have been acting strategically on behalf of their communities, aware that sometimes the risks were different for freedmen and freedwomen who challenged whites. One overseer explained that while freedwomen challenged him, "I did not mind it so much, but when the men took to backing up the women by some of the same talk I asserted my rights as an American Citizen under abuse by at once knocking down and trouncing one of the abusers" (the same overseer suggested that the provost marshal would "be surprised" at the "actions and language" of the freedwomen and freedmen). Still, overseers could and did take their revenge with freedwomen who spoke their minds.[51]

Freedwomen's opposition to the reinstatement of former overseers, like their opposition to the return of planters, also indicated their concerns about developments outside the rice fields. The symbolic violation of freedpeople's homes became one avenue by which planters and their agents attempted to circumscribe the consequences of emancipation, avenge freedpeople's depredations on planter residences at the close of the war, and

reclaim some of their antebellum power over former slaves—both in and outside the rice fields. Former owners and overseers entered and searched freedpeople's homes ostensibly to reclaim stolen property. Of course, given the enthusiasm with which freedpeople had ransacked the planter residences at the close of the war, it was possible—even probable—that many planters actually were trying to recover stolen property. But no less important than the reclamation of that property was the significance of planters and overseers claiming the right to enter and search freedpeople's homes and even their persons. In the process of these searches, planters and their agents performed a ritualistic return to antebellum relations of power on lowcountry plantations, reclaiming their prerogative to violate, and denying freedpeople's claims to the privilege of an inviolable family sphere. One such search was decried by freedman George Singleton as "not only unlawful and cruel but also indecent." Despite his protests and those of the two midwives attending his wife in childbirth, her bed and her person were searched by three white men, allegedly looking for stolen cotton. In this instance and many others, the search also served as an instrument of terror.[52]

Searches were sometimes accomplished with the assistance of an armed guard from a local military post, provoking the disappointment—and outrage—of lowcountry freedpeople who felt betrayed by soldiers' complicity in what they clearly regarded as an invasion and an undesirable return to the past.[53] When a search of this type occurred on Hagley plantation early in 1866, there was trouble "when the freedpeople resisted the soldiers while the latter were making a search of the former's houses for furniture belonging to the estate. One of the men, Corporal Freck, was severely beaten by them, and later in the darkness of the evening missiles were thrown" at an officer and the planter.[54] On another plantation, a planter and a bureau agent made a search of the freedpeople's homes, removing property that the planter identified as stolen. They ordered the freedpeople to carry the items back to the planter residence, but the people refused, saying that their work was done for the day. According to the bureau agent, the freedpeople were "most unruly and impertinent"; they "acknowledged that they had no right in the furniture but wanted to be obstinate." Having accomplished the search on this plantation, the bureau agent then went to a neighboring plantation and performed the same service there.[55] It was not unusual for the bureau to approve planter and overseers' searches made of freed people's homes on the pretext of recovering supposedly stolen crops, or to approve labor contracts that included clauses permitting planters to freely enter and search the homes of contracting freedpeople.[56]

While field laborers endeavored to derail the patterns of invasion and exploitation that had been so common to antebellum life and threatened their freedom, freedwomen who worked in planter residences developed their own strategies to reshape life and labor. Just before the war, from one-third to one-half of the slave workforce on lowcountry rice plantations consisted of domestic servants, artisans, and other slaves with specialized work assignments; these slaves, involved in plantation operations outside the rice fields or waiting on the families of planters or overseers, had an experience of slavery very different from that of field hands.[57] Without the apparent separation between "master's time" and their own time that the task system permitted, house servants faced a more personal and daily struggle to limit the demands made of them. Female house servants were subject to a forced intimacy with slaveowning families, including a degree of vulnerability to sexual exploitation.

With the arrival of Union troops, former slave women began to abandon the mask of subservience they had been forced to wear as domestic slaves, and, in the immediate aftermath of war, female domestic servants, like field hands, first resorted to a work stoppage. Some servants preferred to leave their former owners and find new employers rather than fight with former owners over what they would and would not continue to do now that they were free. Planters' families frequently complained to each other of having to perform their own domestic labor, "their servants having all left them." Since planters viewed the training of new servants as burdensome, some forcibly prevented their former servants from seeking employment elsewhere. Fifteen-year-old Rebecca Jane Grant knew "we had been done freed," but still her uncle "stole me by night from my Missus," so that she could return to her own family.[58] Other planters asked ex-Confederate guerrillas to track down and punish or return house servants who fled their former owners.[59]

Some freedwomen who tried to exercise their new mobility suffered the painful consequences of a domestic slave's constant proximity to slaveowners. Mistresses who had treated the children of their domestic slaves as pets resisted separation from those children when freedwomen decided it was time to leave. Even worse, the children themselves may have resisted separation, having formed strong attachments to the white women who undoubtedly had more time to spend with them than did their enslaved mothers. Wartime diarist Mary Chesnut recorded the drama of a three-year-old child, "a great pet," who "did not wish to go even with his mother." The child was "torn" from the arms of the mistress by "ruthless Yanks" and turned over to his mother. The mother—whose torment and fury over slavery's interference with her child's loyalties and attachments can only be imagined—was described by the mistress as running away with her child, "whipping this screaming little rebel darky every foot of the way." Like other former slaves who found their freedom so quickly revoked, this mother and her child were soon forcibly returned by rebel pickets. The three-year-old was denied the opportunity to renew his confused attachments; both mother and child were banished from the house by the angry and jealous mistress.[60]

When house servants began to reappear voluntarily at planter residences during the summer and fall of 1865 in search of employment, they tried to implement important changes in their work and in their relations with the white women who now employed, rather than owned, them. Former mistresses complained (mostly to each other) that former slave women studiously transgressed the rituals of subservience; they "just drop down into a chair if they come to talk to you about anything & are as free as possible."[61] In attempting to distinguish their work as wage laborers from their experience of slavery, freedwomen focused many of their efforts on undermining the fundamental demand for the undivided attention and loyalty of domestic servants. Freedwomen challenged this expectation in two fundamental ways: by trying to focus their employment on the tasks to be performed rather than the people to be served; and by explicitly preferring labor arrangements designed to accommodate their own familial interests and responsibilities.

To the consternation of many women of the planter families, freedwomen insisted that domestic service be broken down into specific tasks or skills: washing, cooking, cleaning, and nursing became separate jobs. For example, Hagar, a former slave and house servant, insisted she "was not strong enough" to do the laundry and refused to wash "even a towel fit to look at." She could carry water and clean the rooms, but she would not do the laundry, nor would she turn and beat the mattresses. Months later, her employer still had not found a house servant who would agree to do washing as well as cooking.[62] Freedwomen also began to insist on their right to reject particularly arduous or demeaning labor, prompting complaints by women of one planter family when a domestic servant refused to wash her employer's "necessaries"—her menstrual rags.[63] Freedwomen may have gained considerable satisfaction not only from freeing themselves of what they felt was demeaning labor, but also from knowing that former slaveowning women were now forced to perform such labor on their own.

Making their family responsibilities an explicit consideration in their labor arrangements, some freedwomen insisted, for example, on bringing their children along to their employer's house, or limiting the hours or days they worked, as they tried to balance the demands of wage work and child care.[64] Many white women began to view the families of domestic servants as encumbrances and distractions; they tried their best to employ servants without families, a "quality" some prospective employers valued above cleanliness, industry, and even deference.[65] Employers resented the demands of young children on their domestic servants ("her infant monopolizes her attentions," one plantation mistress complained), but welcomed the employment of mothers who were willing to put their older children to work as well.[66]

Freedwomen in domestic service also challenged the very nature of their relationship to planter families, seeking a new level of dignity even as servants. "Have you noticed with the negroes at home," inquired one planter's wife to another, "that when you call they will never answer, every body [sic] up here finds it the case, they seem to think it is a sign of their freedom, heard one of them say, 'My Miss don't like it because I won't answer, but I ain't got no call to answer now.'" White employers sometimes faced the difficult choice of firing servants or finding a way to put up with the changes freedom was bringing into their households; others began what seemed like an endless search for the perfectly deferential and obedient servant, as promising servants proved themselves too assertive for the job ("she was too impudent for anything"). White women treasured those servants they could hire who still acted "humble & civil."[67]

When freedwomen employed as domestic servants attempted to define their own terms of labor, their efforts were made all the more difficult by the fact that plantation mistresses—no less than planters—were unwilling to concede the end of slavery and their loss of ownership and control over former slaves. When freedwomen struck at the core of the antebellum mythology of domestic servitude—that slave women had no lives, priorities, or identity outside their service to white families—slaveowners-turned-employers planned and schemed to prevent the return of formerly enslaved servants to their family and friends. Freed women became the target of considerable hostility and bitter resentment when they chose to abandon their former owners in search of their own families and lives.[68] Setting new boundaries and new terms on their household labor, freedwomen also challenged their employers' presumptions of intimacy and mutual dependency with their former slaves, while at the same time undermining the plantation mistress's veneer of authority in her ability to command and manage a household of servants.[69] Thus, the "servant problem" described by so many elite white South Carolinians in the postbellum period referred not only to the shrinking supply of labor, but also to the assertiveness of freedwomen in shaping the terms and conditions of their employment.

When freedwomen sought control over their paid and unpaid labor, they were driven not only by their determination to shape the meaning of free labor in lowcountry rice fields and planter residences, but also by the increased demands on their domestic production in households stripped of the most basic tools and necessities. White observers seemed convinced that it was a desire not to work that motivated freedwomen, rather than an effort to negotiate the terms of their contracted work, or the necessity of devoting more of their time and resources to the direct care and support of their families, households, and independent crops. But when Union troops moved through the lowcountry at the close of the war, they had laid waste to the region's plantation infrastructure. Union soldiers destroyed or stole the household possessions of innumerable lowcountry slaves. Soldiers confiscated what little reserve of food or farm animals and poultry remained; even pots, pans, bedding and mattresses were stripped from slave quarters. For many freedwomen, the material condition of their households was worse than it had been in slavery, and military and bureau officials had quickly forgotten their own role in making this so. However, the physical devastation of the countryside, the shortage of food and clothing and the most basic necessities, and the poor crops of the 1860s, all heavily increased freedwomen's labor in their own homes. With their own survival and that of their families in the balance, laziness or an escape from hard work were luxuries they could not easily afford.

Freedwomen's "sweet Dreams of freedom" may be difficult to recover from the historical record, but their impact on South Carolina's transition to a free labor society cannot be denied. Far from passive or retreating figures withdrawing to the shadows of southern life, freedwomen played a visible and instrumental role in the reconstruction of life and labor in the postbellum South. They fought for greater freedom of movement between their household and family economies and the plantation economy, for greater insularity from the supervision of overseers and other hated figures from their recent past, and for the freedom to make their own decisions about how best to allocate their time and their labor. In nearly every arena of postbellum conflict, freedwomen also struggled to replace the antebellum configuration of plantation power relations with a new autonomy for African-American women, one which protected their freedom both in the rice fields and plantation residences and outside them. Freedwomen assumed both the right to define black freedom and the responsibility for defending it, and our histories of slavery, war and Reconstruction have yet to acknowledge their bold lessons about the meaning of freedom in America.

NOTES

I would like to thank Elsa Barkley Brown, Daniel Letwin, Steven Hahn, and Tera Hunter for their comments on earlier versions of this research presented at the 1992 North American Labor History Conference and the 1992 meeting of the Southern Historical Association. I would also like to thank Kathleen Brown, Noralee Frankel, Linda Gordon, Leslie Reagan, Susan Smith, and Doris Stormoen for their suggestions and support. This research was funded in part by a grant from the National Endowment for the Humanities.

[1]Charles Manigault, "The Close of the War—The Negro, etc.," Manigault Family Papers, *Records of Ante-Bellum Southern Plantations*, Series (Ser.) J, Pt. 4, Reel (R) 1.

[2]See, for example, Ira Berlin, Joseph P. Reidy, and Leslie S. Rowland, eds., *Freedom: A Documentary History of Emancipation, 1861–1867*, Ser. II: *The Black Military Experience* (Cambridge: Cambridge University Press, 1982); Ira Berlin, Barbara J. Fields, Thavolia Glymph, Joseph P. Reidy, and Leslie S. Rowland, eds., *Freedom: A Documentary History of Emancipation, 1861–1867*, Ser. I, vol. 1: *The Destruction of Slavery* (Cambridge: Cambridge University Press, 1985); Ira Berlin, Thavolia Glymph, Steven F. Miller, Joseph P. Reidy, Leslie S. Rowland, and Julie Saville, eds., *Freedom: A Documentary History of Emancipation, 1861–1867*, Ser. I, vol. 3: *The Wartime Genesis of Free Labor: The Lower South* (Cambridge: Cambridge University Press, 1990); Barbara Jeanne Fields, *Slavery and Freedom on the Middle Ground: Maryland during the Nineteenth Century* (New Haven: Yale University Press, 1985); Eric Foner, *Nothing but Freedom: Emancipation and Its Legacy* (Baton Rouge: Louisiana State University Press, 1983) and *Reconstruction: America's Unfinished Revolution, 1863–1877* (New York: Harper and Row, 1988); Thavolia Glymph and John J. Kushma, eds., *Essays on the Postbellum Southern Economy* (College Station: University of Texas Press, 1985).

[3]The conflicts and alliances among and between southern and northern participants in Reconstruction also continue to be described as though women were not a part of the social landscape and as though gender was peripheral to the expression of power and domination in American cultures. The important exceptions include Jacqueline Jones, *Labor of Love, Labor of Sorrow: Black Women, Work, and the Family from Slavery to the Present* (New York: Basic Books, 1985); Susan A. Mann, "Slavery, Sharecropping, and Sexual Inequality," *Signs: A Journal of Women in Culture and Society* 14, no. 4 (1989): 774–98; Noralee Frankel, "The Southern Side of 'Glory': Mississippi African-American Women during the Civil War," in *"We Specialize in the Wholly Impossible": A Reader in Black Women's History*, ed. Darlene Clark Hine, Wilma King, and Linda Reed (Brooklyn: Carlson Publishing, 1995), 335–42; Laura F. Edwards, "Sexual Violence, Gender, Reconstruction, and the Extension of Patriarchy in Granville County, North Carolina," *North Carolina Historical Review* LXVIII, no. 3 (1991): 237–60; Catherine Clinton, "Reconstructing Freedwomen," in *Divided Houses: Gender and the Civil War*, ed. Catherine Clinton and Nina Silber (New York: Oxford University Press, 1992), 306–19; Victoria E. Bynum, *Unruly Women: The Politics of Social and Sexual Control in the Old South, 1840–1865* (Chapel Hill: University of North Carolina Press, 1992), and Elsa Barkley Brown, "Negotiating and Transforming the Public Sphere: African American Political Life in the Transition from Slavery to Freedom," *Public Culture* 7 (1994): 107–46. See also Drew Gilpin Faust, " 'Trying to Do a Man's Business': Slavery, Violence, and Gender in the American Civil War," *Gender & History* 4, no. 2 (1992): 197–214.

[4]See Roger L. Ransom and Richard Sutch, *One Kind of Freedom: The Economic Consequences of Emancipation* (Cambridge: Cambridge University Press, 1977), 44–47 and 232–36, for their estimate of the rate of freedwomen's retreat from the paid workforce in select districts of the Cotton South. Their study is often used to support assertions about the prevalence of women's withdrawal, despite the implicit and explicit limitations of their estimates. Ransom and Sutch did not address, for example, how variations in family size and household make-up, plantation size, or the process and organization of agricultural production affected the amount of work performed by women in slavery or freedom, nor examine the propagandistic intent of such sources as Freedmen's Bureau estimates of work. Historians have tended to overlook the limitations of Ransom and Sutch's findings. Jacqueline Jones uses *One Kind of Freedom* as the basis for her assertion about the prevalence of withdrawal (in *Labor of Love, Labor of Sorrow*), but also emphasizes that first-hand observations about withdrawal were common (58–63). Both Lawrence Powell (*New Masters: Northern Planters during the Civil War and Reconstruction* [New Haven: Yale University Press, 1980], 108–9) and Jones attempt to contextualize women's withdrawal in terms of the exploitation and oppression they encountered in the postbellum organization of free labor.

[5]See, for example, William Cohen, *At Freedom's Edge: Black Mobility and the Southern White Quest for Racial Control, 1861–1875* (Baton Rouge: Louisiana State University Press, 1991), 14; and Herbert G. Gutman, *The Black Family in Slavery and Freedom, 1750–1925* (New York: Pantheon Press, 1976), 167–68. Leon F. Litwack suggests that by insisting on the withdrawal of their wives from the workforce, freedmen attempted to "reinforce their position as the head of the family in accordance with the accepted norms of the dominant society" (Leon F. Litwack, *Been in the Storm So Long: The Aftermath of Slavery* [New York: Knopf, 1979], 245), but in a following paragraph also portrays withdrawal as a strategy by which freedwomen gained control over the allocation and conditions of their paid labor.

[6]Jones, *Labor of Love, Labor of Sorrow,* 58; see also Ira Berlin, Steven F. Miller, and Leslie S. Rowland, "Afro-American Families in the Transition from Slavery to Freedom," *Radical History Review* 42 (1988): 89–121. In his work *Branches without Roots: Genesis of the Black Working Class in the American South* (New York: Oxford University Press, 1986), Gerald Jaynes challenges the presumption of universality by historians who have described freedwomen's work choices. He contrasts the rate of women's participation in different plantation systems, and finds significantly less participation by women in postbellum sugar, as opposed to cotton, plantation agriculture (228–33). Jaynes also argues that the purchasing power of women's wage work lagged behind the value of women's unpaid social and reproductive labor, making "withdrawal" from the wage labor force and increased work in independent gardens and cash crops a logical and rational choice.

[7]Sharon Ann Holt, "Making Freedom Pay: Freedpeople Working for Themselves, North Carolina, 1865–1900," *The Journal of Southern History* LX, no. 2 (1994): 228–62; and Elsa Barkley Brown, "Negotiating and Transforming the Public Sphere."

[8]See Geo. E. Pingree to Maj. Edw. Deane, 31 August 1867, R 35, National Archives Microfilm Publication (M) 869, and "Recent Election in South Carolina: Testimony Taken by the Select Committee on the Recent Election in South Carolina," House Miscellaneous Document No. 31, 44th Congress, 2d Session (Washington, D.C.: Government Printing Office, 1877), 15, 19, 24, 27, 35, 38, 40, 55, 63.

[9]See Leslie A. Schwalm, "The Meaning of Freedom: African-American Women and Their Transition from Slavery to Freedom in Lowcountry South Carolina" (Ph.D. diss., University of Wisconsin, 1991).

[10]On emancipation and Reconstruction in lowcountry South Carolina, see Willie Lee Rose, *Rehearsal for Reconstruction: The Port Royal Experiment* (Indianapolis: Bobbs-Merrill, 1976); Joel Williamson, *After Slavery: The Negro in South Carolina during Reconstruction, 1861–1877* (Chapel Hill: University of North Carolina Press, 1965); Thomas C. Holt, *Black over White: Negro Political Leadership in South Carolina during Reconstruction* (Urbana: University of Illinois Press, 1977); Charles Joyner, *Down by the Riverside: A South Carolina Slave Community* (Urbana: University of Illinois Press, 1984); John Scott Strickland, "Traditional Culture and Moral Economy: Social and Economic Change in the South Carolina Lowcountry, 1865–1910," in *The Countryside in the Age of Capitalist Transformation,* ed. Steven Hahn and Jonathon Prude (Chapel Hill: University of North Carolina Press, 1985), 141–78 and " 'No More Mud Work': The Struggle for the Control of Labor and Production in Low Country South Carolina, 1863–1880," in *The Southern Enigma: Essays on Race, Class, and Folk Culture,* ed. Walter J. Fraser, Jr. and Winfred B. Moore, Jr. (Westport, Conn.: Greenwood Press, 1983), 43–62; Philip Morgan, "Work and Culture: The Task System and the World of Lowcountry Blacks, 1700 to 1880," *William and Mary Quarterly,* 3rd Ser. 39 (1982): 563–99; and Julie Saville, *The Work of Reconstruction: From Slave to Wage Laborer in South Carolina, 1860–1870* (Cambridge: Cambridge University Press, 1994).

[11]Ira Berlin and Philip D. Morgan, "Labor and the Shaping of Slave Life in the Americas," in *Cultivation and Culture: Labor and the Shaping of Slave Life in the Americas,* ed. Ira Berlin and Philip D. Morgan (Charlottesville: University Press of Virginia, 1993), 1.

[12]See Richard H. Sewell, *A House Divided: Sectionalism and Civil War, 1848–1865* (Baltimore: The Johns Hopkins University Press, 1988), 101–25; Paul W. Gates, *Agriculture and the Civil War* (New York: Alfred A. Knopf, 1965), 3–45; Emory M. Thomas, *The Confederate Nation, 1861–1865* (New York: Harper and Row, 1979), 236–42; and James L. Roark, *Masters without Slaves: Southern Planters in the Civil War and Reconstruction* (New York: Norton, 1977).

[13]J. H. Easterby, ed., *The South Carolina Rice Plantation As Revealed in the Papers of Robert F. W. Allston* (Chicago: University of Chicago Press, 1945), 291–92, 309, 312, 314, 316; Adele Petigru Allston to Charles Allston, 8 July 1863, and Adele Petigru Allston to Benjamin Allston, 30 June 1864, both in R. F. W. Allston Family Papers, South Caroliniana Library, University of South Carolina (SCL); William Capers to Louis Manigault, 20 August and 24 September 1863, Louis Manigault Papers, Ser. F, Part (Pt.) II, R6, *Records of Ante-Bellum Southern Plantations.*

[14]James M. Clifton, ed., *Life and Labor on Argyle Island: Letters and Documents of a Savannah River Rice Plantation, 1833–1867* (Savannah: The Beehive Press, 1978), 320; C. Vann Woodward, ed., *Mary Chesnut's Civil War* (New Haven: Yale University Press, 1981), 48, 78, 234, 464; Mary Elliott Johnstone to Mamma [Mrs. William Elliott], 1861 or 1862, Elliott and Gonzales Family Papers [Ser. 1.7, Folder 67], Southern Historical Collection, University of North Carolina (SHC).

[15]Elizabeth Hyde Botume, *First Days amongst the Contrabands* (1893; reprint, New York: Arno, 1968), 124–27; Ira Berlin et al., eds., *The Wartime Genesis of Free Labor,* 316–19; Virginia M. Adams, ed., *On the Altar of Freedom: A Black Soldier's Civil War Letters from the Front: Corporal James Henry Gooding* (Amherst: University of Massachusetts Press, 1991), 110–11; Rupert Sargent Holland, ed., *Letters and Diaries of Laura M. Towne* (1912; reprint, New York: Negro Universities Press, 1969), 20–22, 56, 140, 144–45; Elizabeth Ware Pearson, ed. *Letters and Diaries from Port Royal, 1862–1866* (1906; reprint, New York: Arno Press, 1969), 250, 303–4; see also Leslie A. Schwalm, *"A Hard Fight for We": Women's Transition from Slavery to Freedom in South Carolina* (University of Illinois Press, forthcoming), chap. 4.

[16]*Charleston Daily Courier,* 31 May 1866.

[17]Following Johnson's February 1866 veto of the Freedmen's Bureau Bill, including the bill's 3-year extension on the possessory titles freedpeople held to Sea Island lands, the bureau and the military department in the state yielded to the inevitability of restoration. By March 1866, the possessory titles to Sea Island land held by freedpeople were subject to closer scrutiny, and those who held no title or who had settled on land other than that specified in the title were subject to eviction. See Martin Abbott, *The Freedmen's Bureau in South Carolina, 1865–1872* (Chapel Hill: University of North Carolina Press, 1967), 60–62; Foner, *Reconstruction,* 161–63; and Williamson, *After Slavery,* 84–86.

[18]Lt. Col. B. F. Smith to Maj. Genl. Devens, 20 January 1866, Letters Received, Ser. 2392, 4th Subdist., Mil. Dist. of Charleston SC, National Archives Record Group (RG) 393, Pt. II, No. 142; and George C. Fox to Lt. Col. A. J. Willard, 2 November 1865, Registered Letters Received, Ser. 3202, Georgetown SC Subasst. Comr., RG 105.

[19]W. C. Munnerlyn to Maj. Genl. Saxton, 29 December 1865, Unregistered Letters Received, R 21, M 869; Geo. C. Fox, Monthly Land Report for the State of South Carolina, 31 October 1865, Misc. Records, Ser. 3212, Georgetown SC Subasst. Comr., RG 105.

[20]George C. Rogers, Jr., *The History of Georgetown County, South Carolina* (Columbia: University of South Carolina Press, 1970), 407; testimony of Job Mayzeck, 11 March 1873, and testimony of Dennis Hazel, 12 March 1873,

both in claim of Job Mayzeck, Disallowed Claims, RG 233; and testimony of Dennis Hazel, 18 March 1873, claim of Alonzo Jackson, Southern Claims Commission, RG 217.

[21]Testimony of Dennis Hazel, 4 April 1866; Statement of Francis S. Parker, Jr., 4 April 1866; Charges and Specifications against Jim, Job, and Stewart, 2 April 1866; Charges against Sukey, 1 April 1866; Charges against Becky, 1 April 1866; Francis S. Parker, Jr., to Col. Smith, 31 March 1866, and undated, unsigned list of fourteen names, all in Letters Received, Ser. 2392, 4th Subdist., Mil. Dist. of Charleston SC, RG 393, Pt. 2, No. 142 [C–1606]. See also Lt. Col. Smith to Capt. M. N. Rice, 7 April 1866, vol. 156 Depart-ment of the South (DS), pp. 62–63, Letters Sent, Ser. 2389, 4th Subdist., Mil. Dist. of Charleston SC, RG 393, Pt. 2, No. 142; Capt. B. F. Smith to Major H. W. Smith, 6 April 1866, Reports of Conditions and Operations, Georgetown, R 34, M 869; and Capt. B. F. Smith, "Semi-Monthly Report of Persons Arrested," 15 May 1866, Reports of Arrests of Civilians, Ser. 4161, Department of the Carolinas, RG 393, Pt. I. Lt. Col. A. J. Willard to Capt. Geo. W. Hooker, 20 October 1865, Vol. 156 DS, pp. 8–10, Letters Sent, Ser. 2389, 4th Subdist., Mil. Dist. of Charleston SC, RG 393, Pt. II, No. 142 [C–1614]. Bracketed letters and numbers (e.g., [C–1614]) refer to file numbers assigned to documents copied from the National Archives by the editors of the Freedmen and Southern Society Project at the University of Maryland, source of the multi-volume history, *Freedom: A Documentary History of Emancipation, 1861–1867.*

[22]James C. Scott (*Domination and the Arts of Resistance: Hidden Transcripts* [New Haven: Yale University Press, 1990]) of-fers a theory of confrontations between dominant and sub-ordinate groups which is helpful to understanding the changing relations between former slaveowners and for-mer slaves in the postbellum South.

[23]Williams Middleton to J. Frances Fisher, 17 November 1865, Middleton Family Papers, South Carolina Historical Soci-ety (SCHS).

[24]Entry for 24 August 1865, James Chaplin Beecher Memo-randum Book, 1865–1866, James Chaplin Beecher Papers, Perkins Library, Duke University (PL).

[25]Wm. G. Robert to Captain [Upham], 20 November 1865, Ser. 2384, Letters Received, Subdistrict of Coosawatchie, RG 393, Pt. 2, No. 141 [C–1581].

[26]Statement by W. M. Robertson, 15 September 1865, and "List of Negroes with their Characters . . . ," undated, both enclosed in Lt. W. Wood to Lt. S. Baker, 16 September 1865, Letters Received, Ser. 2384, Subdistrict of Coosawatchie SC, RG 393, DS, Pt. II, No. 141 [C–1593].

[27]One planter complained to military authorities that "All male hands but two have left the place . . . so I have my houses, filled with women and children, 12 (twelve) women who are full hands, but will not work, 6 (six) half hands, 4 (four) old and crippled, 21 (twenty-one) children fit for no work of any kind, 43 (forty-three) in all" (Benj. R. Bostick to Capt. Upham, 17 October 1865, Letters Re-ceived, Ser. 2384, Subdistrict of Coosawatchie SC, RG 393, DS, Pt. 2, No. 141 [C–1585]).

[28]J. S. Bostick to Capt., n.d. [September 1865?], Letters Re-ceived, Ser. 2384, Subdistrict of Coosawatchie SC, RG 393, DS, Pt. 2, No. 141 [C–1588].

[29]William Robert to Capt. Upham, 13 and 28 September 1865, and to Captain [Upham], 20 November 1865, all in Letters Received, Ser. 2384, Subdistrict of Coosawatchie, RG 393, Pt. 2, No. 141 [C–1581].

[30]Elizabeth Catherine Porcher to Philip Edward Porcher, 23 March 1865, typed transcript, Folder 19, Palmer Family

Papers, SCL; Easterby, ed., *The South Carolina Rice Planta-tion,* 208; Col. James C. Beecher to Gilbert Pillsbury, 11 August 1865, and G. Pillsbury to Col. James C. Beecher, 16 August 1865, both in R 34, M 869; entry for 10 August 1865, James Chaplin Beecher Memorandum Book, 1865–66, James Chaplin Beecher Papers, PL.

[31]G. G. Batchelder to Maj. Genl. R. Saxton, 10 October 1865, R 20, M 869.

[32]G. Pillsbury to Maj. H. W. Smith, 30 December 1865, Un-registered Letters Received, R 20, M 869.

[33]This issue has been explored by Catherine Clinton, "Recon-structing Freedwomen," in Clinton and Silber, eds., *Di-vided Houses,* 306–19, and by Laura F. Edwards, "Sexual Violence," 237–60. For an example of violence against lowcountry freedwomen, see Lt. Col. Garrett Nagle, Report of Outrages Committed, 31 July 1866, Colleton District, Ser. 3353, RG 105.

[34]Planters' exaggerated hopes for what restoration could ac-complish are well documented in Daniel E. Huger Smith, Alice R. Huger Smith, and Arney R. Childs, eds., *Mason Smith Family Letters, 1860–1868* (Columbia: University of South Carolina Press, 1950).

[35]Major James P. Roy to Lt. Col. W. L. M. Burger, 9 December 1865 and 1 February 1866, both in Letters Received, Ser. 4109, Dept. of SC, RG 393, Pt. 1.

[36]*Charleston Daily Courier,* 24 January 1866; William Bull Pringle to Gen. Sickles, 18 January 1866, RG 98; Bvt. Lt. Col. B. F. Smith to 1st Lt. M. N. Rice, 21 January 1866, Vol. 156 DS, pp. 40–41, Letters Sent, Ser. 2389, 4th Sub-dist., Military Dist. of Charleston, RG 393, Pt. 2, No. 142 [C–1616]; Bvt. Lt. Col. B. F. Smith to 1st Lt. M. N. Rice, 21 January 1866, Vol. 156 DS, pp. 40–41, Letters Sent, Ser. 2389, 4th Subdistrict, Military Dist. of Charleston, RG 393, Pt. 2, No. 142 [C–1616]; Wm. R. Maxwell to Genl. Sickles and Genl. Bennet, 1 March 1866, Letters Received, Ser. 2392, RG 393, Pt. II, No. 142.

[37]W. St. J. Mazyck to Col. Smith, 4 February 1866, Letters Received, Ser. 2392, 4th Subdist., Mil. Dist. of Charleston SC, RG 393, Pt. II, No. 142.

[38]Maj. Gen. D. E. Sickles to James L. Orr, 17 December 1865, South Carolina Governors' Papers; Capt. D. T. Corbin to Maj. H. W. Smith, 28 February 1866, Mt. Pleasant, Reports of Conditions and Operations, R 34, M 869; Gen. R. K. Scott, Circular Letter to the Landlords and Laborers of the State of South Carolina, 26 December 1866, *Charleston Daily Courier,* 5 January 1867; Gen. R. K. Scott to Maj. Gen. O. O. Howard, 21 February 1866, reprinted in U.S., Senate, *Senate Executive Documents,* 39th Congress, 1st Ses-sion, No. 27, p. 25.

[39][?] McKim to Capt. F. W. Liedtke, 25 June 1866, and J. Calhoun Cain to Capt. F. W. Liedtke, 11 August 1866, both in Letters Received, Ser. 3277, Moncks Corner SC, Subasst. Comr., RG 105.

[40]Barney [Edward Barnwell Heyward] to Tab [Catherine Hey-ward], 5 May 1867, Heyward Family Papers, SCL.

[41]John William DeForest, *A Union Officer in the Reconstruction* (New Haven: Yale University Press, 1948), 94.

[42]*Charleston Daily Courier,* 25 May 1866; Olney Harleston to General R. K. Scott, 21 January 1867, Testimony, Reports, and Other Records Relating to Court Cases and Complaints, Ser. 3284, Moncks Corner SC, Subasst. Comr., RG 105.

[43]The labor contracts discussed here are located in Ser. 3210 and 3211, Labor Contracts, Georgetown SC Subasst. Comr., RG 105. Information from additional contracts which are not themselves extant can be found in the Re-

ports of Contracts Approved in the Subdistricts, Ser. 2930, SC Assist. Commr., RG 105, reproduced in R 42, M 869. The problems associated with this particular kind of evidence include the casual enforcement of contract terms and constant efforts by both employers and employees to overturn the contract terms; whether the contracts were representative of labor arrangements, given the likelihood that many plantations operated without contracts; and difficulties in transcribing the documents, particularly in identifying the assignees by sex.

[44] The data represented here are an imperfect and incomplete representation of postbellum labor arrangements. Judging from the total number of contracts which are extant for Georgetown District, there were more plantations operating without labor contracts than operating with. For these and other reasons, the contracts can only be considered a closed universe, rather than representative of all plantation labor in this particular lowcountry district.

[45] E. Francis Fischer to Williams Middleton, 10 February 1866, Middleton Family Papers, SCHS.

[46] On rape, violence, and women's experience of slavery, see Catherine Clinton, " 'Southern Dishonor': Flesh, Blood, Race, and Bondage," in *In Joy and In Sorrow: Women, Family, and Marriage in the Victorian South,* ed. Carol Blesser (New York: Oxford University Press, 1991), 52–68.

[47] Rev. C. W. Howard, "Conditions and Resources of Georgia," *Report of the Commissioner of Agriculture for the Year 1866* (Washington, D.C.: Department of the South, 1867), 567–80.

[48] C. P. [illeg.] to Mary Elliott Johnstone, 2 March 1868, Ser. 1.8, Elliott-Gonzales Papers, SHC.

[49] Edwin M. Tilton to Col. Smith, 18 January 1866, Vol. 156 DS, Letters Sent, Ser. 2392, Post of Georgetown SC, RG 393, Pt. 2, No. 142; and Gen. James C. Beecher to Lieut. M. N. Rice, 21 January 1866, Letters and Reports Received, Ser. 4112, Department of SC, RG 393, Pt. 1.

[50] B. H. Pinners to Col. Smith, 1 May 1866, Letters Received, Ser. 2392, Post of Georgetown SC, RG 393, Pt. II, No. 142.

[51] Edwin M. Tilton to Col. Smith, 16 January 1866 and B. H. Pinners to Col. Smith, 1 May 1866, both in Letters Received, Ser. 2392, Post of Georgetown SC, RG 393, Pt. II, No. 142.

[52] See George Singleton vs. John Henry Porcher and Samuel Ravenel, Proceedings of Provost Courts, Military Tribunals, and Post Court Martial Cases tried in North and South Carolina, Ser. 4251A, Judge Advocate, RG 393. For another example of how white men used the pretense of searching freedpeople's homes as a means of terrorizing them, see freedman Austin Elmore's charges against Peter Bird, who entered the Elmore home, beat Austin, his wife, and mother with a pistol and an iron, and smashed earthenware, provisions, and other property in the cabin; see Affidavit by Austin Elmore, 24 December 1866, Misc. Records, Ser. 3353, Summerville SC, Subasst. Comr., RG 105.

[53] For an example of the violence which accompanied these searches, see Affidavit of Austin Elmore, 24 September 1866, Colleton Dist., Ser. 3353, RG 105.

[54] Lt. Col. B. F. Smith to Lt. M. N. Rice, 20 February 1866, vol. 156 DS, pp. 53–54, Letters Sent, Ser. 2389, 4th Subdist., Mil. Dist. of Charleston, RG 393, Pt. 2, No. 142 [C–1616].

[55] C. V. Wilson to Major O'Brien, 18 July 1866, Testimony, Reports, and Other Records Relating to Court Cases and Complaints, Ser. 3284, Moncks Corner SC, Subasst. Comr., RG 105.

[56] Entry for 10 October 1866, vol. 239, Register of Complaints, Ser. 3283, Moncks Corner SC, Subasst. Comr., RG 105; Smith et al., eds., *Mason Smith Family Letters,* 264–65; Contract between A. G. Heriot and Freedmen, 1 February 1866, Labor Contracts, Ser. 3211, Georgetown SC, Subassist. Comr., RG 105.

[57] Based on slave lists from plantations belonging to Charles Manigault in 1845 (Clifton, ed., *Life and Labor on Argyle Island,* 31–32), and plantations belonging to James R. Sparkman in 1847 and 1858 ("Task Hands 1847 June," 1827–1845, and "Dirleton 1858" and "Task Hands Birdfield January 1 1858," 1857–1859, James Ritchie Sparkman Papers, Ser. A, Pt. II, R6, *Records of Ante-Bellum Southern Plantations*).

[58] George P. Rawick, ed., *The American Slave: A Composite Autobiography* (Westport, Conn.: Greenwood Press, 1972), South Carolina, Vol. 2, Pt. 2: 179–80. In Virginia Ingraham Burr, ed., *The Secret Eye: The Journal of Ella Gertrude Clanton Thomas, 1848–1889* (Chapel Hill: University of North Carolina Press, 1990), Thomas describes a very similar postwar scenario where a young girl, a house servant and previously her slave, conspires with her mother—sold away for bad behavior—and "escaped" from the Thomas household, much to Thomas's disappointment (267–68).

[59] Susan R. Jervey and Charlotte St. J. Ravenel, *Two Diaries from Middle St. John's, Berkeley, South Carolina, February–May 1865* (Charleston, South Carolina: St. John's Hunting Club, 1921), 42.

[60] C. Vann Woodward and Elisabeth Muhlenfeld, eds., *The Private Mary Chesnut: The Unpublished Civil War Diaries* (New York: Oxford University Press, 1984), 246.

[61] Elizabeth Catherine Porcher to Hattie, 25 October 1865, Palmer Family Papers, SCL.

[62] Alice A. Palmer to Hattie, 20 July and 2 August 1865, Folder 19, Palmer Family Papers, SCL.

[63] Alice A. Palmer to Hattie, 17 October 1866, and Elizabeth Catherine Porcher to Hattie, 25 October 1865, both in Palmer Family Papers, SCL. See also Major Jos. Totten to Inspector General, 9 May 1866, T–19 1866, Letters Received, Ser. 15, RG 159 [J–51] for a description of the changes freedwomen made in domestic service.

[64] Elizabeth Catherine Porcher to [My Dear Hattie], 5 August [1866], and E. L. Porcher to Harriet [?], [1870], Palmer Family Papers, SCL; Meta M. Grimball to J. B. Grimball, 5 January 1866, John Berkeley Grimball Papers, PL.

[65] Hattie [Harriet Rutledge Elliott Gonzales] to Mama [Ann Hutchinson Smith Elliott], Monday 11th [1867–68], Ser. 1.8, Elliott-Gonzales Papers, SHC.

[66] Mary Elliott Johnstone to Mrs. William Elliott, 10 January 1866, Ser. 1.7, Elliott-Gonzales Papers, SHC, and E. C. P. to Hattie, [1866] and 24 May 1868, both in Palmer Family Papers, SCL.

[67] Alice Palmer to [My Dear Hattie], 19 September 1866, and E. C. P. to Hattie, 25 September [1866], and 28 November 1867, all in Palmer Family Papers, SCL.

[68] Mary Elliott Johnstone to Mrs. William Elliott, 10 January 1866, and Mary Elliott Johnstone to Ralph E. Elliott, 9 July 1865, both in Ser. 1.7, Elliot-Gonzales Papers, SHC.

[69] Elizabeth Fox-Genovese has explored white women's identities as household mistresses in *Within the Plantation Household: Black and White Women of the Old South* (Chapel Hill: University of North Carolina Press, 1988); see also Emily Elliott to Mary Elliott Johnstone, 21 September 1866, Elliott-Gonzales Papers, SHC.

Unit 6

Unit Selections

22. **When White Hoods Were in Flower,** Bernard A. Weisberger

23. **"If You Can't Push, Pull, If You Can't Pull, Please Get Out of the Way": The Phyllis Wheatley Club and Home in Chicago, 1896 to 1920,** Anne Meis Knupfer

24. **Claude McKay and the New Negro of the 1920's,** Wayne Cooper

25. **In the Race Riot of 1919, a Glimpse of Struggles to Come,** Peter Perl

Key Points to Consider

❖ Briefly describe the history of the Ku Klux Klan. What is its status today?

❖ How did African American women's clubs ease the way for recent migrants to urban communities?

❖ What was the Negro Renaissance? In what ways did writer Claude McKay give voice to the New Negro movement?

❖ Unlike previous white-on-black violence, what was different about the Washington, D.C. riot of 1919? What part did the media play in the situation? How did the riot end?

 **Links**   **www.dushkin.com/online/**

These sites are annotated on pages 4 and 5.

African Americans responded to the violence and uncertainty of the twentieth century with hope and creativity. In the South, blacks faced both lynching and the Knights of the Ku Klux Klan (KKK). Between 1882 and 1926, over 3,000 blacks were lynched in the South. Frederick Douglass immediately understood that the southern lynch laws were directly aimed at controlling those blacks who dared to assert their manhood, to attempt to improve their status, or who were simply too intelligent. These were dangerous blacks who had to be taught a lesson. The original Klan came into existence as a southern response to Reconstruction. Through the use of fires, floggings, and lynchings, the Klan accomplished its primary purpose of keeping recently freed blacks and their northern allies in their place. It was formally outlawed in 1870, but was resurrected in 1915. This radically transformed clan also operated in areas outside of the South. In the 1920's the KKK was so large that it was able to influence national and presidential politics.

Racial intimidation, disfranchisement, and economic conditions caused thousands of blacks to leave the South in what has been termed the Great Migration. The North did not prove to be any more hospitable. Black women, responding to these conditions, began the club movement in America. African American women's clubs were critical in the development of settlements, kindergartens, nurseries, youth clubs, homes for the aged, and homes for young girls and women throughout the black community. This article profiles the Phyllis Wheatley Club and Home, which developed and provided services, especially for southern migrating black females, at the turn of the century.

As blacks became the dominant element in many northern urban communities, intellectuals and activists began challenging blacks to change, to transform themselves, to creatively respond to their plight. Out of these strivings came the New Negro movement and a group of young writers of the Harlem Renaissance. Claude McKay, a dominant figure among the Negro Renaissance writers, was one of the first to express the spirit of what was termed the "New Negro." His writings gave voice to the new spirit awakening among blacks in the twenties. The Negro Renaissance signaled a general revolt by writers against the gross materialism and outmoded moral values of America's new industrial society.

Throughout the country, blacks began pushing for a greater piece of the pie. Whites, feeling the economic crunch of heightened competition, pushed back. In some northern cities blacks were not even permitted in the city limits. In others blacks were greeted with lynchings and riots. One of the most shocking of the northern riots occurred in Washington D.C., in 1919. Postwar Washington, which was roughly 75 percent white, was ripe for a race riot. Many whites resented the presumed affluence of the black community. Housing and good jobs were in short supply, and unemployed whites bitterly envied those blacks with even menial government jobs. Racial resentment was aggravated even more as thousands of hopeful black veterans returned home.

When White Hoods Were in Flower

Bernard A. Weisberger

This month's historical reflections are inspired by the presidential candidacy of David Duke, a former Imperial Wizard of the Ku Klux Klan, whose elevation to at least marginal respectability reminds me uncomfortably of a time when the Klan was functioning openly and above-ground and was a very palpable force in American politics.

The "original" Knights of the Ku Klux Klan, the "invisible empire" of hooded nightriders immortalized in *The Birth of a Nation* and *Gone with the Wind,* got its start in 1866 in the defeated former Confederacy. Whatever its exact origins, its purpose soon became to drive freed blacks and their Northern allies away from the polling places and back into a state of economic and political subservience. It "persuaded" by fires, floggings, and lynchings. Forget the romantic mush; it was an outlawed terrorist organization, designed to undo Reconstruction. And with its help, Reconstruction was undone. But so, by 1872, was the Klan. However, in 1915 it underwent a second ten- to fifteen-year incarnation, of which more in a moment. That is the main story here.

During the 1950s a third, "new" Klan—or perhaps several successive new Klans—emerged, in reaction to the legal dismantling of Jim Crow, sometimes called the Second Reconstruction. Like the original KKK, the groups functioned in the South, and they were responsible for bombings and the gunshot murders of at least five civil rights workers. Post-1970 Klans have had a large, changing, Cold War–influenced list of

enemies, allies, and strategies. All have led a furtive existence under legal surveillance and almost universal repudiation.

But it wasn't so with that "middle" Klan that lived in the atmosphere of World War I and the 1920s. That one targeted Catholics, Jews, and foreigners as well as blacks. In so doing, it expanded its base beyond Dixie and had more national influence than is pleasant to think about.

The evidence? How about a parade of forty thousand robed and proud-of-it Klansmen down Pennsylvania Avenue in Washington, D.C.? Or a state—Indiana—whose KKK "Grand Dragon" held a political IOU—one of many—from the mayor of Indianapolis promising to appoint no person to the Board of Public Works without his endorsement? Or a Democratic National Convention of 1924 that split down the middle of a vote to condemn the Klan by name, with just over half the delegates refusing?

This new Klan was the creation of Alabama-born "Colonel" William J. Simmons, who resuscitated fading memories of the original Knights in a Thanksgiving Day cross-burning ceremony atop Stone Mountain, Georgia, in 1915. Its credo not only pledged members to be "true to the faithful maintenance of White Supremacy" but restricted the membership to "native born American citizens who believe in the tenets of the Christian religion and owe no allegiance ... to any foreign Government, nation, political institution, sect, people or person." The "person" was the Pope,

and the new KKK tapped into a long-standing tradition of nativism that went back at least as far as the American or Know-Nothing party of the 1850s, which flared transiently in the cloudy political skies just before the Civil War.

Simmons kept and improved on the primal Klan's ritual mumbo jumbo, including secret initiations and an array of officeholders with titles like Imperial Wizard, Exalted Cyclopes, and Grand Goblin. He struck an alliance with a publicist named Edward Clarke who helped devise a deft recruiting scheme. Recruiters called Kleagles signed up members for local chapters (Klaverns) at ten dollars a head. The Kleagle kept four dollars; one dollar went to the state's King Kleagle, fifty cents to the Grand Goblin, and so on up the chain of command, with two dollars to Simmons himself.

For many native-born, white, Gentile Americans, joiners by nature, the new Klan became a special lodge, like the Elks, the Rotarians, or Woodmen of the World, for which Simmons had been a field organizer. There were four million Klansmen by 1924, according to some estimates, in a population that turned out only about thirty million voters in that year's presidential election. So it became prudent for some politicians, President Harding included, to join the KKK or at least seek its support. According to Wyn C. Wade, author of *The Fiery Cross,* one of the latest books on the Klan, the number of municipal officials elected nationwide by Klan votes has yet to be counted. The organization likewise had input in the choice of more than a dozen senators and eleven governors.

The Klan's greatest victories were in Indiana, whose Grand Dragon, purple-robed David C. Stephenson, was a gifted publicist who organized a women's auxiliary and staged barbecues and picnics, which he visited by dropping from the sky in an airplane with gilded wings. He made enough on the regalia and literature concessions to live in princely style, with lots of clandestine booze and women available. And he endorsed a slate of state candidates that swept Indiana's Republican Convention in 1924 and followed Calvin Coolidge to victory in the fall. Stephenson's dreams of the future for himself included a Senate seat and perhaps even the White House.

What made these astonishing successes possible? Was the whole country gripped by a fever of hatred? Yes and no. Racism and xenophobia actually were enjoying a favorable climate. The KKK's rebirth in 1915 coincided with the success of *The Birth of a Nation*, which depicted the original Klan as a necessity to save Southern civilization from barbaric blacks egged on by Radical Republican plunderers. This was not much of an exaggeration of the "official" version of Reconstruction then embalmed in scholarly histories, but D. W. Griffith's cinematic skills burned it into the popular mind.

At the same time, a wave of immigration from Southern and Eastern Europe troubled "old stock" American. In 1924 the immigration laws were rewritten specifically to keep out such indigestible Catholic and Jewish hordes, as they were considered.

Then there was the experience of World War I, in which "100 percent Americanism" was enforced by vigilante groups and by the government, armed with Espionage and Sedition acts. Following that, the Bolshevik Revolution inaugurated a Red scare that brought a frantic search for "agitators" to arrest or deport.

All these forces predisposed potential Klan members to accept its exclusionary message without much analysis—and to overlook incidents of violence. But there was more. Thousands of fundamentalist Christians, beleaguered and bewildered by the Progressive Era victories of evolution and the social gospel—not to mention jazz, gin, and short skirts—saw the Klan as the savior of oldtime religion. The KKK played to their anxiety by supporting Prohibition and the teaching of religion in the schools. Had the Moral Majority then been in existence, it might have absorbed some who instead became Klan followers.

In the 1920s the KKK expanded its base beyond Dixie and had far more national influence than is pleasant to think about.

It was the onrush of change, the shakeups brought by radio and film and the auto, that spooked so many Americans. My friend David Chalmers, author of *Hooded Americanism,* put it neatly to me by phone. "They couldn't blame Henry Ford or Charles Steinmetz [the socialist engineering genius of the General Electric Company], but happily they found 'the dago on the Tiber' " instead.

But change could not be held back for long. In the mid-twenties the Klan's strength dropped off dramatically, to forty-five thousand by 1930. There were many reasons. One was internal feuding among Klan leaders over control of the organization's assets. Another was the exposure of Klan-led bombings, beatings, threats, and atrocities by courageous newspapers like the Indianapolis *Times,* the Memphis *Commercial Appeal,* and the Columbus (Georgia) *Enquirer-Sun.* They resisted boycotts and other forms of pressure in the heart of the enemy's country and told the truth. So did many courageous politicians who repudiated the votes of bigotry. Revelations that some Klan officials were given to liquor, loot, and lechery also defaced the "knightly" image. The biggest scandal of all sent Grand Dragon Stephenson to jail for the brutal rape of Madge Oberholtzer, a young state employee, who afterward committed suicide. Stephenson, outraged that the Indiana authorities did not set him above the law, avenged himself by squealing on his political puppets and ruining their subsequent careers.

And over time the second Klan was repudiated because it collided with the fundamental American values of inclusiveness and pluralism. The trouble is that it also expressed equally durable American attitudes: the ongoing quest for an unalloyed "Americanism," the perverse pressure to conform to a single majority standard, and the tendency to substitute mob "justice" for the unsatisfying ambiguities of legal verdicts.

It seems that current historians, unencumbered by having lived through the period's hostilities, are more inclined to explain than to condemn the Klan of the twenties. Most of its members, they suggest, were tradition-bound outsiders to the emerging new urban money culture, more frightened than vicious. I am unpersuaded, even while acknowledging that "good" people can join "bad" associations out of understandable frustrations. But the Klan could not be separated from its hateful implications then, and the Klan spirit cannot be so separated now, however prettified, sanitized, and shorn of wacky costumes and titles. Scapegoating of "the other," assurances that "we" must safeguard our system, our heritage, and our values from "them"—these notions inevitably carry implications of violence and repression.

Yet under certain conditions they can become widespread, unless watched and guarded against. As the evidence presented shows, it has happened. Here. And not so long ago.

"IF YOU CAN'T PUSH, PULL, IF YOU CAN'T PULL, PLEASE GET OUT OF THE WAY": THE PHYLLIS WHEATLEY CLUB AND HOME IN CHICAGO, 1896 TO 1920

By
Anne Meis Knupfer*

In 1978, Gerda Lerner noted that the activities and significance of African-American's women's clubs had not received proper attention from historians.[1] Since that time, the scholarship on African-American women's clubs has increased substantially. Studies have explored individual club women's lives and contributions; social institutions and facilities created by the clubs; collaborative efforts between clubs on the regional, state, and local levels; and African-American women's exclusion from white women's clubs.[2]

To date, though, there has not been a thorough analysis, much less chronicling, of African-American women's clubs and their activities in Chicago. Chicago is a critical locus for study as it had one of the largest African-American urban populations in the early twentieth century, due largely to the substantial southern migration there. Chicago was also known for its social reformers and settlement workers, including Jane Addams, Edith Abbott, Mary McDowell, Ida B. Wells, Fannie Barrier Williams, and Mary Waring. Although African-American and white social workers and reformers occasionally worked side by side, more often than not the Chicago settlements and other social institutions were racially segregated. This necessitated the creation and sustenance by African-American women's clubs of community institutions such as settlements, kindergartens, nurseries, youth clubs, homes for the aged, and homes for young girls and women.

One such African-American women's club was the Phyllis Wheatley Club. Founded in 1896 by Elizabeth Lindsay Davis, a prominent state and national organizer in the African-American women's club movement, the Phyllis Wheatley Club was one of the oldest African-American women's clubs in Chicago. The original interests of the Club, in conjunction with the National Association of Colored Women's Clubs (NACW) centered on "all things pertaining to the elevation of home among all women."[3] However, particularly from 1905 to 1918, poverty, segregation and discrimination increased, particularly in the city's Black Belt. To alleviate the dire living and employment conditions which newly-arrived African-American women faced, the Phyllis Wheatley Home was founded by the Club in 1907. It offered "wholesome surroundings for colored girls and women who [we]re strangers in the city and to house them until they [found] safe and comfortable quarters."[4]

Although frequent references have been made to the Home and Club in the African-American women's club scholarship and in historical studies of Chicago, there has been no complete analysis of either the Club or the Home.[5] This is most likely due to the dearth of primary historical sources available on Chicago's African-American women's clubs.[6] The most useful historical sources have been two Chicago African-American newspapers from this time period, the *Broad Ax* and the *Chicago Defender*. Not only did they publish many of the women's clubs annual reports, but also weekly accounts of club

*Anne Meis Knupfer is a professor in the Department of Educational Studies at Purdue University, West Lafayette, Indiana.

From the *Journal of Negro History,* Spring 1997, pp. 223-231. © 1997 by the Association for the Study of African-American Life and History, Inc. Reprinted by permission.

meetings, fund-raisers, and other club activities in the society, church, and women's columns. Such accounts, along with editorials and articles written by club women, provide rich contextual information an the Phyllis Wheatley Club and Home.

Using such documentation, this article will examine the activities of the Phyllis Wheatley Club, particularly those which focused on the Home. The first section will describe the Club's early activities, goals, and members prior to the creation of the Home. The second section will examine the conditions in Chicago which precipitated the founding of the Home, followed by an analysis of the Home and the Club activities associated with it.

THE PHYLLIS WHEATLEY CLUB

The Phyllis Wheatley Club was organized in 1896 in accordance with the National Association of Colored Women's (NACW) departments of Home, Education, Domestic Science, Philanthropy, Industry, Literature, Art, Suffrage, and Patriotism. Consistent with the NACW's motto, "lifting as we climb," the Club functioned on two levels. First, the Club assisted those who were less fortunate through the provisions of social welfare, charity cases, and later, the Home's accommodations and employment referral services. Secondly, the Club promoted the self-education of its members through a series of addresses, speeches, poetry readings, dramatic renditions, and musical performances. Thus, the Club not only provided community service and camaraderie, but also served as a marker of social class, status, and prestige. These multiple activities and roles of club women were not contradictory, but rather reflected the complexities of social reform ideology and social uplift practices during the Progressive Era. Although social class differences cut across the African-American communities in Chicago, and were evident in the women's clubs, club women and other community members united in their efforts to combat racism and discrimination in employment, housing and access to public facilities. Because club women were well aware of the double burden of racism and sexism which all African-American women faced, more often than not they reached 'across" rather than "down" to their less fortunate sisters.

However, this is not to deny that most of the Phyllis Wheatley Club members led lives which were far different from the recipients of their charitable deeds. The founder of the Club and Home, Elizabeth Lindsay Davis, was illustrative of the typical background of the African-American club women in Chicago. A former teacher, Davis came to Chicago in 1885, where she immediately took up club and church work. Not only did she found the Phyllis Wheatley Club, but she was active in other clubs, including the Ida B. Wells' Club, the Giles Charity Club, and the Woman's City Club.[7] Like many other club women, Davis was college educated, of middle-class

status, and subscribed to the ideology of domestic feminism. More specifically, she and club women perceived their roles of mother, wife, and homemaker as cornerstones to "race uplift" and progress. To fulfill their domestic roles properly and fully, it was necessary that they extend their duties and responsibilities outward into the community. Their concerns with child and youth welfare naturally resulted in the founding of kindergartens, nurseries, orphanages, settlements, and youth clubs.[8]

An examination of other club members background reveals that many were either professional women or were married to prominent men in the community. For example, three of the club members—Fannie Emanuel, Anna Cooper, and Carrie Golden—were medical doctors. Another member, Carry Warner, owned several chiropody and manicure parlors. A long-standing member, Mrs. Daniel Williams, was the wife of a prominent doctor who founded Provident Hospital in Chicago; Mrs. Julius Taylor was married to the editor of the newspaper, *Broad Ax*. With the founding of the Home in 1907, a second generation of younger women, many of whom were educators, social workers, and settlement workers, joined the club. These members include Lena Perry, a truant officer, and Elizabeth Haynes and Sophie Boas, workers with the Wendell Phillips Settlement.[9] They, along with the older club women, advocated industrial education to solve the employment dilemma of the female migrants. Accordingly, they encouraged the young women residing at the Home to learn sewing, cooking, and other domestic skills to insure themselves an income, albeit a meager one. This training differed greatly from the educative experiences offered at club meetings, which included literary discussions, the study of classical art, and informative talks by physicians, educators, and community leaders.

Papers, addresses, presentations and discussions were mainstays for the Club's Literary Section. According to newspaper accounts, male speakers gave lectures and addresses, whereas female club members gave readings or presentations, even though many of the club members' presentations were original writings. Topics were diverse. Mr. Moore, for example, lectured on the teachings of Zeno, Socrates, Marcus Aurelius, Seneca, and other "profound" thinkers and writers. Extending his subject to the club women, he admonished them about the importance of "good" books in the home, and concluded with the advice that young, as well as middle-aged, women should cease from aping women whose highest ambitions were wearing fine clothes but whose minds were aimless."[10] Similar advice was also offered by Dr. Jeffrey, a physician, following his lecture of the "formation of the brain" and its relationship to philanthropy. He advised women to follow the tenets of "brotherly love" and to "cease from being puffed up and self-conceited creatures."[11] This is not to suggest that women took such advice without debate. When Dr. Jeffrey argued the advantages of polygamy at one meeting, the women vehemently disagreed. One newspaper account of his lecture jokingly remarked that he spoke as if he had a D.D. rather than an M.D.[12]

Although the emphasis seemed to be on classical literature and philosophy, efforts were also devoted to African-American literature. Paul Lawrence Dunbar's poetry was frequently read, cited and discussed. A synopsis of "The Black Fairy" by Fenton Johnson, an African-American journalist and poet, was given by club president, Elizabeth Lindsay Davis. At several meetings, Robert Jackson, an African-American poet and artist, recited his poems, as well as displayed paintings. Writings by W. E. B. Du Bois were also studied.[13]

As with the Literature Section, the Music and Art Sections focused on both classical and African-American artists and musicians. Interest in classical art was evident in talks by Mrs. Daniel Williams, who gave an overview of the history of music from Roman times to the present, and Mrs. W. B. Anderson, who read an original paper on the Renaissance painters. But art work by African-American artists, Henry Tanner and William Harper, was also discussed. So, too, did the Club support course work at the Chicago Art Institute for young African-American woman, Nellie Toler, a budding artist and musician. Musical activities demonstrated that much attention was given to classical music, often listened to during "high teas," as well as to contemporary African-American music. Popular music was played on the victrola during meetings, as well as at dances and dramatic productions. Professor Elgar's Orchestra, an African-American student orchestra, regularly performed for the club meetings and their events. Lastly, individual club women were recognized for their musical talent, including Dr. Mary Waring, who composed the club song; Amelia Scott, considered "a natural born and talented young musician"; and others who performed on the piano, violin, and cornet.[14]

Paper topics for the Home and Industry Sections fit well within the prevailing ideologies of Tayloristic management in domestic science, as well as Booker T. Washington's emphasis on home care, thrift, and industry. They included the "scientific method" of housekeeping, the value of sanitation, consumption, ventilation, and the importance of water (both for drinking and for bathing), sanitary plumbing, and "pure food.[15] Dr. Wilberforce Williams, who wrote a weekly health column for the Chicago African-American newspapers, was a regular speaker at the Phyllis Wheatley Club.

The Industry Section frequently reflected the ongoing debate on industrial versus academic education. Papers were read which advocated industrial education, such as "Should the Education of the Negro be Wholly or Chiefly Industrial?," and "The Importance of Industrial Training." At a meeting in 1901, Mrs. Reverend Gray argued that young boys, as well as girls, should be taught to work. She extended this topic by "scorning" those men who did not financially provide for their families, but

instead depended upon their wives. Consensus on the topic was evident in the group's response: "Mrs. Gray was loudly applauded during her remarks."[16] Dr. Anna Cooper, however, at another meeting, extended the work issue beyond individuals or families to the community. She argued that part of the African-Americans' economic dilemma was due to their not patronizing businesses in their own communities, but relying upon white persons for their financial support instead.[17] Unfortunately, there were no records kept of club members' responses to her talk.

The Philanthropy Section seemed to be the most active in terms of social reform. Dr. Carrie Golden's paper, "The Sanitary Conditions of the City and Its Relation to the Home(s)," was based on her committee's inspection in 1900 of over six-hundred homes on Chicago's South Side. Although she stressed the importance of keeping a home "clean and attractive," she provided political and social commentary by criticizing the tenement owners whose lodgings were dilapidated and crowded, and who charged higher rents to African-Americans than to whites. She concluded her talk by urging the club women to exert a greater influence over their husbands' vote.[18] Other speakers on philanthropy supported similar social reform. Mrs. Fannie Emanuel, a medical doctor who founded the Emanuel Settlement in Chicago, talked about issues of health and hygiene, as well as settlement work. Mrs. Ophelia Ward Bush, a writer and social worker at the Robert Gould Shaw House in Boston, visited and spoke about conditions in her city; Dr. Mary Waring, who directed the Dunbar Tubercular Sanitarium and the Red Cross Auxiliary in Chicago, spoke of child welfare. The activities of the Philanthropic Section prompted Julius Taylor of the *Broad Ax* to endorse the Club, which he stated performed "good deeds" and did not "pander to cake walks and jim-crowism."[19]

As evident from the above descriptions, the activities and the interests of the Club members were varied and extensive. Much of the learning that occurred was directly translated into social reform. In fact, with the founding of the Home, the Club's literary and musical activities diminished, and the Club devoted more attention to the Home's management.

SOCIAL CONDITIONS IN CHICAGO

The housing issue was one of the most pressing issues for African-Americans in Chicago, especially after 1910. Many discriminatory practices prevailed, including higher rental fees for African-Americans, dilapidated and unsanitary housing conditions, neighborhood bombings, and the formation of neighborhood associations which red-lined African-Americans from residing in certain Chicago communities.[20] The situation for poorer Southern African-Americans, new to the city, was especially difficult. Most settled in or near the Black Belt, an area variously described as impoverished, unsanitary, crowded, and segregated. There, tenement owners charged such high rates that renters were forced to take in lodgers. In a comparative study of the number of lodgers per dwelling, the Chicago Commission on Race Relations found that 35 percent of African-Americans were lodgers living in 62 per cent of the households.[21] These percentages far exceeded those of any immigrant group. Bowen's investigation, *The Colored People of Chicago*, corroborated these findings. She claimed that nearly one-third of the African-American population on the South Side were lodgers.[22]

Problems associated with crowded housing were also discussed in studies and reports, including issues of proper home life, child care, and African-American female employment. Bowen argued that lodging posed a "danger" to family life, particularly for those families who lived in or near what was called the vice district; she cited the evils of prostitution, idleness, and the lack of wholesome recreation for youth. An excerpt from the Chicago newspaper, *The Conservator*, decried such conditions and their harmful influences on the young:

> We are calling attention to the fact that a number of our girls and boys are on the road to ruin. The boys rioting in the Clark and 4th Avenue dives, and the girls walking the streets in gaudy attire. . . . How sad it is to see the girls we have known in their innocent childhood, change their lives, just when life's days should be brightest, change from piety, virtue, and happiness to vice, dissipation and woe.[23]

Although blame was occasionally attributed to absent mothers or fathers, most social workers and club women acknowledged the larger issues: lack of suitable employment and of child care Most poorer African-American mothers in Chicago, as elsewhere, worked as domestic servants, thereby necessitating their being absent from their homes for as long as fourteen hours a day. As of 1910, over 63 percent of the African-American women in Chicago were employed as domestic servants or laundry women. In Bowen's investigation, the percentages were even higher; out of one hundred case records taken from the Juvenile Protective Association, at least eighty-six of the African-American women worked outside of the home.[24] More often than not, the mothers left their young children in the care of an older sibling or lodger. Not only could poorer mothers not afford the fees of nurseries and kindergartens, but, as previously mentioned, many of these facilities were racially segregated.

Similarly, for older children and young women new to the city, there were few employment or educational opportunities available to them. Many did not attend high schools, industrial schools, nor colleges because of discriminatory practice. Many who had been promised employment, especially young southern girls who had recently arrived in Chicago, found that they were prey to the scruples of those who often confiscated their luggage or their money, without providing employment. Some found that the nursing job they had been offered was little more than a domestic servant position, or that there was no position at all. With no relatives or friends to take them in, many young girls moved to the Black Belt, where lodging was cheap and some type of marginal employment could be had.

Club women in Chicago, as well as in other Northern and Southern cities, realized the gravity of the situation, and accordingly established nurseries and kindergartens for the young, and homes for working girls. So, too, did they provide assistance in procuring more suitable employment and creating "wholesome" recreational clubs for young women. In the South, African-American club women often networked with educational institutions, such as Hampton and Tuskegee Institutes, to assist poor, rural families; in their outreach efforts, they especially sought to improve home life through mothers' and girls' clubs, home-making lessons, and instruction in hygiene, child care, and health matters. In Northern cities, club women relied more upon the constellation of African-American organizations, including sister clubs in various cities and states, the NAACP, the Urban League, and national women's organizations. Despite these regional differences, the issues addressed by most African-American women's clubs were mutual and included child welfare, family life, and housing for the elderly, orphans, the poor, and working girls and women.[25]

Homes for the young women established in Chicago included the Elaine Home Club and Johnson Home for Girls. The Illinois Technical School for Colored Girls, a Catholic agency, not only provided technical training to about one hundred young girls, but also provided board. In 1915, a segregated YWCA was opened by African-American club women. Although only a small group of girls lived there because of limited space, the YWCA created a directory of "safe" homes for girls who were new to the city and without families. Through its Industrial Section, the YWCA also assisted girls in locating employment.[26] Phyllis Wheatley Home, however, was the best known home for young working girls, and one that was supported and maintained through the fund-raising activities of the Phyllis Wheatley Club and many sister clubs in Chicago.

THE PHYLLIS WHEATLEY HOME

The concerns of the Phyllis Wheatley Club dovetailed into the formation of the Home. Even before the opening of the nursery and the Home, Phyllis Wheatley Club members were concerned with poorer African-Americans' home life, generally, and young women, particularly. In the late 1800's, the Club had opened a sewing school, which accommodated nearly one hundred young girls; taught by club members, the facility closed after five years. As early as 1899, Mrs. Ida Taylor had written and read a paper in regard to a Mr. Monroe Clark, who had opened a newsboys' home on Wabash Avenue. In 1900, Dr. Anna Cooper had spoken on practical charity for poorer families. The topics at a 1905 meeting, "Aiding the Nurseries" and "Founding a Clubroom" no doubt laid the ground work for the creation of the nursery and the Home.[27]

In 1906, a nursery was organized, and in the following year, the Club incorporated the Phyllis Wheatley Home, a nine-room, two-story house. The purpose of the Home was to "befriend the Colored girls and women who come into this great city seeking work, often without relatives, friends or money."[28] The Home not only provided a Christian influence, but assisted homeless girls and women in securing employment, especially by "elevating" the standards of domestic service. This latter effort was achieved by providing the girls with encouragement and sympathy, as well as giving them practical experience through the upkeep of the Home's laundry, sewing, and other household duties. The Home accommodated twenty girls, at the cost of one dollar and twenty-five cents per week, and twenty-five cents per night for "transients." As of 1914, the Home had been a source of lodging for more than three hundred girls, and had assisted over five hundred girls in locating jobs.[29]

The Club organized seven standing Home Committees whose responsibilities ranged from cleaning and furnishing the Home, prompting members to contribute to the Home's taxes, to soliciting the membership and support of other clubs and church members, and investigating individual cases of welfare. All this was necessary for "proper home life conditions." The motto of the housecleaning committee was testimony to the Club's determination: "If you can't push, pull, and if you can't pull, please get out of the way." The same determination was evident in their fund-raising committees. The Club wasted little time or energy in raising funds for the Home. As early as 1906, the Phyllis Wheatley Club sponsored a lawn fete with dancing and other forms of amusement; the proceeds went directly toward the new Home. Handmade items were made and raffled off, as was the case of a "beautiful, hand-made lingerie skirt" sewn by Mrs. Martha Walton. On another occasion, a hand-embroidered skirt quilt, "made from sixteen gentlemen's handkerchiefs . . . put together in the most artistic manner" was exhibited and raffled off, netting over two hundred and thirty dollars. In 1915, an "apron/shop" was opened at the Home, providing a small but steady source of support.[30]

Concerts and drama productions were other successful fund-raising events. In 1913, a "Celebrity Party" was held for the benefit of the Home. This program highlighted prominent African-American authors and composers, such as Paul Lawrence Dunbar, Samuel Coleridge-Taylor, and Fenton Johnson. A benefit drama was sponsored by the Elete [sic] Social and Charity Club, a club which "work[ed] wholly for the Phyllis Wheatley

Home." In 1913, the Willing Dramatic Club produced a four-act drama, "The Dust of the Earth," as a fund-raiser. In 1915, the Phyllis Wheatley Club produced a three-act drama, "A Woman's Honor," directed by Madam B. L. Hensley, an organizer with the Elete [sic] Social and Charity Club. Fenton Johnson, as well, donated one of his one-act dramas to a Thanksgiving Day matinee.[31]

Dances and balls also raised much needed monies, as well as provided social entertainment for young girls and club women. A Benefit Dance for young people was held, as were fall dances, with Authur Stewart's Orchestra entertaining. Invitations to these events were often exclusive. For example, a pre-Lenten ball in 1917 was considered "the grandest society affair that Chicago has ever had, [and] has taken not only the city but the entire state by storm." Prominent African-American citizens participated in organizing the event, including Eva Jenifer, president of the YWCA, and Julius Avendorph, a prominent businessman. Julius Avendorph, "Chicago's arbiter elegantarium," was in charge of the floor committee; the ushers were some of "the most popular and beautiful young ladies and debutantes of the season." Reporters, including Fenton Johnson of the *Champion Magazine*, Robert Abbott of *the Chicago Defender*, Kathryn Williams of *The Half Century Magazine* and Julius Taylor of the *Broad Ax*, devoted much press coverage to the occasion.[32]

Monies raised from these events were sorely needed as there was talk of purchasing a larger home in 1914 because of the increased number of applications. This was due to another wave of southern migration to Chicago. From 1910–1920 alone, the African-American population in the city had increased from 44,103 to 109,594, or by 148.5%.[33] Many of the migrants were young women who sought lodging and employment through the Travelers' Aid which, in turn, requested assistance from the Home. Applications also came from young women wishing to attend the University of Chicago, but with little money for housing. That the young women were grateful for such assistance was made public at a picnic given by the Club, at which "all expressed the highest appreciation of the Home, which means so much to so many of our girls struggling to make their way through school and in other avenues of life. . . ."[34] In 1915, a new home was finally purchased, with a substantial amount paid toward the mortgage by the Elete [sic] Social and Charity Club. Improvements were continually made to the new Home through the women's club efforts, including the installation of electric lights in 1918. By 1920 the Home accommodated as many as forty-four girls at a single time.[35]

Although the usual fund-raising events were balls, dramas, and dances, the Phyllis Wheatley Club also organized a number of other creative fund-raising endeavors to support the Home. For example, a "mysterious social" involved the solving of a mystery, with the simple clue of "they are all 'peaches' and herein lies the mystery." The mystery brought in over one hundred dollars. A Halloween Party was given at the Home, where dinner was served and prizes were awarded for "most artistic and most comical costumes." An "experience meeting" was held, in which each member earned a dollar and told how it was earned. Money was directed toward payment of the furnace bill. Dr. Fannie Emanuel visited the Club and "filled five feet of pennies" toward an effort to raise money by making a "mile of pennies."[36]

Other sister clubs were generous in their collaborative efforts and donations to the Phyllis Wheatley Home. A list of requests in 1914 mentioned furniture, bedding, kitchen utensils, and other household materials. That these requests were met was evident in the in-kind goods donated by the various clubs, such as soap, towels, sheets, new beds, a kitchen floor, curtains, three chairs, one wash boiler, a davenport, a center table, small brackets, pillows, bed spreads, couch, a chenille couch cover, and a dozen pillow cases. The Gaudeamus Club alone donated one dozen pillow cases and towels, most likely made by club members. The same year, the Tiliman Club from Hannibal, Missouri, sent a pair of pillow cases for a pillow case shower which the club held for the Home. Other donors of the above necessities included the Chicago Woman's Club, the North Side Women's Club, the Hyde Park Woman's Club, the Samaritan Club, the Lady Elliot Circle C.O.F., and the Necessity Club.[37] Such cooperation and networking sustained long-standing institutions, such as the Phyllis Wheatley Home, through fundraising and social uplift programs, as well as provided entertainment and camaraderie to its club members.

This article has presented only a sampling of activities carried out by the Phyllis Wheatley Club. The maintenance of the Phyllis Wheatley Home absorbed much of the time and commitment of its members after 1907. The arduous task of providing safe living quarters for many African-American girls was accomplished through the creative efforts and organizational skills of members of the Club. Although the Club featured selective topics in literature, art, and music, much of its discussion also led to social reform, including the upkeep of the home, the creation of a nursery, or the teaching of sewing to young women.

Although some scholars have emphasized the social class distinctions between club women and their poorer sisters, in the case of the Phyllis Wheatley Club, these differences seemed to be less distinct than those of other African-American clubs in Chicago. Although many of the fund-raising activities, such as balls, dances, theatre, and musicals, reflected a "cultural capital" not enjoyed by poorer African-Americans, these efforts were almost always directed toward philanthropic purposes. Unlike some of the other women's clubs, whose time was spent in whist and other card games, or in the study of classical music, the Phyllis Wheatley Club combined "much good will" with informed discussion and study.[38] Thus, activism and intellectual debates were mutual and reciprocal, a testimony to uplift of both mind and heart.

NOTES

1. Gerda Lerner, "Early Community Work of Black Club Women," *Journal Negro History*, 59 (1978): 158–167.
2. Although this list is not comprehensive, see Darlene Clark Hine, ed., *Black Women in United States History*, (16 vols.; Brooklyn, 1990); Paula Giddings, *Where and When I Enter. The Impact of Black Women on Race and Sex in America* (New York, 1984); Gerda Lerner, ed., *Black Women in White America* (New York, 1992); Cynthia Neverdon-Morton, *Afro-American Women of the South and the Advancement of the Race, 1895–1925* (Knoxville, 1985); Anne Firor Scott, "Most Invisible of All: Black Women's Voluntary Associations," *Journal of Southern History* 56 (February 1990): 5–22; Anne Firor Scott, *Natural Allies. Women's Associations in American History* (Urbana: University of Illinois Press, 1992); Dorothy Sterling, ed., *We Are Your Sisters. Black Women in the Nineteenth Century* (New York, 1984).
3. *Historical Records of Conventions of 1895–1896 of the Colored Women of America* (Washington, DC: NACW, n.d.), 108.
4. St. Clair Drake, *Churches and Voluntary Association in the Chicago Negro Community* (Chicago Work Projects Administration, 1940), 146.
5. Primary sources include Chicago Commission of Race Relations, *The Negro in Chicago. A Study of Race Relations and a Race Riot in 1919* (New York, 1968; Chicago, 1922), 142; Junius Wood, *The Negro in Chicago* (Chicago, 1916), 20; Elizabeth Lindsay Davis, *Lifting As They Climb* (Washington, DC: National Association of Colored Women, 1933), 136–138; W. E. B. Du Bois, *Efforts for a Social Betterment* (Atlanta, 1909), 100; "Phyllis Wheatley Home," *Co-Operation* 8 (June 1908): 179–180. Secondary sources are Dorothy Salem, *To Better Our World. Black Women in Organized Reform, 1890–1920*, vol. 14 of *Black Women in United States History* (Brooklyn, 1990), 91, 124, 202; Allen Spear, *Black Chicago. The Making of a Negro Ghetto, 1890–1920* (Chicago, 1967), 102.
6. There are few collections available in Chicago's African-American women's clubs or individual club women for the time period 1890 to 1920. Records were not yet archived through the city, state or national associations. The only collections concerning Phyllis Wheatley Club and Home are the Phyllis Wheatley Association Records, Special Collections, The University Library, The University of Illinois at Chicago. This collection contains only a few descriptions of the Home, Club or its members from 1896 to 1920. The Ida B. Wells Papers and the Julius Rosenwald Papers at the University of Chicago's Special Collections Department have yielded some biographical information on Ida B. Wells and a few other club women. The Irene McCoy-Gaines Papers at the Chicago Historical Society pertain mostly to McCoy-Gaines' club life from the 1920s to 1940s. The Hull House Records at the University of Illinois in Chicago contained little information on African-Americans. So, too, did the Elizabeth Harrison Papers at St. Louis University contain little information on African-American kindergartens, most of which were founded by club women. Lastly, the Newberry Library's collections were mostly concerned with immigrant settlements, although 1916–1918 editions of the charity magazines, *Co-Operation*, did contain some descriptions of African-American organizations in Chicago. This predicament is not peculiar to Chicago clubs, as there is still a great need for diaries, letters, club memos and records to be collected and catalogued. See Deborah Gray White, "Mining the Forgotten: Manuscript Sources for Black Women's History," *Journal of American History* 74 (June 1987), 237–243.
7. Phyllis Wheatley Association Records, Special Collections, The University Library, The University of Illinois at Chicago, n.p.
8. This is not to suggest that African-American women followed white women's prescriptions of domestic feminism or the cult of true womanhood. Rather, they mediated and redefined their roles as mothers and wives, which had historically been denied full expression.

9. This information is from various listings of new members and club officers which were regularly featured in newspaper accounts of weekly activities.

10. *Broad Ax,* Nov. 4, 1899.

11. *Broad Ax,* Nov. 11, 1899.

12. *Broad Ax,* June 23, 1900.

13. *Broad Ax,* Apr. 23, 1910; *Chicago Defender,* Apr. 29, 1911; *Broad Ax,* Dec. 1, 1900.

14. *Broad Ax,* Nov. 25, 1899; *Broad Ax,* Mar. 2, 1901; *Broad Ax,* Apr. 25, 1903.

15. *Broad Ax,* Dec. 2, 1899; *Broad Ax,* Mar. 17, 1900; *Broad Ax,* Oct. 13, 1900; Broad Ax, Dec. 1, 1900; *Broad Ax,* Oct. 31, 1903.

16. *Broad Ax,* Apr. 7, 1900; *Broad Ax,* Oct. 27, 1900; *Broad Ax,* May 4, 1901.

17. *Broad Ax,* Apr. 7, 1900.

18. *Broad Ax,* July 13, 1912; *Broad Ax,* Oct. 29, 1916; *Broad Ax,* Oct. 21, 1911; *Broad Ax,* Nov. 26, 1910; *Chicago Defender,* May 4, 1912.

19. *Broad Ax,* Nov. 4, 1899.

20. For further information on the Black Belt, see Allen Spear, "The Rise of the Chicago Black Belt," in *The Rise of the Ghetto,* eds. E. Franklin Frazier, John H. Bracey, Jr., August Meler, and Elliott Rudwick (Belmont, CA, 1971), 57–69. For further information on the bombings and violence directed at African-Americans as they attempted to move into Hyde Park and other predominantly white, middle-class neighborhoods, see William Tuttle, Jr., "Contested Neighborhoods and Racial Violence: Prelude to the Chicago Riot of 1919," *Journal of Negro History* 55 (October 1970): 266–288.

21. Chicago Commission on Race Relations, *The Negro in Chicago. A Study of Race Relations and a Race Riot in 1919* (Chicago, 1922), 158.

22. Louise de Koven Bowen, *The Colored People of Chicago. An Investigation Made for the Juvenile Protective Association* (Chicago, 1913), unnumbered pages.

23. Cited in *Chicago Tribune,* Aug. 11, 1889, p. 12.

24. Bowen, *Colored People of Chicago.*

25. For a more complete analysis of southern African-American women's clubs, see Cynthia Neverdon-Morton, *Afro-American Women of the South and the Advancement of the Race, 1895–1925.*

26. Chicago Commission, *The Negro in Chicago,* 142.

27. *Broad Ax,* Dec. 2, 1899; *Broad Ax,* Oct. 29, 1900; *Broad Ax,* Apr. 8, 1905.

28. *Broad Ax,* Mar. 27, 1909.

29. *Broad Ax,* Apr. 14, 1914.

30. *Broad Ax,* July 28, 1906; *Broad Ax,* Mar. 23, 1912; *Chicago Defender,* Dec. 30, 1913; *Broad Ax,* Mar. 14, 1914.

31. *Chicago Defender,* Oct. 11, 1911; *Broad Ax,* Nov. 15, 1913; *Chicago Defender,* June 28, 1913; *Broad Ax,* June 5, 1916; Sept. 20, 1917.

32. *Broad Ax,* Feb. 11, 1917.

33. Chicago Commission of Race Relations, "The Migration of Negroes from the South, 1916–1918," in *The Rise of the Ghetto,* eds. E. Franklin Frazier, John H. Bracey, Jr., August Meier, and Elliott Rudwick (Belmont, California, 1971), 44.

34. *Broad Ax,* Aug. 9, 1913.

35. *Chicago Defender,* Feb. 7, 1920.

36. *Broad Ax,* Apr. 14, 1900.

37. *Chicago Defender,* May 21, 1914; *Broad Ax,* Mar. 7, 1914; *Broad Ax,* Apr. 6, 1912.

38. *Chicago Defender,* Nov. 4, 1899. Particularly after 1910, the number of whist, lawn tennis, and other social clubs increased amongst the growing middle-class African-American communities in Chicago. Even so, most of these clubs devoted part of their efforts to philanthropic and charitable causes.

Claude McKay and the New Negro of the 1920's

By WAYNE COOPER

As USED IN THE 1920's, the term "New Negro" referred to more than the writers then active in the Negro Renaissance. The New Negro also included the Negro masses and especially the young. "For the younger generation," Alain Locke wrote in 1925, "is vibrant with a new psychology."[1] This new spirit he described as basically a renewal of "self-respect and self-dependence."[2]

The new confidence which characterized Negroes in the twenties resulted from many forces. Prior to World War I, militant new leaders had arisen. By demanding immediately full civil liberties and an end to segregation, men such as W. E. B. DuBois had inspired a greater self-assertiveness in their people. World War I and the resulting mass migration of Negroes to the urban North further disrupted old patterns of life and created new hopes, as well as new problems. The fight for democracy abroad led to greater expectations at home. The bloody race riots of 1919 did not kill these hopes, although the remarkable popularity of Marcus Garvey and his black nationalism indicated the Negro masses could not forever contain their frustrated aspirations.[3] As the Negro people entered the twenties, the "promised land" of the old spirituals still seemed far away. But their new militancy demonstrated that the long journey down the bitter desert years of history had strengthened, not weakened, their determination to reach the good life ahead.

That sudden flowering in literature called the Negro Renaissance gave voice to the new spirit awakening in Negroes in the twenties.[4] In addition, the Negro Renaissance became a part of the general revolt by the writers of the decade against the gross materialism and outmoded moral values of America's new industrial society. Negro writers found new strength in their own folk culture. As Robert Bone has written, "The Negro Renaissance was essentially a period of self-discovery, marked by a sudden growth of interest in things Negro."[5]

Of all the Renaissance writers, Claude McKay was one of the first to express the spirit of the New Negro.[6] His first American poems appeared in 1917. Before the decade of the Negro Renaissance had begun, he was already winning recognition as an exciting new voice in Negro literature.[7] A brief examination of his early career will perhaps reveal more clearly some of the important characteristics of the New Negro of the 1920's.

Claude McKay was born September 15, 1889, on the British West Indian island of Jamaica. There he grew to manhood. In 1912, at the age of twenty-three, he came to the United States to study agriculture at Tuskegee Institute, In Jamaica, McKay had already established a local reputation as a poet, having produced before he left two volumes of dialect poetry, *Song of Jamaica* and *Constab Ballads.*[8]

These volumes revealed McKay to be a sensitive, intelligent observer of Jamaican life. Of black peasant origin himself, he used the English dialect of rural Jamaica to record lyrically the life of his people. In evaluating McKay's Jamaican verse, Jean Wagner has recently written:

> Here, we are far from the dialect of the Dunbar school, inherited from the whites, who had forged it in order to perpetuate the stereotype of Negro inferiority, and at best fix them in their role of buffoons charged with diverting the white race. . . .[9] All things being equal, McKay's portrait of the Jamaican peasant is in substance that of the peasant the world over. Profoundly attached to the earth, he works the soil with a knowledge gained from age long habit; although a hard worker, the Jamaican, like his counterpart the world over, is condemned to exploitation.[10]

On the eve of his departure to the United States, McKay appeared to be an ambitious, talented young man with a fine future in Jamaica. In his poetry he had closely identified himself with its people. He had also revealed a deeply sensitive,

---

[1] Alain Locke (ed.), *The New Negro* (New York, 1925), p. 3.

[2] *Ibid.,* p. 4.

[3] Two recent general discussions of the New Negro of the twenties are found in Robert A. Bone, *The Negro Novel in America* (New Haven, 1958), pp. 51–107; and Jean Wagner, *Les Poetes Negres des États-Unis* (Paris: Librairie Istra, 1963), pp. 161–207.

[4] Wagner, *op. cit.,* p. 161.

[5] Bone, *op. cit.,* p. 62.

[6] Wagner, *op. cit.,* p. 211.

[7] McKay first became widely known after the appearance of his poem, "If We Must Die," in *The Liberator* (July, 1919), 20–21.

[8] Claude McKay, *Songs of Jamaica* (Kingston: Aston W. Gardner and Co., 1912); *Constab Ballads* (London, 1912).

[9] Wagner, *op. cit.,* p. 219.

[10] *Ibid.,* p. 220.

From *Phylon*, Fall 1964, pp. 297-306. © 1964 by Wayne Cooper. Reprinted by permission.

independent spirit, keenly responsive to the good and evil in both man and nature.

Like many before him, however, he was strongly attracted to the United States. Years later, he wrote that America then seemed to him, "a new land to which all people who had youth and a youthful mind turned. Surely there would be opportunity in this land, even for a Negro."[11] Although far from naïve, McKay had never experienced firsthand American racial prejudice, and he seemed to have been totally unprepared for its vicious effects.

His initiation into the realities of Negro American life must certainly have been a swift one. Landing in Charleston, South Carolina, in the summer of 1912, he proceeded to Alabama's Tuskegee Institute. In 1918, Mckay recorded in *Pearson's Magazine* his first reaction to Southern racial prejudice.

It was the first time I had ever come face to face with such manifest, implacable hate of my race, and my feelings were indescribable. At first I was horrified; my spirit revolted against the ignoble cruelty and blindness of it all.... Then I found myself hating in return, but this feeling could not last long for to hate is to be miserable.[12]

Accompanying this statement were several poems, which, McKay said, had been written during his first year in America. "I sent them so that you may see what my state of mind was at the time."[13] Among them was one of his most eloquent polemics—"To the White Fiends." This poem shows a personality unaccustomed to servility and murderously aroused against the brutish debasement of Southern prejudice. If the poet could not physically defeat it, he, nevertheless, could throw a revealing light on its moral inferiority.

Think you I am not fiend and savage too?
Think you I could not arm me with a gun
And shoot down ten of you for every one of my black
    brothers murdered, burnt by you?
Be not deceived, for every deed you do
I could match—out-match: Am I not Afric's son,
Black of that black land where black deeds are done?
But the Almighty from the darkness drew
My soul and said: Even thou shalt be a light
Awhile to burn on the benighted earth,
Thy dusky face I set among the white
For thee to prove thyself of higher worth;
Before the world is swallowed up in night,
To show thy little lamp: go forth, go forth![14]

Soon tiring of what he described as "the semi-military, machine-like existence"[15] at Tuskegee, McKay transferred to Kansas State College, where he remained until 1914. In that year

he was given several thousand dollars by an English friend.[16] Having decided his future lay in writing, not agricultural science, he took the money and went to New York City.

Once there, literary success did not come quickly. In fact, during his first year in New York, little time seems to have been devoted to writing. As he described it, through "high-living" and "bad investments" he soon managed to lose all his money.[17] His marriage to a Jamaican girl shortly after his arrival in New York lasted almost as briefly as his money.[18] "My wife," McKay wrote in 1918, "wearied of the life [in New York] in six months and went back to Jamaica."[19] McKay himself made a different decision. "I hated to go back after having failed at nearly everything so I just stayed here and worked—porter ... janitor ... waiter—anything that came handy."[20]

He also wrote, "If I would not," he said, "graduate as a bachelor of arts, I would graduate as a poet."[21] Within two years, Waldo Frank and James Oppehheim accepted for *Seven Arts Magazine* two of his sonnets, "The Harlem Dancer" and "Invocation."[22] A year later he was discovered by Frank Harris, who brought him to public notice again in *Pearson's Magazine*. Shortly afterwards, McKay met Max Eastman and his sister, Crystal. A lifelong friendship resulted.

At the time, Max Eastman was editor of *The Liberator*, then America's most openly Marxist literary magazine.[23] Through the *Liberator*, McKay quickly became identified with the radical-bohemian set in Greenwich Village. In 1919, Eastman and his staff were eagerly praising the young communist government of Russia, violently denouncing the repressive post-war hysteria at home, and writing stories and poems that ranged from fighting proletariat propaganda to tender pieces of home and mother. Few magazines, then or now, could match the *Liberator* in enthusiasm. Despite its flamboyancy, however, it was rich in talents. "On the surface," Robert Aaron has written, "*The Liberator* reflected the aimless, pointless life of the village." Yet, as Aaron pointed out, after World War I, it displayed a "toughness and militancy in its social attitudes,"[24] which belied its bohemian character.

Into such an atmosphere McKay fitted well. Eastman has described him then as a very black, handsome, high-spirited young man, with peculiar, arched eyebrows which gave him a perpetually quizzical expression.[25] Another old radical, Joseph Freeman, remembered also in his autobiography McKay's charm and wit.[26]

---

[11]McKay, *My Green Hills of Jamaica* (Unpublished mss. in the Schomburg Collection, New York Public Library), p. 80, written in the mid-1940's.
[12]*Pearson's Magazine* (September, 1918), 275.
[13]*Ibid.*
[14]*Ibid.*, p. 276.
[15]*Ibid.*

[16]Letter from McKay to James Weldon Johnson, March 10, 1928, in the McKay folder of Johnson Correspondence (James Weldon Johnson Collection, Yale University Library).
[17]Countee Cullen (ed.), *Caroling Dusk, An Anthology of Verse by Negro Poets* (New York, 1927), p. 82.
[18]Marriage certificate in the McKay Papers (Yale University Library).
[19]*Pearson's Magazine* (September, 1918), 276.
[20]*Ibid.*
[21]McKay, *A Long Way From Home* (New York, 1937), p. 4.
[22]Wagner, *op. cit.*, p. 215.
[23]For a good discussion of *The Liberator* and its origins see, Daniel Aaron, *Writers on the Left, Episodes in American Literary Communism* (New York, 1961), pp. 5–108.
[24]*Ibid.*, p. 92.
[25]In McKay, *The Selected Poems of Claude McKay* (New York, 1953). p. 110.
[26]Joseph Freeman, *An American Testament, A Narrative of Rebels and Romantics* (New York, 1936), pp. 243, 245–46, 254.

If McKay was sometimes given to abandoned gaiety, in the summer of 1919 he had good reason to exhibit a greater seriousness, as well as toughness. 1919 was the year of the Great Red Scare, one desperate phase of the effort to return to pre-war "normalcy." For Negroes, the year turned into a nightmare of bloody riots and violent death.[27] From June until January there occurred no less than twenty-five riots in major urban centers throughout the country.[28] The Chicago riot of July was the worst. When it was over, authorities counted 38 Negroes and whites dead, over 520 injured, and 1,000 families homeless.[29] Like all Negroes, McKay felt the emotional effects of such battles.

In the July issue of the *Liberator*[30] there appeared, along with six other poems, his now famous "If We Must Die." Today, it is the one poem by which McKay is most widely known. "If We Must Die" was a desperate shout of defiance; almost, it seemed a statement of tragic hopelessness. At the same time, it loudly proclaimed that in Negroes the spirit of human courage remained fully alive. Here is the poem which brought McKay to the alert attention of the Negro world. If not a great poem it, nevertheless, must certainly have expressed the attitude of many Negroes in 1919.

If we must die, let it not be like hogs
Hunted and penned in an inglorious spot,
While round us bark the mad and hungry dogs,
Making their mock at our accursed lot.
If we must die, O let us nobly die,
So that our precious blood may not be shed in vain;
   then even the monsters we defy
Shall be constrained to honor us though dead!

. . . .

What though before us lies the open grave?
Like men we'll face the murderous, cowardly pack,
Pressed to the wall, dying, but fighting back!

After his appearance in *The Liberator*, McKay entered more fully into the literary world. His career through the twenties reads, in fact, like a romance of the decade itself. Through the generosity of friends, he went to England in late 1919 and stayed for more than a year, working part of the time for Sylvia Pankhurst's socialist paper, *The Workers' Dreadnought*. While there his third book of poems, *Spring in New Hampshire*, appeared.[31]

Upon his return to the United States in 1921, he became for a brief time co-editor of *The Liberator* with Michael Gold. Before leaving that job because of policy differences with Gold,[32] McKay's first American book of poems, *Harlem Shad-*

ows,[33] appeared. During this period, he also made a brief first acquaintance with many leading Negro intellectuals, among them James W. Johnson and W. E. B. DuBois.[34] But before the end of 1922, he was off again, this time to Russia.

McKay was among the first Negroes to go to Russia after the Civil War which had brought the Communists into undisputed power. He arrived during Lenin's period of ideological retrenchment, when the New Economic Policy allowed a limited amount of free enterprise and personal freedom. Because of his black complexion, McKay immediately attracted the attention of people in the street. Although not a party member, or even definitely committed to Marxist principles, McKay's popularity with the crowds in Moscow and Leningrad helped win him favor among higher party circles. Sen Katayama, then Japan's leading Communist, got McKay admitted to the Fourth Congress of the Communist International.[35] But above all, as McKay wrote James Weldon Johnson in 1935, "It was the popular interest that irresistibly pushed me forward."[36] His trip soon turned into one long triumph of personal popularity.

After meeting Trotsky in Moscow, he was sent on a long and elaborate tour of Soviet army and naval bases. Besides Trotsky, he met Zinoviev and other top Communists, as well as many leading Russian literary figures.

Despite McKay's sincere attraction to the Communist Revolution, he never fully committed himself to its ideology. In the 1930's, he was viciously attacked by American Communists for going back on his principles; but, as he wrote James Weldon Johnson in 1935, he went to Russia as "a writer and free spirit"[37] and left the same. He wrote Johnson then and later repeated in his autobiography that he had desired in 1922 the title, "creative writer," and had felt it would mean more to Negroes in the long run.[38]

Throughout the twenties, and to a large extent throughout his life, McKay remained what Frederick Hoffman called the "aesthetic radical."[39] This was the artist who, typical of the twenties, stoutly affirmed the value of his non-social personality. He considered himself "the natural man," willing in an age of conformity to be only himself. That McKay shared this attitude is evident in all his writings.

Like other Negro writers of the twenties (most notably, Langston Hughes), he shared, to some degree, the same feeling of alienation that characterized Gertrude Stein's "lost generation." Thus, in 1918, McKay could write: "And now this great catastrophe [World War I] has come upon the world, proving the real hollowness of nationhood, patriotism, racial pride, and most of the things one was taught to respect and reverence."[40]

[27]John Hope Franklin, *From Slavery to Freedom, A History of American Negroes* (New York, 1947), pp. 471–73.
[28]*Ibid.*
[29]*Ibid.*, pp. 473–74.
[30]*The Liberator* (July, 1919), 20–21.
[31]McKay, *A Long Way From Home*, pp. 59–91.
[32]*Ibid.*, pp. 138–41. See also, Aaron, *op. cit.*, p. 93.
[33]McKay, *Harlem Shadows* (New York, 1922).
[34]McKay, *A Long Way From Home*, pp. 108–15.
[35]*Ibid.*, pp. 165–66.
[36]Letters from McKay to James Weldon Johnson, May 8, 1935, in the McKay folder of the Johnson Correspondence (James Weldon Johnson Collection, Yale University Library).
[37]*Ibid.*
[38]*Ibid.*
[39]Frederick J. Hoffman, *The Twenties, American Writings in the Postwar Decade* (New York, 1955), pp. 382–84.
[40]*Pearson's Magazine* (September, 1918), 276.

His affiliation with *The Liberator* and his trip to Russia were part of a personal search for new moral and social standards.

McKay's trip to Russia marked the beginning of his long twelve-year exile in Europe. From Russia, he went briefly to Germany, then to France, where he lived for a number of years. In the late twenties, he journeyed to Spain and then to Morocco in North Africa where he remained until his return to the United States in 1934.[41]

Why did McKay spend twelve years wandering through Europe and North Africa? He never felt himself to be a typical expatriate. In this autobiography, he gave perhaps the main reason for his long expatriation.

> Color consciousness was the fundamental of my restlessness ... my white fellow-expatriates could sympathize but ... they could not altogether understand ... unable to see deep into the profundity of blackness, some even thought ... I might have preferred to be white like them ... they couldn't understand the instinctive ... pride of a black person resolute in being himself and yet living a simple civilized life like themselves.[42]

The place of Negroes in the modern world was the one great problem that obsessed McKay from his arrival in the United States until his death in 1948.[43] For a while after World War I, he undoubtedly thought that in Communism Negroes might find a great world brotherhood.

In the twenties, he turned from international communism but not from the common Negro, with whom he had always closely identified. He came to the conclusion that in Negro working people there existed an uninhibited creativity and joy in life which Europeans, including Americans, had lost. In their folk culture lay strength enough for their salvation. McKay felt Negroes should not lose sight of their own uniqueness and the value of their own creations while taking what was valuable from the larger European civilization. He laid much emphasis on the need of Negroes to develop a group spirit.[44]

Among Negro writers of the twenties, McKay was not alone in his discovery of the folk. In fact, of central importance to the Negro Renaissance was its emphasis on Negro folk culture. Jean Toomer, for example, celebrated the black peasants of Georgia, and in the following verses, associated himself with their slave past:

O Negro slaves, dark purple ripened plums
Squeezed, and bursting in the pine-wood air,
Passing, before they stripped the old tree bare
One plum was saved for me, one seen becomes

An everlasting song, a singing tree,
Caroling softly souls of slavery,
What they were, and what they are to me,
Caroling softly souls of slavery.[45]

In enthusiastic outbursts, youthful Langston Hughes was also loudly proclaiming the worth of the common folk.[46]

To a certain extent, the New Negro's emphasis on the folk was heightened by the new attitude toward Negroes exhibited by many white writers of the twenties. After World War I certain white writers such as Gertrude Stein and Waldo Frank thought they saw in Negroes beings whose naturally creative expressiveness had not been completely inhibited by the evil forces of modern civilization.[47] As the twenties progressed, Negroes and their arts enjoyed a considerable vogue. Primitive African art became popular among many intellectuals. Jazz, of course, became popular in the twenties. Negro singers found a greater public receptivity, and the blues entered American music. In many respects, American Negroes had in the twenties a favorable opportunity for a reassessment of their past accomplishments and future potentials.

The great emphasis on the primitive and the folk led however to some naïve delusions. Just as whites had previously built a stereotype of the happy, simpleminded plantation Negro, many people in the twenties stereotyped Negroes as unfettered children of nature, bubbling over with uninhibited sexual joy and child-like originality. To the extent that Negro writers accepted such an image, they limited the depth and richness of their own evaluations of American Negro life.[48]

While he was in Europe, McKay produced three novels which reflected his own interest in the Negro folk. They were *Home to Harlem* (1928),[49] *Banjo* (1929), and *Banana Bottom* (1933). He also produced a volume of short stories entitled *Gingertown* in 1932.[50] To a considerable extent, McKay's view of the Negro common folk was influenced by the newer stereotype of Negroes. *Home to Harlem,* his first novel, is the story of Jake, a Negro doughboy, and his joyful return to Harlem after World War I. Jake seems to have been McKay's ideal type—an honest, carefree worker whose existence, if a rather aimless one, is not complicated by pettiness or unnecessary worry over things that do not immediately concern him. Contrasted to Jake is Ray (McKay himself), an educated Negro, who is torn between two ways of life—Jake's and the more serious though conventional one imposed upon him by education. While the virtues of the common folk are contrasted to the doubts and confusion of the educated, McKay takes the reader on a tour of Harlem cabarets and rent parties.

[41]McKay, *A Long Way From Home,* pp. 153–341, contains an account of his travels through Europe and North Africa. A briefer account is in Wagner, *op. cit.,* pp. 215–17.
[42]McKay, *A Long Way From Home,* p. 245.
[43]For McKay's views on race toward the end of his life, his "Right Turn to Catholicism" (typewritten ms. in the Schomburg Collection, New York Public Library) is especially important.
[44]These ideas were presented by McKay in two novels, *Banjo* (New York, 1929), and *Banana Bottom* (New York, 1933). He discussed the idea of a "group soul" in *A Long Way From Home,* pp. 349–54.

[45]In Wagner, *op. cit.,* p. 292.
[46]Langton Hughes, "The Negro Artist and the Racial Mountain," *The Nation* (June 23, 1926), 694.
[47]For a general discussion of this topic, see Wagner, *op. cit.,* pp. 174–77. Also, see Hoffman, *op. cit.,* pp. 269–71.
[48]Bone, *op. cit.,* pp. 58–61.
[49]*Home to Harlem* (New York, 1928).
[50]*Gingertown* (New York, 1932).

His unvarnished view of Harlem night life delighted many white readers of the twenties and dismayed not a few middle-class Negroes.[51] The latter felt that an undue emphasis on the Negro lower class would damage their fight for civil rights and further delay their just battle for liberty. McKay was not the only writer of the Negro Renaissance to upset respectable Negro society.[52] One of the chief results of the Negro Renaissance was to force the Negro middle class to reevaluate their relationship to the Negro masses.

McKay's second novel, *Banjo,* told the story of the Negro beachboys of Marseilles, and further contrasted the free life of common Negroes with the frustrations of those caught in the more sophisticated web of modern civilization. In his third novel, *Banana Bottom,* he idealized the folk culture of Jamaica.

In some ways, Claude McKay differed radically from the typical New Negro writer of the twenties. For one thing, he was a Jamaican and did not become an American citizen until 1940. For another, he was older by some ten years than most writers of the Negro Renaissance; and except for a brief period, he did not live in the United States at all in the twenties.

He was also unique in the extent to which he associated with the larger literary world. Most Negro writers of the twenties had depended on Negro publications for a start. McKay's first successes were in white magazines—*Seven Arts, Pearson's,* and *The Liberator.* As an editor of *The Liberator* for a

brief while, he was probably the only Negro writer of the time to hold such a position on an important American publication. McKay was at least partly responsible for the greater degree of communication that existed between Negro and white writers in the twenties. On the eve of his departure for Russia in 1922, James Weldon Johnson gave him a farewell party, and invited prominent writers of both races. Years later Johnson wrote to McKay concerning that event:

> We often speak of that party back in '22. . . . Do you know that was the first getting together of the black and white literati on a purely social plane. Such parties are now common in New York, but I doubt if any has been more representative. You will remember there were present Heywood Broun, Ruth Hale, F. P. Adams, John Farrar, Carl Van Doren, Freda Kirchwey, Peggy Tucker, Roy Nash—on our side you, DuBois, Walter White, Jessie Fauset, [Arthur] Schomburg, J. Rosamond Johnson—I think that party started something.[53]

Although McKay's career differed somewhat from that of the typical Negro writer of the twenties, he represented much that was characteristic of the New Negro. His movement from rural Jamaica to the big city and the literary world of the twenties is itself symbolic of the larger movement by Negro people from the rural South to the broader horizons of the urban North. His early interest in Communism was only one indication that the New Negro would no longer be unaffected by world events. World War I had ended American isolation for both Negroes and whites.

In his prose, McKay stressed the value of the common Negro and joined other Negro Renaissance writers in a rediscovery of Negro folk culture. But it is for his poetry that McKay will be longest remembered. For in his poetry, he best expressed the New Negro's determination to protect his human dignity, his cultural worth, and his right to a decent life.

---

[51]Here are two extreme views of McKay's *Home to Harlem.* The first reflects Negro middle-class opinion.

> Again, white people think we are buffoons, thugs and rotters anyway. Why should we waste so much energy to prove it? That's what Claude McKay has done. (Clipping from the *Chicago Defender,* March 17, 1928, in McKay Folder, Schomburg Collection, New York Public Library.)

Now, another view:

> [*Home to Harlem* is] . . . beaten through with the rhythm of life that is the jazz rhythm . . . the real thing is rightness. . . . It is the real stuff, the low-down on Harlem, the dope from the inside. (John R. Chamberlain, Review of *Home to Harlem, New York Times,* March 11, 1928, p. 5.)

[52]Langston Hughes, *The Big Sea, An Autobiography* (New York, 1945), pp. 265–66.

---

[53]Letter from Johnson to McKay, August 21, 1930, in the McKay Correspondence (Yale University Library).

In the Race Riot of 1919, a Glimpse of Struggles to Come

By Peter Perl
Washington Post Staff Writer

Another in a biweekly series of stories about the people and events that shaped Washington in the 20th century.

Nobody knows precisely how or where it started, but on a steamy Saturday night, July 19, 1919, the word began to spread among the saloons and pool halls of downtown Washington, where crowds of soldiers, sailors and Marines freshly home from the Great War were taking weekend liberty.

A black suspect, questioned in an attempted sexual assault on a white woman, had been released by the Metropolitan Police. The woman was the wife of a Navy man. So the booze-fueled mutterings about revenge flowed quickly among hundreds of men in uniform, white men who were having trouble finding jobs in a crowded, sweltering capital.

Late that night, they started to move. The mob drew strength from a seedy neighborhood off Pennsylvania Avenue NW called "Murder Bay," known for its brawlers and brothels. The crowd crossed the tree-covered Mall heading toward a predominantly poor black section of Southwest. They picked up clubs, lead pipes and pieces of lumber as they went.

Near Ninth and D streets SW, they fell upon an unsuspecting black man named Charles Linton Ralls, who was out with his wife, Mary. Ralls was chased down and beaten severely. The mob then attacked a second black man, George Montgomery, 55, who was returning home with groceries. They fractured his skull with a brick.

The rampage by about 400 whites initially drew only scattered resistance in the black community, and the police were nowhere to be seen. When the Metropolitan Police Department finally arrived in force, its white officers arrested more blacks than whites, sending a clear signal about their sympathies.

It was only the beginning. The white mob—whose actions were triggered in large part by weeks of sensational newspaper accounts of alleged sex crimes by a "negro fiend"—unleashed a wave of violence that swept over the city for four days. Nine people were killed in brutal street fighting, and an estimated 30 more would die eventually from their wounds. More than 150 men, women and children were clubbed, beaten and shot by mobs of both races. Several Marine guards and six D.C. policemen were shot, two fatally.

"A mob of sailors and soldiers jumped on the [street]car and pulled me off, beating me unmercifully from head to foot, leaving me in such a condition that I could hardly crawl back home," Francis Thomas, a frail black 17-year-old, said in a statement to the NAACP. Thomas said he saw three other blacks being beaten, including two women. "Before I became unconscious, I could hear them pleading with the Lord to keep them from being killed."

The Washington riot was one of more than 20 that took place that summer. With rioting in Chicago, Omaha, Knoxville, Tenn., Charleston, S.C., and other cities, the bloody interval came to be known as "the Red Summer." Unlike virtually all the disturbances that preceded it—in which white-on-black violence dominated—the Washington riot of 1919 was distinguished by strong, organized and armed black resistance, foreshadowing the civil rights struggles later in the century.

Postwar Washington, roughly 75 percent white, was a racial tinderbox. Housing was in short supply and jobs so scarce that ex-doughboys in uniform panhandled along Pennsylvania Avenue. Unemployed whites bitterly envied the relatively few blacks who had been fortunate enough to procure such low-level government jobs as messenger and clerk. Many whites also resented the black "invasion" of previously segregated neighborhoods around Capitol Hill, Foggy Bottom and the old downtown.

Washington's black community was then the largest and most prosperous in the country, with a small but impressive upper class of teachers, ministers, lawyers and businessmen concentrated in the LeDroit Park neighborhood near Howard University. But black Washingtonians were increasingly resentful of the growing dominance of the Jim Crow system that had been imported from the Deep South.

Racial resentment was particularly intense among Washington's several thousand returning black war veterans. They had proudly served their country in such units as the District's 1st Separate Battalion, part of the segregated Army force that fought in France. These men had been forced to fight for the right to serve in combat because the Army at first refused to draft blacks for any role other than laborer. They returned home hopeful that their military service would earn them fair treatment.

Instead, they saw race relations worsening in an administration dominated by conservative Southern whites brought here by Woodrow Wilson, a Virginian. Wilson's promise of a "New Freedom" had won him more black voters than any Democrat before him, but they were cruelly disappointed: Previously integrated departments such as the Post Office and the Treasury had now set up "Jim Crow corners" with separate washrooms and lunchrooms for "colored only." Meanwhile, the Ku Klux Klan was being revived in Maryland and Virginia, as racial hatred burst forth with the resurgence of lynching of black men and women around the country—28 public lynchings in the first six months of 1919 alone, including seven black veterans killed while still wearing their Army uniforms.

Washington's newspapers made a tense situation worse, with an unrelenting series of sensational stories of alleged sexual assaults by an unknown black perpetrator upon white women. The headlines dominated the city's four daily papers—the Evening Star, the Times, the Herald and The Post—for more than a month. A sampling of these July headlines illustrates the growing lynch-mob mentality: 13 SUSPECTS ARRESTED IN NEGRO HUNT; POSSES KEEP UP HUNT FOR NEGRO; HUNT COLORED ASSAILANT; NEGRO FIEND SOUGHT ANEW. Washington's newly formed chapter of the NAACP was so concerned that on July 9—10 days before the bloodshed—it sent a letter to the four daily papers saying they were "sowing the seeds of a race riot by their inflammatory headlines."

Violence escalated on the second night, Sunday, July 20, when white mobs sensed the 700-member police department was unwilling or unable to stop them. Blacks were beaten in front of the White House, at the giant Center Market on Seventh Street NW, and throughout the city, where roving bands of whites pulled them off streetcars.

One of black Washington's leading citizens, author and historian Carter G. Woodson, 43, the new dean at Howard University, was caught up in that night's horror. Walking home on Pennsylvania Avenue, Woodson was forced to hide in the shadows of a storefront as a white mob approached. "They had caught a Negro and deliberately held him as one would a beef for slaughter," he recalled, "and when they had conveniently adjusted him for lynching, they shot him. I heard him groaning in his struggle as I hurried away as fast as I could without running, expecting every moment to be lynched myself."

The Parents League, a black citizens group that had been formed primarily to improve the "colored schools," printed and distributed about 50,000 copies of a Notice to the Colored Citizens, a handbill that advised "our people, in the interest of law and order and to avoid the loss of life and injury, to go home before dark and to remain quietly and to protect themselves."

The city's chief executive, Louis Brownlow, the chairman of the District Commissioners, issued an urgent appeal: "The actions of the men who attacked innocent Negroes cannot be too strongly condemned, and it is the duty of every citizen to express his support of law and order by refraining from any inciting conversation or the repetition of inciting rumor and tales."

But a crucial event had already occurred that morning that would overwhelm Brownlow's good intention. The Washington Post published a front-page article that would be singled out by the NAACP, and later by historians, as a contributing cause of the riot's escalation. Under the words "Mobilization for Tonight," The Post erroneously reported that all available servicemen had been ordered to report to Pennsylvania Avenue and Seventh Street at 9 p.m. for a "clean-up" operation.

It was never clear how this fictional mobilization call was issued, but it became a self-fulfilling prophecy, as white rioters gathered and blacks began arming themselves in defense. Longtime Post reporter Chalmers Roberts, in his history of The Washington Post, called the paper's riot coverage "shamefully irresponsible."

As blacks realized that authorities were not protecting them, many took up arms. More than 500 guns were sold by pawnshops and gun dealers that Monday, when the worst violence occurred. White mobs were met by black mobs up and down the Seventh Street commercial corridor. Black Army veterans took out their old guns; sharpshooters climbed to the roof of the Howard Theatre; blacks manned barricades at New Jersey Avenue and at U Street.

Black men were driving around the city firing randomly at whites. Blacks turned the tables and pulled whites off streetcars. At Seventh and G streets NW, a black rioter emptied his revolver into a crowded streetcar before taking five bullets from police. At 12th and G NW, a 17-year-old black girl barricaded herself in her house and shot and killed an MPD detective. In all, 10 whites and five blacks were killed or mortally wounded that night.

James Scott, a World War I veteran, boarded a streetcar at Seventh Street and Florida Avenue NW late Monday night and quickly noticed he was the only black man on board. As he headed for a vacant seat, a white soldier barred his way and shouted, "Where are you going, nigger?"

"Lynch him!" yelled another white. "Kill him! . . . Throw him out the window," others yelled.

"I was being grabbed from all sides. I forced my way to the rear door and was hit by something as I stepped off, which cut my ear and bruised my head," Scott recalled in a statement to the NAACP. "As the car moved away, the conductor fired three shots at me."

Finally, on Tuesday, as city leaders and members of Congress realized the situation was out of hand, President Wilson mobilized about 2,000 troops to stop the rioting—cavalry from Fort Myer, Marines from Quantico, Army troops from Camp Meade and sailors from ships in the Potomac. City officials and businessmen closed the saloons, movie houses and billiard rooms in neighborhoods where violence erupted.

Despite the federal troops, white mobs gathered again. But a strong summer downpour doused their spirits and heavy rains continued through the night, effectively ending the riot of 1919.

In the ensuing months, the NAACP and others pushed for hearings into the riot. But the episode became a mostly forgotten chapter of Washington history, largely because conservative Southern congressmen blocked further inquiry.

Sociologist Arthur Waskow, who interviewed riot survivors in the 1960s, said the experience gave them a new self-respect and "a readiness to face white society as equals. . . . The Washington riot demonstrated that neither the silent mass of 'alley Negroes' nor the articulate leaders of the Negro community could be counted on to knuckle under."

Unit Selections

Key Points to Consider

❖ How did Adolph Hitler's racist philosophies affect blacks following World War I and during World War II?

❖ Describe the experiences of African American women during World War II. What happened in the 1950s to shatter their American dream?

❖ Why did some black leaders warn against service in the military during World War II?

❖ What were the major accomplishments of the black baseball leagues? What, if any, economic impact did the leagues have on African American communities?

 **Links** **www.dushkin.com/online/**

These sites are annotated on pages 4 and 5.

For many African Americans, the period from the Great Depression to World War II was a period of protest and nationalism. The New Deal, with its promise of social equality, was filled with controversy and contradictions. Black wage earners who, in theory, should have benefited the most, actually benefited the least. Many black leaders, tired of the same old promises, sought once again to gain the upper hand by redefining their purpose and identity. Black nationalism was seen as the vehicle for this transformation. But it, too, had to be transformed.

Black nationalism was significantly transformed from its primarily conservative nineteenth century moorings, which tended to embrace Western values, to a more radical one that was highly critical of Western culture. The black nationalism that emerged during this period was anything but monolithic. The three foremost black leaders of the day reflect three distinctly different variants of what would later become modern black nationalism. The three leaders were Marcus Garvey, who called for the total separation of the races and a back-to-Africa movement; W.E. B. Du Bois, who stressed education and believed that the ultimate goal should be the total integration of blacks into American society; and Claude McKay, who sought to use black nationalism (primitivism) as a critique of the dominant white culture and as a means of avoiding bourgeois morality.

In many regards the dialogue between these three giants was cut short as conflict engulfed America and much of Europe into yet another World War. An evil, more sinister than any that had been produced to date in America, threatened to drench the world in the blood of not only Jews and Gypsies, but blacks as well. Adolf Hitler equated blacks with Jews in his autobiography, *Mein Kampf.* His racist philosophies not only crippled and eradicated millions of European nationals, especially Jews and Gypsies, but also some blacks from Europe, Africa, and the United States.

Prior to World War II, 85 percent of African American women worked as domestics, earning as little as $35 a month. As the war got under way, industrial America forced unions to accept black workers. Black women, benefiting from the convoluted logic of racism and sexism, found it easier to get high-paying industrial jobs than did black men.

Both black and national leaders grappled with how blacks should be utilized in the military during World War II. While some black leaders demanded total integration, the War Department and civil authorities insisted upon maintaining the status quo.

Many Americans saw black baseball played for the first time during the World War. While their accomplishments are often ignored in the official statistics, many are becoming aware of the accomplishments of the Negro leagues. Black baseball teams, despite incomparably worse conditions, produced as many stars and records as their white counterparts.

Finally, while many in the nation were consumed with World War II, a small handful of scholars under the leadership of Hubert Branch Crouch started the National Institute of Science. The primary purpose of these efforts was aimed at encouraging the development of the sciences in black colleges.

FORGOTTEN VICTIMS:
BLACKS IN THE HOLOCAUST

By Robert W. Kesting

Most scholars agree that the Holocaust was a time of oppression and destruction for millions of European nationals, especially Jews, Gypsies, and others. Adolph Hitler's irrational racial philosophies not only crippled and eradicated generations of Europeans, but some blacks from Europe, Africa, and the United States were also victimized by his madness. Even though their losses were minimal compared to other groups, their torment and suffering were no different. Current debates by Holocaust scholars about degree of participation, mortality statistics, and who were programmed targets for destruction never will be satisfactorily resolved. Neither will black involvement, because unlike Jews, Gypsies, and others, blacks, by comparison, never inhabited Europe in large numbers. Therefore, scant evidence exists as to their participation.

Hitler included blacks with Jews in his autobiography, *Mein Kampf*. He was affected by a world-wide white supremacy movement which was prevalent prior to World War I, and in-

creased in popularity as a result of the political and economic chaos following the war. In the United States, there was a rebirth of the Ku Klux Klan after the war, with membership reaching millions by the mid 1920s. Hitler was also greatly influenced by Social-Darwinism, and its propagandists, such as the upcoming eugenicists or race scientists. He rationalized that someone was to blame for his perception of world collapse. Therefore, liberalized and wealthy Jews as well as supposedly parasitic and ignorant blacks became the scapegoats. Politically, he used them to affect the minds of the white European masses. Unlike other white supremacist movements, his disciples tried to effectively implement and enforce every word he preached. They perceived that once the tide of National Socialism engulfed the world these members of society would be eliminated. Evidence to support this conclusion exists in the deliberate attempt to exterminate European Jewry. If Nazi racists succeeded in occupying Africa and countries of the Western Hemisphere which possessed large black populations, the carnage perhaps would have been horrific. But for the most part, blacks were not considered an immediate threat like the Jews.

However, the few who resided in Europe as well as black Allied soldiers and airmen who encountered devout Nazi racists were chosen to be eliminated. This essay presents some little known black experiences with Nazi racists.

According to a war crimes investigation dated February 15, 1946, on June 21, 1944, near Raids, France, the commander of the 1st Battalion, 17th SS Infantry Division ordered "no Negro prisoners of war were to be taken alive." This allegation was made in a statement given by a captured Dutch national who was a member of the unit. He further alleged he saw at least "one American Negro being executed." After several weeks trying to confirm his story and attempting to locate the prime suspect, the United States Deputy Judge Advocate, Colonel Pfifer, decided to close the case unless other information was received to warrant its reactivation.[1]

Another investigation, dated July 14, 1945, alleged that Fritz Scholz, commander of the 2nd Battalion, SS Regiment, "Der Fuehrer," in August 1944, near Tours, France, ordered "100 Negro prisoners of war to be executed once they completed the task of digging their own graves."

Robert W. Kesting is an archivist with the United States Holocaust Memorial Museum in Washington, D.C.

From the *Journal of Negro History,* Winter 1992, pp. 30-36. © 1992 by the Association for the Study of African-American Life and History, Inc. Reprinted by permission.

These allegations were made by two former members of the battalion. After several months attempting to find Scholz, the case was closed because investigators interviewed the wrong suspect, and they failed to locate the correct one.[2]

On July 16, 1945, another investigation alleged that 1,000 black Senegalese soldiers, who were used as slave laborers at a factory located at Fritzlar, Germany, were executed on orders given by Alfred Moretao, who was a member of the SS, burgermeister, and owner of the business. According to the statements of four French surviving prisoners of war, Moretao had ordered the executions because "they were stealing potatoes from the field." They also alleged "potatoes were stolen, because Moretao was deliberately starving them." The case was closed and the information was transferred to French war crimes officials, so they could continue or close the case.[3] Accordingly, American interests in war crimes focused on atrocities and other mistreatments directed at American nationals, including military personnel.

On December 17, 1944, near the town of Wereth, Belgium, eleven Afro-American soldiers of the 333rd Field Artillery Battalion were brutally executed and their bodies hideously mutilated before and after the executions. Their bodies were discovered lying in a cattle ditch partially covered by snow. These facts were revealed during an investigation conducted by war crimes investigators, and autopsies performed by a medical pathologist on March 18, 1945. Also, statements were collected from the townspeople. These interrogations produced additional information that "an unknown SS unit committed the heinous crimes." It was later learned that 1st and 2nd SS Panzer Divisions were operating in that area. But jurists decided to close the case, because the perpetrators could not be positively identified.[4] From the hundreds of cases that were tried and not tried involving American prisoners of war, these cases contained one common element: similar sadistical mutila-

tions had occurred within the same area of operation during the same time period.[5]

In an account given to British war crimes investigators on November 22, 1944, a female Polish Jew alleged that in February 1944 she overheard her supervisor, Doctor Prima, who was responsible for a municipal hospital in Salzburg, Austria, boasting to a colleague that on February 20, 1944, he was called upon to render assistance to some American flyers who had crashed nearby. Upon his arrival, he noticed that "four Negro airmen were unharmed, while two others were seriously injured or dead." Prima claimed to have executed the remaining ones who were alive. The explanation for their terminations was "Americans were paying enormous sums to niggers for each flight." Additionally, the witness alleged Prima held a military rank, and occasionally wore his black uniform. He was probably a member of the SS. Jurists recommended the case be closed, because the primary allegation was based on hearsay.[6]

In another investigation dated July 11, 1945, it was alleged that on March 18, 1945, a black South African was executed by a SS guard while cutting down the tall grass around the fenced perimeter of Stalag VII-A located at Moosburg, Germany. The excuse given to the other inmates was "he was trying to escape." On April 1, 1945, at the same camp, an Afro-American soldier was also executed, but unlike the first incident, the SS guard did not provide an explanation. Former prisoners of war of the camp provided the allegations, but also they stated the South African was performing his job, and there was no attempted escape. But the case was closed, because the prime suspects were not located.[7]

During the month of December 1944, two Afro-American airmen were shot down over the town of Debrecen, Hungary. Upon landing, they were clubbed to death by Hungarian SS troops. Witnesses alleged the reason they were executed was that "Hungarians do not like Negroes."

Within the same case file is a statement made by an American sergeant. He alleged that on December 18, 1944, while being held captive in a jail located at Sopron, Hungary, an Afro-American pilot, who was in the next cell, was executed. Later, the witness overheard a conversation between two Gestapo guards who stated "Hungarians do this to all Negroes." Both cases were closed, because of jurisdictional difficulties.[8]

On December 18, 1944, an Afro-American soldier was allegedly singled out and executed by SS guards for no apparent reason, while being marched to Stalag IV-B located at Muehlberg, Germany. The case was closed pending receipt of additional evidence.[9]

On or about September 1, 1944, near Merzig, Germany, two former SS guards alleged they saw "Negro American soldiers being executed after they were ordered to dig their own graves." Also, they alleged "Negroes were not to be taken prisoner." But the case was closed, because the prime suspects were not found.[10]

In a related case or maybe the same aforementioned incident, a citizen of Merzig, Germany alleged that on September 1, 1944, he saw "20 Negro soldiers detained in a Hotel." Their fates rested in the hands of a local Gestapo officer named [FNU] Frick. He also alleged that they were taken to a nearby forest and executed. During the investigation, the witness showed investigators the mass burial site. However, jurists closed the case, because the alleged perpetrators were not found.[11]

On May 5, 1944, witnesses alleged "three colored American pilots" were executed by the Gestapo while being incarcerated in a prison located at Budapest, Hungary. The method of execution was death by hanging in a public square. The case was closed because of jurisdictional problems.[12]

In August 1942 at Stalag II-C located near Bremen, Germany, witnessed allegedly saw an SS guard, Ludwig Hach, execute an Afro-American soldier for no apparent reason. The case was closed, because investigators were unable to find the suspect.[13]

On March 28, 1945, Americans captured a German SS officer, Otto Vetter. In his possession was a personal letter alleging that he witnessed "two colored airmen clubbed to death by the townspeople of Weinboella, Germany, after they were directed to perform the executions by the local Gestapo. Jurists decided to close the case, because the letter was hearsay evidence.[14]

On October 3, 1944, two former officers of the SS Regiment, "Der Fuehrer," admitted to French investigators they ordered the executions of "two Negro soldiers" near Toulon, France.[15] However, further information or documentation regarding adjudication of these war crimes suspects by the French currently cannot be located.

On March 28, 1945, near Iserlohn, Germany, a witness alleged "a Negro American airman was brutally executed by the townspeople of Iserlohn upon orders issued by the local Gestapo." The method of execution was by "dung fork and other implements." The case was closed, because investigators were unable to identify the prime suspects.[16]

In a witness statement dated May 12, 1945, Hans Pasch, a Polish national and former inmate of the Gross-Rosen concentration camp, alleged he recorded the deaths of inmates in the camp's death registers. He claimed to have recorded the names of many nationalities including "Negroes." Because these registers are currently not extant and presumably destroyed, it must be theorized that these blacks were either French, Belgians, or Africans residing in France or Belgium. Perhaps, some were the missing "Rhineland mulattoes."[17]

At the conclusion of World War I, some significant events occurred which ultimately affected the lives of the few blacks residing in Nazi Germany and some Nazi occupied territories. As a result of the French occupation of the Rhineland by African colonial troops, mulattoes were born because of interracial relationships. Another result was that Germany lost its colonies in Africa. Therefore, interracial couples and their offspring returned to Germany. Collectively, these blacks suffered and several disappeared without a trace, because of Nazi racism. It must be mentioned, however, that the blacks from the German-African colonies were exposed to white racism prior to the war. Furthermore, prewar and postwar Germany also witnessed the ascent to prominence of eugenicists and race scientists. These pseudoscientists not only devised scientific explanations for the doctrine of racial purity but they also provided Hitler and his disciples with pseudo-moral, ethical, and legal justifications for the elimination of supposedly inferior races, or as the Germans commonly called them, "Race Polluters." Jews, Gypsies, and blacks were victimized by this scientific madness. Additionally, they provided the scientific reasoning for the eventual euthanasia and sterilization programs, which not only affected these aforementioned racial groups but many German nationals who were mentally and physically handicapped as well as children and the elderly who were afflicted with mental or physical maladies. The nadir of their success arrived with the passage of a series of well-known race laws from 1933 to 1938.[18]

Collectively, the Rhineland mulattoes were among the first to suffer under the sterilization program of 1933. However, the sterilizations were not performed until 1937, because some German scientists, physicians, and jurists argued that "sterilizations of German colored children were illegal." But these verbal and written protests did not deter Nazi racists from conducting these illegal sterilizations. After 1937, nearly 385 black children disappeared without a trace.[19] There has been speculation that they were deported to "Killing Centers." Yet, the only documentation known to exist citing blacks in a concentration camp is in the investigative file of Gross-Rosen.[20]

But even with the revelations just presented, some Holocaust scholars suggest that Afro-American and black African soldiers and airmen did not qualify as Holocaust victims, because they were paid and prepared to die. Others will state that many white soldiers and airmen also perished, because some German commanders and commandants of prisoner of war camps did not honor specific clauses dealing with the treatment of prisoners of war under the Geneva Convention, and there were orders issued from the German High Command, SS and the Gestapo, particularly about parachute troops and commandos, stating these troops were to be immediately executed. Some will argue that Wehrmacht and Waffen SS units were not logistically able to support large numbers of Allied prisoners; therefore, many were killed. All of these arguments have some merit, but they do not explain the element of racism. In each case cited, Gestapo or SS personnel were ordering, instigating, or performing the executions. These units usually were the enforcers of Nazi racism. Furthermore, some American Jewish soldiers and airmen who were captured by Gestapo or SS units experienced similar fates.[21] But devout Nazi racists made distinctions between Jews and blacks.

In a lecture dated June 20, 1939, Professor Fischer, a well-known anthropoligist and race scientist, exclaimed:

> When a people wants, somehow or other, to preserve its own nature, it must reject alien racial elements, and when these have already insinuated themselves, it must suppress them and eliminate them. The Jew is such an alien and, therefore, when he wants to insinuate himself, he must be warded off. This is self-defense. In saying this, I do not characterize every Jew as inferior, as *Negroes,* and I do not underestimate the greatest enemy with whom we have to fight. . . .[22]

Therefore, blacks were relegated to the lowest anthropological and social strata within the Nazi world order. Furthermore, operational orders created and issued by the headquarters of the Security Police, SS, and OKW, especially in France and Belgium, were to select and murder not only Jews, but other "intolerables." Black civilians and prisoners of war were perhaps also included within this definition.[23]

The story of blacks in the Holocaust has sadly been neglected, but the townspeople of Wereth, Belgium, recently remembered those Afro-Americans who suffered and died by the sadistic hands of devout Nazi racists. In 1989, a monument was dedicated in their honor. Holocaust scholars, not unlike the townspeople of Wereth, must continue the search, and add to this testament in order that blacks in the Holocaust be remembered for their sacrifices.[24]

Notes

1. Report of Investigation and Witness Statement; February 15, 1946; War Crimes Case File, 0–4, box 1; Records of the Deputy Judge Advocate General, United States Forces, European Theater, 7708th War Crimes Group, 1945–1947; Records of the United States Army Commands, 1942–; Record Group 338; National Archives in Suitland, Maryland.

2. Report of Investigation and Witness Statements; July 14, 1945; War Crimes Case File, 11–256, box 66; Records of the Deputy Judge Advocate General, United States Forces, European Theater, 7708th War Crimes Group, 1945–1947; Records of United States Army Commands, 1942–; Record Group 338; National Archives in Suitland, Maryland.

3. Report of Investigation and Witness Statements; July 16, 1945; War Crimes Case File 000–12–185A, box 471; Records of the Deputy Judge Advocate General, United States Forces, European Theater, 7708th War Crimes Group, 1945–1947; Records of United States Army Commands, 1942–; Record Group 338; National Archives in Suitland, Maryland.

4. Report of Investigation, Witness Statements, and Photographs; March 18, 1945; War Crimes Case File, 6–102, box 26; Records of the Deputy Judge Advocate General, United States Forces, European Theater, 7708th War Crimes Group, 1945–1947; Records of United States Army Commands, 1942–; Record Group 338; National Archives in Suitland, Maryland.

5. Report of Investigation and Prosecution Exhibits; 1944–1946; Malmedy Massacre Case; War Crimes Case File, 6–24, boxes 4–10; Records of the Deputy Judge Advocate General, United States Forces, European Theater, 7708th War Crimes Group, 1945–1947; Records of United States Army Commands, 1942–; Record Group 338; National Archives in Suitland, Maryland.

6. Report of Investigation and Witness Statement; August 31, 1945; War Crimes Case File, 5–17, box 4; Records of the Deputy Judge Advocate General, United States Forces, European Theater, 7708th War Crimes Group, 1945–1947; Records of United States Army Commands, 1942–; Record Group 338; National Archives in Suitland, Maryland.

7. Report of Investigation and Witness Statements; July 11, 1945; War Crimes Case File 000–12–495, box 493; Records of the Deputy Judge Advocate General, United States Forces, European Theater, 7708th War Crimes Group, 1945–1947; Records of United States Army Command, 1942–; Record Group 338; National Archives in Suitland, Maryland.

8. Report of Investigation and Witness Statement; June 18, 1945; War Crimes Case File, 15–3, box 259; Records of the Deputy Judge Advocate General, United States Forces, European Theater, 7708th War Crimes Group, 1945–1947; Records of the United States Army Commands, 1942–; Record Group 338; National Archives in Suitland, Maryland.

9. Report of Investigation and Witness Statements; July 9, 1945; War Crimes Case File, 12–2009, box 190; Records of the Deputy Judge Advocate General, United States Forces, European Theater, 7708th. War Crimes Group, 1945–1947; Records of United States Army Commands, 1942–; Record Group 338; National Archives in Suitland, Maryland.

10. Report of Investigation and Witness Statements; June 29, 1945; War Crimes Case File, 12–2620, box 213; Records of the Deputy Judge Advocate General, United States Forces, European Theater, 7708th War Crimes Group, 1945–1947; Records of United States Army Commands, 1942–; Record Group 338; National Archives in Suitland, Maryland.

11. Report of Investigation and Witness Statement; July 6, 1945; War Crimes Case File, 12-2635, box 214; Records of the Deputy Judge Advocate General, United States Forces, European Theater, 7708th War Crimes Group, 1945–1947; Records of United States Army Commands, 1942–; Record Group 338; National Archives in Suitland, Maryland.

12. Report of Investigation and Witness Statements; May 24, 1945; War Crimes Case File, 15–32, box 261; Records of the Deputy Judge Advocate General, United States Forces, European Theater, 7708th War Crimes Group, 1945–1947, Records of United States Army Commands, 1942–; Record Group 338; National Archives in Suitland, Maryland.

13. Report of Investigation and Witness Statements; June 10, 1945; War Crimes Case File, 12–1138, box 138; Records of the Deputy Judge Advocate General, United States Forces, European Theater, 7708th War Crimes Group, 1945–1947; Record of United States Army Commands, 1942–; Record Group 338; National Archives in Suitland, Maryland.

14. Report of Investigation and Exhibit; June 5, 1945; War Crimes Case File, 12–2008, box 176; Records of the Deputy Judge Ad-vocate General, United States Forces, European Theater, 7708th War Crimes Group, 1945–1947, Records of United States Army Commands, 1942–; Record Group 338; National Archives in Suitland, Maryland.

15. Report of Investigation; January 5, 1945; Folder 1, box 117; Records of the Supreme Headquarters, Allied Expeditionary Forces, Psychological Warfare Division, 1944–1945; Records of Allied Commands, 1942–1945; Record Group 331; National Archives in Washington, D.C.

16. Report of Investigation and Witness Statement; May 17, 1945; War Crimes Case File, 12-2165, box 187; Records of the Deputy Judge Advocate General, United States Forces, European Theater, 7708th War Crimes Group, 1945–1947; Records of United States Army Commands, 1942–; Record Group 338; National Archives in Suitland, Maryland.

17. Witness statement of Hans Pasch; May 12, 1945; War Crimes Case File, 000–50–14, box 524; Records of the Deputy Judge Advocate General, United States Forces, European Theater, 7708th War Crimes Group, 1945–1947; Records of United States Army Commands, 1942–; Record Group 338; National Archives in Suitland, Maryland.

18. Benno Mueller-Hill; translated by George R. Fraser, *Murderous Science.* (New York, 1988), pp. 10–12.

19. *Ibid.,* pp. 10–12, 30, 138, 172.

20. Witness Statement of Hans Pasch; May 12, 1945; WCCF, 0005–50–14, box 524; Recds of DJAG, USFET, 7708th WCG, 45–47; Recds of USA Cmds, 42–; RG–338; NARA in Suitland, Md. Mueller-Hill, p. 138. Mueller-Hill stated that he personally knew one Black male adolescent who was sent to a concentration camp, but he does not specify whether his source was authenticated by documentation. Further, their is another male mulatto who claimed to be at Dachau, but again there are no documents to verify his allegation.

21. War Crimes Cases Regarding the Executions and Mistreatment of American Jewish Soldiers and Airmen by German Nationals; 1945–1947; War Crimes Case Files, 15–46/box 261, 40–IIA/boxes 280–281, 40–IXB/boxes 320–325, 41–64/boxes 381–382, 12–2782/box 224, 12–3249/box 253; Records of the Deputy Judge Advocate General, United States Forces, European Theater, 7708th War Crimes Group, 1945–1947; Records of United States Army Commands, 1942–; Record Group 338; National Archives in Suitland, Md.

22. Mueller-Hill, p. 12.

23. Adalbert Rueckel; translated by Derek Rutten, *The Investigation of Nazi Crimes, 1945–1978,* (Heidelberg-Karlsrude, 1979), pp. 22–23.

24. In a conversation with Doctor Sybil Milton of the United States Holocaust Memorial Museum, she explained to me that she had recently returned from a trip to Armenia and Germany in April 1990. She further stated that a colleague in Potsdam had discovered a scheme used by the Nazis to record blacks as mixed bloods (mishlinges). Doctor Milton is the museum's historian, and a well-known author and scholar on Holocaust History.

Work and Hope:

African American Women in Southern California during World War II

Paul R. Spickard

SOUTHERN California during World War II was a magnet for hundreds of thousands of people from all over the United States. Drawn by the explosive growth of war industries, migrants from every region, of every class and color, made their way to greater Los Angeles. Among them were more than 100,000 African Americans. More than half of those were women. They transformed the Southern California African American community. They came seeking opportunity; they found hard work and, for a time, they found hope.

Before World War II, African American women and their families lived in an old black neighborhood just southeast of downtown Los Angeles near the corner of Central and Pico within earshot of the tracks of the Southern Pacific Railway. Many of the early African American men worked as porters or laborers on this line. Their wives and children stayed in Los Angeles while the men worked lines all over the Southwest. Around them grew a modest-sized community of tens of thousands of African Americans in the 1920s and 1930s. They were surrounded by a welter of other people: Russians and other European immigrants in Boyle Heights to the east, Mexicans in East Los Angeles a little farther east, Japanese in Little Tokyo to the north, Chinatown just beyond that. There were small clusters of African Americans in other parts of Southern California—in San Diego, Calexico, Long Beach, Pasadena, and elsewhere—but the Los Angeles black community was the largest, and the hub around which the others turned.

By 1940, the Los Angeles African American community had reached 60,000 in number and stretched in all directions from this central zone south along Central Avenue, the main thoroughfare of black culture in the West. It was quite a wonderful place, as any old-time resident is eager to recount. As one drove slowly down Central Avenue in 1941, the decaying southern fringes of downtown were left behind for a black city teeming with street life. The Avenue's many stores, humble and grand, all boasted shoppers. And families with small children

as well as the unemployed—the fruit of the Depression—"hung out" and were shooting dice. There were moviegoers at the Lincoln Theater, earnest black dentists, and secretaries from the offices of Golden State Mutual Insurance. And there were also prostitutes and drug pushers, Garveyites and disciples of Father Divine, as well as newcomers, just walking the streets and gawking.

At the corner of 41st Street, about a mile and a half south of Pico, stood the Dunbar Hotel, the jewel of Cen-

Some women went to war. Anna Marie Greaux in uniform. (Courtesy of Security Pacific National Bank Photograph Collection/Los Angeles Public Library)

Reprinted with permission from *Journal of the West*, July 1993, pp. 70-79. © 1993 by Journal of the West, 1531 Yuma, Manhattan, KS 66505-1009, USA.

tral Avenue. Built in 1928 as the Somerville, this luxury hotel was where notable African Americans came to stay. Mary White Ovington, W E. B. DuBois, and Jack Johnson stayed at the Dunbar. Billie Holiday, Lionel Hampton, and Bessie Smith stayed there, too, and played in the Big Apple, the Club Alabam, and the Savoy nearby. Hollywood actresses Louise Beavers and Ethel Waters came down from their swank homes on Sugar Hill to see and be seen. Central Avenue was also the center of West Coast jazz. It was the most exciting street west of Chicago.

Central Avenue was part of the glamour that African Americans in the South associated with Los Angeles, part of what drew them to Southern California. Times were hard for Southern black women in the 1930s and early 1940s, as they were for many other Americans. Prices for cotton and other crops were low. Lots of families who had owned farms became tenants, and tenants became laborers. Men thrown out of work went looking for jobs and did not always come back. Women were often left to support families in the midst of hard times. Throughout the 1930s, large numbers of black women left the rural South, sometimes with husbands but often without, frequently with children in tow, and headed for nearby towns and cities in search of work. Some went farther. For Mississippians who left the South, the natural place to go by virtue of habit, proximity, and ease of transport, was Chicago. For Carolinians it was New York. For those from the Southwest—Texas and Oklahoma—and the Southeast—Louisiana and Arkansas—the West Coast was a possibility. Nearly half of the African Americans who came to Los Angeles came from those four states. Texas was the largest contributor; there was a regular pipeline of black people from Houston to Los Angeles from the 1920s on.

Yet it was more than proximity that drew them. For blacks as for whites, California was not just a place but an idea. In California, the world was made new every day. It was a place where the living was easy, where people could pick fruit right from the trees, where they could own their own homes, where they could find work and hope to retire someday. Those economic dreams seemed especially promising in the early 1940s when the impending Second World War brought new industries to Los Angeles. Shipyards, steel plants, and aircraft factories meant jobs with relatively high pay and high status. African American women and men left their homes in the South and headed for California.

Tina Hill was typical. Hard times in the 1930s had forced her and her sister to drop out of high school in Prairie View, Texas. She related in 1938,

> [W]e finally decided to break up housekeeping and go to the city. I decided I wanted to make more money, and I went to a little small town—Tyler, Texas. . . . [But] the only thing I could do there for a living was domestic work and it didn't pay very much. . . . So I decided I'd better get out of this town. I didn't like Dallas because that was too rough. Then someone told me. "Well, why don't you try California?" So then I got Los Angeles in my mind.[1]

In 1940, she invested her savings in a train ticket and headed for California.

Black women came on their own, or with their children, or sometimes following their husbands. Frequently they already had a relative living in California who offered to help them make a start. Some came via the Southern Pacific Railway, but trains were expensive. More came by bus or by car, across the hot dusty stretches of U.S. Highways 66, 80, and 60. Texas, Arizona, and New Mexico were segregated states in those days, with no hotel rooms for black people, so they camped out along the way or, if they were lucky, stayed in the homes of the few African Americans who lived in Amarillo and Santa Fe, Albuquerque and Flagstaff, Phoenix and Barstow.

The inflow of African Americans during World War II was large and sudden. The state officials who counted migrants at the border noted only about 100 blacks per month bound for Los Angeles in the period 1940 to 1942. But toward the end of 1942, some aircraft plants, as well as the Southern Pacific Railway and other major employers, were driven by labor shortages, black

Three friends on the town. The war did not keep people from enjoying Central Avenue nightspots, but men were in short supply. (Courtesy of Security Pacific National Bank Photograph Collection/Los Angeles Public Library)

protests, and federal government pressure to begin to employ African American workers. Word spread quickly that there was good money to be made in Southern California. In short order, thousands of blacks poured in—as many as 10,000 to 12,000 per month during the summer of 1943. In those months, blacks constituted two-thirds to three-quarters of the total migration to Los Angeles. Altogether, over 140,000 African Americans were added to the population of Los Angeles County in the decade of the 1940s.

The African American women who came to California found their situation was not so pleasant as they had imagined. They did find work, but more often it was in somebody's kitchen at moderate pay rather than in a war plant at high pay. When World War II began, very few African Americans held jobs in the industrial sector of Los Angeles. Eighty-five percent of the black women before the war (and half of the men) were engaged as domestic servants. Early any morning, one could see them on street corners along Central Avenue, waiting for the buses that would take them to Bel Air and Santa Monica and Glendale to their day's work. Tina Hill described her experience as a domestic:

Charlene McKinney on her pony, 1944. (Courtesy of Security Pacific National Bank Photograph Collection/Los Angeles Public Library)

Patriotism ran high for Mary Patterson. (Courtesy of Security Pacific National Bank Photograph Collection/Los Angeles Public Library)

In less than ten days I had found a job living on the place doing domestic work. I started there from some time in August until Christmas. I was making thirty-five dollars a month. That was so much better than what I was making at home, which was twelve dollars a month. I saved my money and I bought everybody a Christmas present and sent it. Oh, I was the happiest thing in the world!

The family I worked for lived in Westwood. I had to cook breakfast, serve. They had a man and a wife and four kids. The smallest ones was twins and they wasn't too old. They had a nurse that took care of the twins. So I had to wash and iron, clean the house, cook. That was my job. So it was all day or practically, and I had very little time for myself. I had every Thursday off and every other Sunday. That just killed me to have to work on a Sunday, but I told myself I wasn't going to cry because I was coming out to do better and I would do better sooner or later.[2]

She quit that job soon enough and tried several others, but was not able to crack the industrial work force until 1943.

Much of the reason for the small number of black women and men in aircraft, steel, shipbuilding, and the other industrial enterprises can be laid at the door of white discrimination. Both management and labor did their part. For example, the manager of industrial relations at Consolidated-Vultee, an aircraft manufacturer, told representatives of the National Negro Congress, "I regret to say that it is not the policy of this company to employ people other than the Caucasian race, consequently we are not in a position to offer your people employment at this time."[3] The president of North American Aviation (later Rockwell International) echoed those sentiments: "Regardless of their training as aircraft workers we will not employ Negroes in the North American Plant. It is against company policy."[4] But labor, if anything, outdid management in discriminating against African American workers. The AFL-affiliated International Association of Machinists first refused black applicants for membership, then segregated them into a separate unit, the Jim Crow auxiliary local that lacked full voting rights or an independent voice. At the beginning of the war, despite a racially open national policy, Los Angeles CIO union organizers were only marginally more receptive to black membership. African Americans were shut out of the aircraft industry until the spring and summer of 1943, when it became apparent that the war-induced labor shortage would not go away. Then management at Lockheed and North American led the way in hiring and training black industrial workers and bulldozed the unions into accepting them.

Because of the convoluted logic of racism and sexism at that time, it was easier for black women than for black men to get the higher paying industrial jobs. At North American, it was hard for an African American man to get a production line job, because men, black or white, were viewed as permanent employees. To put a black man on the line was, in white eyes, to overturn the prewar racial system; so African American men had a hard time laying down the broom and picking up the rivet gun. But to hire an African American woman for an industrial job was not seen as such a threat to the prevailing racial hierarchy. Women of whatever race were viewed as only temporary employees, because the prevailing ideology said they would go back to being housewives at the war's end (never mind that most had been wage workers before the war). So, even though factory managers' sexism kept them from regarding women as fully competent workers, they still could see their way clear to hiring black women for industrial jobs. Tina Hill went to a school on Figueroa Street for four weeks. She took psychological tests, then learned to drill and rivet and file pieces of metal, all the while earning 60 cents an hour. Margaret Wright did the same thing, and then took her place on the line at Lockheed:

> I worked an eight-hour shift. If they asked me to work overtime I got paid for overtime. . . . It was a bit boring at times, but all in all I was doing the same work that other people were doing. If things didn't work right, I could always go to the union. . . . I could either quit, pack up and leave, or whatever, but I did have some say so and a job in the factory. There was another difference,

too. Instead of working alone all the time like they do in domestic work, somewhere in the kitchen or wherever you were at by yourself, I was always with a bunch of other women.[5]

Even when they got jobs, however, African American workers generally were denied positions commensurate with their skill level, and they frequently received lower pay than white workers for the same work. They also found themselves on segregated work teams, often with white foremen. Tina Hill recalled, "They did everything they could to keep you separated. They just did not like for a Negro and a white person to get together and talk."[6] Segregation diminished as the years went by and some blacks did manage to ascend to team leader positions, but usually only supervising other African Americans.

Sometimes racial tensions flared on the job. Lyn Childs, a woman who worked in a San Francisco ship repair yard, described a scene perhaps more vivid than, but not fundamentally unlike, many that occurred in Los Angeles:

> I was working down in the hold of the ship and there were about six Filipino men and over these men was a nineteen-year-old officer of the ship, and this big White guy went over and started to kick this poor Filipino and none of the Black men that was working down there in the hold with him said one word to this guy. And I sat

Some African American women worked in offices—outside the Selective Service office. (Courtesy of Security Pacific National Bank Photograph Collection/Los Angeles Public Library)

Before and during the war, most African Americans lived in substandard housing. (Courtesy of Security Pacific National Bank Photograph Collection/Los Angeles Public Library)

there and was getting madder and madder by the minute. I sprang to my feet, turned on my torch, and I had a flame about six to seven feet out in front of me, and I walked up to him and I said (you want me to say the real language?) I said to him "You so-and-so. If you go lift one more foot, I'll cut your guts out." That was my exact words. I was so mad with him.

Then he started to tell me that he had been trained in boot camp that any national group who was dark-skinned was beneath all White people. So he started to cry. I felt sorry for him, because he was crying, really crying. He was frightened, and I was frightened. I didn't know what I was doing, so in the end I turned my torch off and I sat down on the steps with him.

About that time the intercom on board the ship started to announce, "Lyn Childs, report to Colonel Hickman immediately." So I said, "I guess this is it." So I went up to Colonel Hickman's office, and behind me came all these men, and they lined up behind me, and I said, "Where are you guys going?" They said, "We're going with you." He said (Colonel Hickman), "I just wanted to see Lyn Childs," and they said, "You'll see all of us, because we were all down there. We all did not have guts enough to do what she did, and we're with her."

Colonel Hickman said, "Come into this office." He had one of the guards take me into the office real fast and close the door real fast and keep them out, and he said, "What kind of communist activity are you carrying on down there?" [I said], "A communist! What is that?" He said, "You know what I am talking about. You're a communist." [I said], "A communist! Forget you!" I said, "The kind of treatment that man was putting on the Filipinos, and to come to their rescue. Then I am the biggest communist you ever seen in your life. That is great. I am a communist." He said, "Don't say that so loud." I said, "Well, you asked me was I a communist. You're saying I am. I'm saying I'm a..." [He said], "Shh! Shh! Shh! Hush! Don't say that so loud." He said, "I think you ought to get out of here and get back to work." [I said], "Well, you called me. Why did you call me?" He said, "Never mind what I called you for. Go back to work."[7]

Those opportunities that did open up for African American women were not simply a product of the forces or the labor market. They were also the result of a series of campaigns for jobs by African American organizations. A black woman, Charlotta Bass, was a central figure in the drive to compel businesses to hire blacks. Bass was the crusading editor of the *California Eagle,* the state's largest African American newspaper. Since the 1910s she had covered strikes, lynchings, the Ku Klux Klan, race riots in Houston, housing discrimination in Los Angeles, the case of the Scottsboro Boys, and other stories both topical and dangerous. The *Eagle* was also the daily monitor of activities and achievements among African Americans in Southern California.

During the war, the *Eagle* kept up a constant barrage of front-page stories and editorials aimed at getting jobs and housing for African Americans and at ending harassment. Teaming with the Reverend Clayton Russell of the Negro Victory Committee and other black leaders, Bass daily hammered on city, state, and federal officials to do something about discrimination against African American workers in war industries. Bass, Russell, and their allies petitioned national and local officials for redress. They marched and picketed. They shamed the War Manpower Commission (WMC) and the U.S. Fair Employment Practices Committee into taking action against local companies that refused to hire African Americans.

An example will illustrate their tactics and general success. In July 1942, an official of the U.S. Employment Service (USES) expressed the opinion that black women were not interested in jobs in war industries, that they were better fitted for domestic work. Russell got into the *Eagle* and on the radio and gathered several hundred followers, together with representatives of the NAACP (National Association for the Advancement of Colored People) and the Urban League. They marched on the USES office. Women filled the lines downstairs applying for jobs, while members of the Victory Committee were upstairs negotiating with USES officials. The government agreed to have the WMC investigate; and after several months of continuing pressure, African American women began to find jobs building aircraft and ships. Charlotta Bass kept her *Eagle*-eye out for cases of discrimination—in the municipal railway system, the boilermaker's union, the post office, and elsewhere—and trumpeted the names and details in the pages of her newspaper. By 1944, the combination of worker shortage and militant activism by this fiery woman and her colleagues had achieved black integration into the work force in all major industrial enterprises.

By the war's end, significant numbers of African Americans, women and men, were working in skilled positions in each of the heavy industries that the war had brought to Southern California. Precisely how many is not clear, because the only figures available are from the U.S. Census. The war ended in 1945, but numbers are available only for 1940 and 1950. As the war-spurred industrial boom wound down in 1945 and collapsed in 1946, black women, even more than black men and white women, lost the jobs they had found in industry. As Lyn Childs described it: "The women were laid off first, and then the less senior Black men were laid off next, and

After the war, housing projects like Aliso Village brought hope for the future. (Courtesy of Security Pacific National Bank Photograph Collection/Los Angeles Public Library)

last, but as time went on, finally many of the White workers were laid off. But originally the first number that were laid off were women."[8] Margaret Wright recalled: "I knew how to rivet. I knew how to weld. I knew how to work on assembly lines. I knew how to run a dolly—you know [what] the good jobs are. I thought I had several skills that, you know, [were] very good, and I wouldn't have any problems getting a job anywhere else." But she was laid off by Lockheed, and "I had to fall back on the only other thing that I knew, and that was doing domestic work."[9] Tina Hill also worked cleaning people's homes, then in a garment factory reweaving damaged clothing.

Women's income plummeted, but not their independence and self-esteem. The war had permanently changed the job scene for African American women. As Tina Hill put it: "The war made me live better, it really did. . . . Hitler was the one that got us out of the white folks' kitchen."[10] Contrary to most people's expectations, the Depression did not return at the war's end. Manufacturing picked up again, and the companies started calling back their workers. By 1950, half of the black working women were in domestic service, but the other half were back in the skilled industrial, white collar, or professional positions that they had occupied during the war. In this they were unlike their white sisters; more of the whites remained out of the work force. Tina Hill remembered,

When North American called me back, was I a happy soul! I dropped that job [in the garment factory] and went back. That was a dollar an hour. So, from sixty cents an hour, when I first hired in there, up to one dollar. That wasn't traveling fast, but it was better than anything else because you had hours to work by and you had benefits and you come home at night with your family. So it was a good deal.[11]

She worked for North American Aviation for almost forty years.

Loss of jobs was not the only problem black women faced. Once the color bar in employment had been broken, the biggest problem for Los Angeles African Americans was housing. Los Angeles was a segregated metropolis. African Americans were not barred by law from white towns and neighborhoods, but white antagonism kept them near the city's core nonetheless. More than one black family felt the necessity to display a shotgun prominently and keep it near at hand when they moved out of the central black district and into a white area. As the African American population increased and inched southward during the war, residents of some all-white, working-class suburbs adopted racially restrictive covenants (some had used such covenants since the 1920s) that made it illegal for anyone to sell a house to a black family. These kept the African American population bottled up in Watts and Willowbrook, for instance, and out of such neighboring communities as Southgate and Huntington Park. One woman described her experience in trying to buy a house just outside the black zone:

My husband and I, who worked very hard during World War II in order to save enough to buy a decent house for our family, were confronted by hostile White realtors who tried to discourage us from wanting to move into an area recently integrated by Blacks in a surrounding community. They refused to take our deposit on a house. The realtors told us that the house was already sold and that there were no other houses in that area for sale.[12]

Sometimes the resistance in white areas was less subtle. In late 1945, Helen Short, her husband, and two small children bought five acres in Fontana, a working-class suburb east of Los Angeles, and started to build a house. After a string of threats from local whites, the Shorts' burned bodies were found in the ashes of their oil-soaked home. No one was prosecuted. Just after the war, in 1946, Klansmen visited ten African American families who had moved into white neighborhoods and burned crosses on their lawns.

Such opposition from whites left African Americans confined to a central ghetto that expanded only very gradually, never enough to accommodate their growing numbers. Most housing in black areas was substandard and overcrowded even before the war; by the war's end, conditions were far worse. In 1940, Little Tokyo had 30,000 Japanese American residents. Four years later, it had been renamed Bronzeville and held 80,000 (mostly African American) inhabitants. Dorothy Baruch described Little Tokyo storefronts that had been converted into housing:

In place after place children lived in windowless rooms, amid peeling plaster, rats, and the flies that gathered thick around food that stood on open shelves or kitchen-bedroom tables. Ordinarily there was no bathtub; never more than a single washroom or lavatory. Sometimes as many as forty people shared one toilet. Families were separated only by sheets strung up between beds. Many of the beds were "hot," with people taking turns sleeping in them.[13]

Willowbrook and Watts, along with some previously white working-class suburbs, swelled with African American migrants. They housed their inhabitants somewhat more graciously—typically in one-story, two-bedroom bungalows of cheap construction. Such structures by war's end frequently housed two or three black families, with another put up in a makeshift structure out back. Chicken coops and garages became houses. People showered at work and went next door to use the toilet or outhouse. They cooked on open firepits and wood stoves.

Not all African Americans were poor renters in need of public housing. Over a third were home owners. Most owned the small, cheaply constructed bungalows that filled the corridor around Central Avenue as it made its way south to Watts. But there were middle-class blacks, too. Many old-time residents and a few newcomers who had a little cash moved west after the war into the Crenshaw and West Adams districts. There they bought or built more substantial single-family homes with wide lawns and gardens along quiet streets. Previously these had been all-white districts, and both white residents and public authorities resisted the black incursion. A series of cases challenging the racially restricted covenants made their way through state courts. Pauletta Fears and her parents did time in jail for contempt when they refused to vacate their home on 92nd Street in 1945, despite protests from the *Eagle* and a picket line of sympathizers. But in 1948 a Michigan case reached the U.S. Supreme Court, and the restrictive covenants were overturned. African Americans in larger numbers began to move west and south into previously all-white areas, but these did not become completely black neighborhoods. In Crenshaw especially, African Americans mixed with Japanese Americans returning from wartime concentration camps and with others to form a polyethnic, middle-class neighborhood that endures to this day.

Related to the housing problem was the difficulty of transport. Public war housing—flimsy temporary buildings and trailers—was built by the state, county and federal governments to house war industry workers. But only 1,510 units were built in the Central, Vernon, and Watts black districts. Over 5,800 units were built in Wilmington and San Pedro, where the shipbuilding jobs were: almost all of these were segregated units designated for whites. There was little public housing—and none at all for African Americans—in places like Long Beach, Inglewood, and Fontana, where most steel and aircraft manufacturing took place. The concentration of black housing in south central Los Angeles, combined with the scattering of industrial plants far to the south, west, north, and east, meant that African Americans had to travel long distances to work. Typically, a woman from

Watts or Central Avenue would spend an hour and a half each way in a car pool or riding the Los Angeles Railway's Red Car. Pauletta Fears recalls getting up at 4:00 in the morning, walking from Florence down to Watts, catching the Red Car for San Pedro, riding for over an hour, then walking the last mile to her job at California Shipbuilding.

All this commuting, together with long hours in the factory kept black women away from their homes and children for long hours, sometimes days. Lyn Childs recalled:

> While I came to ... work in the shipyard, I had a little child that I had to leave behind. I had to leave her with my mother because up here I didn't think I would have any place for her to stay and I was going into a new community and a new town, and I didn't want to bring my child with me. I left her with my mother, and that's one of the most awful things that I did to anybody, because even today that child hurts because I promised her that, "Give me one year and I will come back for you." That one year stretched into two years and finally into three years, and ended up almost five years before I could go back and get her. That's one of the things that is very sad. If there had been any kind of conditions under which I could have brought her with me, I certainly would have brought her.[14]

Margaret Wright did not have to leave her children. Her challenge was to manage them and her job at the same time: "My kids were little, and so I worked at nights so I would get home in the morning. I didn't have a washing machine, and so I washed by hand, hung the clothes on the line. Then I would have to clean the house, bathe the babies. Then I would have to go shopping."[15]

These difficulties were compounded by the fact that many men were off in the war. Women were left to handle their jobs, children, finances, housing, and other matters on their own. Even when men were present, they were not always helpful. Margaret Wright complained that "[Y]our husband [would] come home, you know, prop his feet up, get his can of beer while you fixed dinner. Or even if we weren't working the same shift, you fixed dinner and left it where it would be convenient for him to get."[16] There was a lot for a woman to do.

As the war went on and more African Americans secured defense jobs, they managed to integrate some of the housing projects in the Long Beach Harbor industrial area. Mixing black and white, Latino and Asian in these projects proved inflammatory in several instances. But the conflict was not bad enough to dissuade public housing authorities from continuing the experiment in social engineering after the war. Between 1945 and 1952, most of the wartime "temporary" housing projects were converted to permanent status. A dozen other larger and better constructed housing projects were built, from Little Tokyo down to Watts, and more were planned. They bore names like Avalon Gardens, Aliso Village, William Mead Homes, and Nickerson Gardens that bespoke their sylvan aspirations. At first these were pretty spartan places, but soon they began to live up to the illusory term "gardens" that was often part of their names. Those that survive do not look much like gardens now. But that was the ideal—to create a cheaper, smaller, but recognizably similar version of the bungalows that were going up for middle-class whites out in Orange County and the San Fernando Valley for poor, inner-city African Americans.

The 1940s were not an easy time for African American women in Southern California, but they were a time of hope, and the number of black women grew. They had to work hard, often at menial tasks. They had difficulty finding good jobs, housing, and transportation, managing families with men absent, making stable lives for themselves and their children. They endured discrimination, both subtle and overt, sometimes extending to violence. But they fought back, worked hard, and won places for themselves. They found good jobs and better pay than they had ever dreamed was possible. Their children received better education than could be had in the South; many were graduating from high school, and some were going on to college. Housing, though crowded, was better—even the slums had plumbing and electricity, and the housing projects seemed like gardens. By the end of World War II, blacks and whites went to the same beaches and sometimes shared the same municipal pools. Social relations between the races were not close, but there was little of the domination and hostility many had known in the South. This was a hopeful era for most Angeleno African Americans.

Then in the 1950s, the hope began to recede. The destruction of the war-era dreams of Los Angeles African Americans is the subject of another paper, but a few summary comments here will mark the way of the future. In the late 1940s and early 1950s, the Los Angeles African American community was ripped apart by allegations of communist involvement in the NAACP. Charges and countercharges flew around the community and were inflated in the *Los Angeles Times* and other organs of white opinion. Charlotta Bass and other community leaders were called to testify before witch-hunting Congressional committees. The *Times*, realtors' organizations, Chief of Police William H. Parker, and others mounted a campaign to prevent the housing authority from building any more public housing projects, and to cut the funding for maintenance at existing ones. With black leadership immobilized, with the dream of good housing gone bust, and with other looming disasters in jobs, education, and relations with the police, Los Angeles blacks began to lose the faith in their future that the war years had created. For Southern California African Americans, women and men, hard work continued, but hope had begun to ebb. By the mid-1960s, the tide was out, and the African American community exploded in the Watts riot of 1965. The story of black women in that disaster has yet to be told.

NOTES

1. Sherna Berger Gluck, *Rosie the Riveter Revisited* (New York, New American Library. 1988), 31–32.
2. *Ibid.*, 33.
3. National Negro Congress, *Jim Crow in National Defense* (Los Angeles. CA: National Negro Congress, 1940).
4. James R. Wilburn, "Social and Economic Aspects of the Aircraft Industry in Metropolitan Los Angeles During World War II," Ph.D. diss., University of California at Los Angeles, 1971, 165–166.
5. Connie Field, "The Life and Times of Rosie the Riveter" (Emeryville. CA: Rosie the Riveter Film Project. 1980).
6. Gluck, *Rosie the Riveter Revisited*, 43.
7. Field, "The Life and Times of Rosie the Riveter."
8. *Ibid.*
9. *Ibid.*
10. Gluck, *Rosie the Riveter Revisited*, 23.
11. *Ibid.*, 41–42.
12. Keith E. Collins, *Black Los Angeles: The Maturing of the Ghetto, 1940–1950* (Saratoga, CA: Century Twenty One Publishing, 1980), 72–74.
13. Dorothy W. Baruch, "Sleep Comes Hard," *Nation*, 160 (Jan. 27, 1945): 95–96.
14. Field, "The Life and Times of Rosie the Riveter."
15. *Ibid.*
16. *Ibid.*

BIBLIOGRAPHY

Adler, Patricia R. "Watts: From Suburb to Black Ghetto," Ph.D. diss., University of Southern California, Los Angeles, 1977.

Anderson, E. Frederick. *The Development of Leadership and Organization Building in the Black Community of Los Angeles from 1900 through World War II* (Saratoga, CA: Century Twenty One Publishing, 1980).

Bass, Charlotta, *Forty Years* (Los Angeles, CA: *California Eagle*, 1960).

Collins, Keith E. *Black Los Angeles: The Maturing of the Ghetto, 1940–1950* (Saratoga, CA: Century Twenty One Publishing, 1980).

DeGraaf, Lawrence B. "Negro Migration to Los Angeles, 1930 to 1950," Ph.D. diss., University of California at Los Angeles, 1962.

Field, Connie. *The Life and Times of Rosie the Riveter* (Emeryville, CA: Rosie the Riveter Film Project, 1980).

Gluck, Sherna Berger. *Rosie the Riveter Revisited: Women, the War, and Social Change* (New York: New American Library, 1988).

Himes, Chester. *If He Hollers Let Him Go* (New York: New American Library, 1971).

Kraus, Henry. *In the City Was a Garden* (New York: Renaissance Press, 1951).

Sandoval, Sally J. "Ghetto Growing Pains: The Impact of Negro Migration on the City of Los Angeles. 1940–1960." M.A. thesis, California State University. Fullerton, 1973.

Smith, Alonzo N. "Black Employment in the Los Angeles Area, 1938–1948." Ph.D. diss., University of California at Los Angeles, 1978.

Wilburn, James R. "Social and Economic Aspects of the Aircraft Industry in Metropolitan Los Angeles During World war II," Ph.D. diss., University of California at Los Angeles, 1971.

Williams, Dorothy S. "Ecology of Negro Communities in Los Angeles: 1940–1959." Ph.D. diss., University of Southern California, Los Angeles, 1961.

Paul R. Spickard teaches history and chairs the division of social sciences at Brigham Young University-Hawaii. His previous books include the award-winning *Mixed Blood: Intermarriage and Ethnic Identity in Twentieth-Century America* (1989). This article is part of an ongoing study, *Black Los Angeles: The Worlds of African American Migrants, 1930–1955*.

DESEGREGATION OF THE ARMED FORCES:

BLACK LEADERSHIP, PROTEST AND WORLD WAR II

By Phillip McGuire

The integration and usage of black Americans in the armed forces became grave questions for both the military and the black community during World War II. While segments of black America demanded integration and full opportunity for its black soldiers, War Department officials and politicians insisted that the military should not be used as a "sociological laboratory" for effecting social change.[1] Although this attitude reflected the overall policies of the War Department, the Army, however reluctantly and belatedly, did undergo some noteworthy shifts during the war.

But just as black Americans in the larger society found the American "dream" an illusion, black soldiers in particular experienced racial discrimination in the armed forces. Most of them were never accepted as military equals to white soldiers. Blacks were relegated to segregated and distinct combat units, to separate training schools, and to segregated camp facilities. More often than not they made up the service and supply units and, even within these, black troops faced what they considered to be unwarranted degrees of discrimination. The soldiers claimed they did their duty and fought proudly to make the world "safe for democracy." Yet, for them, the vestiges of racism were inescapable. In their letters, the soldiers told of these debilitating experiences from the day they entered the Army to the day of their discharge.[2]

When the Selective Service and Training Act became law on September 16, 1940, black leaders considered it a milestone for black soldiers because of two antidiscrimination clauses. The first provided that all men between the ages of 18 and 36 were eligible to volunteer for service in the land and naval forces of the United States. The second clause prohibited discrimination (based on race and color) in the selection and training of men. However, a third provision gave the War Department final authority in deciding who would or would not be accepted in the military, prompting leaders in the black community to voice their concern about the intention of the legislation. Sensitive to racist implicatons, they argued that the provision could be implemented so as to leave blacks desiring to enlist no redress if they were rejected, possibly rendering the antidiscrimination clauses in the Selective Service Act virtually ineffective.[3]

Phillip McGuire is an Associate Professor of History at The University of North Carolina, Wilmington, N.C.

From the *Journal of Negro History,* Spring 1983, pp. 147-158. © 1983 by the Association for the Study of African-American Life and History, Inc. Reprinted by permission.

Evidence suggests that such concern was appropriate. As blacks were given the opportunity to serve in the army, they volunteered for induction in record numbers. Many were turned away, however, and as the black community had feared, the law provided no method or means to redress the grievance of any black American on rejection.

The reasons for rejection ranged from overt Army actions to more subtle excuses. The First Army Headquarters (one of nine geographical service commands that included Maine, Connecticut, Massachusetts, New Hampshire, Rhode Island, and Vermont) sent secret orders to its draft boards requesting that no blacks be inducted in the first draft. Although the order to Connecticut was rescinded when Governor Raymond Baldwin threatened to expose it to the public and to President Roosevelt, the antiblack request did not fade away. Late in 1940 the War Department itself ordered Connecticut's draft boards to fill their quotas with white men only, and it fell to Governor Robert Hurley, Baldwin's successor, to instruct the draft boards to ignore the War Department's order.[4]

A survey by Roy Wilkins showed that twenty-five cities in seventeen states had no blacks on the draft boards. Moreover, white recruiting officers often failed to serve induction notices to black I-A registrants, despite the War Department's promise to create more black ground units to absorb the new inductees. When pressed, the War Department claimed that separate facilities were inadequate to house the new inductees.[5]

Another factor may have been the absence of black advisors in the office of the director of the Selective Service and in the War Department. One who addressed this issue was Mary McLeod Bethune, director of the Division of Negro Affairs of the National Youth Administration. Ms. Bethune asked Mrs. Roosevelt, whom Secretary of War Henry L. Stimson regarded as an agitator, to urge the President to appoint black advisors to the office of the director of the Selective Service and to the War Department. She stressed that the request was a result of long consultation with other black leaders, all of whom agreed that these appointments were necessary to ensure that the policies of the War Department were effectively carried out. Mrs. Bethune also assured Mrs. Roosevelt that she and the other leaders were prepared to offer the names of the best qualified men for these positions.[6]

Illiteracy was another major factor that prevented the inclusion of blacks. Over 75 percent of the black inductees who failed the Army Classification Test came from the South and border states, which accounted for only 25 percent of the white inductees. According to a study conducted by Professors Eli Ginzberg and Douglas Bray of Columbia University, 90 percent of the blacks who failed the test had been deprived of adequate educational and cultural opportunities. Their conclusions were anticipated by Major Campbell C. Johnson, who later became special assistant to the director of the Selective Service. As early as 1944, Johnson blamed the South for the high rate of illiteracy among black inductees.[7]

Furthermore, the War Department apparently seized the opportunity to use illiteracy as a tactic to discriminate against blacks while accepting illiterate whites without question. According to his diary, Secretary of War Henry L. Stimson had sanctioned this policy. He admitted that "the Army had adopted rigid requirements for literacy mainly to keep down the number of colored troops and this is reacting badly in preventing us from getting in some very good but illiterate [white] recruits from the southern mountain states." To solve the manpower shortage, at least from the southern region of the country, Stimson recommended that the Army embark upon a voluntary recruitment program aimed at bringing more whites into the service. Thus the War Department was willing to actively recruit illiterate whites but unwilling to do the same for illiterate blacks.[8]

On October 9, 1940, the War Department finally announced the confidential guidelines established in 1937 for the treatment of black personnel in the army. The policy itself might have received a favorable response from black leaders had it not been accompanied by a general statement that "the policy of the War Department is not to intermingle colored and white enlisted personnel in the same regimental organization. This policy has proven satisfactory over a long period of years and to make changes would produce situations destructive to morale and detrimental to the preparation for National defense." The statement continued, "for similar reasons the department does not contemplate assigning colored Reserve Officers other than of the Medical Corps and Chaplains to existing Negro combat units of the Regular Army. These regular units are going concerns, accustomed through many years to the present system. Their morale is splendid, their rate of reenlistment is exceptionally high and their field training is well advanced." The final sentence was probably the most devastating to the hopes of black leaders. The department refused to accept the idea of experimenting with mixed units and used as its rationale the war as a time too critical for such experimentation.[9]

Because the War Department had rejected the idea of integration, blacks renewed their challenges to President Roosevelt and to the War Department for failure to end segregation. Black leaders based their protest on three basic principles: (1) segregation was morally wrong since it embodied an undemocratic doctrine of racial inferiority; (2) segregation denied full military opportunities to black soldiers, relegated them to an infe-rior status, and destroyed their esprit de corps; and (3) segregation was an unnecessary luxury. These leaders also believed that had the War Department been aware of the considerably greater expense involved in maintaining a segregated army, official zeal for a black and white military would have wavered.[10]

Eugene K. Jones, successor to George E. Haynes as executive secretary of the National Urban League, sent a letter to President Roosevelt in protest of the October 9 announcement. He declared: "We deny that the segregationist policy of the War Department, though it has been pursued over a long period of years, has been satisfactory to thoughtful Negro citizens. We deny also that to make changes in this policy would produce situations destructive to morale." Jones also called the President's attention to a unanimous resolution adopted at the League's 30th annual conference. In summary, the resolution stated: "The National Urban League is unalterably opposed to the policy and practice of racial discrimination and segregation in the Army, Navy, Air Force, and Marine Corps of the United States."[11]

More adamant in its tone than the Urban League, the Citizens' Nonpartisan Committee for Equal Rights in National Defense demanded that the War Department's policy be revised. In telegrams to President Roosevelt and to the War Department the committee stated: "We want no discrimination or segregation in the Army, Navy, Air Corps, or Industrial Defense. This is our just desert in a democratic Government, and the need for national unity demands immediate revision of the stated policy."[12]

In an effort to quiet or delude the black community, Roosevelt's press secretary, Stephen Early, released a statement to the press implying that military segregation had been sanctioned by A. Phillip Randolph, president of the Brotherhood of Sleeping Car Porters, Walter White, and T. Arnold Hill, director of the National Urban League's Department of Industrial Relations, at their White House meeting on September 27. Randolph, White and Hill, however, denounced Early's statement as a gross fabrication of the truth and demanded that Roosevelt make a public statement exculpating them of any participation in such an agreement. In a letter to White, Early made it clear that the White House could not be held responsible for inferences drawn from press releases.[13] White was not satisfied, insisting that Early's words, "as a result of that conference," conveyed to the public that he, Randolph, and Hill supported segregation in the armed forces when in fact they were diametrically opposed to it. The moral implications of the statement worried these leaders, who feared that if Roosevelt did not exonerate them publicly the black community would think the struggle for integration had come to a halt. Therefore, they reiterated to President Roosevelt that whatever Early's intentions, Americans, black and white, would accept the erroneous inferences as truth. Roosevelt finally capitulated and wrote a letter to each of the men, which was reprinted in the official news organ of their respective organizations. The President assured them that he regretted that Early's remarks had been misunderstood, and expressed sorrow that their positions, the White House, and the position of the War Department had not been made clear to the public. Roosevelt ended his letter remarking that "these measures [components of the October 9 policy statement] represents a very substantial advance over what has been the practice in past years. You may rest assured that Negroes are given fair treatment on a nondiscriminatory basis."[14] Roosevelt's letter notwithstanding, Walter White and Roy Wilkins subsequently went on a nationwide speaking tour. They spoke in every major city in an effort to solidify black support, which had fluctuated because of Early's statement.[15]

Meanwhile, shortly before the 1940 presidential election, two damaging incidents occurred that proved politically advantageous for the black community. First, the *New York Age* editorialized rumors that Colonel Benjamin O. Davis, Sr., was resigning his commission because President Roosevelt had ignored him in appointing thirty-four white colonels to brigadier general. The second incident was a political embarrassment. Following a speech Roosevelt had delivered in Madison Square Garden, Stephen Early kicked James Sloan, a black policeman, in the groin for unknowingly blocking Early's entrance to a presidential train bound for Washington, D.C. This incident made news headlines in major newspapers across the country. Although Early had publicly apologized to Sloan and to the New York Police Commissioner, black leaders were outraged.[16]

President Roosevelt also apologized publicly for Early's conduct. But black leaders were not satisfied. Hastie, White, Weaver (special advisor to Secretary of Interior Harold Ickes), Hill, Jones, Marshall, Randolph, Houston, Will W. Alexander (presidential advisor on black affairs), and Wilkins formulated strategy to quell the crisis, but they used the incident and the threat of the black vote to gain some military concessions from the government. Secretary of War Stimson apparently felt pressure from the leaders as he noted in his diary that "there is a tremendous drive going on by the Negroes, taking advantages of the last weeks of the campaign in order to force the Army and Navy into doing things for their race which would not otherwise be done and which are certainly not in the interest of sound national defense." Finally, Stimson wrote, "but they are making such progress in their drive that the friends of Mr. Roosevelt are very much troubled and are asking us to do anything we can."[17]

In the meantime, Roosevelt and his aides were discussing and mapping strategy at the White House. Because they felt the black vote was important to the outcome of the 1940 presidential election, Harry Hopkins, chief aide, called in Will Alexander to help resolve the President's dilemma. Black leaders had already met with and instructed Alexander to state four basic demands in return for the black vote. Thus he informed Hopkins that the black community wanted segregation abolished in the armed forces, Colonel Benjamin O. Davis, Sr. promoted to brigadier general, Major Campbell C. Johnson appointed assistant to the selective service director, and Judge William H. Hastie appointed assistant secretary in the War Department.[18]

Except for the abolition of segregation, the government yielded to black demands, and shortly after the political crisis three significant appointments were made: National Director General Lewis B. Hershey announced the appointment of Major Johnson as executive assistant to the office of the Selective Service; President Roosevelt promoted Colonel Davis to brigadier general; and the War Department announced the appointment of Hastie as civilian aide to the Secretary of War. Johnson and Davis accepted their positions without hesitation. Their appointments were praiseworthy mainly because they were firsts for black Americans. However, Secretary Stimson considered Davis' promotion political appeasement and having no substantive value. He remarked sarcastically that "I had a good deal of fun with Knox over the necessity that he was facing of appointing a colored Admiral and a battle fleet full of colored sailors according [to] a Resolution passed by the Colored Federal Employees Association and I told him that when I called next time at the Navy Department with my colored Brigadier General I expected to be met with the colored Admiral."[19]

Unlike the appointments of Davis and Johnson, Hastie's appointment became a controversial issue, and he delayed acceptance of the post. Hastie's attitude toward the newly created position was based largely on his conviction that the office of the civilian aide was just another bureaucratic office established to appease the black community and capture its vote in the 1940 presidential election. Then, too, his knowledge of Emmett J. Scott's role as the black special assistant to Secretary of War Newton Baker during World War I worried him. He viewed Scott as an adjuster of racial ills and black complaints rather than a leading voice for justice and social change within the military establishment. Hastie was particularly concerned that the black community might view him an as appeaser on racial matters. Consequently, Hastie refused to accept the post until the War Department announced publicly that he had been persuaded to represent

the interest of blacks in the War Department although he strongly opposed a segregated military.[20]

Hastie eventually accepted the post, and in a letter to Hastie, Secretary Stimson spelled out his duties in detail. They included aid to the department in developing plans that would ensure the most effective use of black manpower, recommending ways to improve the department's plan to organize black units in all branches of the services, assisting in the employment of civilian blacks at military installations, investigating discriminatory complaints of black soldiers as well as those of black civilians, and cooperating with blacks on the Selective Service Committee and other agencies concerned with blacks in the armed forces.[21]

Hastie was not exactly sure what Stimson's letter meant. He noted, however that it did not include a specific statement that the War Department was committed to the elimination of segregation and the other discriminatory policies that were major sources of frustration in the black community. He and other black leaders were anxious to have such a commitment in writing. But Stimson refused to provide one either in writing or verbally. In fact, the War Department's official position regarding black and white relations remained the same: "The Army would not be used as a sociological laboratory for effecting social change within the military establishment." In light of the department's stance, Hastie publicly responded to his appointment in such a way as to ensure that his opposition to segregation and discrimination was well known. He declared: "I have always been constantly opposed to any policy of discrimination and segregation in the Armed Forces of this country. I am assuming this post in the hope that I will be able to work effectively toward the integration of the Negro into the Army and to facilitate his placement, training, and promotion."[22]

Shortly after Hastie's appointment, Secretary Stimson remarked that "he seems like a rather decent negro [sic] who is now Dean of Law in the Law School of Howard University in this city." By October 1942, Stimson would accuse Hastie of having an unrealistic attitude toward solving the race problem in the armed forces, but at the time of Hastie's appointment, Stimson was probably aware that black leaders, the black press, and the black community expected Hastie to be "more than a rubber stamp official" who would work toward integration and the elimination of the inequalities blacks experienced in the armed services. Stimson probably was also aware that Hastie's determination to do an effective job stemmed from his sources of power and his previous career as a public servant and lawyer for the NAACP. Drawing on his capacity to articulate the facts and the immorality of racism and segregation, Hastie was always supported by a majority of the black press and black leaders. All the black national pressure organizations, many white liberals and, to some degree, white national organizations also supported Hastie. As nongovernmental opponents of racism and segregation, these elements were instrumental in exposing the discriminatory policies and practices of the armed forces.[23]

Since Hastie and the other black leaders expected little sympathy from the War Department, they felt it was equally important for them to constantly stress to black soldiers that while they fought for the elimination of discrimination within and outside the government, it was necessary to maintain good discipline and the highest possible rate of military efficiency. Hastie summed up the leaders' aspirations as he prepared to lead the campaign for integration within the War Department. He said: "The man in uniform must grit his teeth, square his shoulders and do his best as a soldier, confident that there are millions of Americans outside the armed forces, and more persons than he knows in high places within the military establishment, who will never cease fighting to remove all social barriers and every humiliating practice which now confronts him. But only by being, at all times, a first-rate soldier can the man in uniform help in this battle which shall be fought and won."[24]

Thus Hastie and the black leaders all agreed that the time was right for them to put pressure on the federal government to take the initiative in promoting equal opportunity and the integration of the armed forces. To this end, Hastie suggested to Walter White and A. Philip Randolph that in their upcoming meeting with President Roosevelt they should emphasize three major points: (1) that blacks vigorously opposed segregated army units; (2) that many whites supported this opposition; and (3) that the Army was not, as Congress had mandated, training blacks for the Army Air Corps. He also wanted them to inquire whether all black units would be officered by blacks; whether blacks would be included in medical training programs; and whether the War Department would make sincere efforts to prevent discrimination against civilian blacks in awarding defense contracts. In all these matters, Hastie urged White and Randolph to convey to the President as strongly as they could the idea that the black community was diametrically opposed to segregation and the attitude of the federal government toward its black soldiers. Hastie then noted, "If such inquires are made, I will undoubtedly be asked what the situation is with reference to particular matters. I think between us we will be able to give a more comprehensive picture of the seriousness and diversity of the problems than the persons in authority now have."[25]

Although Hastie and the other black leaders demonstrated solidarity on the issue of army integration, the NAACP and the National Urban League, sensing some confusion and antipathy in the black community, called a black leadership conference in New York City shortly after the Japanese attack on Pearl Harbor. Sixty prominent blacks met to consider the black community's part in the war effort. Judge William H. Hastie, now civilian aide to the Secretary of War, introduced a resolution, with only five dissenting votes, which stated that "colored people are not wholeheartedly and unreservedly all out in support of the present war effort." Walter White summed up the sentiments of the group and attributed the apathy among blacks to discrimination and segregation in the armed services and war industries.[26]

A faction, however, had developed in the black community. A small group of black accommodationists opposed integration while the war was in progress. For example, Eddie W. Reevers, editor of the *Messenger*, voiced the sentiments of conservative blacks who felt that such men as Hastie, White, and Randolph, as well as the leading black press, such as the *Pittsburgh Courier*, had incited racial hatred among the black masses. As early as August 1941, Reevers had written to Secretary of War Stimson claiming that millions of loyal blacks supported the policies of the War Department. In the same spirit, Charles M. Thomas, editor of the *Washington Tribune*, sent a letter to Stephen Early, stating that there was general dissatisfaction with Hastie's performance as civilian aide. Dr. William Pickens, former director of branches for the NAACP, echoed the same feelings. In May 1942, he was quoted in the *Richmond Times-Dispatch*, a southern white newspaper, as having said that the black community was loyal as a group but suffered from the traitorous influences of some foolish leaders in its midst. Pickens further stated: "It [the Army] is planning to win a war in spite of segregation of those who oppose segregation. Blacks could demand their full citizenship rights after Hitler and the Axis powers had been defeated. Everything must be sacrificed in winning this war. Such sacrifices are not sacrifices at all."[27]

While Pickens, Thomas, and Reevers, and the conservative black press supported segregation during the war, their position did not arouse much enthusiasm among the black masses. Instead, integrationists such as Hastie, White, and Randolph, major civil rights organizations, and an overwhelming majority of the black press wielded the most influence. Thus, in spite of the black conservatives, the integrationists continued to spearhead the black community's thrust toward desegregating the armed forces.[28]

In March 1942, however, the black press startled its white colleagues by assuming a more determined stance, one that was made visible by the adoption of the "Double V" symbol for victory at home as well as abroad. Despite admonitions from Director of the Office of War Information, Archibald MacLeish, and criticisms from members of their own community, black editors insisted that they would not cease the "Double V" campaign until blacks in the military and in the larger community were accorded their full constitutional rights as citizens and soldiers. Besides, said the editors, 91.2 percent of black community approved of their efforts to force the government to integrate the military.[29]

The case of Winfred W. Lynn furnished an example of blacks' dedication to eliminating segregation and racial discrimination in the military. Lynn was notified in June 1942 by Local Board 261 of Jamaica, New York, that he had been classified I-A. He replied: "Gentlemen: I am in receipt of my draft-reclassification notice. Please be informed that I am ready to serve in any unit of the armed forces of my country which is not segregated by race. Unless I am assured that I can serve in a mixed regiment and that I will not be compelled to serve in a unit undemocratically selected as a Negro group, I will refuse to report for induction."[30]

Not receiving the assurances he wanted, Lynn refused to report for duty, claiming that his induction into segregated units violated Section 4(A) of the 1940 Draft Act, which states: "In the selection and training of men under this act, and in the interpretation and execution of the provisions of this act, there shall be no discrimination against any person on account of race or color." The Act also states " . . . in classifying a registrant there shall be no discrimination for or against him because of his race, creed, or color." Subsequently, Lynn was arrested and indicted for draft evasion. Thus with his case began a two-year saga of the only legal challenge to the Jim Crow practices of the military in the Second World War.[31]

A lower court judge informed Lynn that to have his case heard he had to submit to induction and then file suit against his superior officer. He did so, and the Federal District Court in New York ruled against him by refusing to hear the case. Thereupon the case was appealed to the U.S. Circuit Court of Appeals. There, the lower court's decision was upheld. Finally, his case reached the U.S. Supreme Court in 1944. The justices refused to hear the case on the grounds that Lynn was on active duty overseas and, therefore, outside the jurisdiction of the court, and that the military officer against whom he had originally brought the suit had retired from active service. The Supreme Court also declared that " . . . if Congress had intended to prohibit separate white and Negro quotas and calls we believe it would have expressed such intention more definitely than by the general prohibition against discrimination appearing in Section 4."[32]

Although Lynn's case generated almost no press coverage, Selective Service Director

General Lewis B. Hershey reacted to his charge that discriminatory segregation and racial quotas violated the Draft Act by commenting publicly that he regretted the case, "but unfortunately the army gets the final say." Hershey went on to say, "what we are doing, of course, is simply transferring discrimination from everyday life into the army. Men who make up the army staff have the same ideas [about blacks] as they had before they went into the army."[33]

In view of Lynn's case, black leaders had raised questions in 1940 about the Draft Act clause that made the Army the final arbiter in determining the circumstances under which it could draft men. Lynn's case confirmed their earlier fears that the Army could strip virtually all force from the antidiscrimination clause of the Draft Act.[34]

Unfortunately for blacks, the Supreme Court had come down on the side of the Army and adopted discriminatory segregation and racial quotas as official military policy. The Lynn case, nevertheless, dramatized the extent to which blacks were willing to go to redress their grievances.

So the battle went on between the black leadership and other advocates of integration and those military and political voices who maintained that military efficiency demanded segregation. A *prima facie* case can be made that the military's policy of segregation, which resulted in racial discrimination, was maintained throughout the war.[35] However, important shifts in policies affecting blacks and the changing status of black Americans in the larger society suggested the beginning of an end to an old order of restrictive outlooks and actions toward black soldiers in the armed services.

Although black soldiers and the black community had not achieved their single-most objective—integration of the armed forces—the Army Air Force, for example, began training black pilots in 1941, and in 1942 the Navy began enlisting blacks other than for messman duty.[36]

Other significant changes affecting black soldiers also occurred: an increasing number were attending officer candidate schools; the War Department banned the use of racial epithets by commanding officers; a film on black contributions to the war effort was made and distributed throughout the country; more blacks were enrolled in and graduated from the Army's special training schools on an integrated basis, although they were returned to segregated army units in the regular army; black schools participated in the Air Force Enlistment Program; more black medical personnel were commissioned with the establishment of two black medical facilities at Fort Huachuca, Arizona, and Tuskegee Air Base; the Army and Navy, in conjunction with the Red Cross, agreed to accept blood donations from blacks; the Army Air Forces allowed blacks to fly combat missions over North Africa; and in 1944

fatigued black and white soldiers returning from Europe were assigned to the same distribution centers.[37]

With the aim of eliminating racial prejudice in all camps, the Army also published and distributed magazines such as *Army Talk,* and made available to black and white soldiers alike pamphlets on race relations. Moreover, notables such as boxing champion Joe Louis and black band leader Noble Sissle appeared at army camps in an effort to raise the level of morale among black troops.[38]

The military was not alone in relaxing major restrictions and racial attitudes toward black soldiers. Race relations in the larger society had also changed. The Second World War had created a new social and political climate in which black Americans could forge ahead in their determination to eliminate discrimination and racial segregation. The ballot gave them new political power, and black migration from the South provided new economic and educational opportunities. Such was the racial climate that encouraged the black leadership, black pressure organizations, notably the NAACP, and the black press to work even more vigorously to obtain racial equality for blacks in the armed forces.

NOTES

1. "Colonial Eugene Householder's Remarks at the Conference of Negro Newspaper Representatives," Washington, D.C., December 8–9, 1941, Civilian Aide to the Secretary of War Subject File, 1940–1947, National Archives Record Group (hereafter cited as NARG) 107; Judge William H. Hastie, private interview with author, United States Court of Appeals, Washington, D.C., March 6, 1974.

2. Phillip McGuire, *Taps for a Jim Crow Army: Letters from Black Soldiers in World War II* (Santa Barbara, California: Clio Books, 1983).

3. Jean Byers, *A Study of the Negro in Military Service* (Washington, D.C.: Department of Defense, 1947), 6–9; John P. Davis, "The Negro in the Armed Forces of America," in John P. Davis, editor, *The Negro Reference Book* (New Jersey; Prentice-Hall, 1966), 627; "Army Can Dodge Anti-Discrimination Clause on Selective Service System," *The Pittsburgh Courier,* November 30, 1940.

4. "Secret Army Orders Barred," *The Pittsburgh Courier,* November 23, 1940; "Army Jim Crow Orders Defied By Connecticut," *The Pittsburgh Courier,* January 4, 1941.

5. Roy Wilkins, "No Negro Draft Board Members in Many States, says NAACP Survey," *The Crisis* XLVIII (January, 1941), 22.

6. Letter, Mary McLeod Bethune to Eleanor Roosevelt, October 5, 1940, Box 151, Judge Robert P. Patterson Papers, Manuscript Division, Library of Congress, Washington, D.C.; Henry L. Stimson Diary, January 24, 1942, Yale University Library, New Haven, Connecticut; Walter White, *A Man Called White: The Autobiography of Walter White* (New York: The Viking Press, Inc., 1948).

186–187: Colonel Campbell C. Johnson, *Selective Service System: Special Groups: Special Monograph No. 10* (Washington, D.C.: United States Printing Office, 1953), 3, 94: "U.S. Plans New Units of Race Troops," *Norfolk Journal and Guide,* July 6, 1940; Charles S. Johnson, *To Stem This Tide: A Survey of Racial Tension Areas in the United States* (Boston: The Pilgrim Press, 1943), 81; "Only Whites Are Called; Boards All White," *The Pittsburgh Courier,* January 4, 1941.

7. Byers, *A Study of the Negro in Military Service,* 17; Eli Ginzberg and Douglas W. Bray, *The Uneducated* (New York: Colombia University Press, 1953), 240–245; Colonel Noel F. Parrish, "The Segregation of Negroes in the Army Air Forces" (unpublished M. A. thesis, Air University, 1947), 10–11; War Department Pamphlet, *Command of Negro Troops* (Washington, D.C.: United States Government Printing Office, 1944), 9.

8. Stimson Diary, May 12, 1942.

9. "War Department Press Release," The Adjutant General's Office, October 9, 1940, NARG 407.

10. Byers, *A Study of the Negro in Military Service,* 80–82; Horace R. Clayton, "Fighting For White Folks?," *Nation,* CLV (September 26, 1943), 267–269; Evelyn P. Meyers, *The Case Against Jim Crow Army Demands Investigation By the U.S. Congress* (Washington, D.C.: United States Government Printing Office, 1947), 5; "President O.K.'s Strange Request As Fellowmen Fight For Equality," *Chicago Defender,* October 9, 1940.

11. *New York Age,* October 26, 1940. The letter from Jones and the resolution adopted by the National Urban League were reprinted in this black newspaper.

12. Telegrams, Citizens' Nonpartisan Committee For Equal Rights in National Defense to Roosevelt, October 20, 1940, Franklin D. Roosevelt Papers, Franklin D. Roosevelt Library, Hyde Park, New York; to War Department, October 20, 1940, Box 151, Patterson Papers.

13. Letter, Stephen Early to White, October 18, 1940, Roosevelt Papers; James C. Evans, private interview with author, 3533 Warder Street, Washington, D.C., October 6, 1974; James C. Evans was the last black American to hold the position titled civilian aide to the Secretary of War. He assumed the post in 1947.

14. Letters, White to Early and Roosevelt, October 21, 1940; Roosevelt to Randolph, Hill, and White, October 25, 1940, Roosevelt Papers.

15. *New York Amsterdam News,* October 26, 1940.

16. *New York Age,* October 12, 1940. On November 1, 1940, the "Stephen Early Incident" made headlines in the following: *New York Times, New York Amsterdam News, The Oregon Statesman, Norfolk Journal and Guide, The Washington Afro-American, The Pittsburgh Courier, The Washington Post, Chicago Defender, The Richmond Times-Dispatch, The Los Angeles Times, The Greensboro Daily News, The Vicksburg Herald, The Baltimore Sun, The New Orleans Times, The Savannah Morning News, The Montgomery Advertiser, The Boston Daily Globe, The California Eagle, The Chicago Daily News, The Philadelphia Tribune, The Houston Post,*

The Detroit News, The Atlanta Daily World, The Atlanta Constitution, The Philadelphia Record, The People's Voice, The Cleveland Gazette, and *The Indianapolis News.*

17. Walter White, *A Man Called White,* 188–189; Samual A. Stouffer and Others, *The American Soldier, Adjustment During Army Life,* Volume 1 (New Jersey: Princeton University Press, 1949), 489–490; Richard Bardolph, *The Negro Vanguard* (New York: Vintage Books, 1959), 353; Stimson Diary, October 23, 1940, Finkle, "Forum For Protest: The Black Press and World War II," 197.

18. Bardolph, *The Negro Vanguard,* 354; Richard M. Dalfiume, *Desegregation of the United States Armed Forces; Fighting On Two Fronts, 1939–1953* (Missouri: University of Missouri Press, 1969), 40–41; White, *A Man Called White,* 187.

19. Press Release, Democratic National Committee Publicity Department Colored Division, October 30, 1940; Stimson Diary, October 22, 25, 1940; Lee, *The Employment of Negro Troops,* 79; "First Race General in History of United States Army Appointed," *Norfolk Journal and Guide,* November 2, 1940.

20. Hastie, private interview with author, March 4, 1974; memorandums, Associate Justice Felix Frankfurter to Robert P. Patterson, no date, and Huntington Thomas to Patterson, October 2, 1940, Box 151, Patterson Papers.

21. Letter, Stimson to Hastie, October 25, 1940, Box 151, Patterson Papers.

22. Hastie, private interview with author, March 6, 1974; "Colonel Eugene Householder's Remarks at the Conference of Negro Newspapers Representatives," December 8–9, 1941, NARG 107; *New York Amsterdam News,* November 2, 1940, *Norfolk Journal and Guide,* November 2, 1940.

23. Stimson Diary, October 23, 28, 1940, and October 19, 1942; Editorial, *The New York Age,* November 9, 1940; Editorial, *The Cleveland Gazette,* November 2, 1940, Editorial, *The Chicago Defender,* November 2, 1940; Editorial, *Norfolk Journal and Guide,* November 2, 1940; Editorial, *The Pittsburgh Courier,* November 2, 1940; Finkle, "Forum For Protest: The Black Press and World War II," 197; White, *A Man Called White,* 188–189; Bardolph, *The Negro Vanguard,* 353; Henry I. Stimson and McGeorge Bundy, *On Active Service in Peace and War* (New York: Harper, 1948), 463, Office Memorandum, "Conference of the Chicago Council of Negro Organizations With Under Secretary Robert P. Patterson," March 29, 1941, NARG 107.

24. Memorandum, Huntington Thomas to Patterson, October 21, 1940, Box 151, Patterson Papers; Hastie, private interview with author, March 6, 1974; William H. Hastie, *On Clipped Wings; the Story of Jim Crow in the Army Air Corps* (New York: National Association for the Advance of Colored People, 1943), 1.

25. Letter, Hastie to White and Randolph, December 21, 1940, Box 264, NAACP Papers; Rackham Holt, *Mary McLeod Bethune* (New York: Doubleday and Company, 1964), 196–197.

26. Roi Ottley, *'New World A-Coming': Inside Black America* (Boston, Houghton Mifflin Company, 1943), 314–315.

27. *The Richmond Times-Dispatch,* May 17, 1942; Letter, Eddie W. Reevers to Henry L. Stimson, August 8, 1941; Letter, Charles M. Thomas to Stephen Early, March 3, 1942, Roosevelt Papers; Warren H. Brown, "A Negro Looks At The Negro Press," *Saturday Review of Literature,* XXV (December 19, 1942), 5; Finkle, "Forum For Protest: The Black Press and World War II," 172; Sheldon B. Avery, "Up From Washington: William Pickens and the Negro Struggle For Equality 1900–1954" (unpublished Ph.D. dissertation, University of Oregon, 1970), 243–246.

28. For detailed discussions of the black community's consensus on army integration see Roi Ottley, *'New World A-Coming': Inside Black America* (Boston: Houghton Mifflin Company, 1943): William H. Hastie, *On Clipped Wings: the Story of Jim Crow in the Army Air Corps* (New York: NAACP, 1943): Richard J. Stillman, *Integration of the Negro in the U.S. Armed Forces* (New York: Frederick A. Praeger, 1968): Richard M. Dalfiume, *Desegregation of the United States Armed Forces, 1939–1953* (Missouri: University of Missouri Press, 1969): Phillip McGuire, "Black Civilian Aides And The Problems of Racism and Segregation in The United States Armed Forces: 1940–1950" (unpublished Ph.D. dissertation, Howard University, 1975); Neil A. Wynn, *The Afro-American and the Second World War* (New York: Holmes and Meier Publishers, 1976); A Russell Buchanan, *Black Americans in World War II* (Santa Barbara, California: ABC-Clio Press, 1977); Alan M. Osur, *Black In The Army Air Forces During World War II* (Washington, D.C.: United States Printing Office, 1977).

29. Ottley, "The Negro Press," *Common Ground* (Spring 1943), 11–16, Ottley; *'New World A-Coming',* 269–270.

30. Quoted in Dwight MacDonald, "The Novel Case of Winfred Lynn," *The Nation,* CLVI (February 20, 1943), 263.

31. Memorandum of Law, United States ex rel. Winfred W. Lynn against Colonel John W. Downer, William H. Hastie papers, Howard University Law School, Washington, D.C.: Gerald R. Gill, "Religious, Constitutional, and Racial Objections to the United States Involvement in World War II 1939–1945" (unpublished M. A. thesis, Howard University, 1974), 52; MacDonald, "The Novel Case of Winfred Lynn," 263–264.

32. Quoted in S. P. Breckinridge, "The Winfred Lynn Case Again: Segregation in the Armed Forces," *Social Service Review,* XVIII (September, 1944), 370; MacDonald, "The Novel Case of Winfred Lynn," 264–70; MacDonald, "The Supreme Court's New Moot Suit," *The Nation,* CLIX (July 1, 1944), 13–14; Letter, Winfred L. Kerr, chairman of the Lynn Committee To Abolish Segregation In The Armed Forces, to Hastie, April, 4, 1944, Hastie Papers.

33. MacDonald, "The Novel Case of Winfred Lynn," 268.

34. Byers, *A Study of the Negro in Military Service,* 6–9; Davis, "The Negro in the Armed Forces of America," 627; "Army Can Dodge Anti-Discrimination Clause on Selective Service System," *The Pittsburgh Courier,* November 30, 1940.

35. McGuire, *Taps for a Jim Crow Army: Letters from Black Soldiers in World War II,* (Santa Barbara, California: Clio Books, 1983).

36. For detailed discussions of blacks in the U.S. Navy and Army Air Forces during World War II see Dennis D. Nelson, *The Integration of the Negro into the U.S. Navy* (New York: Farrar, Straus & Young, 1951); Alan M. Osur, *Blacks in the Army Air Forces during World War II* (Washington, D.C.: United States Printing Office, 1977); Frederick S. Harrod, "Integration of the Navy 1941–1978," *United States Naval Institute Proceedings,* CV (October 1979), 41–47; Phillip McGuire, "Black Civilian Aides and the Problems of Racism and Segregation in the United States Armed Forces, 1940–1950" (unpublished Ph.D. dissertation, Howard University, 1975), 119–27.

37. McGuire, "Black Civilian Aides," 101–119.

38. Ibid.

Sacrifice Play

The Negro Baseball Leagues Remembered

David Conrads

You don't have to be a baseball fan to know Jackie Robinson broke the color line—the unwritten rule barring blacks from playing in the major leagues—when he joined the Brooklyn Dodgers in 1947. Yet, until recently, even avid fans knew little or nothing about the Negro leagues or the rich culture of black baseball that preceded the Robinson era by a half century and flourished even before the color line was drawn in the 1890s.

They played for teams like the Pittsburgh Crawfords, the Birmingham Black Barons, the Cleveland Buckeyes, and the Chicago American Giants. In a sport renowned for nicknames, they sported some of the best: Cool Papa, Smokey Joe, Big Mitt, Highpockets, Double Duty. It is said they were good enough—but not white enough—to play in the major leagues. Indeed, the players in the Negro leagues were among the greatest the game has ever seen. But until recently, these players and this chapter in American history have been mostly ignored.

Now, after decades of neglect, there is a greater awareness of the Negro leagues than at any time since they dissolved in the mid-1950s. There has been a steady increase in interest since the early 1970s, when nine Negro league greats—a mythical all-star team—were inducted into the Baseball Hall of Fame in Co-

operstown, New York. Robert Peterson's *Only the Ball Was White*, the first history of black baseball, was published in 1970. With a latter-day flood of books on the subject, it introduced the reading public to this shadow league. Ken Burns' television documentary *Baseball* brought the Negro leagues to the attention of even-greater numbers of television viewers. Many who knew nothing about the Negro leagues learned that before integration black ballplayers were not just sitting on their gloves waiting for the door to "organized" baseball to open. They formed their own teams and leagues

and, despite incomparably worse conditions, played the game with as much skill and enthusiasm as their white counterparts.

'It wasn't easy street'

Black baseball was tough," recalls Walter "Buck" Leonard, arguably the greatest first baseman in the history of black baseball, in his recent autobiography. "We'd play our way into shape. We didn't have time for somebody to teach us fundamentals and inside baseball like the major leaguers did

NEGRO BASEBALL LEAGUERS

The Monarchs' team bus. Many players look back with fondness on the friendships forged on the road.

This article originally appeared in *The World & I,* February 1996, pp. 185-195. Reprinted by permission of *The World & I,* a publication of the Washington Times Corporation. © 1996.

in the spring. As for backup plays, relays, cutoffs, and things like that, we learned by playing. We'd play every day. Anybody, anywhere, anytime."

Roy Campanella, who played for ten years with the Baltimore Elite Giants before going on to a Hall-of-Fame career with the Brooklyn Dodgers, recalls in his memoirs, "We traveled in a big bus and many's the time we never bothered to take off our uniforms going from one place to another. . . . The bus was our home, dressing room, dining room, and hotel."

Chet Brewer, a pitcher whose twenty-three-year career was spent mostly with the Kansas City Monarchs, summarized the Negro league experience succinctly: "We'd just eat and ride and play," he said. "That

was the size of it. It wasn't easy street."

Although the Negro leagues have become synonymous with grueling bus rides, low pay, poor playing conditions, and living with the constant indignities of racism and segregation, some of the surviving players are quick to point out that life in the Negro leagues was not all privation and misery. "It was a hardship," recalls Max Manning, a star pitcher in the 1940s with the Newark (New Jersey) Eagles. "But there was so much joy and pleasure that came out of the associations you had. The fun you had on the bus ride—talking and jiving, singing and telling jokes. It sort of took the pain away."

"Life in the Negro leagues was better than a lot of people thought," says John "Buck" O'Neil. A fixture at first base during some of the Kansas City Mon archs' greatest years, O'Neil later became the team's manager. "Travel was grueling, but not as bad as people have made it out to be. The Monarchs may have had it a little better than a lot of other teams. We stayed in the best hotels and ate at the best restaurants. They just happened to be black owned."

In an era when baseball and boxing were the only professional sports where money could be made, baseball players were among the earliest black sports heroes. In Kansas City, the black community was centered around

Eighteenth and Vine Streets, an area that boasted scores of nightclubs featuring some of the best jazz in the country. The Monarchs were celebrities and rubbed elbows with the likes of Count Basie, Duke Ellington, and Billie Holiday. While players had to endure punishing travel schedules, for most young black men, the opportunity to see the country and even play in foreign lands, like Mexico, Cuba, and the Dominican Republic, was the opportunity of a lifetime.

Much is made of the low salaries; Negro leaguers made about a quarter of what their counterparts in the major leagues were making. But the big stars of black baseball did well. Satchel Paige, the legendary pitcher and biggest star of that era, took a pay cut when he finally made it to the majors in 1948. Josh Gibson, the second-biggest name and one of the greatest hitters in the history of baseball, made $1,200 a month playing for the Homestead (Pennsylvania) Grays in the 1940s. Although that was more than the average major leaguer earned at the time, it was far less than the salaries of Ted Williams and Joe DiMaggio, the white stars of Gibson's stature.

For all the players, a stint with a Negro league team was a good job and a chance to get paid to do something they loved. "We made good money compared to general salaries," asserts Manning. "I made $650 a month in my last years with the Eagles. How many blacks made that kind of money? I made enough to buy a house and a car and raise my family."

Misconceptions abound

After forty years, what is remembered about the Negro leagues is a blend of fact and folklore. The revival of interest has given surviving players an opportunity to correct some of the many misconceptions about black baseball.

NEGRO BASEBALL LEAGUERS

Satchel Paige is considered by some to have been the greatest pitcher ever, and large crowds turned out whenever he was scheduled to pitch.

One of the biggest is that the Negro leagues were less an organized league and more a motley band of itinerant showmen—part ballplayers, part minstrel-show performers—roaming the country in beat-up cars, picking up games where they could. A low-budget baseball version of the Harlem Globetrotters. Such distortions are painful to the players who were there.

"The Negro leagues were very organized," insists O'Neil. "We had spring training. We had an all-star game. We had a world series. When I came out of spring training, I knew where I would be every single night of the season. It wasn't just pick up a game here and pick up a game there."

This misapprehension is not purely the figment of bigoted minds. Many early black teams combined showmanship with baseball to enhance their drawing power. Teams like the Zulu Cannibal Giants (who sported war paint and grass skirts), the Ethiopian Clowns (who played under names like Selassie, Wahoo, and Tarzan), and the Indianapolis Clowns, while hardly the norm in black baseball, were very popular for a time. Photographs of these teams reproduced in modern books make a big impression. *The Bingo Long Traveling All-Stars and Motor Kings*, a 1976 movie about a barnstorming black baseball team, reinforced the stereotype.

Oddly enough, Paige, black baseball's most illustrious star, contributed to the misleading association of black baseball with comedy. Paige may have been the greatest pitcher ever. He was said to warm up by throwing the ball over a chewing gum wrapper and guaranteed to strike out the first nine batters in a game. He once walked two batters in a Negro league World Series game to pitch to Gibson, then struck him out. Dizzy Dean, whose all-star teams played many lucrative exhibition games against black all-star teams led by Paige, once said: "My fastball looks like a change of pace alongside that little bullet old Satchel shoots up to the plate."

NEGRO BASEBALL LEAGUERS

Eighteenth and Vine Streets in Kansas City. By attracting business to black-owned hotels and restaurants, Negro league teams helped foster the community's economic progress.

Paige was equally renowned for his antics on and off the field. Forsaking the team bus, he sped around the country in his own car, frequently arriving late, then shuffled out to the mound like he had all the time in the world. He was one of the first athletes to realize that sport is show business and the name of the game is entertainment. He gave his pitches names such as "Big Tom," "Be Ball," "Bat Dodger," and "Midnight Creeper." He scoffed at training (one of his famous Rules for Living was "Avoid running at all times"), yet managed to pitch well into his forties. He once pitched with all seven fielders behind him sitting down. Though he did this rarely, the possibility of it happening in any given game was enough to keep the turnstiles spinning wherever he appeared.

Contributions

The Negro leagues made an enormous contribution to African-American society and the country as a whole. Their contributions to the game itself are impressive and underappreciated. The shin guard and batting helmet are both said to have their origin in black baseball. Andrew "Rube" Foster, called the "father of black baseball" for his instrumental role in founding the Negro National League, is credited with developing the hit-and-run bunt during his days as a highly successful and innovative manager. And J.L. Wilkinson, the white owner of the Kansas City Monarchs, introduced the world to night baseball five years before lights were used in the major leagues.

First and foremost, says Edward Beasley, a cultural historian and vice president of the Association for the Study of Afro-American Life and History, "the black teams provided heroes to black youth. Sure they identified with white baseball players, but here they had an opportunity to get to know their own heroes, on a one-to-one basis in many cases."

From Harlem to Kansas City, from the Black Bottom section of Detroit to Beale Street in Memphis, the

The 'Gentlemen's Agreement'

In 1867, the black Philadelphia Pythians applied to join the National Association of Base Ball Players, the sport's first governing body. Hovever, the nominating committee voted "unanimously . . . against the admission of any club which may be composed of one or more colored persons." With those words, a wall keeping blacks out of organized baseball was erected, and the next thirty years were spent sealing up the cracks. Future leagues didn't have a written regulation barring blacks, but their "gentlemen's agreement" proved to be as binding as any law.

Because the injunction applied only to black teams, a few individual black players managed to play on predominantly white teams. But as the nineteenth century drew to a close, attitudes toward race hardened, and the few black players in organized baseball found their positions more and more precarious. Threats of violence from white fans became increasingly common, and, with pressure from white teammates, the last black player was forced out in 1898.

Blacks had long realized that they would have to form their own teams if they wanted to play. In 1885, waiters at the Argyle Hotel, a resort in Babylon, New York, formed the first all-black salaried team. Calling themselves the Cuban Giants they spoke gibberish on the field that they hoped to pass off as Spanish. (Interestingly, it was skin color, not genealogy, that was of greatest concern to whites. Light-skinned African Americans could "pass," while darker individuals found their major league careers cut short.) By the turn of the century, there were five known professional black teams, and there were more than sixty by 1910.

In 1920, the owners of seven midwestern black teams, under the leadership of Andrew "Rube" Foster, formed the Negro National League. The rival Eastern Colored League formed three years later. Buth leagues folded during the Depression but soon regrouped. They flourished in the 1940s, but baseball's integration in 1947 sounded their death knell. After 1955, the Negro American League was down to four teams. By 1965, only the Indianapolis Clowns remained as a remnant of the days of segregation.

—D.C.

players and teams in the Negro leagues were an immense source of pride among blacks. In many racially divided cities, the local black baseball team was just about the only entertainment available to the African-American community.

Though only the larger cities had teams in one of the leagues, the players were well known to black fans around the country through the pages of national black weekly newspapers, especially the *Pittsburgh Courier* and the *Chicago Defender*. O'Neil grew up with two sets of heroes. "We knew all about the major league teams and major league players," he recalls. "Ruth, Gehrig, Foxx, and all those guys were big heroes to us. It didn't matter what color their skin was. But we also had our black heroes. Oscar Charleston, Pop Lloyd, Biz Mackey. Whites didn't know anything about our leagues, but we had the best of both worlds."

Black players had many opportunities to see just how they measured up against white major leaguers. Both before and after the advent of organized leagues, exhibition games between black teams and white teams were a perennially popular attraction. (Additionally, blacks and whites often played together on winter league teams in Cuba, Puerto Rico, Mexico, and the Dominican Republic.)

Over the decades, black teams played 445 recorded games against white teams, winning 61 percent of them. Black teams did so well against major league teams that baseball commissioner Kenesaw Mountain Landis, embarrassed by the losses, put a stop to the practice.

"When black teams were beating white teams, as many of them were, there was a great sense of pride, especially at a time when blacks were

NEGRO BASEBALL LEAGUERS

Cecil Travis, Dizzy Dean, and Paige. Over the decades, black teams occasionally competed against and frequently defeated teams of white all-stars, a source of pride and inspiration to their fans.

NEGRO BASEBALL LEAGUERS

Jackie Robinson and Brooklyn Dodgers general manager Branch Rickey.

a whole generation of people. It had to be an uplifting feeling."

The leagues made a substantial economic impact on the African-American communities where they operated, providing jobs to players and other employees, as well as business to hotels and restaurants where they traveled. The owners of the black teams were among the earliest successful black entrepreneurs. By the end of World War II, when they were at their peak, the Negro leagues were a $2 million empire, one of the largest black-dominated businesses in the country.

And blacks were not the only ones profiting from the Negro leagues. The Pittsburgh Crawfords and the Memphis Red Sox played in their own stadiums, but the rest of the teams rented ballparks, many from major league organizations. The Yankees earned $100,000 a year renting out stadiums in Kansas City, Newark, and Norfolk, Virginia (as well as Yankee Stadium itself) to black teams.

being told they couldn't beat a white person doing anything," says Phil Dixon, coauthor of *The Negro Baseball Leagues: A Photographic History.* "And yet it was being done day in and day out. I think to be able to witness that kind of equality so easily through the sporting arena helped transform

NATIONAL BASEBALL LIBRARY & ARCHIVE

Crowd appeal. The desire to attract black audiences may have been a factor in the integration of the major leagues.

NATIONAL BASEBALL LIBRARY AND ARCHIVE

Commissioner Bowie Kuhn (right) welcomes Cool Papa Bell into the Baseball Hall of Fame.

African-American baseball fans represented a lucrative market. This was amply demonstrated every year in Chicago at black baseball's premier event, the East-West All-Star Game. Started in 1933, the same year as the major leagues' all-star game, the East-West game attracted black fans from all over the country. The first game, played during the depth of the Great Depression, drew twenty thousand spectators. In 1943, the game drew nearly fifty-two thousand fans. The attendance at these games puts to rest the mistaken notion that nobody saw the great black players and black teams of that era.

And it wasn't only blacks who patronized the games, although they made up the large majority of paying spectators. Many league teams at-tracted white fans to their games on a regular basis. All teams supplemented their league schedule with exhibition games against non-league teams (games that did not count in the standings). The Monarchs barnstormed throughout the West and Midwest, even into Canada, bringing big-city entertainment to small towns with few if any black residents. For many small towns in rural America, hosting a professional black baseball game was the biggest event of the year.

By the 1940s the Negro leagues had fostered the development of a black economic market that was largely, though not entirely, inde-pendent of white participation. This did not go unnoticed by the white majority. Among those watching the popular East-West games, either from the stands or from afar, were the white owners of major league baseball who longed to attract some of these black fans into their stadiums.

Thus, the Negro leagues turned out to be more than an economic phenomenon; they were a powerful force for acculturation. Indeed, the success of the Negro leagues and the sight of so many African Americans paying money to attend a baseball game hastened the integration of the major leagues. Whether or not Branch Rickey, the general manager of the Brooklyn Dodgers who signed Jackie Robinson to a major league contract, was motivated more by money than morals, the fact remains that, in the realm of integration, baseball was a forerunner. The integration of the major leagues pre-dated all the early civil rights landmarks, including President Tru-man's desegregating of the armed forces (1948), the *Brown vs. Board of Education* decision (1954), the Mont-gomery bus boycott (1955), and the civil rights marches of the early 1960s. As historian and author Larry Lester put it: "Jackie Robinson did more than any lawyer, more than any politician, and more than any civil rights activist to promote the civil rights movement." The circum-stances that brought Robinson to his momentous role are hard to imagine separated from the proving ground of the Negro baseball leagues.

No bitterness

One of the most striking things about meeting for-mer players from the Negro leagues is their nearly universal lack of bitterness over being kept out of the major leagues. Some, like pitcher Clifford "Connie" Johnson of the Monarchs, did get a chance, playing for the Chicago White Sox and the Baltimore Orioles. O'Neil, who was thirty-six when the color wall fell, knew the major leagues were look-ing for young players. Still, he vehe-mently rejects the idea that he was born too soon, noting that everyone who played before integration con-tributed to paving the way for Ro-binson. Although he never got to play in the majors, O'Neil neverthe-less blazed another trail. Hired in 1956 as a scout by the Chicago Cubs, he was made the first African-American coach in major league his-tory in 1962. "I didn't come along too early," he is fond of saying, em-bracing his place in history. "I was right on time."

The death of the Negro leagues went entirely unheralded. At the time, few took note of their slow, steady demise, as African Americans—most of them instant Dodgers fans—turned their attention to the major leagues. The Negro leagues had outlived their usefulness. Now, forty years later, there is an appreciation and regard for those days, for this rediscovered period of American history and the players who participated in it.

Today, the survivors of the Negro league era find themselves celebrities again. They are invited to card shows, sought after by the media, and honored with special days at major league ballparks. It is a welcome opportunity for these men to get some long-overdue recognition, and most are enjoying their newfound fame. Whatever deprivations and injustices they suffered tend to disappear in the rosy glow of hindsight. Manning sums up his Negro league experience this way: "Winning was nice and all, but it was fun just to be playing. Just to play ball and play it right and strive to be a complete ballplayer. It was a beautiful experience."

Additional Reading

Janet Bruce, *The Kansas City Monarchs: Champions of Black Baseball*, University Press of Kansas, Lawrence, 1985.

Phil Dixon and Patrick Hannigan, *The Negro Baseball Leagues: A Photographic History*, Amereon House, Mattituck, N.Y., 1992.

John Holway, *Voices from the Great Black Baseball Leagues*, revised edition, Da Capo Press, New York, 1992.

Robert Peterson, *Only the Ball Was White*, Oxford University Press, New York, 1992 (first published by Prentice Hall, 1970).

Mark Ribowsky, *Don't Look Back: Satchel Paige on the Shadows of Baseball*, Simon & Schuster, New York, 1994.

For young adult readers (ages 9–13):

Michael Cooper, *Playing America's Game: The Story of Negro League Baseball*, Lodestar, New York, 1993.

David Conrads is a writer and editor in Kansas City, Missouri. He is the coauthor, with Steve Wulf, of I Was Right on Time, *the autobiography of Buck O'Neil, to be published by Simon & Schuster in April 1996.*

Unit Selections

Key Points to Consider

❖ How did Martin Luther King Jr. explain his presence and purpose in Birmingham, Alabama, to the eight white religious leaders who had issued a public statement of concern? Describe your thoughts about King's letter now that more than 35 years have passed since it was written and after knowing what has transpired during the years that followed.

❖ Describe the progress or lack of progress that has occurred in Mississippi since 1962. Do you concur with the commentary (see "The South's History Rises, Again and Again") that confronting the past can be cathartic, but that it can also provoke resentment. Expand your answer.

❖ In what ways did black women contribute to the modern civil rights movement? After reading "Black Women Activists and the Student Nonviolent Coordinating Committee: The Case of Ruby Doris Smith Robinson," do you agree or disagree with the statement "black female activist efforts have routinely been tied to a negative assessment of black womanhood"? Defend your answer.

 **Links** | **www.dushkin.com/online/**

These sites are annotated on pages 4 and 5.

The 1960s marked the beginning of what many have termed the modern civil rights movement in the United States. This period, with it sit-ins and marches, protests and boycotts, work stoppages and riots, significantly redefined the character of America and the struggle for equal rights. In August 1963, in answer to a "statement of concern and caution" issued by eight white religious leaders in the South, Martin Luther King Jr. wrote a longhand letter in prison that explained the purposes of the nonviolent demonstrations against segregation. In that letter he said "Over the last few years I have consistently preached that nonviolence demands that the means we use must be as pure as the ends we seek." While not all black leaders acted out of this point of view, King's statement provided the impetus for much of the period's protests.

Looking back at that time, Kevin Sack, in "The South's History Rises, Again and Again," points out that while confronting past violent civil rights events today can be cathartic, it can also provoke renewed resentment.

Black women have been a significant part of the the struggle against racism and oppression. "Against the backdrop of the peculiar status of African American women in U.S. society, black female activist efforts have routinely been tied to a negative assessment of black womanhood," claims Cynthia Fleming in an article about the case of Ruby Doris Smith Robinson, a black female activist who sought to define her womanwhood as she gained power within the Student Nonviolent Coordinating Committee (SNCC).

Modern Civil Rights

The Negro Is Your Brother

From the Birmingham jail, where he was imprisoned
as a participant in nonviolent demonstrations against segregation,
Dr. Martin Luther King, Jr., wrote in longhand the letter which
follows. It was his response to a public statement of concern and
caution issued by eight white religious leaders of the South.
Dr. King, who was born in 1929, did his undergraduate work at
Morehouse College; attended the integrated Crozer Theological
Seminary in Chester, Pennsylvania, one of six Negroes among a
hundred students, and the president of his class; and
won a fellowship to Boston University for his Ph.D.

by Martin Luther King, Jr.

WHILE confined here in the Birmingham city jail, I came across your recent statement calling our present activities "unwise and untimely." Seldom, if ever, do I pause to answer criticism of my work and ideas. If I sought to answer all of the criticisms that cross my desk, my secretaries would be engaged in little else in the course of the day, and I would have no time for constructive work. But since I feel that you are men of genuine good will and your criticisms are sincerely set forth, I would like to answer your statement in what I hope will be patient and reasonable terms.

I think I should give the reason for my being in Birmingham, since you have been influenced by the argument of "outsiders coming in." I have the honor of serving as president of the Southern Christian Leadership Conference, an organization operating in every Southern state, with headquarters in Atlanta, Georgia.

We have some eighty-five affiliate organizations all across the South, one being the Alabama Christian Movement for Human Rights. Whenever necessary and possible, we share staff, educational and financial resources with our affiliates. Several months ago our local affiliate here in Birmingham invited us to be on call to engage in a nonviolent direct-action program if such were deemed necessary. We readily consented, and when the hour came we lived up to our promises. So I am here, along with several members of my staff, because we were invited here. I am here because I have basic organizational ties here.

Beyond this, I am in Birmingham because injustice is here. Just as the eighth-century prophets left their little villages and carried their "thus saith the Lord" far beyond the boundaries of their hometowns; and just as the Apostle Paul left his little village of Tarsus and carried the gospel of Jesus Christ to practically every hamlet and city of the Greco-Roman world, I too am compelled to carry the gospel of freedom beyond my particular hometown. Like Paul, I must constantly respond to the Macedonian call for aid.

Moreover, I am cognizant of the interrelatedness of all communities and states. I cannot sit idly by in Atlanta and not be concerned about what happens in Birmingham. Injustice anywhere is a threat to justice everywhere. We are caught in an inescapable network of mutuality, tied in a single garment of destiny. Whatever affects one directly affects all indirectly. Never again can we afford to live with the narrow, provincial "outside agitator" idea. Anyone who lives inside the United States can never be considered an outsider.

You deplore the demonstrations that are presently taking place in Birmingham. But I am sorry that your statement did not express a similar concern for the conditions that brought the demonstrations into being. I am sure that each of you would want to go beyond the superficial social analyst who looks merely at effects and does not grapple with underlying causes. I would not hesitate to say that it is unfortunate that so-called demonstrations are taking place in Birmingham at this time, but I would say in more emphatic terms that it is even more unfortunate that the white power structure of this city left the Negro community with no other alternative.

IN ANY nonviolent campaign there are four basic steps: collection of the facts to determine whether injustices are alive, negotiation, self-purification, and direct action. We have gone through all of these steps in Birmingham. There can be no gainsaying of the fact that racial injustice engulfs this community. Birmingham is probably the most thoroughly segregated city in the United States. Its ugly record of police brutality is known in every section of this country. Its unjust treatment of Negroes in the courts is a notorious reality. There have been more unsolved bombings of Negro homes and churches in Birmingham than in any other city in this nation. These are the hard, brutal, and unbelievable facts. On the basis of them, Negro leaders sought to negotiate with the city fathers. But the political leaders consistently refused to engage in good-faith negotiation.

Then came the opportunity last September to talk with some of the leaders of the economic community. In these negotiating sessions certain promises were made by the merchants, such as the promise to remove the humiliating racial signs from the stores. On the basis of these promises, Reverend Shuttlesworth and the leaders of the Alabama Christian Movement for Human Rights agreed to call a moratorium on any type of demonstration. As the weeks and months unfolded, we realized that we were the victims of a broken promise. The signs remained. As in so many experiences of the past, we were confronted with blasted hopes, and the dark shadow of a deep disappointment settled upon us. So we had no alternative except that of preparing for direct action, whereby we would present our very bodies as a means of laying our case before the conscience of the local and national community. We were not unmindful of the difficulties involved. So we decided to go through a process of self-purification. We started having workshops on nonviolence and repeatedly asked ourselves the questions, "Are you able to accept blows without retaliating?" and "Are you able to endure the ordeals of jail?" We decided to set our direct-action program around the Easter season, realizing that, with exception of Christmas, this was the largest shopping period of the year. Knowing that a strong economic withdrawal program would be the by-product of direct action, we felt that this was the best time to bring pressure on the merchants for the needed changes. Then it occurred to us that the March election was ahead, and so we speedily decided to postpone action until after election day. When we discovered that Mr. Conner was in the runoff, we decided again to postpone action so that the demonstration could not be used to cloud the issues. At this time we agreed to begin our nonviolent witness the day after the runoff.

This reveals that we did not move irresponsibly into direct action. We, too, wanted to see Mr. Conner defeated, so we went through postponement after postponement to aid in this community need. After this we felt that direct action could be delayed no longer.

You may well ask, "Why direct action, why sit-ins, marches, and so forth? Isn't negotiation a better path?" You are exactly right in your call for negotiation. Indeed, this is the purpose of direct action. Nonviolent direct action seeks to create such a crisis and establish such creative tension that a community that has consistently refused to negotiate is forced to confront the issue. It seeks so to dramatize the issue that it can no longer be ignored. I just referred to the creation of tension as a part of the work of the nonviolent resister. This may sound rather shocking. But I must confess that I am not afraid of the word "tension." I have earnestly worked and preached against violent tension, but there is a type of constructive nonviolent tension that is necessary for growth. Just as Socrates felt that it was necessary to create a tension in the mind so that individuals could rise from the bondage of myths and half-truths to the unfettered realm of creative analysis and objective appraisal, we must see the need of having nonviolent gadflies to create the kind of tension in society that will help men to rise from the dark depths of prejudice and racism to the majestic heights of understanding and brotherhood. So, the purpose of direct action is to create a situation so crisis-packed that it will inevitably open the door to negotiation. We therefore concur with you in your call for negotiation. Too long has our beloved Southland been bogged down in the tragic attempt to live in monologue rather than dialogue.

One of the basic points in your statement is that our acts are untimely. Some have asked, "Why didn't you give the new administration time to act?" The only answer that I can give to this inquiry is that the new administration must be prodded about as much as the outgoing one before it acts. We will be sadly mistaken if we feel that the election of Mr. Boutwell will bring the millennium to Birmingham. While Mr. Boutwell is much more articulate and gentle than Mr. Conner, they are both segregationists, dedicated to the task of maintaining the status quo. The hope I see in Mr. Boutwell is that he will be reasonable enough to see the futility of massive resistance to desegregation. But he will not see this without pressure from the devotees of civil rights. My friends, I must say to you that we have not made a single gain in civil rights without determined legal and nonviolent pressure. History is the long and tragic story of the fact that privileged groups seldom give up their privileges voluntarily. Individuals may see the moral light and voluntarily give up their unjust posture; but, as Reinhold Niebuhr has reminded us, groups are more immoral than individuals.

We know through painful experience that freedom is never voluntarily given by the oppressor; it must be demanded by the oppressed. Frankly, I have never yet engaged in a direct-action movement that was "well timed" according to the timetable of those who have not suffered unduly from the disease of segregation. For years now I have heard the word "wait." It rings in the ear of every Negro with a piercing familiarity. This "wait" has almost always meant "never." It has been a tranquilizing thalidomide, relieving the emotional stress for a moment, only to give birth to an ill-formed infant of frustration. We must come to see with the distinguished jurist of yesterday that "justice too long delayed is justice denied." We have waited for more than three hundred and forty years for our God-given and constitutional rights. The nations of Asia and Africa are moving with jetlike speed toward the goal of political independence, and we still creep at horse-and-buggy pace toward the gaining of a cup of coffee at a lunch counter. I guess it is easy for those who have never felt the stinging darts of segregation to say "wait." But when you have seen vicious mobs lynch your mothers and fathers at will and drown your sisters and brothers at whim; when you have seen hate-filled policemen curse, kick, brutalize, and even kill your black brothers and sisters with impunity; when you see the vast majority of your twenty million Negro brothers smothering in an airtight cage of poverty in the midst of an affluent society; when you suddenly find your tongue twisted and your speech stammering as you seek to explain to your six-year-old daughter why she cannot go to the public amusement park that has just been advertised on television, and see tears welling up in her little eyes when she is told that Funtown is closed to colored children, and see the depressing clouds of inferiority begin to form in her little mental sky, and see her begin to distort her little personality by unconsciously developing a bitterness toward white people; when you have to concoct an answer for a five-year-old son asking in agonizing pathos, "Daddy, why do white people treat colored people so mean?"; when you take a cross-country drive and find it necessary to sleep night after night in the uncomfortable corners of your automobile because no motel will accept you; when you are humiliated day in and day out by nagging signs reading "white" and "colored"; when your first name becomes "nigger" and your middle name becomes "boy" (however old you are) and your last name becomes "John," and when your wife and mother are never given the respected title "Mrs."; when you are harried by day and haunted by night by the fact that you are a Negro, living constantly at tiptoe stance, never knowing what to expect next, and plagued with inner fears and outer resentments; when you are forever fighting a degenerating sense of "nobodyness"—then you will understand why we find it difficult to wait. There comes a time when the cup of endurance runs over and men are no longer willing to be plunged into an abyss of injustice where they experience the bleakness of corroding despair. I hope, sirs, you can understand our legitimate and unavoidable impatience.

YOU express a great deal of anxiety over our willingness to break laws. This is certainly a legitimate concern. Since we so diligently urge people to obey the Supreme Court's decision of 1954 outlawing segregation in the public schools, it is rather strange and paradoxical to find us consciously breaking laws. One may well ask, "How can you advocate breaking some laws and obeying others?" The answer is found in the fact that there are two types of laws: there are just laws, and there are unjust laws. I would agree with St. Augustine that "An unjust law is no law at all."

Now, what is the difference between the two? How does one determine when a law is just or unjust? A just law is a man-made code that squares with the moral law, or the law of God. An unjust law is a code that is out of harmony with the moral law. To put it in the terms of St. Thomas Aquinas, an unjust law is a human law that is not rooted in eternal and natural law. Any law that uplifts human personality is just. Any law that degrades human personality is unjust. All segregation statutes are unjust because segregation distorts the soul and damages the personality. It gives the segregator a false sense of superiority and the segregated a false sense of inferiority. To use the words of Martin Buber, the great Jewish philosopher, segregation substitutes an "I—it" relationship for the "I—thou" relationship and ends up relegating persons to the status of things. So segregation is not only politically, economically, and sociologically unsound, but it is morally wrong and sinful. Paul Tillich has said that sin is separation. Isn't segregation an existential expression of man's tragic separation, an expression of his awful estrangement, his terrible sinfulness? So I can urge men to obey the 1954 decision of the Supreme Court because it is morally right, and I can urge them to disobey segregation ordinances because they are morally wrong.

Let us turn to a more concrete example of just and unjust laws. An unjust law is a code that a majority inflicts on a minority that is not binding on itself. This is difference made legal. On the other hand, a just law is a code that a majority compels a minority to follow, and that it is willing to follow itself. This is sameness made legal.

Let me give another explanation. An unjust law is a code inflicted upon a minority which that minority had no part in enacting or creating because it did not have the unhampered right to vote. Who can say that the legislature of Alabama which set up the segregation laws was democratically elected? Throughout the state of Alabama all types of conniving methods are used to prevent Negroes from becoming registered voters, and there are some counties without a single Negro registered to vote, despite the fact that the Negroes constitute a majority of the population. Can any law set up in such a state be considered democratically structured?

These are just a few examples of unjust and just laws. There are some instances when a law is just on its face and unjust in its application. For instance, I was arrested Friday on a charge of parading without a permit. Now, there is nothing wrong with an ordinance which requires a permit for a parade, but when the ordinance is used to preserve segregation and to deny citizens the First Amendment privilege of peaceful assembly and peaceful protest, then it becomes unjust.

Of course, there is nothing new about this kind of civil disobedience. It was seen sublimely in the refusal of Shadrach, Meshach, and Abednego to obey the laws of Nebuchadnezzar because a higher moral law was involved. It was practiced superbly by the early Christians, who were willing to face hungry lions and the excruciating pain of chopping blocks before submitting to certain unjust laws of the Roman Empire. To a degree, academic freedom is a reality today because Socrates practiced civil disobedience.

We can never forget that everything Hitler did in Germany was "legal" and everything the Hungarian freedom fighters did in Hungary was "illegal." It was "illegal" to aid and comfort a Jew in Hitler's Germany. But I am sure that if I had lived in Germany during that time, I would have aided and comforted my Jewish brothers even though it was illegal. If I lived in a Communist country today where certain principles dear to the Christian faith are suppressed, I believe I would openly advocate disobeying these anti-religious laws.

I MUST make two honest confessions to you, my Christian and Jewish brothers. First, I must confess that over the last few years I have been gravely disappointed with the white moderate. I have almost reached the regrettable conclusion that the Negro's great stumbling block in the stride toward freedom is not the White Citizens Councillor or the Ku Klux Klanner but the white moderate who is more devoted to order than to justice; who prefers a negative peace which is the absence of tension to a positive peace which is the presence of justice; who constantly says, "I agree with you in the goal you seek, but I can't agree with your methods of direct action"; who paternalistically feels that he can set the timetable for another man's freedom; who lives by the myth of time; and who constantly advises the Negro to wait until a "more convenient season." Shallow understanding from people of good will is more frustrating than absolute misunderstanding from people of ill will. Lukewarm acceptance is much more bewildering than outright rejection.

In your statement you asserted that our actions, even though peaceful, must be condemned because they precipitate violence. But can this assertion be logically made? Isn't this like condemning the robbed man because his possession of money precipitated the evil act of robbery? Isn't this like condemning Socrates because his unswerving commitment to truth and his philosophical delvings precipitated the misguided popular mind to make him drink the hemlock? Isn't this like condemning Jesus because His unique God-consciousness and never-ceasing devotion to His will precipitated the evil act of crucifixion? We must come to see, as federal courts have consistently affirmed, that it is immoral to urge an individual to withdraw his efforts to gain his basic constitutional rights because the quest precipitates violence. Society must protect the robbed and punish the robber.

I had also hoped that the white moderate would reject the myth of time. I received a letter this morning from a white brother in Texas which said, "All Christians know that the colored people will receive equal rights eventually, but is it possible that you are in too great of a religious hurry? It has taken Christianity almost 2000 years to accomplish what it has. The teachings of Christ take time to come to earth." All that is said here grows out of a tragic misconception of time. It is the strangely irrational notion that there is something in the very flow of time that will inevitably cure all ills. Actually, time is neutral. It can be used either destructively or constructively. I am coming to feel that the people of ill will have used time much more effectively than the people of good will. We will have to repent in this generation not merely for the vitriolic words and actions of the bad people but for the appalling silence of the good people. We must come to see that human progress never rolls in on wheels of inevitability. It comes through the tireless efforts and persistent work of men willing to be coworkers with God, and without this hard work time itself becomes an ally of the forces of social stagnation.

YOU spoke of our activity in Birmingham as extreme. At first I was rather disappointed that fellow clergymen would see my nonviolent efforts as those of an extremist. I started thinking about the fact that I stand in the middle of two opposing forces in the Negro community. One is a force of complacency made up of Negroes who, as a result of long years of oppression, have been so completely drained of self-respect and a sense of "somebodyness" that they have adjusted to segregation, and, on the other hand, of a few Negroes in the middle class who, because of a degree of academic and economic security and because at points they profit by segregation, have unconsciously become insensitive to the problems of the masses. The other force is one of bitterness and hatred and comes perilously close to advocating violence. It is expressed in the various black nationalist groups that are springing up over the nation, the largest and best known being Elijah Muhammad's Muslim movement. This movement is nourished by the contemporary frustration over the continued existence of racial discrimination. It is made up of people who have lost faith in America, who have absolutely repudiated Christianity, and who have concluded that the white man is an incurable devil. I have tried to stand between these two forces, saying that we need not follow the do-nothingism of the complacent or the hatred and despair of the black nationalist. There is a more excellent way, of love and nonviolent protest. I'm grateful to God that, through the Negro church, the dimension of nonviolence entered our struggle. If this philosophy had not emerged, I am convinced that by now many streets of the South would be flowing with floods of blood. And I am further convinced that if our white brothers dismiss as "rabble-rousers" and "outside agitators" those of us who are working through the channels of nonviolent direct action and refuse to support our nonviolent efforts, millions of Negroes, out of frustration and despair, will seek solace and security in black nationalist ideologies, a development that will lead inevitably to a frightening racial nightmare.

Oppressed people cannot remain oppressed forever. The urge for freedom will eventually come. This is what has happened to the American Negro. Something within has reminded him of his birthright of freedom; something without has reminded him that he can gain it. Consciously and unconsciously, he has been swept in by what the Germans call the *Zeitgeist*, and with his black brothers of Africa and his brown and yellow brothers of Asia, South America, and the Caribbean, he is moving with a sense of cosmic urgency toward the promised land of racial justice. Recognizing this vital urge that has engulfed the Negro community, one should readily understand public demonstrations. The Negro has many pent-up resentments and latent frustrations. He has to get them out. So let him march sometime; let him have his prayer pilgrimages to the city hall; understand why he must have sit-ins and freedom rides. If his repressed emotions do not come out in these nonviolent ways, they will come out in ominous expressions of violence. This is not a threat; it is a fact of history. So I have not said to my people, "Get rid of your discontent." But I have tried to say that this normal and healthy discontent can be channeled through the creative outlet of nonviolent direct action. Now this approach is being dismissed as extremist. I must admit that I was initially disappointed in being so categorized.

But as I continued to think about the matter, I gradually gained a bit of satisfaction from being considered an extremist. Was not Jesus an extremist in love?—"Love your enemies, bless them that curse you, pray for them that despitefully use you." Was not Amos an extremist for justice?—"Let justice roll down like waters and righteousness like a mighty stream." Was not Paul an extremist for the gospel of Jesus Christ?—"I bear in my body the marks of the Lord Jesus." Was not Martin Luther an extremist?—"Here I stand; I can do no other so help me God." Was not John Bunyan an extremist?—"I will stay in jail to the end of my days before I make a mockery of my conscience." Was not Abraham Lincoln an extremist?—"This nation cannot survive half slave and half free." Was not Thomas Jefferson an extremist?—"We hold these truths to be self-evident, that all men are created equal." So the question is not whether we will be extremist, but what kind of extremists we will be. Will we be extremists for hate, or will we be extremists for love? Will we be extremists for the preservation of injustice, or will we be extremists for the cause of justice?

I had hoped that the white moderate would see this. Maybe I was too optimistic. Maybe I expected too much. I guess I should have realized that few members of a race that has oppressed another race can understand or appreciate the deep groans and passionate yearnings of those that have been oppressed, and still fewer have the vision to see that injustice must be rooted out by strong, persistent, and determined action. I am thankful, however, that some of our white brothers have grasped the meaning of this social revolution and committed themselves to it. They are still all too small in quantity, but they are big in quality. Some, like Ralph McGill, Lillian Smith, Harry Golden, and James Dabbs, have written about our struggle in eloquent, prophetic, and understanding terms. Others have marched with us down nameless streets of the South. They sat in with us at lunch counters and rode in with us on the freedom rides. They have languished in fifty roach-infested jails, suffering the abuse and brutality of angry policemen who see them as "dirty nigger lovers." They, unlike many of their moderate brothers, have recognized the urgency of the moment and sensed the need for powerful "action" antidotes to combat the disease of segregation.

LET me rush on to mention my other disappointment. I have been disappointed with the white church and its leadership. Of course, there are some notable exceptions. I am not unmindful of the fact that each of you has taken some significant stands on this issue. I commend you, Reverend Stallings, for your Christian stand this past Sunday in welcoming Negroes to your Baptist Church worship service on a nonsegregated basis. I commend the Catholic leaders of this state for integrating Springhill College several years ago.

But despite these notable exceptions, I must honestly reiterate that I have been disappointed with the church. I do not say that as one of those negative critics who can always find something wrong with the church. I say it as a minister of the gospel who loves the church, who was nurtured in its bosom, who has been sustained by its Spiritual blessings, and who will remain true to it as long as the cord of life shall lengthen.

I had the strange feeling when I was suddenly catapulted into the leadership of the bus protest in Montgomery several years ago that we would have the support of the white church. I felt that the white ministers, priests, and rabbis of the South would be some of our strongest allies. Instead, some few have been outright opponents, refusing to understand the freedom movement and misrepresenting its leaders; all too many others have been more cautious than courageous and have remained silent behind the anesthetizing security of stained-glass windows.

In spite of my shattered dreams of the past, I came to Birmingham with the hope that the white religious leadership of this community would see the justice of our cause and with deep moral concern serve as the channel through which our just grievances could get to the power structure. I had hoped that each of you would understand. But again I have been disappointed.

I have heard numerous religious leaders of the South call upon their worshipers to comply with a desegregation decision because it is the law, but I have longed to hear white ministers say, follow this decree because integration is morally right and the Negro is your brother. In the midst of blatant injustices inflicted upon the Negro, I have watched white churches stand on the sidelines and merely mouth pious irrelevancies and sanctimonious trivialities. In the midst of a mighty struggle to rid our nation of racial and economic injustice, I have heard so many ministers say, "Those are social issues which the gospel has nothing to do with," and I have watched so many churches commit themselves to a completely otherworldly religion which made a strange distinction between bodies and souls, the sacred and the secular.

There was a time when the church was very powerful. It was during that period that the early Christians rejoiced when they were deemed worthy to suffer for what they believed. In those days the church was not merely a thermometer that recorded the ideas and principles of popular opinion; it was the thermostat that transformed the mores of society. Wherever the early Christians entered a town the power structure got disturbed and immediately sought to convict them for being "disturbers of the peace" and "outside agitators." But they went on with the conviction that they were "a colony of heaven" and had to obey God rather than man. They were small in number but big in commitment. They were too God-intoxicated to be "astronomically intimidated." They brought an end to such ancient evils as infanticide and gladiatorial contest.

Things are different now. The contemporary church is so often a weak, ineffectual voice with an uncertain sound. It is so often the arch supporter of the status quo. Far from being disturbed by the presence of the church, the power structure of the average community is consoled by the church's often vocal sanction of things as they are.

But the judgment of God is upon the church as never before. If the church of today does not recapture the sacrificial spirit of the early church, it will lose its authentic ring, forfeit the loyalty of millions, and be dismissed as an irrelevant social club with no meaning for the twentieth century. I meet young people every day whose disappointment with the church has risen to outright disgust.

I hope the church as a whole will meet the challenge of this decisive hour. But even if the church does not come to the aid of justice, I have no despair about the future. I have no fear about the outcome of our struggle in Birmingham, even if our motives are presently misunderstood. We will reach the goal of freedom in Birmingham and all over the nation, because the goal of America is freedom. Abused and scorned though we may be, our destiny is tied up with the destiny of America. Before the Pilgrims landed at Plymouth, we were here. Before the pen of Jefferson scratched across the pages of history the majestic word of the Declaration of Independence, we were here. For more than two centuries our foreparents labored here without wages; they made cotton king; and they built the homes of their masters in the midst of brutal injustice and shameful humiliation—and yet out of a bottomless vitality our people continue to thrive and develop. If the inexpressible cruelties of slavery could not stop us, the opposition we now face will surely fail. We will win our freedom because the sacred heritage of our nation and the eternal will of God are embodied in our echoing demands.

I must close now. But before closing I am impelled to mention one other point in your statement that troubled me profoundly. You warmly commended the Birmingham police force for keeping "order" and "preventing violence." I don't believe you would have so warmly commended the police force if you had seen its angry violent dogs literally biting six unarmed, nonviolent Negroes. I don't believe you would so quickly commend the policemen if you would observe their ugly and inhuman treatment of Negroes here in the city jail; if you would watch them push and curse old Negro women and young Negro girls; if you would see them slap and kick old Negro men and young boys, if you would observe them, as they did on two occasions, refusing to give us food because we wanted to sing our grace together. I'm sorry that I can't join you in your praise for the police department.

It is true that they have been rather disciplined in their public handling of the demonstrators. In this sense they have been publicly "nonviolent." But for what purpose? To preserve the evil system of segregation. Over the last few years I have consistently preached that nonviolence demands that the means we use must be as pure as the ends we seek. So I have tried to make it clear that it is wrong to use immoral means to attain moral ends. But now I must affirm that it is just as wrong, or even more, to use moral means to preserve immoral ends.

I wish you had commended the Negro demonstrators of Birmingham for their sublime courage, their willingness to suffer, and their amazing discipline in the midst of the most inhuman provocation. One day the South will recognize its real heroes. They will be the James Merediths, courageously and with a majestic sense of purpose facing jeering and hostile mobs and the agonizing loneliness that characterizes the life of the pioneer. They will be old, oppressed, battered Negro women, symbolized in a seventy-two-year-old woman of Montgomery, Alabama, who rose up with a sense of dignity and with her people decided not to ride the segregated buses, and responded to one who inquired about her tiredness with ungrammatical profundity, "My feets is tired, but my soul is rested." They will be young high school and college students, young ministers of the gospel and a host of their elders courageously and nonviolently sitting in at lunch counters and willingly going to jail for conscience's sake. One day the South will know that when these disinherited children of God sat down at lunch counters they were in reality standing up for the best in the American dream and the most sacred values in our Judeo-Christian heritage.

Never before have I written a letter this long—or should I say a book? I'm afraid that it is much too long to take your precious time. I can assure you that it would have been much shorter if I had been writing from a comfortable desk, but what else is there to do when you are alone for days in the dull monotony of a narrow jail cell other than write long letters, think strange thoughts, and pray long prayers?

If I have said anything in this letter that is an understatement of the truth and is indicative of an unreasonable impatience, I beg you to forgive me. If I have said anything in this letter that is an overstatement of the truth and is indicative of my having a patience that makes me patient with anything less than brotherhood, I beg God to forgive me.

Yours for the cause of Peace and Brotherhood,

MARTIN LUTHER KING, JR.

The South's History Rises, Again and Again

By KEVIN SACK

JACKSON, Miss.—Like an anthology of short stories threaded by a common theme, a confluence of events in Mississippi last week provided a poignant test of William Faulkner's wry observation that "the past is never dead; it's not even past."

Clearly that was more true in the mythic South of Faulkner's fiction than in the modern South that promotes itself so relentlessly as New. But as developments in Mississippi last week demonstrated, the region's noble ambitions are still weighed down by the transgressions of the past. Hard as it tries—and it tries more earnestly with each passing day—the South never quite pulls free of the most repellent aspects of its history.

The week began with a contentious forum held by the President's Advisory Board on Race at the University of Mississippi, an institution still coming to terms with the deadly riots of 1962 that greeted the enrollment of its first black student, James Meredith. Next came the unsealing of 124,000 pages of documents from the state's defunct Sovereignty Commission, a domestic spy agency disbanded in 1977 after waging an illegal, 21-year war on the civil rights movement.

And the week ended with an ugly confrontation in the state Capitol between legislators and Gov. Kirk Fordice over a voting rights bill that has generated yet another debate over states' rights and race.

Anguish and Anger

At the intersection of all three events there is reason to believe that many in this most Southern of states have concluded that they must address their past forthrightly to move forward. But in doing so they must inevitably confront anguish and anger—evoked by haunting images of Medgar Evers and other civil rights martyrs.

> Confronting the past is cathartic. But it also provokes resentment.

And they face a paradox: the fact that revisiting the past both stimulates catharsis and stokes resentment. Whether it ultimately speeds healing or retards it is hard to know.

"Medgar Evers and James Meredith both said that if we ever turn the corner on race, Mississippi will be the best place in the world to live," said David Sansing, a University of Mississippi historian, who turned to the metaphor of a traffic circle to explain the South's progress. "We have turned the corner, but it's not a 90-degree turn," he said. "It's like one of those things that I drove in England last summer,

a roundabout. Maybe we'll get off of it one day. But at least we're in motion, and that's more than you can say for much of the country."

That race relations in the South do not always advance in a straight line could be seen Tuesday morning at the Mississippi Department of Archives and History, where the Sovereignty Commission files were unsealed.

Ellie Dahmer, the widow of Vernon Dahmer, a leader for the National Association for the Advancement of Colored People in Hattiesburg whose 1966 firebombing death is being reinvestigated, was there with her two children, hoping to discover something in her late husband's file that would implicate a local Ku Klux Klan leader, Sam Bowers. "At last, Mississippi is willing to rebuild some of its past," said Mrs. Dahmer, clutching the agency's surveillance records on her husband.

But also on hand was Richard Barrett, a white lawyer from Jackson who defended the members of the Sovereignty Commission as patriots. He handed out fliers arguing that Mississippi's streets were safer and its schools were better when the commission was at work.

The commission, supported by tax dollars and housed in the Capitol, was, in the words of a longtime Mississippi journalist, Bill Minor, the "KGB of the cotton patches." As the civil rights movement was sustained by the Federal courts, Mississippi and several other Southern states institutionalized their resistance by creating such agencies to track the activities, associations, political affiliations and sexual proclivities of their citizens.

When the Mississippi Legislature shut the agency, it sealed the records—those that had not been destroyed—for 50 years. The American Civil Liberties Union and several other plaintiffs challenged the closing of the files, and succeeded in opening them 29 years early.

The records show that the commission used both physical and economic intimidation to fight its foes. A 1958 memorandum from a commission investigator, for example, noted approvingly that steps had been taken to silence a black preacher, W.B. Ridgeway of Hattiesburg, who had testified before a congressional committee about the curtailment of black voting rights.

"Economic pressure had been applied to members of his congregation in such a way that they got on Ridgeway pretty hard and effectively," wrote the investigator, Zack VanLandingham, "and since that time there has been nothing heard out of Ridgeway."

Few details were too inconsequential for the commission's records. The purchase of a new Singer sewing machine was noted in the file on Rita Schwerner, a civil rights worker whose husband, Michael, was later murdered. License plate numbers were collected and traced. Marital spats were detailed.

States' Rights Redux

Against that legacy, it was hard to miss the irony unfolding in the Capitol, where lawmakers argued last week with Fordice, a Republi-

can, over his insistence that voters show identification at the polls.

Last month, Fordice vetoed a bill that would have made Mississippi the final state to adhere to the National Voter Registration Act of 1993, which requires states to make registration forms available in drivers' license bureaus, social service agencies and other state offices. Fordice has said the "motor voter" law should be renamed the "welfare voter" law, and has charged that it is an unconstitutional imposition on his state's rights.

Under pressure from the Justice Department, however, he has said he would sign a bill that included a mandatory voter identification provision to deter fraud. The Legislature has rejected that proposal, specifically because of objections from black Mississippians who harbor fresh memories of the obstacles erected by the state to keep them from voting in the past.

State Sen. John Horhn, a black Democrat from Jackson, said black Mississippians were very suspicious of the voter identification requirement, given that the state once had an agency charged with the surveillance of its citizens and the abridgment of their rights. "It's something that we are very wary of and that we don't trust," he said.

Fordice charged last week that many of the legislators opposing his proposal "are here because of voter fraud." Horhn responded by saying that the governor "has repeatedly shown himself to be a callous, unthinking dolt."

Monday and Tuesday in Oxford, members of the President's Advisory Board on Race gathered at the University of Mississippi for a forum dedicated to gauging the community's progress on race. Again,

the old South and the new one clashed.

A black student and a white student from Oxford High School declared their friendship with a heartfelt hug, but also pointed out that black and white students segregated themselves at lunch. Black speakers complained about the lack of a black doctor in town, adding that a nonwhite physician would have trouble attracting white patients. When a white man in the audience stood to proclaim that it was his "freedom" to wave the Confederate flag at Ole Miss football games, a white student responded by saying that most students would appreciate it if he did not.

Former Gov. William Winter, a member of the advisory panel, and John Hope Franklin, the historian who serves as its chairman, both commented on the progress reflected in the simple fact that such a discussion was being held at Ole Miss, a place with such a history of racial strife. The university's chancellor, Robert Khayat, who has tried to tone down Confederate symbolism at the school, said events in the South "move forward and backward, seldom in a straight line."

Such acknowledgements of the region's complexities are becoming more common across the South, as are apologies for past behavior. Last fall, at a 40th anniversary commemoration of the desegregation of Little Rock Central High School, Arkansas' Republican governor, Mike Huckabee, said the violent white resistance to school's integration "may be forgivable, but it is not excusable."

"In the Proverbs," added Huckabee, formerly a Baptist preacher, "it says that he who conceals his sins does not prosper. But whoever professes and renounces them will find mercy."

BLACK WOMEN ACTIVISTS AND THE STUDENT NONVIOLENT COORDINATING COMMITTEE:

The Case of Ruby Doris Smith Robinson

Cynthia Griggs Fleming

Since their earliest days in American society, many people of African descent have worked to combat the racism and oppression confronting them. Some of these activists were women, and a select few of them even became famous. Names like Sojourner Truth and Harriet Tubman are familiar to most Americans. Yet, those few African-American female freedom fighters who have been elevated to legendary status have often been forced to confront a very personal issue in the midst of their efforts to free their people: the issue of redefining their womanhood. Against the backdrop of the peculiar status of African-American women in U.S. society, black female activist efforts have routinely been tied to a negative assessment of black womanhood.

This is a consequence of negative notions of African-American women that are firmly anchored in the nineteenth century and slavery. In fact, slaveholders defined African-American womanhood in their own best interests, shift-

From the *Journal of Women's History,* Winter 1993, pp. 64-82. © 1993 by Indiana University Press. Reprinted by permission.

ing their treatment of female slaves to meet their needs:

> Where work was concerned, strength and productivity under the threat of the whip outweighed considerations of sex. In this sense, the oppression of women was identical to the oppression of men.
>
> But women suffered in different ways as well, for they were victims of sexual abuse and other barbarous mistreatment that could only be inflicted on women.[1]

In short, "when it was profitable to exploit them [slave women] as if they were men, they were regarded, in effect, as genderless, but when they could be exploited, punished and repressed in ways suited only for women, they were locked into their exclusively female roles."[2]

At the same time, critical nineteenth-century political and economic changes began to have a profound impact on definitions of white womanhood. It was at this time that sharply differentiated gender roles emerged. Many middle-class nineteenth-century white Americans became convinced that men and women were so different that their duties, obligations, and responsibilities actually constituted "separate spheres."[3] In this context expectations of proper female behavior came to be defined by women's domestic duties. "Women's activities were increasingly limited to the care of children, the nurturing of [the] husband, and the physical maintenance of the home."[4]

Negative views of African-American womanhood combined with restrictive notions of white womanhood and persisted until well into the twentieth century. Both black and white women were affected by them—but in very different ways. Many white women were intent on questioning and testing the old established limits. At the same time, this white female restlessness contrasted sharply with black female aspirations. As black economic expectations rose during the post-World War II period, many African-American women would have been only too happy to stay home and cultivate a separate female sphere for a change.[5] Yet, at this time financial realities continued to push large numbers of African-American women out of the home and into the job market. In such an atmosphere questions about black womanhood and white womanhood persisted. It was a confusing and unsettling time.

In this volatile and fluid atmosphere one modern African-American female activist who sought to define her womanhood as she gained power within the Student Nonviolent Coordinating Committee (SNCC) was Ruby Doris Smith Robinson. Robinson began her activist career in the Atlanta Student Movement. She was a freshman at Spelman College in Atlanta when the sit-ins first started. Early on, though, Robinson began to look beyond Atlanta and concentrate her efforts on the national arena and SNCC. Over two decades after Robinson's most active period, many of her movement colleagues still have vivid memories of her. Friends and associates were able to recall with remarkable clarity a wealth of detail about Robinson's activist career and her personal life. Consequently, I conducted interviews with a number of those who were close to her, including family members, childhood friends, Atlanta University Center associates, and SNCC comrades.

Regardless of the circumstances of their relationship with Robinson, most associates identified her as a powerful woman. In many instances this identification resulted in curious perceptions of the importance of Robinson's gender in relation to her power. For example, co-worker Courtland Cox insisted that people in SNCC "didn't view her as a man or a woman, they viewed her as a strength."[6] SNCC organizer Mukasa (Willie Ricks) insisted that gender was not an issue since "her personality was so strong . . . didn't nothing else matter."[7] One of her earlier acquaintances, Reverend Albert Brinson, had a chance to observe Ruby when she was a Spelman College student just beginning her movement work. Brinson remembered that a typical Spelman student was "always taught to be a lady. A lady stood back and waited to be waited upon by a man." Robinson did not fit in this atmosphere, though, since "she was not the lady-like kind. . . . She was rather aggressive."[8]

The existence of such perceptions of Robinson raises crucial questions. How did she see this issue of gender in view of her growing power within the Student Nonviolent Coordinating Committee? Also, what influences in Robinson's early life shaped the balance that she would eventually strike between her activism and her gender identity? Indeed, an examination of her upbringing reveals intriguing glimpses of the influences that provoked her activism and shaped her views of proper gender roles.

Ruby Doris Smith was born in Atlanta, Georgia, on April 25, 1942, the second oldest of seven children. She was raised in the city's black Summerhill neighborhood. The family home at 794 Fraser Street was a large frame structure that had both a store and a beauty shop attached to it. Ruby Smith's mother, Alice Smith, supplemented the family income by operating the beauty shop, while her father, J. T. Smith, operated the store and engaged in a variety of other occupations. Smith drove a cab, owned a used furniture store, tried his hand at the moving business, and operated a restaurant. Later, when Ruby Smith was in high school, her father became a Baptist minister. He eventually founded his own church.[9] Even though the family did not have a lot of money, J. T. and Alice Smith were able to provide a comfortable living for their children. Just as important as the income they provided was the example they set: the source of their income was dependent on black patronage rather than white support.

As Robinson grew to maturity she became involved in a variety of social activities. In 1958, with the enthusiastic blessing of her family, she became a debutante, just as her older sister, Mary Ann, had done a year earlier. The Smith sisters' formal introduction to African-American social life clearly indicates the family's and their daughters' acceptance of African-American middle-class standards for proper female behavior. Other actions and attitudes that characterized Robinson's formative years also suggest that she accepted the 1950s notions of proper African-American middle-class female behavior. For example, she was head majorette with the Price High School marching band. She was very concerned about her appearance and particularly liked expensive clothes that would flatter her figure.

Ruby Smith and her sisters and brothers enjoyed a secure existence in their separate black world as they grew to maturity. They had strong adult support, and they had their own churches, schools, and social activities. Also, within the confines of the middle-class value system that governed their lives, the Smith children comfortably embraced the gender roles that were a part of that value system. No matter how insulated and comfortable they were, though, the reality of racism and segregation in the United States managed to intrude from time to time. Moreover, the injurious effects of segregation were equally traumatic for males and females. In the segregated South of the 1950s gender counted for much less than race.

African-American youngsters of this generation reacted in a variety of ways to the ugly reality of segregation. Ruby Smith's older sister Mary Ann (Wilson) remembered that she was aware of segregation, but "everything was so separated you just didn't think about it."[10] Despite this perception, confrontation was inevitable. Wilson sharply recalled the pain resulting from one of those confrontations. One day she boarded a bus on her way home from school. Since the bus on this route was usually filled with African-American passengers, most of them generally sat wherever they chose. Consequently, without even thinking, Wilson sat down right behind the driver. But there was a white woman sitting behind her, and when Wilson realized this, she jumped up and moved behind this woman. At that moment Wilson knew something was terribly wrong.[11]

When young Ruby Doris Smith encountered segregation she reacted to it quite strongly. Her younger sister Catherine witnessed one encounter that occurred in a drugstore located at the corner of Capitol and Georgia Avenue. The Smith children often bought ice cream from this drugstore. Catherine Robinson recalled that store clerks generally seemed reluctant to serve black customers. That reluctance was particularly apparent one day when the Smith sisters ordered an ice cream cone. "So, they pulled the cone down. . . . [Ruby] waited till they fixed it and got ready for her to pay. . . . She said, 'Oh, you can keep that one, I won't be eating that one.' " The baffled and annoyed clerk could not understand Ruby's behavior. She angrily insisted, " 'You ordered this.' " "An equally angry Ruby explained, " 'But you're not going to put your hands on my cone.' She knew that when whites came in, they used a tissue to pull the cone down; and when blacks came in, they would use their hands."[12] This was not the only time she confronted the reality of racism during her early years. Robinson recalled, "I was conscious of my blackness. Every young Negro growing up in the South has thoughts about the racial situation."[13] She also remembered her reaction to the white people with whom she came in contact when she was a youngster. "I didn't recognize their existence and they didn't recognize mine. . . . My only involvement was in throwing rocks at them."[14]

As Ruby Doris Smith Robinson passed through adolescence during the 1950s, she was keenly aware of the broader issues of racial injustice. She saw others suffer the same indignities that confronted her. Yet, she also saw the signs of change: the Montgomery Bus Boycott, the Brown Decision, and the integration of Little Rock's Central High School were powerful symbols for this generation. At the same time, the African-American teachers at Price High School where Robinson was a student routinely discussed issues of race with their students. They encouraged these youngsters to think critically and to consider possibilities for change.

This heightened consciousness regarding segregation that characterized the 1950s occurred amidst the growing interest in reassessing gender roles in the modern U.S. This juxtaposition of race and gender issues served to focus particular attention on African-American women. Consequently, the efforts of white journalists, scholars, and physicians to examine the female role generally were complemented by a special interest in black women's roles by various members of the African-American community. Studies produced by scholars along with articles in the African-American press during this era contained mixed signals about black female prospects and accomplishments.

An article in the popular black press entitled "What's Wrong With Negro Women?" provides a graphic example of the negative assessment accepted by some. The author of that article, Roi Ottley, criticized African-American women in practically every area of life. He declared that African-American women were not interested in furthering their education, and that they were culturally backward as well. He went on to insist that they were shallow dilettantes who were primarily interested in embracing the vulgar trappings of middle-class life. Above all, these women were not fulfilling one of their most important responsibilities, Ottley charged: *"Too few Negro women contribute to the race fight* [emphasis added]. Beyond one or two national organizations and sororities, they do not even organize for their own rights as women. . . ."[15]

While the Ottley article is extremely critical, it is also quite revealing. It clearly suggests that the proper role for the modern African-American woman should include civil rights activism and an emphasis on educational achievement. A more thoughtful and sympathetic view is provided by author Lerone Bennett in a 1960 edition of *Ebony* magazine. In an article entitled "The Negro Woman," Bennett asserted that most people accepted the notion that the African-American woman's role was one of domination. This history of domination resulted in a healthy sense of independence. Yet, it was that very independence that created a dilemma for African-American women. "Independence, as many white women have recently discovered, is not an unmixed blessing. . . . One result of the traditional independence of the Negro woman is that she is more in conflict with her innate biological role than the white woman."[16]

Thus, by the 1950s some members of the African-American community began to express concern about the issue of black women's roles. In many instances African-American sentiment tended to favor a far more inclusive role than the restrictive and traditional view that tied women's roles more firmly to the home. But, there was still a lot of uncertainty. It was during this volatile period that Ruby Doris Smith began her college career; she entered Spelman College as a freshman in the fall of 1959.

Even though there was a strain of conservatism at many black colleges and universities—including the Atlanta University Center schools[17]—this conservatism existed in the midst of an atmosphere that encouraged students to question the South's racial etiquette. Some faculty and administrators in Atlanta University Center schools regularly reminded students that they must play a role in their own liberation. Others, however, were not nearly as supportive as Howard Zinn, a Spelman history professor who noted that:

> The new Spelman girl is having an effect on faculty and administrators. Many who were distressed and critical when they first learned their sweet young things were sitting behind bars, later joined in the applause of the Negro community and the nation at large.[18]

While Spelman worked hard to provide a nurturing and supportive atmosphere that encouraged students to think critically and act assertively, it also provided training in etiquette that rivaled any charm school. Throughout the 1950s many of the college's faculty members and administrators clearly remained committed to training proper "ladies" for the black middle class. Thus, the Spelman College that shaped the young Ruby Doris Smith Robinson accepted expanded limits for African-American women's roles, but also expected traditional behavior. In short, young African-American women of this generation were told that they could and should do it all.

In this hospitable atmosphere Robinson, like many other young black people of her generation, became convinced that change was possible.[19] Furthermore, many saw themselves as the agents of that change. Then Greensboro happened. The start of sit-ins there galvanized black college students all over the South. Robinson immediately considered the prospect of sit-ins in Atlanta, but was not prepared to take the initiative. When the Atlanta University Center students formed the Atlanta Committee on Appeal for Human Rights, though, she enthusiastically joined. The group quickly staged its first demonstration at the state capitol, and Robinson was with them. She described the events:

> I went through the food line in the restaurant at the State Capitol with six other students, but when we got to the cashier, she wouldn't take our money. She ran upstairs to get the Governor. The Lieutenant-Governor came down and told us to leave. We didn't, and went to the county jail.[20]

This was only the beginning of Robinson's activist career. She became heavily involved in the

Atlanta student movement. While she did not assume a leadership role, she did gain a reputation for bravery and assertiveness. Atlanta Student Movement colleague Julian Bond witnessed one of the incidents that added to her reputation. Bond recalled that on one occasion a group of Atlanta students decided to desegregate Grady Hospital—a large, public hospital. Although Grady admitted African-American patients, it had segregated entrances. When black Atlanta students went in the hospital's white entrance the receptionist just inside the door immediately told them they could not enter on that side; "and besides," she insisted, "you're not sick anyway."[21] As the students stood in the entrance trying to decide how to proceed, Robinson boldly walked up to the receptionist's desk, looked her in the eye, bent over and vomited all over the desk, straightened up and demanded to know, "Is that sick enough for you?"[22]

While Robinson continued to work with the Atlanta Student Movement, she became involved on the national scene as early as February of 1961. At that time the new Student Nonviolent Coordinating Committee decided to initiate a "jail no bail" policy. The arrest of a group of Friendship College students, who were jailed for protesting in Rock Hill, South Carolina, provided the occasion for the initiation of this new policy. Throughout the fall of 1960 members of SNCC had debated the wisdom of pursuing this strategy. Most recognized that the increasing number of students jailed for protesting activities was beginning to strain the financial resources of the black community to the limit. In many instances members of these communities—even those in difficult financial circumstances—were generous contributors to bail funds. It was not uncommon for property owners to pledge their houses in an effort to raise bail money. By late 1960 some in SNCC expressed alarm that the depletion of community resources might begin to strangle the life out of the movement.

On the other hand, if protestors insisted on serving their full sentences, this could put pressure on the white community that might hasten movement victories. As white southerners were faced with the logistical and financial nightmare of housing and feeding increasing numbers of demonstrators serving jail time, many reasoned, white tax payers would become much more willing to accede to movement demands. Once SNCC voted to pursue the jail no bail strategy, the organization immediately dispatched a delegation to Rock Hill. They were directed to demonstrate and refuse bail once they were arrested. When the delegation was chosen, Robinson was not among them, but her older sister Mary Ann was. Mary

Ann Wilson vividly recalled that when she went home to pack, she began to have second thoughts. At the same time, Robinson began to express an interest in going. "So what happened eventually is Ruby Doris talked it up, and I just bowed out and let her go."[23] After Robinson and the other students were arrested in Rock Hill, they spent thirty days in the York County, South Carolina, jail. Upon completion of her sentence, Robinson returned to Atlanta on March 18, 1961. At that time the *Atlanta Inquirer* reported that she was "ready, if necessary, to do it again."[24]

Ruby Doris Robinson soon got her chance to do it again. By May of 1961 she decided to join the Freedom Rides. After being menaced by white mobs, she and the other riders were arrested and jailed. She eventually served a sixty-day jail sentence in Mississippi. Shortly after her scheduled release on August 11, 1961, Robinson decided to work with some of her SNCC colleagues involved in voter registration in McComb, Mississippi.[25] She was always willing to volunteer for the most hazardous movement duty. Furthermore, in such circumstances colleagues could depend on Robinson to be bold and daring.

Because of her attitude and her actions, Ruby Doris Smith Robinson soon became a legend—even among the bold and brave young people of SNCC. Most people in the early days of SNCC could recount at least one Ruby Doris Robinson story. For example, Julian Bond remembered that when a delegation of SNCC staff was preparing to board a plane for Africa in the fall of 1964, an airline representative told them that the plane was full even though they had tickets. He wanted to know if they would wait and take a later flight. This angered Robinson so much that, without consulting the rest of the group, she went and sat down in the jetway and refused to move. They were given seats on that flight.[26]

James Bond, who worked in the SNCC print shop, witnessed another incident. The incident occurred when a group of SNCC staff, including Robinson, went to the airport to meet some of the organization's celebrity supporters. The first plane the group met had Marlon Brando and Tony Franciosa on it. The group then went to a different gate to meet a second plane:

> And as we stood out at the gate waiting—and the first person to come off the plane was Governor [George] Wallace. And Ruby Doris went up to him and said "How are you Governor," and introduced herself and said, "I've spent some time in your jails." And he said, "Well, I hope they treated you well, and if you're ever back, look me up."[27]

She never did.

While Robinson's assertiveness, brashness, and courage were important, they were not unique. Rather, her actions and her attitude fit comfortably in a context of boldness displayed by many African-American women over time. A number of cases illustrating this attitude exist within the civil rights movement. Consider the example of Annie Pearl Avery. During the course of a demonstration in Montgomery, Alabama, Avery came face-to-face with a white policeman who had a billy club aimed straight at her head. He had already beaten several others. Avery "reached up, grabbed the club and said, 'Now what you going to do, mother——?' " The policeman was awed. Avery slipped back into the crowd of demonstrators.[28] Cynthia Washington, on the other hand, became a SNCC project director in a rural Alabama County where there had previously not been any civil rights workers. Because she was convinced that a car would make her too conspicuous a target for racist authorities, Washington ditched the car and organized the county from the back of a mule.[29]

Even though the behavior of African-American women activists like these did not always fit contemporary notions of proper female behavior, they still fit comfortably into that established tradition of African-American female assertiveness that came straight out of slavery. Yet, what was considered acceptable and normal in the black community was not necessarily acceptable to white American society. Consequently, African-American women whose actions were applauded by other African Americans received the message from the larger American society that those actions were somehow unladylike. Furthermore, regardless of how they acted, their race had always consigned black women to a category other than female. For over three centuries they had been treated differently from white women in a society that eagerly embraced a white female standard of beauty and propriety.

In view of such differential treatment, gender roles and black and white female perspectives on issues of oppression were necessarily quite different. As young white women of the sixties generation explored the gender limitations imposed by their society, they collided with African-American women who came out of a black tradition that had a less restricted vision. Cynthia Washington clearly recalled how different their perspectives were. In the fall of 1964 Washington's white co-worker Casey Hayden complained that women were being limited to office work. An exasperated Washington simply could not understand Hayden's complaint:

What she said didn't make any particular sense to me because, at the time, I had my own project in Bolivar County, Mississippi. A number of other black women also directed their own projects. What Casey and other white women seemed to want was an opportunity to prove they could do something other than office work. I assumed that if they could do something else, they'd probably be doing that.[30]

Washington recognized how hard the work of a project director was, and besides, "it wasn't much fun." Because of her insider's view she was at a loss to understand why white women were complaining about their assignments. In fact, their discontent over such issues only convinced Washington "how crazy they [white women] were."[31]

While white women's perspectives were very difficult for African-American women to understand, white society's disrespect for their womanhood was almost too painful to bear. One African-American female civil rights worker frankly expressed that pain:

We've been getting beaten up for years trying to integrate lunch counters, movies, and so on, and nobody has ever paid us no attention or wrote about us. But these white girls come down here for a few months and get all the publicity. Everybody talks about how brave and courageous *they* are. What about us?[32]

Another black female civil rights worker was both angered and amazed by the treatment she received. When she was with a group demonstrating at a bus station "a cop grabbed me by the arm and slapped my face. I don't know why I was surprised, but I really was." She decided to remind him of a basic tenet of southern etiquette. "I looked at him and I say, 'Listen Man, take another look at me. I'm a woman! You don't hit a woman! Didn't they teach you that?' He looked kinda sorry, but he say, 'You're a niggah and that's all you are!' "[33]

Such a pervasive and negative view was bound to wound black women's views of their own womanhood. As a blunt, outspoken, black, female activist Ruby Doris Smith Robinson was clearly the victim of such negative views. There is an additional factor in Robinson's case, however, that further reinforced negative views of her womanhood. That additional factor was her appearance. Robinson grew to maturity in a society that, from its earliest days, had judged African women by a European standard of beauty. Many women of African descent had only to look in the mirror to see that they could never measure up physically. But many tried, and it was often quite painful.

Zohara Simmons, one of Robinson's SNCC colleagues and a fellow Spelman student, was keenly aware of the European standard of beauty that was idealized by so many. That awareness was born of Simmons's painful experience on the Spelman campus. Spelman was famous for the beauty of its student body, which, translated, meant that a fairly high proportion of the students had light skin, keen features, and straight or nearly straight hair. Because Simmons was dark skinned, she experienced a great deal of pain. But, it was often caused less by white reaction than by black rejection. She insisted, "Some of the Morehouse guys were so nasty to a person who looked like myself. OVERT. I mean, straight up. . . ."[34] Appearance was important, but African-American women were powerless to change their appearance, at least permanently. Feelings of insecurity about their looks could and did lead to the application of desperate measures: "Cosmetic preparations for lightening skin and straightening hair represent a multi-million dollar market among Negroes not favored with Caucasoid features." In fact, according to some, the African-American female concern about appearance led many women to pursue an "unending search for some approximation of the white ideal."[35] It was a terrible burden to carry around.

Ruby Doris Robinson had to carry her share of this black woman's burden. She was not particularly light skinned, she had broad features, and her hair was not naturally straight. Like so many African-American women of her generation she wrestled with negative views of who and what she was that were popularized by white society, but then embraced, at least in part, by African-American society. Evidence of black acceptance of such negative assessments was abundant and pervasive. In fact, the African-American author of one popular magazine article noted that such black acceptance had a profound impact:

Negro women, according to the consensus of male opinion, have some sort of inferiority complex where white women are concerned. . . . Unwittingly, much of this feeling, if it exists is inspired by men themselves—at least, as far as I can see. Too many Negro men have loudly sang [sic] the praises of white women they have known.[36]

Such pervasive negative notions of black female character, combined with Robinson's assertive activist demeanor in the field, helped shape perceptions of her by movement colleagues in the early years. By late 1962, however, Robinson became much less active in the field. At that point she became a permanent fixture in SNCC's central office in Atlanta. In this setting colleagues continued to recognize her assertiveness; and she soon gained a reputation as an uncompromising administrator. She eventually became the only female Executive Secretary the organization ever had. Co-workers agreed that Robinson was an exceptionally talented administrator. "She had great facility with words. She had such quick ability to think and conceptualize."[37] Through it all, Robinson was tough. She demanded hard work and dedication from all of those around her. She would not allow anyone to shirk his or her responsibilities. Jack Minnis, a member of SNCC's research staff, insisted that people were never able to fool Ruby because she had a "100 percent effective shit detector."[38]

As SNCC's membership enlarged and its character changed over time, it became increasingly difficult to administer. But Robinson tried. She made hard decisions, and she eventually had a great deal of influence in SNCC. She used whatever tactics were necessary to keep people on the job so that the organization could continue to function. Robinson would threaten, cajole, insist, and demand. Such administrative tactics provoked a wide range of reactions from movement colleagues. Mukasa described some of those reactions. "She's nice, she was kind, she was in charge, she was hateful. She was mean, and at different points you would hate her. You dislike her, you disagreed with her, and you agreed with her, and you liked her, and you loved her."[39]

Robinson's reputation as a tough female administrator constituted an important challenge to general notions of woman's place in the 1960s in the U.S. At the same time, even in the context of more broadly defined women's roles in the African-American community, Robinson's position as a leader in a male-dominated organization still made her an anomaly. Of course, SNCC was more egalitarian in many respects than the other civil rights groups: the organization had a number of black female field secretaries, project directors, and local leaders. Yet, even in SNCC, there was a great deal of "male posturing" in the early 1960s, and "overt sexism" by the end of the decade when Black Power became popular.[40] Regardless of her gender, though, SNCC colleagues insist that Robinson was respected by her co-workers—both male and female. In an effort to keep that respect, some suspected that she carefully and consciously emphasized the assertive, blunt, and independent part of her nature.

On the other hand, some in SNCC looked beyond her leadership and observed another side of Ruby Doris Smith Robinson. Kwame Ture [Stokely Carmichael], for example, remembered, "I found Ruby Doris to be a real pretty sister with a pleasant smile. . . . If she wasn't my sister, you know, I'd say she had a fine body."[41] SNCC co-worker Mildred Forman recalled the tender and domestic side of Ruby that was especially evident after the birth of her son.

> That was, I think, one of the best moments of her life. She was ecstatic over the baby and the husband; and she was a good mother. And she was always mothering that baby ... she just beamed and glowed with the baby.[42]

Ruby only knew Clifford Robinson a few months before she married him in 1963. In fact their courtship was so brief and so private that the two were married before many of Robinson's SNCC colleagues even realized they were seriously involved. SNCC co-worker Stanley Wise clearly recalled his surprise. "I mean I never saw them stand together, I never saw them hold hands, I mean I didn't even know they were married until I went to their house and saw that's who Cliff was."[43] SNCC staffer Bobbi Yancey recalled that secretive romances were not that uncommon among the organization's members. Furthermore, Yancey reasoned, Robinson may have been concerned about how marriage might affect her colleagues' perceptions of her. After all, the tough, blunt, and uncompromising image Ruby projected as a leader was incompatible with the qualities many Americans in the 1960s thought a good wife should possess. Yancey concluded, "She [Ruby] may have felt that it was going against her image to have this person on the side."[44]

Many were particularly surprised that Robinson's new husband was an outsider. Clifford Robinson did not remain an outsider very long, however. He soon joined the SNCC staff as a mechanic and worked on the cars in the Sojourner Motor Fleet. Even though he joined the organization, he was less committed to the movement than he was to his new wife. Many SNCC colleagues agree that he joined SNCC because he loved Ruby Smith and she was committed to the movement. Essentially, when Clifford Robinson married twenty-one-year-old Ruby Doris Smith, he also married the Student Nonviolent Coordinating Committee. By this time she had been working in SNCC for over three years and a large part of her identity was inextricably bound up in the organization. Movement coworker Reginald Robinson remembered the way in which many of Robinson's colleagues viewed her husband. In Reginald Robinson's estimation, "he was not involved—he was Ruby's husband."[45] In fact, Clifford Robinson freely admitted that if he and Ruby Smith had not been married he never would have joined SNCC. Mukasa succinctly described the newlyweds' relationship to SNCC. "Cliff was the

husband, but Ruby Doris was the boss [in the organization]."[46] Regardless of the extent of his involvement, Clifford Robinson had to cope with an uncommon situation. He was married to one of the most powerful women in a major civil rights organization, and that meant that he and his new wife faced a number of difficult issues. Strains were inevitable.

One of the most important issues the Robinsons had to resolve was the question of establishing a balance of power in their relationship. Obviously, Ruby Robinson exercised a fair amount of power in SNCC. But what about her power within the marriage? Some insist that she dominated the relationship. SNCC colleague Dorie Ladner agreed. She remarked, "He seemed to have been in awe of her, and under her spell."[47] Ladner continued:

> I was a little surprised that she got married as early as she did. I always [pictured] her staying single much longer and uh, being more or less the woman who was in charge and ... see the other side of it was that she wanted a family ... but her husband was also very supportive of her. And I saw him as being weaker than she.... And he looked up to her.... When I met Cliff and saw his bearing, I knew that she was in control.[48]

Others in the organization viewed the marriage very differently. Ruby Robinson's friend and colleague Freddie Biddle insisted that Ruby "had this husband who wanted to really dominate her."[49] According to Biddle, "she [Ruby] was definitely sensitive to what he liked and what he didn't like. But yet she tried as much as possible not to, not to be dominated by that whole process."[50] In all likelihood both descriptions of the Robinsons' relationship are accurate. As newlyweds they were undoubtedly testing limits and trying to establish a balance of power in their relationship. The fact of their unique position as a husband/powerful wife team in SNCC made the establishment of that balance a difficult proposition, indeed.

Regardless of how hard the Robinsons worked to keep their relationship in balance, evidence of strain soon became apparent. Movement colleague Emma Bell Moses clearly recalled witnessing incidents that indicated strains. Zohara Simmons also remembered seeing evidence of strains. She described a particularly illustrative incident:

> I can remember ..., you run in the office and he's [Clifford] standing there waiting on her to go. And ..., everybody's saying, "Ruby Doris, so and so and so." And he's saying. "Look, we got to go." And she's saying, "Cliff, wait a minute ... I got to take care of this." And him stalking off

mad. And she saying, "Oh God . . . later for him, then." I imagine she caught hell when she got home.[51]

Thus, even though her marriage was important, there were times when Ruby Robinson refused to let anything—including marriage—interfere with her SNCC duties.

Clifford Robinson freely acknowledged how consumed Ruby Robinson was by her work in SNCC. It seemed that she never had any free time. Rather, according to Clifford, "it [SNCC work] was going on all the time around the house."[52] In the midst of her responsibilities, however, there were instances when she made extraordinary efforts to plan activities with her SNCC friends that her husband enjoyed. Freddie Biddle clearly recalled that Ruby Robinson would often invite some of the people from the office to their house to play cards. She knew that Clifford enjoyed this and he would participate.

It is clear that there was more than one side to Ruby Doris Smith Robinson. Yet, those characteristics Robinson possessed that were most compatible with popular notions of proper female behavior were often submerged in the intensity of her work. Often, but not always. It would be misleading to try and fit Robinson's life into rigid categories. On the contrary, even in the office there were times when she displayed behavior that some might have considered contradictory to her tough leader image. Co-worker Dion Diamond had vivid recollections of such behavior:

Ruby used her femininity. . . . Ruby was aware that aside from all of these macho men that they were in many respects chauvinist . . . and I think she was aware that her being female that there was something that she could utilize in terms of that chauvinism—she could manipulate the chauvinism."[53]

It seemed, then, that Robinson did not mind engaging in a little light-hearted bantering and mild flirtation of her own. Nevertheless, all agreed that she drew a line: she did not simper, she was not coquettish or coy.

Hence, given her personal characteristics, Robinson was quite comfortable in an assertive and commanding role, and she was equally comfortable with the other side of her personality. Even if people around her saw a contradiction between the various parts of Ruby Doris Smith Robinson, she did not. At the same time, it seemed that she was annoyed by people who attempted to categorize her based on their own limited notions of proper female behavior. Matthew Jones, one of the SNCC Freedom Singers, talked about his perceptions and Robinson's reactions: "Ruby Doris wasn't the kind of woman that you'd say. . . can I talk to her. You never thought that way." She found such perceptions exasperating, Jones remembered, since she really wanted to be treated like a "regular human being."[54]

Robinson's unconventional actions and demeanor were accompanied by attitudes that were a bit surprising and definitely unpredictable. For, despite her strength, her vision, and the reality of her life, Ruby Doris Robinson still embraced some very traditional attitudes about gender roles; and she was not alone. A chorus of strong black female voices echoed similar sentiments. For example, SNCC staffer Jennifer Lawson observed, "Often women might prefer *not* to lead, but there's a responsibility to black people at this time that must be met, and it overshadows this business of being a man or a woman."[55] Carolyn Rivers, a New Yorker working in the Alabama Black Belt, had no doubt that "if Negro men were able to assert themselves fully, they'd be willing to send all the women back home."[56] Rivers did not say whether she thought the women would be willing to go. Finally, Fannie Lou Hamer explained, "But as women, we feel we have done many things that have enabled us to open doors for our men and to show them that when they get their chance, we will be there to back them up all the way."[57]

Like her activist sisters, Robinson also expressed views that were sympathetic to the peculiar trials suffered by African-American men in U.S. society. She believed that the crusade for racial justice was really men's work, after all. Since African-American men had been so victimized by U.S. society, however, they were not yet ready to shoulder the whole burden. Robinson insisted that "fortunately, more men are becoming involved with the movement, and the day might come when women aren't needed for this type of work."[58] Because she was practical and realistic, though, Robinson realized that women would be in the movement for a long time: "But, I don't believe the Negro man will be able to assume his full role until the struggle has progressed to a point that can't even be foreseen—maybe in the next century or so."[59]

Clearly these women, including Ruby Doris Robinson, were suggesting that in the future men, not women, would be *the* leaders of the movement. Women were leading, they insisted, because in the United States of the 1960s this was the most practical approach. On one hand, Robinson and the others could have been reacting to the exhaustion and frustration that came with trying to juggle their traditional female family responsibilities with their leadership commitments. On the other hand, however, this assessment could have been influenced by the increasingly popular notion that black men had somehow been more victimized than black women. Above all, race loyalty undoubtedly overshadowed gender issues in the minds of most African-American female civil rights activists of this era. They wanted to lead but they did not wish to assert themselves at the expense of their men. Such a position was fraught with contradictions.

As Robinson and her colleagues reflected on the issue of gender roles in the movement, their views were filtered through the growing male chauvinism that accompanied the rise of Black Power. One of the distinctive rallying cries of Black Power advocates was black male dominance. For so long, these advocates insisted, African-American men had been virtually emasculated by white society in the U.S. Thus, they must assume leadership roles and reclaim their masculinity as a prerequisite to the empowerment of African-American people. According to some men, they could only assume their rightful place if women would step aside and stop interfering. Such a negative notion of black female leadership was inextricably bound to a twisted assessment that blamed African-American women rather than white society for black male subordination.

Thus, increasingly, strong African-American women were subjected to negative assessments of their character and accomplishments from the black community as well as from the larger white society. Yet, Ruby Doris Smith Robinson refused to surrender to society's negative and limited expectations. She was an extremely complex woman who fought against the stereotypes. But, she had to have been affected by them. Any effort to assess Robinson's contribution to the movement, and the movement's effect on her, must necessarily recognize that part of her struggle was a continuing effort to hang on to her own sense of self in the face of pervasive and pernicious stereotypical images. Despite what anyone else thought or expected, however, Ruby Doris Robinson acted in ways *she* defined as appropriate and did things *she* thought were important. If she had moments of hesitation or indecision, she did not let them stop her. Rather, she fulfilled the roles that were most important to her. She was a leader in the Student Nonviolent Coordinating Committee, and that was important to her. She was also a woman, a wife, and a mother, and that was also important to her. There were some who insisted that Ruby Doris Smith Robinson's refusal to limit her vision of her capabilities led to her premature death from cancer in 1967 at the age of 25:

. . . she died of exhaustion. . . . I don't think it was necessary to assassinate her. What killed Ruby Doris was the constant outpouring of work, work, work, work with being married, having a child, the constant conflicts, the constant struggles that she was subjected to because she was a woman. . . . She was destroyed by the movement.[60]

NOTES

1. Angela Davis, *Women, Race and Class* (New York: Vintage Books, 1983), 6.
2. *Ibid.*
3. Carl Degler, *At Odds: Women and the Family in America From the Revolution to the Present* (New York: Oxford University Press, 1980), 26.
4. *Ibid.*
5. William Chafe, *The Paradox of Change: American Women in the Twentieth Century* (New York: Oxford University Press, 1991), 176.
6. Courtland Cox, interview with author, Washington, D.C., December 16, 1988.
7. Mukasa (Willie Ricks), interview with author, Atlanta, Ga., April 8, 1990.
8. Albert Brinson, interview with author, Atlanta, Ga., November 10, 1990.
9. Mary Ann Wilson, interview with author, Atlanta, Ga., November 19, 1989.
10. *Ibid.*
11. *Ibid.*
12. Catherine Robinson and Ruby O'Neal, interview with author, Atlanta, Ga., March 3, 1990.
13. Phyl Garland, "Builders of a New South," *Ebony* 21 (August 1966): 36.
14. *Ibid.*
15. Roi Ottley, "What's Wrong with Negro Women?" *Negro Digest* 9 (December 1950): 73.
16. Lerone Bennett, "The Negro Woman," *Ebony* 16/17 (August 1960): 40.
17. The Atlanta University schools at that time included all-female Spelman College, all-male Morehouse College, Morris Brown College, Atlanta University, Clark College, and Gammon Theological Seminary.
18. Howard Zinn, "Finishing School for Pickets," *The Nation* (August 6, 1960), 73.
19. Robinson, like many African-American women, did not see the two sides of herself, debutante and activist, as contradictory. She was comfortable with both roles.
20. Howard Zinn, *SNCC, The New Abolitionists* (Boston: Beacon Press, 1964), 17–18.
21. Julian Bond, interview with author, Washington, D.C., December 16,1988.
22. *Ibid.*
23. Benjamin Brown and Mary Ann Wilson, interview with author, Atlanta, Ga., November 11, 1990.
24. The *Atlanta Inquirer,* March 18, 1961.
25. Taylor Branch, *Parting the Waters* (New York: Simon and Schuster, 1988), 496.
26. Julian Bond interview.
27. James Bond, interview with author, Atlanta, Ga., February 8, 1991.
28. Paula Giddings, *When and Where I Enter* (New York: Bantam Books, 1984), 292.
29. *Ibid.*

30. Cynthia Washington, "We Started From Different Ends of the Spectrum," *Southern Exposure* 5 (Winter 1977): 14.

31. *Ibid.*

32. Alvin Poussaint, "The Stresses of the White Female Worker in the Civil Rights Movement in the South," *Journal of American Psychiatry* 123 (October 1966): 403.

33. Josephine Carson, *Silent Voices* (New York: Delacorte Press, 1969), 60.

34. Zohara Simmons, interview with author, Philadelphia, Pa., December 17, 1988.

35. Carson, *Silent Voices,* 160.

36. Roi Ottley, "What's Wrong With Negro Women?" 75.

37. Joyce Ladner, interview with author, Washington, D.C., December 18, 1988.

38. Jack Minnis, interview with author, New Orleans, La., November 4,1990.

39. Mukasa interview.

40. Jacqueline Jones, *Labor of Love, Labor of Sorrow: Black Women, Work and The Family, From Slavery to the Present* (New York: Vintage Books, 1985), 282.

41. Kwame Ture (Stokely Carmichael), interview with author, Knoxville Tenn., March 14, 1990.

42. Mildred Forman, interview with author, Chicago, Ill., November 6, 1989.

43. Stanley Wise, interview with author, Atlanta, Ga., November 11, 1988.

44. Bobbi Yancey, interview with author, New York, N.Y., May 16, 1991.

45. Reginald Robinson and Charles Jones, interview with author, McComb, Miss., June 28, 1991.

46. Mukasa interview.

47. Dorie Ladner, interview with author, Washington, D.C., May 18, 1991.

48. *Ibid.*

49. Freddie Greene Biddle, interview with author, McComb, Miss., June 29, 1991.

50. *Ibid.*

51. Simmons interview.

52. Clifford Robinson, interview with author, Atlanta, Ga., March 17, 1989.

53. Dion Diamond, interview with author, McComb, Miss., June 18, 1991.

54. Matthew Jones, interview with author, Knoxville, Tenn., April 24, 1989.

55. Garland, "Builders of a New South," 37.

56. *Ibid.*

57. *Ibid.*

58. *Ibid.,* 36.

59. *Ibid.*

60. Giddings, *When and Where I Enter,* 315.

Unit Selections

Key Points to Consider

❖ Describe who have been the winners and losers in the recent assault on affirmative action?

❖ What solutions would you project to help solve the educational inadequacies that exist in Florida (and several other states)?

❖ What is womanism and how does it differ from feminism? Describe the challenges that "black women face in defining their role in today's society."

❖ After reading "Pride and Prejudice," do you agree or disagree with the statement that "racist hate groups, fueled by old animosities and new political conflicts, are being energized by talk radio and the Internet"? Defend your answer.

 **Links** | **www.dushkin.com/online/**

These sites are annotated on pages 4 and 5.

In the first article of unit 9, Robert Staples notes that in less than three decades the stereotypical images of blacks have shifted from being "violent criminals, drug dealers, wife beaters, sexual harassers, welfare cheaters and underclass members to privileged members of the middle class, who acquired their jobs through some racial quota system." We are led to believe that the primary victims of these shifts have been white males with superior qualifications who are not being hired.

In Florida, a group of civil rights groups have filed a lawsuit in which they charge the state with failing to provide an adequate education as required by the Constitution. While the majority of the students named in the lawsuit are either black or Hispanic, the suit charges the state with failure to deliver on its promises.

African American women in the last two decades, following the lead of those in previous periods, are in the process of voicing "a self-defined, collective black women's standpoint about black womanhood." This new voice is coupled with new concerns regarding their presence in higher education, capitalist market relations, and increased conflict along the axes of sexuality, social class, nationality, religion, and region.

Racist hate groups, fueled by old animosities and the source of new political conflicts, are being energized by talk radio and the Internet. The spate of church fires across the South and the development of groups like the Lords of Chaos are causing many to question just how much progress we have made since the civil rights struggle. Members of hate groups, only accounting for 5 percent of the perpetrators of hate crimes, are still the most dangerous.

Contemporary Debates and Issues

Black Deprivation-White Privilege: The Assault On Affirmative Action

by Robert Staples

THE CURRENT FUROR over affirmative action has many of us perplexed. Somehow, black Americans have shifted, in image, from being violent criminals, drug dealers, wife beaters, sexual harassers, welfare cheaters and underclass members to privileged members of the middle-class, who acquired their jobs through some racial quota system at the expense of white males who had superior qualifications for those same jobs. It is a testament to the ingenuity of white male politicians, using the race card, that they can exploit the historically ingrained prejudice against black Americans in the direction of the small black middle-class. For the last twenty-five years, the use of racial code issues, such as law and order, revising the welfare system and the tax revolt has served to transform the southern states from a Democratic stronghold to a Republican majority among its white population.

However, Republicans are increasingly becoming victims of their own success. White Democratic candidates have become as vigilantly anti-crime and welfare as their Republican opponents. In the Louisiana gubernatorial race of 1995, even the black candidates reached out to those whites seeking harsher sentences for criminals, the overwhelming majority of offenders being black in that particular state. While this situation illustrates that there is no honor among thieves, i.e. politicians, it also demonstrates that the diminishing returns of the racial code issues have created a dilemma among the Republican right. Into this void steps the issue of affirmative action, an innocuous program devised more than thirty years ago by President John F. Kennedy to increase the employment of blacks in the public sector. It was expanded by President Richard M. Nixon, who personally believed blacks were intellectually inferior, to include other people of color and white women.

All this occurred at a time when white males held an almost total monopoly of all top and mid-level professional and managerial jobs in the US. Blacks and women who were qualified could not penetrate the barriers to white collar employment except in very special niches for white women (e.g. nursing, home economics or teaching) and a small number of professional blacks who serviced the black community. Subsequently, there was some reduction in the exclusive white male monopoly in the white collar occupations and affirmative action was only one of the reasons for the change. The shift from a manufacturing to a service based economy was a big factor in increasing female employment. And the racial violence of the late 1960s convinced the ruling elites that some blacks had to be brought into white dominated institutions to bring about racial tranquility.

As for affirmative action, there is no consensus on what it is, who are its beneficiaries or what it has achieved. I will not try to define it, since the practice runs the gamut from including people of color and women in the pool of applicants for vacant positions to establishing explicit racial and gender quotas in some institutional spheres. The beneficiaries are generally blacks, Latinos, American Indians, sometimes Asians and women, the disabled, and military veterans. It is estimated that as many as five million people of color have gotten their jobs directly through affirmative action. However, such figures cannot be validated because affirmative action operates in such a complex and convoluted way.

WHAT WE DO KNOW is that there has been a small shift in the number of blacks who can be regarded as middle-class. Most estimates are generally in the range of one-third of the Afro-American population. The progress for black women has been greater, as recent census figures show that among young black college graduates, women earn more than men. The progress for white

Reprinted by permission from *The Black Scholar*, Summer 1995, pp. 2-6. © 1995 by The Black Scholar.

women is more complicated to measure, because the majority of them are married to white men and share the same standard of living. Nonetheless, there has been some economic and educational progress for all affected groups and affirmative action is, at least, partly responsible for this progress because it requires employers to be racial and gender inclusive. What has been overshadowed in this debate is that these groups make up about 70 percent of the American population. White males, the alleged victims of affirmative action compose about 30 percent of the population and still hold about 75 percent of the highest earning occupations in this country, and 95 percent at the very top.

Somehow, some way, this whole issue has been distorted into a prevailing belief that white men are the victims of affirmative action and that their rights have been trampled on. Underlying this belief is the assumption that white males are entitled to 100 percent of the high paying occupations, as they had prior to 1965, because they are intellectually superior to people of color and women. That such a notion could have any credence should be absurd on the face of it. Still, it will be upheld in an initiative on the California ballot in 1996, as it was in July of 1995, when the University of California Regents abolished affirmative action in admissions and employment. And this occurred in a state where half the population are people of color and white, non-Hispanic, males compose twenty percent of the state's population.

I will now address the issue of affirmative action in the state of California and at the University of California, where I have lived and taught for the last three decades. About the state: it is a mosaic of geographic, cultural, social and political elements. Its borders house both the radicals of Berkeley and the John Birch Society of Orange County. Not only is California the most populous of the 50 states, it is one of the most racially diverse. Latinos, Asians, blacks and American Indians make up one half of the state's population. Politically it can be a progressive state, since blacks and women have held a higher number of elective offices there than in any other state. Yet, in the last thirty years the state has experienced (1) the passage of a state proposition to legalize racial discrimination in housing, which was declared unconstitutional by the courts (2) The uprooting of every black person, by white groups, from their homes in the town of Taft. (3) The election of a member of the Ku Klux Klan as the Democratic candidate for a US Congressional seat and (4) the passage of proposition 187, which denies medical treatment and education to undocumented aliens and their children, most of whom are considered people of color.

With this historical backdrop, the Board of Regents of the University of California met in San Francisco on July 20, 1995 to vote on the issue of abolishing affirmative action in admissions and employment. Until this date, there had been no ground swell of public desire to end a program that had existed for 25 years, in a state where

blacks and Latinos compose 40 percent of the pool of potential students. But, the Governor, Pete Wilson, who is running for the Republican nomination for president, was way behind in the polls and needed to show he could actually do something about this "wedge issue" that the Republican party discovered in 1995. Typical of 1990s politics, Wilson has a black man, Ward Connerly, himself a beneficiary of affirmative action, to lead the fight to abolish affirmative action. All those involved in the university—the faculty, administration, student groups and alumni were opposed to its abolishment. The vote was a mere formality, as almost all the white male regents were Republican appointees, and by a vote of 15–10, became the first public university to abolish affirmative action.

One would think it a risky political move in a state where people of color make up 50 percent of the population. However, because many Latinos and Asians are recent immigrants, some undocumented, the voting population is 80 percent white. As Mark Di Camillo, of the California Poll commented, "when you do public opinion polling, you see that whites are much more sensitive to issues that relate to the future of California and the position of whites. They probably have greater concern about their own self-interest." Of course, a substantial number of Asians and some Latinos were also opposed to affirmative action at the University of California. The issue is often framed as a black/white one, though blacks make up only 8 percent of the state's population, less than 6 percent of the UC student body and 2 percent of the faculty. By far, the greatest beneficiaries of affirmative action, due to their larger numbers, are white women. Yet they are hardly mentioned in this debate, partly because they are also 52 percent of white voters and their husbands depend on them for their standard of living. The polls show that about two-thirds of white women would vote to abolish affirmative action.

It IS NOT CLEAR WHAT EFFECT the UC Regents' votes will have on the racial and gender balance of the UC campuses. The president of the University of California, Jack Petalson, issued a statement saying, "Few significant changes are likely because UC's employment and contracting programs are governed by state and federal laws, regulations, executive orders and the US Constitution." Because affirmative action is such an innocuous program, it has created strange political bedfellows. Richard Butler, a leading white supremacist and head of the Church of Jesus Christ Christian Aryan Nation hailed Governor Wilson for his support of the UC Regents' decision. He said that "Wilson is beginning to wake up to Aryan views." At the same time, arch conservatives such as Jack Kemp and William Bennett, who are not running for public office, have reaffirmed their support for affirmative action.

This whole debate tends to obscure some of the real issues for the black community. As Jesse Jackson has noted, "There is substantial evidence that affirmative action is inadequately enforced and too narrowly applied." Blacks hold only 4 percent of professional and managerial positions in the US and are a fraction of 1 percent of senior managers in America's major corporations. At the same time, almost a majority of black males are not in the civilian labor force. About 25 percent of young black males are in prison, on probation or parole. Even if white males can reclaim that 4 percent of the executive positions, it will do little to restore them to the 100 percent monopoly they once held.

An essential piece of the attack on affirmative action is that it unfairly discriminates against white males. To accept this premise is to assume that every white male is superior to every woman and person of color. Why else should they control 100 percent of the top positions in the society: for example, in the government contract set asides about 25 percent of the work is often delegated to people of color and women. Presumably, the other 75 percent is held by "deserving" white males. If that aspect of affirmative action is eliminated, white males will get all the hundreds of billions of dollars in taxpayer funds that go to private companies. As for how white males have achieved such an advantage in this one sphere, far in excess of their percentage of the population, it may have more to do with the fact that other white males are making the decisions on whom to award those contracts—not on the merits of a true competition for them.

The center of the white male argument is that they possess skills other groups do not have, particularly as measured by their performance on standardized tests. Thus, they pretend that those tests are valid measures of merit and use them to exclude all but white males from the top paying occupations. It is, indeed, true that they are better test takers than women and people of color—in part because they created and administer the tests. Other research, also by white males, suggests that many of those exams have no relevance to job performance, contain a cultural bias that favors middle-class Anglo males and are not required for most jobs in the US. In many cases, affirmative action was a tool to consider other—often more relevant—measures to evaluate job applicants. And the opponents of affirmative action [are] hard pressed to name many cases where individuals, hired under affirmative action, lack the necessary skills to do a job for which they are hired.

IN REALITY, MOST PEOPLE in this country are capable of performing well at a variety of occupations, because most of what they learn, in performing occupational tasks, is on the job itself. Since there are not enough desirable and high paying jobs for all the qualified applicants, the system devises arbitrary screening devices such as educational requirements and standardized tests to weed out people. Because white males in the US are socialized into a sense of entitlement to the most prestigious and highest paying positions, they are generally better positioned to take advantage of those arbitrary screening devices. Moreover, studies over the years have found that between 35–65 percent Americans find their jobs through contacts made via the friends and kinship network, a practice that partly accounts for the white male dominance of senior positions in both the private and public sector.

Affirmative action has experienced some abuses. Why people of color and women are held responsible for the abuses is a mystery, since white males are chiefly responsible for administering affirmative action programs. The greatest abuses seem to occur in the contract set asides, where a few black and Latinos have served as fronts to get government contracts that actually go to Anglo contractors. Another problem has been the classification of racial minorities. Because people with a small percentage of Indian ancestry can live as white Americans, they face no disadvantage different from other whites in this society. Yet, they have often qualified for affirmative action treatment. The problem of white usurpation of Indian identity was so prevalent that American Indians wanted to retain their original name, albeit a misnomer, because so many whites were claiming the title of Native Americans and receiving benefits designed for oppressed American Indians.

Some opponents of affirmative action have suggested replacing its racial/gender components with that of socioeconomic status, which would also include poor whites. Of course poor whites are already included in university recruitment and admission of students as well as being part of the disabled and military veteran category. However it is unfair to equate a low socioeconomic status with the disadvantages of race and gender. A poor white male who gets a college education and a middle-class job simply increases the number of white males in the ruling elite. His problems are over, while women and people of color will continue to encounter glass ceilings in education and employment. And blacks who are middle-class do not escape anything but the economic problems associated with being black. Because the oppression is aimed at the entire group, the political remedies should go to all visible members of the black population.

FINALLY, THIS ATTACK ON AFFIRMATIVE ACTION is nothing more than a replay of history for Afro-Americans. Slavery was defended with a variety of rationalizations, including the inferiority of blacks, the need to make blacks Christians and the slaveowners' property rights. Racial segregation in schools was defended by the separate but equal doctrine. Southern apartheid was maintained politically under the states' rights defense. Now, we have the anomaly of having white males, a third of the population who make up 95 percent of those who run America, control and distribute 90 percent of the nation's wealth, trying to portray themselves as victims because women and people of color finally broke their grip on all the society's resources. Their attack on affirmative action can only be characterized as political and economic overkill.

However, despite its absurdity, the assault has the potential to succeed. Politicians have had the wisdom to target blacks as the main recipients of affirmative action, while ignoring the fact that white women make up as much as 80 percent of the beneficiaries. This allows them to get the votes of white women, who may act on their interests as whites and ignore their interests as women. To the degree that they empathize and share households with white males, they have less to lose. Single white women, female heads-of-households and lesbians, will be sacrificed on the altar of larger white interests. Blacks, historically, make a convenient scapegoat for the decline of capitalism and the whites who are casualties of that decline. While they comprise a small percentage of those subject to affirmative action, they remain a national target of prejudice and stereotyping in every corner of the nation.

The notion of a color blind society, with no need for affirmative action, is a fantasy at this point. Race is the most divisive variable extant in the US. Whites commonly betray their class interests on its behalf and individual life chances for both blacks and whites are a direct function of it. Affirmative action is but one tool—not a very effective one—to mitigate its effect. The attack on it is part of a white plan to make people of color their servants again, while they continue to obligate them to pay taxes to subsidize white privilege. What whites may find is they may not want to live in the world they are creating.

Rights Groups Suing Florida for Failure to Educate Pupils

By ETHAN BRONNER

A coalition of Florida civil rights groups filed a lawsuit in state court in Tallahassee Friday, accusing the state of violating the rights of tens of thousands of schoolchildren by failing to provide them with an adequate education as required by the state Constitution.

The 31-page complaint names 19 pupils, all members of minorities from poor schools where a large percentage of students fail state reading and mathematics exams. It cites the state constitutional requirement that "adequate provision shall be made by law for a uniform system of free public schools," and says the state has failed to live up to that guarantee.

"All schools are required to provide adequate education and many of these schools are not meeting the state's own minimal standards," said Laura Besvinick, a lawyer for the plaintiffs. "Florida is ranked in the lowest 5 to 10 states in education."

Most of the schools affected have large enrollments of black and Hispanic students, although the lawsuit does not accuse them of discrimination. Rather, as part of a growing trend in such lawsuits, it tries to hold the state to its own word regarding a constitutional promise to educate its citizens.

Theodore Shaw, associate director and counsel of the NAACP Legal Defense and Educational Fund, which is not involved in the suit, said, "I think we are going to see more of these suits because the quality of education is so abysmally poor and these schools are being used as warehouses with no expectations of these students, especially students of color.

"With federal desegregation cases now fading, people are looking at educational adequacy as the best hope. They are being pushed in that direction by the courts."

Similar lawsuits have been filed in Alabama, North Carolina, Ohio and Connecticut. But the Florida suit is unusual in its singular focus on educational adequacy rather than on racial imbalances or the inequality of educational resources or spending.

The Florida suit, brought by a group that includes the National Association for the Advancement of Colored People, the League of United Latin American Citizens and the Florida Appleseed Center for Law and Justice Inc. does not seek monetary damages, only an improvement in education.

A state referendum that passed in November and went into effect this week refines the state's obligation as that of providing a "uniform, efficient, safe, secure and high-quality system of free public schools."

John M. Ratliff of the Children First Project at Nova Southeastern University in Fort Lauderdale, a lawyer for the plaintiffs, said the plaintiffs intended to work with the new administration of Gov. Jeb Bush and the Legislature to make sure the new provisions were met.

"We are in the courts to insure that this opportunity is not missed," Ratliff said.

He said the schools in greatest crisis were in large urban centers and rural areas. But the lawsuit was filed in the name of the 1.4 million pupils—a third of whom have failed the state exams—in all the schools where an adequate education toward functional literacy had not been provided.

WHAT'S IN A NAME?

Womanism, Black Feminism, and Beyond

by Patricia Hill Collins

BLACK WOMEN ARE AT A DECISION POINT that in many ways mirrors that faced by African Americans as a collectivity. Building on the pathbreaking works by Toni Cade Bambara, Ntozake Shange, Angela Davis, Toni Morrison, June Jordan, Alice Walker, Audre Lorde and other black women who "broke silence" in the 1970s, African American women in the 1980s and 1990s developed a "voice," a self-defined, collective black women's standpoint about black womanhood (Collins 1990). Moreover, black women used this standpoint to "talk back" concerning black women's representation in dominant discourses (hooks 1989). As a result of this struggle, African American women's ideas and experiences have achieved a visibility unthinkable in the past.

But African American women now stand at a different historical moment. Black women appear to have a voice, and with this new-found voice comes a new series of concerns. For example, we must be attentive to the seductive absorption of black women's voices in classrooms of higher education where black women's texts are still much more welcomed than black women ourselves. Giving the illusion of change, this strategy of symbolic inclusion masks how the everyday institutional policies and arrangements that suppress and exclude African Americans as a collectivity remain virtually untouched (Carby 1992; Du Cille 1994). Similarly, capitalist market relations that transformed black women's writing into a hot commodity threaten to strip their works of their critical edge. Initially, entering public space via books, movies, and print media proved invigorating. But in increasingly competitive global markets where anything that sells will be sold regardless of the consequences, black women's "voices" now flood the market. Like other commodities exchanged in capitalist markets, surplus cheapens value, and the fad of today becomes the nostalgic memory of tomorrow.

While a public voice initially proved dangerous, black women's coming to voice ironically fostered the emergence of a new challenge. The new public safe space provided by black women's success allowed longstanding differences among black women structured along axes of sexuality, social class, nationality, religion, and region to emerge. At this point, whether African American women can fashion a singular "voice" about the black *woman's* position remains less an issue than how black women's voices collectively construct, affirm, and maintain a dynamic black *women's* self-defined standpoint. Given the increasingly troublesome political context affecting black women as a group (Massey and Denton 1993; Squires 1994), such solidarity is essential. Thus, ensuring group unity while recognizing the tremendous heterogeneity that operates within the boundaries of the term "black women" comprises one fundamental challenge now confronting African American women.

CURRENT DEBATES about whether black women's standpoint should be named "womanism" or "black feminism" reflect this basic challenge of accommodating diversity among black women. In her acclaimed volume of essays, *In Search of Our Mothers' Gardens*, Alice Walker (1983) introduced four meanings of the term "womanist." According to Walker's first definition, a "womanist" was "a black feminist or feminist of color" (xi). Thus, on some basic level, Walker herself uses the two terms as being virtually interchangeable. Like Walker, many African American women see little difference between the two since both support a common agenda of black women's self-definition and self-determination. As Barbara Omolade points out, "black feminism is sometimes referred to as womanism because both are concerned with struggles against sexism and racism by black women who are themselves part of the black community's efforts to achieve equity and liberty" (Omolade 1994; xx).

But despite similar beliefs expressed by African American women who define themselves as black feminists, as womanists, as both, or, in some cases, as neither, increasing attention seems devoted to delineating the differences, if any, between groups naming themselves as "womanists" or "black feminists." The *name* given to black women's collective standpoint seems to matter, but why?

In this paper, I explore some of the theoretical implications of using the terms "womanism" and "black feminism" to name a black women's standpoint. My purpose is not to classify either the works of black women or African American women themselves into one category or the other. Rather, I aim to examine how the effort to categorize obscures more basic challenges that confront African American women as a group.

Womanism

ALICE WALKER'S MULTIPLE DEFINITIONS of the term "womanism" in *In Search of Our Mothers' Gardens*, shed light on the issue of why many African American women prefer the term womanism to black feminism. Walker offers two contradictory meanings of "womanism." On the one hand, Walker clearly sees womanism as rooted in black women's concrete history in racial and gender oppression. Taking the term from the Southern black folk expression of mothers to female children "you acting womanish," Walker suggests that black women's concrete history fosters a womanist worldview accessible primarily and perhaps exclusively to black women. "Womanish" girls acted in outrageous, courageous, and willful ways, attributes that freed them from the conventions long limiting white women. Womanish girls wanted to know more and in greater depth than what

was considered good for them. They were responsible, in charge, and serious.

Despite her disclaimer that womanists are "traditionally universalist," a philosophy invoked by her metaphor of the garden where room exists for all flowers to bloom equally and differently, Walker simultaneously implies that black women are somehow superior to white women because of this black folk tradition. Defining womanish as the opposite of the "frivolous, irresponsible, not serious" girlish, Walker constructs black women's experiences in opposition to those of white women. This meaning of womanism sees it as being different from and superior to feminism, a difference allegedly stemming from black and white women's different histories with American racism. Walker's much cited phrase, "womanist is to feminist as purple to lavender (1983, xii)" clearly seems designed to set up this type of comparison—black women are "womanist" while white women remain merely "feminist."

This usage sits squarely in black nationalist traditions premised on the belief that blacks and whites cannot function as equals while inhabiting the same territory or participating in the same social institutions (Pinkney 1976; Van Deburg 1992). Since black nationalist philosophy posits that white people as a group have a vested interest in continuing a system of white supremacy, it typically sees little use for black integration or assimilation into a system predicated on black subjugation. Black nationalist approaches also support a black moral superiority over whites because of black suffering.

Walker's use of the term womanism promises black women who both operate within these black nationalist assumptions and who simultaneously see the need to address "feminist" issues within African American communities partial reconciliation of these two seemingly incompatible philosophies. Womanism offers a distance from the "enemy," in this case, whites generally and white women in particular, yet still raises the issue of gender. Due to its endorsement of racial separatism, this interpretation of womanism offers a vocabulary for addressing gender issues within African American communities without challenging the racially segregated terrain that characterizes American social institutions.

This use of womanism sidesteps an issue central to many white feminists, namely, finding ways to foster interracial cooperation among women. African American women embracing black nationalist philosophies typically express little interest in working with white women—in fact, white women are defined as part of the problem. Moreover, womanism appears to provide an avenue to foster stronger relationships between black women and black men, another very important issue for African American women regardless of political perspective. Again, Walker's definition provides guidance where she notes that womanists are "committed to survival and wholeness of entire people, male *and* female" (xi). Many black women view feminism as a movement that at best, is exclusively for women and, at worst, dedicated to attacking or eliminating men. Sherley Williams takes this view when she notes that in contrast to feminism, "womanist inquiry . . . assumes that it can talk both effectively and productively about men (1990, 70). Womanism seemingly supplies a way for black women to address gender oppression without attacking black men.

Walker also presents a visionary meaning for womanism. As part of her second definition, Walker has a black girl pose the question "Mama, why are we brown, pink, and yellow, and our cousins are white, beige, and black?" (xi). The response of "the colored race is just like a flower garden, with every color flower represented," both criticizes colorism within African American communities and broadens the notion of humanity to make all people people of color. Reading this passage as a metaphor, womanism thus furnishes a vision where the women and men of different colors coexist like flowers in a garden yet retain their cultural distinctiveness and integrity.

This meaning of womanism seems rooted in another major political tradition within African American politics, namely, a pluralist version of black empowerment (Van Deburg 1992). Pluralism views society as being composed of various ethnic and interest groups, all of whom compete for goods and services. Equity lies in providing equal opportunities, rights, and respect to all groups. By retaining black cultural distinctiveness and integrity, pluralism offers a modified version of racial integration premised not on individual assimilation but on *group* integration. Clearly rejecting what they perceive as being the limited vision of feminism projected by North American white women, many black women theorists have been attracted to this joining of pluralism and racial integration in this interpretation of Walker's "womanism." For example,

black feminist theologian Katie Geneva Cannon's (1988) work *Black Womanist Ethics* invokes this sense of the visionary content of womanism. As an ethical system, womanism is always in the making—it is not a closed fixed system of ideas but one that continually evolves through its rejection of all forms of oppression and commitment to social justice.

Walker's definition thus manages to invoke three important yet contradictory philosophies that frame black social and political thought, namely, black nationalism via her claims of black women's moral and epistemological superiority via suffering under racial and gender oppression, pluralism via the cultural integrity provided by the metaphor of the garden, and integration/assimilation via her claims that black women are "traditionally universalist" (Van Deburg 1992). Just as black nationalism and racial integration coexist in uneasy partnership, with pluralism occupying the contested terrain between the two, Walker's definitions of womanism demonstrate comparable contradictions. By both grounding womanism in the concrete experiences of African American women and generalizing about the potential for realizing a humanist vision of community via the experiences of African American women, Walker depicts the potential for oppressed people to possess a moral vision and standpoint on society that grows from their situation of oppression. This standpoint also emerges as an incipient foundation for a more humanistic, just society. Overall, these uses of Walker's term "womanism" creates conceptual space that reflects bona fide philosophical differences that exist among African-American women.[1]

Oɴᴇ ᴘᴀʀᴛɪᴄᴜʟᴀʀʟʏ sɪɢɴɪꜰɪᴄᴀɴᴛ ꜰᴇᴀᴛᴜʀᴇ of black women's use of womanism concerns the part of Walker's definition that remains neglected. A more troublesome line for those self-defining as womanist precedes the often cited passage, "committed to survival and wholeness of entire people, male *and* female" (xi). Just before Walker offers the admonition that womanists, by definition, are committed to wholeness, she states that a womanist is also "a woman who loves other women, sexually and/or nonsexually" (xi). The relative silence of womanists on this dimension of womanism speaks to black women's continued ambivalence in dealing with the links between race, gender and sexuality, in this case, the "taboo" sexuality of lesbianism. In her essay "The Truth That Never Hurts: Black Lesbians in Fiction in the 1980s," black feminist critic Barbara Smith (1990) points out that African American women have yet to come to terms with homophobia in African American communities. Smith applauds the growth of black women's fiction in the 1980s, but also observes that within black feminist intellectual production, black lesbians continue to be ignored. Despite the fact that some of the most prominent and powerful black women thinkers claimed by both womanists and black feminists were and are lesbians, this precept often remains unacknowledged in the work of African American writers. In the same way that many people read the Bible, carefully selecting the parts that agree with their worldview and rejecting the rest, selective readings of Walker's womanism produce comparable results.

Another significant feature of black women's multiple uses of womanism concerns the potential for a slippage between the real and the ideal. To me, there is a distinction between describing black women's historical responses to racial and gender oppression as being womanist, and using womanism as a visionary term delineating an ethical or ideal vision of humanity for all people. Identifying the liberatory *potential* within black women's communities that emerges from concrete, historical experiences remains quite different from claiming that black women have already *arrived* at this ideal, "womanist" endpoint. Refusing to distinguish carefully between these two meanings of womanism thus collapses the historically real and the future ideal into one privileged position for African American women in the present. Taking this position is reminiscent of the response of some black women to the admittedly narrow feminist agenda forwarded by white women in the early 1970s. Those black women proclaimed that they were already "liberated" while in actuality, this was far from the truth.

Black Feminism

AFRICAN AMERICAN WOMEN who use the term black feminism also attach varying interpretations to this term. As black feminist theorist and activist Pearl Cleage defines it, feminism is "the belief that women are full human beings capable of participation and leadership in the full range of human activities—intellectual, political, social, sexual, spiritual and economic" (1993, 28). In its broadest sense, feminism constitutes both an ideology and a global political movement that confronts sexism, a social relationship in which males as a group have authority over females as a group.

Globally, a feminist agenda encompasses several major areas. First and foremost, the economic status of women and issues associated with women's global poverty, such as educational opportunities, industrial development, environmental racism, employment policies, prostitution, and inheritance laws concerning property, constitute a fundamental global women's issue. Political rights for women; such as gaining the vote, rights of assembly, traveling in public, officeholding, the rights of political prisoners, and basic human rights violations against women such as rape and torture constitute a second area of concern. A third area of global concern consists of marital and family issues such as marriage and divorce laws, child custody policies, and domestic labor. Women's health and survival issues, such as reproductive rights, pregnancy, sexuality, and AIDS constitute another area of global feminist concern. This broad global feminist agenda finds varying expressions in different regions of the world and among diverse populations.

Using the term "black feminism" positions African American women to examine how the particular constellation of issues affecting black women in the United States are part of issues of women's emancipation struggles globally (Davis 1989; James and Busia 1994). In the context of feminism as a global political movement for women's rights and emancipation, the patterns of feminist knowledge and politics that African American women encounter in the United States represent but a narrow segment refracted through the dichotomous racial politics of white supremacy in the United States. Because the media in the United States portrays feminism as a for-whites-only movement, and because many white women have accepted this view of American apartheid that leads to segregated institutions of all types, including feminist organizations, feminism is often viewed by both black and whites as the cultural property of white women (Caraway 1991).

DESPITE THEIR MEDIA ERASURE, many African American women have long struggled against this exclusionary feminism and have long participated in what appear to be for-whites-only feminist activity. In some cases, some black women have long directly challenged the racism within feminist organizations controlled by white women. Sojourner Truth's often cited phrase "ain't I a woman" typifies this longstanding tradition (Joseph 1990). At other times, even though black women's participation in feminist organizations remains largely invisible, for example, Pauli Murray's lack of recognition as a founding member of NOW, black women participated in feminist organizations in positions of leadership. In still other cases, black women combine allegedly divergent political agendas. For example, Pearl Cleage observes that black feminist politics and black nationalist politics need not be contradictory. She notes, "I don't think you can be a true Black Nationalist, dedicated to the freedom of black people *without* being a feminist, black *people* being made up of both men and *women*, after all, and feminism being nothing more or less than a belief in the political, social and legal equality of women" (1994, 180).

Using the term "black feminism" disrupts the racism inherent in presenting feminism as a for-whites-only ideology and political movement. Inserting the adjective "black" challenges the assumed whiteness of feminism and disrupts the false universal of this term for both white and black women. Since many white women think that black women lack feminist consciousness, the term "black feminist" both highlights the contradictions underlying the assumed whiteness of feminism and serves to remind white women that they comprise neither the only nor the normative "feminists." The term "black feminism" also makes many African American women uncomfortable because it challenges black women to confront their own views on sexism and women's oppression. Because the majority of African American women encounter their own experiences repackaged in racist school curricula and media, even though they may support the very ideas on which feminism rests, large numbers of African American women reject the term "feminism" because of what they perceive as its association with whiteness. Many see feminism as operating exclusively within the terms white and American and perceive its opposite as being black and American. When given these

two narrow and false choices, black women routinely choose "race" and let the lesser question of "gender" go. In this situation, those black women who identify with feminism must be recoded as being either non-black or less authentically black. The term "black feminist" also disrupts a longstanding and largely unquestioned reliance on black racial solidarity as a deep tap root in black political philosophies, especially black nationalist and cultural pluralist frameworks (Dyson 1993). Using family rhetoric that views black family, community, race and nation as a series of nested boxes, each gaining meaning from the other, certain rules apply to all levels of this "family" organization. Just as families have internal naturalized hierarchies that give, for example, older siblings authority over younger ones or males over females, groups defining themselves as racial-families invoke similar rules (Collins forthcoming). Within African American communities, one such rule is that black women will support black men, no matter what, an unwritten family rule that was manipulated quite successfully during the Clarence Thomas confirmation hearings. Even if Anita Hill was harassed by Clarence Thomas, many proclaimed in barber shops and beauty parlors, she should have kept her mouth shut and not "aired dirty laundry." Even though Thomas recast the life of his own sister through the framework of an unworthy welfare queen, in deference to rules of racial solidarity, black women should have kept our collective mouths shut. By counseling black women not to remain silent in the face of abuse, whoever does it, black feminism comes into conflict with codes of silence such as these.

SEVERAL DIFFICULTIES accompany the use of the term "black feminism." One involves the problem of balancing the genuine concerns of black women against continual pressures to absorb and recast such interests within white feminist frameworks. For example, ensuring political rights and economic development via collective action to change social institutions remains a strong focal point in the feminism of African American women and women of color. Yet the emphasis on themes such as personal identity, understanding "difference," deconstructing women's multiple selves, and the simplistic model of the political expressed through the slogan the "personal is political," that currently permeate North American white women's feminism in the academy can work to sap black feminism of its critical edge. Efforts of contemporary black women thinkers to explicate a long-standing black women's intellectual tradition bearing the label "black feminism" can attract the attention of white women armed with a different feminist agenda. Issues raised by black women not seen as explicitly "feminist" ones, primarily issues that affect only women, receive much less sanction. In a sense, the constant drumbeat of having to support white women in their efforts to foster an anti-racist feminism that allows black women access to the global network of women's activism diverts black women's energy away from addressing social issues facing African American communities. Because black feminism appears to be so well-received by white women, in the context of dichotomous racial politics of the United States, some black women quite rightfully suspect its motives.

Another challenge facing black feminism concerns the direct conflict between black feminism and selected elements of black religious traditions. For example, the visibility of white lesbians within North American feminism overall comes into direct conflict with many black women's articles of faith that homosexuality is a sin. While individual African American women may be accepting of gays, lesbians and bisexuals as individuals, especially if such individuals are African-American, black women as a collectivity have simultaneously distanced themselves from social movements perceived as requiring acceptance of homosexuality. As one young black woman queried, "why do I have to accept lesbianism in order to support black feminism?" The association of feminism with lesbianism remains a problematic one for black women. Reducing black lesbians to their sexuality, one that chooses women over men, reconfigures black lesbians as enemies of black men. This reduction not only constitutes a serious misreading of black lesbianism—black lesbians have fathers, brothers, and sons of their own and are embedded in a series of relationships as complex as their heterosexual brothers and sisters—it simultaneously diverts attention away from more important issues (Lorde 1984). Who ultimately benefits when the presence of black lesbians in any black social movement leads to its rejection by African Americans?

The theme of lesbianism and its association with feminism in the minds of many African Americans also overlaps with another concern of many African American women, namely their commitment to African American men. Another challenge confronting black feminism concerns its perceived separatism— many African Americans define black feminism as being exclusively for black women only and rejecting black men. In explaining her preference for "womanism," Sherley Ann Williams notes, one of the most disturbing aspects of current black feminist criticism (is) its separatism—its tendency to see not only a *distinct* black female culture but to see that culture as a separate cultural form having more in common with white female experience than with the facticity of Afro-American life" (1990, 70). This is a valid criticism of black feminism, one that in my mind, must be addressed if the major ideas of black feminism expect to avoid the danger of becoming increasingly separated from African American women's experiences and interests. But it also speaks to the larger issue of the continuing difficulty of positioning black feminism between black nationalism and North American white feminism. In effect, black feminism must come to terms with a white feminist agenda incapable of seeing its own racism as well as a black nationalist one resistant to grappling with its own sexism (White 1990). Finding a place that accommodates these seemingly contradictory agendas remains elusive (Christian 1989).

Beyond Naming

AFRICAN AMERICAN WOMEN'S EFFORTS to distinguish between womanism and black feminism illustrates how black women's placement in hierarchical power relations fosters different yet related allegiances to a black women's self-defined standpoint. While the surface differences distinguishing African American women who embrace womanism and black feminism appear to be minimal, black women's varying locations in neighborhoods, schools, and labor markets generate comparably diverse views on the strategies black women feel will ultimately lead to black women's self-determination. In a sense, while womanism's affiliation with black nationalism both taps an historic philosophy and a set of social institutions organized around the centrality of racial solidarity for black survival, this position can work to isolate womanism from global women's issues. At the same time, while black feminism's connections to existing women's struggles both domestically and globally fosters a clearer political agenda regarding gender, its putative affiliation with whiteness fosters its rejection by the very constituency it aims to serve.

No TERM CURRENTLY EXISTS that adequately represents the substance of what diverse groups of black women alternately call "womanism" and "black feminism." Perhaps the time has come to go beyond naming by applying main ideas contributed by both womanists and black feminists to the overarching issue of analyzing the centrality of gender in shaping a range of relationships within African-American communities. Such an examination might encompass several dimensions.

First, it is important to keep in mind that the womanist/black feminist debate occurs primarily among relatively privileged black women. Womanism and black feminism would both benefit by examining the increasing mismatch between what privileged black women, especially those in the academy, identify as important themes and what the large numbers of African American women who stand outside of higher education might deem worthy of attention. While these African American women physically resemble one another and may even occupy the same space, their worlds remain decidedly different. One might ask how closely the thematic content of newly emerging black women's voices in the academy speak for and speak to the masses of African American women still denied literacy. Black women academics explore intriguing issues of centers and margins and work to deconstruct black female identity while large numbers of black women remain trapped in neighborhoods organized around old centers of racial apartheid. Talk of centers and margins, even the process of coming to voice itself, that does not simultaneously address issues of power leaves masses of black women doing the dry cleaning, cooking the fast food, and dusting the computer of the sister who has just written the newest theoretical treatise on black women.

Second, shifting the emphasis from black women's oppression to how institutionalized racism operates in gender-specific ways should provide a clearer perspective on how gender oppression works in tandem with racial oppression for both black women and men. This shift potentially opens up new political choices for African Americans as a group. just as feminism does not automatically reside in female bodies, sexism does not reside in male ones. It may be time to separate political philosophies such as black nationalism, Afrocentrism, and feminism, from the socially constructed categories of individuals created by historical relations of racism and sexism. Black men cannot have black women's experiences but they can support African American women by advocating antiracist and anti-sexist philosophies in their intellectual and political work (see, e.g., Marable 1983; hooks and West 1991; and Awkward 1995). Focusing on gender as a structure of power that works with race should provide the much needed space for dialogues among black women, among black men, and between black women and men.

This approach promises to benefit the black community as a collectivity because it models sensitivity to the heterogeneity concerning not only gender, but class, nationality, sexuality, and age currently operating within the term "black community." Thus, the womanism/black feminism debate also provides an excellent opportunity to model a process of building community via heterogeneity and not sameness. For African American women, breathing life into Alice Walker's seemingly contradictory meanings of "womanist" and "black feminist" means engaging in the difficult task of working through the diverse ways that black women have been affected by interlocking systems of oppression. Some black women will have to grapple with how internalized oppression has affected them because they are poor while others must come to terms with the internalized privilege accompanying their middle and upper-class status. Other black women must grapple with the internalized privileges that accrue to them because they engage in heterosexual behaviors or how American citizenship provides them rights denied to women elsewhere in the Diaspora. Working through the interconnected nature of multiple systems of oppression and potential ways that such intersectionality might foster resistance becomes significant in moving quite diverse African American women forward toward Walker's visionary term "womanism." A commitment to social justice and participatory democracy provide some fundamental ground rules for black women and men concerning how to relate across differences.

FINALLY, DESPITE THE PROMISE of this approach, it is important to consider the limitations of womanism, black feminism, and all other putatively progressive philosophies. Whether labeled "womanism," "black feminism," or something else, African American women could not possibly possess a superior vision of what community would look like, how justice might feel, and the like. This presupposes that such a perspective is arrived at without conflict, intellectual rigor, and political struggle. While black women's particular location provides a distinctive angle of vision on oppression, this perspective comprises neither a privileged nor a complete standpoint. In this sense, grappling with the ideas of heterogeneity within black women's communities and hammering out a self-defined, black women's standpoint leads the way for other groups wishing to follow a similar path. As for black women, we can lead the way or we can follow behind. Things will continue to move on regardless of our choice.

REFERENCES

Awkward, Michael. 1995. *Negotiating Difference: Race, Gender, and the Politics of Positionality*. Chicago: University of Chicago Press.

Cannon, Katie C. 1988. *Black Womanist Ethics*. Atlanta: Scholars Press.

Caraway, Nancie. 1991. *Segregated Sisterhood: Racism and the Politics of American Feminism*. Knoxville: University of Tennessee Press.

Carby, Hazel. 1992. "The Multicultural Wars." Pp. 187–99 in *Black Popular Culture*, edited by Michele Wallace and Gina Dent. Seattle: Bay Press.

Christian, Barbara. 1989. "But Who Do You Really Belong To—Black Studies or Women's Studies?", *Women's Studies* 17, 1–2: 17–23.

Cleage, Pearl. 1993. *Deals With the Devil and Other Reasons to Riot*. New York: Ballantine Books.

Collins, Patricia Hill. 1990. *Black Feminist Thought: Knowledge, Consciousness, and the Politics of Empowerment*. New York: Routledge, Chapman and Hall.

____. forthcoming. "Intersections of Race, Class, Gender, and Nation: Some Implications for Black Family Studies." *Journal of Comparative Family Studies*.

Davis, Angela. 1989. *Women, Culture, and Politics*. New York: Random House.

Dubey, Madhu. 1994. *Black Women Novelists and the Nationalist Aesthetic*. Bloomington: Indiana University Press.

DuCille, Ann. 1994. "The Occult of True Black Womanhood: Critical Demeanor and Black Feminist Studies." *Signs* 19(3): 591–629.

Dyson, Michael. 1993. *Reflecting Black: African-American Cultural Criticism*. Minneapolis: University of Minnesota Press.

hooks, bell. 1989. *Talking Back: Thinking Feminist, Thinking Black*. Boston: South End Press.

____, and Cornel West. 1991. *Breaking Bread: Insurgent Black Intellectual Life*. Boston: South End Press.

James, Stanlie, and Abena Busia, eds. 1994. *Theorizing Black Feminisms*. New York: Routledge.

Jordan, June. 1992. *Technical Difficulties: African-American Notes on the State of the Union*. New York: Pantheon Books.

Joseph, Gloria I. 1990. "Sojourner Truth: Archetypal Black Feminist." Pp. 35–47 in *Wild Women in the Whirlwind*, edited by Joanne Braxton and Andree Nicola McLaughlin. New Brunswick: Rutgers University Press.

Lorde, Audre. 1984. *Sister Outsider*. Trumansburg, NY: The Crossing Press.

Marable, Manning. 1983. "Grounding with My Sisters: Patriarchy and the Exploitation of Black Women." Pp. 69–104 in *How Capitalism Underdeveloped Black America*. Boston: South End Press.

Massey, Douglas S. and Nancy A. Denton. 1993. *American Apartheid: Segregation and the Making of the Underclass*. Cambridge: Harvard University Press.

Omolade, Barbara. 1994. *The Rising Song of African American Women*. New York: Routledge.

Pinkney, Alphonso. 1976. *Red, Black, and Green: Black Nationalism in the United States*. London: Cambridge University Press.

Smith, Barbara. 1990. "The Truth That Never Hurts: Black Lesbians in Fiction in the 1980s." Pp. 213–245 in *Wild Women in the Whirlwind*, edited by Joanne Braxton and Andree Nicola McLaughlin. New Brunswick: Rutgers University Press.

Squires, Gregory D. 1994. *Capital and Communities in Black and White: The Intersections of Race, Class, and Uneven Development*. Albany: SUNY Press.

Van Deburg, William L. 1992. *New Day in Babylon: The Black Power Movement and American Culture, 1965–1975*. Chicago: University of Chicago Press.

Walker, Alice. 1983. *In Search of Our Mothers' Gardens*. New York: Harcourt, Brace Jovanovich.

White, E. Frances. 1990. "Africa on My Mind: Gender, Counter Discourse and African-American Nationalism." *Journal of Women's History* 2, 1 (Spring): 73–97.

Williams, Sherley Ann. 1990. "Some Implications of Womanist Theory." Pp. 68–75 in *Reading Black, Reading Feminist: A Critical Anthology*, edited by Henry Louis Gates. New York: Meridian.

Notes

1. For a detailed treatment of Alice Walker's and other black feminist writers' connection to black nationalist politics, see Dubey (1994).

Pride and prejudice

*Are old animosities, new political conflicts, talk radio
and the Internet fueling a racist revival?*

They called themselves the "Lords of Chaos." Five of them were superior students at Riverdale High School in Fort Myers, Fla., advanced in math, computers and art. The sixth—their leader, police say—was 19-year-old Kevin Foster, who was better known for his hatred of blacks than for his artistic abilities: He allegedly drew a crude cartoon depicting hooded figures standing next to a burning cross holding a crucified black man, with the words "Black BBQ" scrawled below. The Lords "didn't fit the mold of bad boys," says Riverdale principal Robert Durham. "They did all the things parents expect them to do. These could be anyone's kids."

Earlier this year, police say, these Everyman's kids burned an abandoned bottling plant, pulled an armed robbery and stole a car. And authorities charge that after music teacher Mark Schwebes, 32, caught the Lords planning to burn a school auditorium, they went to his house, knocked on his door and killed him with a shotgun blast in the face. After that, police claim, the Lords were planning a "Terror Night" at Disney World in Orlando. The idea was to assault some Disney characters, steal their costumes and walk around the park shooting African-Americans. Five Lords were arrested the night before that was to occur; four of them have been charged with Schwebes's murder.

The existence of groups like the Lords of Chaos and the epidemic of church fires across the South are peeling the lid off an alarming phenomenon: Despite the gains of the civil rights struggle, in-your-face racism is bubbling to the surface again. "There is in our society today, more so than 20 or 30 years ago, a greater tolerance for intolerance," says Abraham Foxman, national director of the Anti-Defamation League of B'nai B'rith.

Mainstream racism. Statistics on hate crimes are soft, and federal data-gathering on the subject lags, so it's hard to draw broad conclusions. But the best estimates are that between 10,000 and 40,000 hate crimes are committed annually in America—about 60 percent by whites, and about 60 percent motivated by racial bias. Whites have no monopoly on hatred: Of the 5,842 hate crimes reported to the FBI for 1994, the most recent year available, 1,901 were racial incidents directed at whites—including 908 antisemitic religious incidents.

Stockton College criminal justice Prof. Brian Levin, formerly of the Southern Poverty Law Center, says 56 percent of bias-related homicides are committed by offenders under 21. Adds Prof. Jack Levin of Northeastern University: "The bad news is that this is coming from the center where most of us live. These are our children—the boy next door, the young man at the next desk—who can't handle diversity and whose rage translates into violence. Many are red-blooded, hot-dog- and-apple-pie Americans. We aren't talking about racism under a rock but in the mainstream of our culture."

There are reasons for the church fires—vandalism, insurance fraud and revenge among them. But "it's plain that racial hostility is behind many," says Assistant U.S. Attorney General Deval Patrick. Federal authorities have not uncovered any broad conspiracy, but now some almost wish they had. "The prospect of a conspiracy is a chilling thing," says Patrick. "But the prospect that these are separate acts of racism is even worse."

That may be the case. A 1993 study of some 4,000 hate crimes by Northeastern University Profs. Jack Levin and Jack McDevitt found the perpetrators were primarily white males in their teens or early 20s who seem to fall into three categories. Sixty percent are thrill seekers who don't belong to an organized group but who in an impromptu act will attack a black person or deface a church simply for the excitement, often after drinking with buddies. The second-largest category, about 35 percent, aren't members of an organized group either but see themselves as turf defenders. They might throw rocks at a new black family in the neighborhood, for instance.

Members of hate groups account for 5 percent of the perpetrators of hate crimes, but they are the most dangerous. "These folks are on a mission," says McDevitt. "They are more likely to be violent, and their violence is most likely to cause injury." A *USA Today* study of 14 white men investigated by the federal government for racially motivated church arsons in the 1990s found the majority to be poor, young and minimally educated. Most had been drinking on the night churches burned, but none had previous felony convictions.

Bad examples? Many hate-crime offenders also seem to be under the influence of an older leader. That might be the case for the best-known church fire suspects, Timothy Welch, 23, and Gary Cox, 22. Currently jailed in Kingstree, S.C., the pair are charged with the June 1995 torchings of the Macedonia Baptist Church in Bloomville, S.C., and the Mount Zion AME Church in nearby Greeleyville. They also are charged with beating and stabbing a retarded black man the same month. Cox and Welch had been attending local Ku Klux Klan recruiting rallies, and Welch was carrying a KKK membership card when he was arrested. Clarendon County Sheriff Hoyt Collins says Cox and Welch were "followers," not leaders. "I think they had encouragement," says Collins. "I'm not sure they had instructions."

A suit against the KKK filed on behalf of the Mount Zion Church by the Southern Poverty Law Center asserts that a speaker at one rally made "disparaging and inflammatory statements about black churches." And Cox had been living with Arthur Haley, 52, a former Klan member who also attended some rallies. Federal agents raided Haley's home in February and came away with guns and Klan paraphernalia but did not arrest him. Horace King, grand dragon of the South Carolina chapter of the Christian Knights of the Ku Klux Klan Invisible Empire, says he knew nothing of the church burnings and would have stopped them if he had. Haley declined to speak with *U.S. News.* Lawyers for Cox and Welch did not return phone calls.

The Klan and other white supremacist groups have long denounced affirmative action, welfare, immigration and race-based congressional districting, and now those issues have become mainstream political controversies. Grand Dragon King told *U.S. News* that African-Americans "hand down welfare from one generation to the next." Klan member Herbert Rowell told the *State* newspaper in Columbia, S.C., that black churches tell members how to get on the dole: "Have you ever noticed that when there's free cheese or milk and stuff? We don't know nothing about it, but they're the first in line."

Affirmative action is another target. "We've given blacks every opportunity in the form of affirmative action and quotas," said a posting on the World Wide Web from "Aryan True." "It's not opportunity they want, they want control of the country." Grand Dragon King was upset by a minority set-aside program at Columbia Metropolitan Airport. "White people have no security because of affirmative action," he said. "They can take away a job and give it to a black. The best qualified ought to get the job and that's it."

Losers? Nonwhite immigrants come in for criticism, too. "The doors should be wide open to our white brothers and sisters from everywhere in the world, and slammed shut to racial aliens," says another recent Internet posting.

More generally, some whites fear they are being shunted aside and are losing control. "Each race deserves its rights," says King, "but no race should infringe upon another race's rights and push them back, and that's what's happening today with the white race."

Civil rights experts think talk radio and the Internet provide new megaphones for bias and hate. The Center for Democratic Renewal says Darrell Flinn, the imperial wizard of the Knights of the White Kamellia in Alabama and Louisiana, has a bimonthly cable show, "The Klan in Akadiana," that reaches as many as 54,000 people. Michael Harrison, editor and publisher of *Talkers* magazine, thinks the incidence of racism and hatred on talk radio is exaggerated, but says 20 to 25 percent of radio talk shows occasionally air such themes. After Commerce Secretary Ron Brown's plane was reported missing, New York talk show host Bob Grant said he feared Brown might have survived "because at heart, I'm a pessimist." Grant was fired but was soon picked up by another station.

Meanwhile, the struggle for racial equality and tolerance appears to be losing out to resignation that de facto segregation is both normal and acceptable. Greenville, S.C., high school students say that even though their schools are integrated, blacks and whites seldom mix, and that that's just the way it is.

In this atmosphere, stereotypes and biases can flourish. "Unfortunately, blacks are considered more lower class," says Jennie Johnson, a 17-year-old senior at Greenville's J. L. Mann High School. "In the black community it's not really 'cool' to be smart, so the majority don't apply themselves academically." Gainesville, Ga., High School held a "Farmer/Redneck Day" as part of its prehomecoming festivities last fall. African-American students say they were called "nigger" all day by white classmates; school officials say the claims may have been exaggerated.

Redneck store. There is no lack of encouragement for this volatile mix of pride and prejudice. South Carolina's legislature passed a law to keep the Confederate flag flying over the state house. Blacks say the flag represents slavery; whites say it celebrates Southern heritage. In Laurens, S.C., John Howard has converted the old Echo Theatre into the Redneck Shop, which is also slated to house a Ku Klux Klan museum. The store, which opened in March, sells Confederate and "redneck" merchandise, including Ku Klux Klan pins and T-shirts with the slogan, "We're here to stay."

"The goal of the shop is just to cater to people that love Confederate flags," says Howard. "And the museum is just to maintain the relics of the Klan that are part of our heritage—not to uplift it, but the history of the Klan needs to be understood. I have no intention of causing racial tension. No one's been hurt but John Howard. I've been ridiculed, persecuted and threatened."

"The Klan came into existence to oppress and inflict pain, and that store is a basic insult to what America claims it stands for," replies the Rev. David Kennedy of New Beginning Missionary Baptist Church in Laurens, who has organized several protests against the Redneck Shop. "There's going to be a fight, and our task is to make sure it's a nonviolent fight, because this town has the possibility of becoming a Little Bosnia. But if they're here to stay, so are we."

With churches still burning throughout the South, it may be hard to ensure that the fight is nonviolent.

─────────

By Gordon Witkin in South Carolina and Jeannye Thornton with Susannah Fox, Jill Jordan Sieder in Atlanta and Allison Walcott in Greenville

AE Article Review Form

We encourage you to photocopy and use this page as a tool to assess how the articles in **Annual Editions** expand on the information in your textbook. By reflecting on the articles you will gain enhanced text information. You can also access this useful form on a product's book support Web site at **http://www.dushkin.com/online/.**

NAME: DATE:

TITLE AND NUMBER OF ARTICLE:

BRIEFLY STATE THE MAIN IDEA OF THIS ARTICLE:

LIST THREE IMPORTANT FACTS THAT THE AUTHOR USES TO SUPPORT THE MAIN IDEA:

WHAT INFORMATION OR IDEAS DISCUSSED IN THIS ARTICLE ARE ALSO DISCUSSED IN YOUR TEXTBOOK OR OTHER READINGS THAT YOU HAVE DONE? LIST THE TEXTBOOK CHAPTERS AND PAGE NUMBERS:

LIST ANY EXAMPLES OF BIAS OR FAULTY REASONING THAT YOU FOUND IN THE ARTICLE:

LIST ANY NEW TERMS/CONCEPTS THAT WERE DISCUSSED IN THE ARTICLE, AND WRITE A SHORT DEFINITION:

ANNUAL EDITIONS revisions depend on two major opinion sources: one is our Advisory Board, listed in the front of this volume, which works with us in scanning the thousands of articles published in the public press each year; the other is you—the person actually using the book. Please help us and the users of the next edition by completing the prepaid article rating form on this page and returning it to us. Thank you for your help!

ANNUAL EDITIONS: African American History 00/01

ARTICLE RATING FORM

Here is an opportunity for you to have direct input into the next revision of this volume. We would like you to rate each of the 36 articles listed below, using the following scale:

1. Excellent: should definitely be retained
2. Above average: should probably be retained
3. Below average: should probably be deleted
4. Poor: should definitely be deleted

Your ratings will play a vital part in the next revision.
So please mail this prepaid form to us just as soon as you complete it.
Thanks for your help!

RATING

ARTICLE

1. The Nile Kingdoms
2. Our Third Root: On African Presence in American Populations
3. Under the Whiplash
4. Who Was Responsible?
5. Encouragement of the Slave-Trade
6. A Multitude of Black People . . . Chained Together
7. The Founding Fathers, Conditional Antislavery, and the Nonradicalism of the American Revolution
8. "Us Colored Women Had To Go through a Plenty": Sexual Exploitation of African-American Slave Women
9. Negro Craftsmanship in Early America
10. American Slave Insurrections before 1861
11. "All We Want Is Make Us Free!"
12. The Long Road to Abolition
13. The Struggle for Black Freedom before Emancipation
14. The Jacksonville Mutiny
15. Pride and Prejudice in the American Civil War
16. Forgotten Rebels: Blacks Who Served the Confederacy
17. Gallantry under Fire
18. Reconstruction
19. Negroes in the First and Second Reconstructions of the South
20. Negro Officials after the Civil War
21. "Sweet Dreams of Freedom": Freedwomen's Reconstruction of Life and Labor in Lowcountry South Carolina

RATING

ARTICLE

22. When White Hoods Were in Flower
23. "If You Can't Push, Pull, If You Can't Pull, Please Get Out of the Way": The Phyllis Wheatley Club and Home in Chicago, 1896 to 1920
24. Claude McKay and the New Negro of the 1920's
25. In the Race Riot of 1919, a Glimpse of Struggles to Come
26. Forgotten Victims: Blacks in the Holocaust
27. Work and Hope: African American Women in Southern California during World War II
28. Desegregation of the Armed Forces: Black Leadership, Protest and World War II
29. Sacrifice Play: The Negro Baseball Leagues Remembered
30. The Negro Is Your Brother
31. The South's History Rises, Again and Again
32. Black Women Activists and the Student Nonviolent Coordinating Committee: The Case of Ruby Doris Smith Robinson
33. Black Deprivation–White Privilege: The Assault on Affirmative Action
34. Rights Group Suing Florida for Failure to Educate Pupils
35. What's in a Name? Womanism, Black Feminism, and Beyond
36. Pride and Prejudice

(Continued on next page)

We Want Your Advice

ANNUAL EDITIONS: AFRICAN AMERICAN HISTORY 00/01

BUSINESS REPLY MAIL
FIRST-CLASS MAIL PERMIT NO. 84 GUILFORD CT

POSTAGE WILL BE PAID BY ADDRESSEE

**Dushkin/McGraw-Hill
Sluice Dock
Guilford, CT 06437-9989**

ABOUT YOU

Name   Date

Are you a teacher? ☐   A student? ☐
Your school's name

Department

Address   City   State   Zip

School telephone #

YOUR COMMENTS ARE IMPORTANT TO US !

Please fill in the following information:
For which course did you use this book?

Did you use a text with this *ANNUAL EDITION*? ☐ yes ☐ no
What was the title of the text?

What are your general reactions to the *Annual Editions* concept?

Have you read any particular articles recently that you think should be included in the next edition?

Are there any articles you feel should be replaced in the next edition? Why?

Are there any World Wide Web sites you feel should be included in the next edition? Please annotate.

May we contact you for editorial input? ☐ yes ☐ no
May we quote your comments? ☐ yes ☐ no